Teaching Social Studies in Middle and Secondary Schools

Fifth Edition

Candy Beal
North Carolina State University

Cheryl Mason Bolick
University of North Carolina at Chapel Hill

Peter H. Martorella
Late of North Carolina State University

Allyn & Bacon
is an imprint of

PEARSON

Boston   New York   San Francisco
Mexico City   Montreal   Toronto   London   Madrid   Munich   Paris
Hong Kong   Singapore   Tokyo   Cape Town   Sydney

Vice President and Executive Publisher: Jeffery W. Johnston
Acquisitions Editor: Meredith D. Fossel
Editorial Assistant: Maren Vigilante
Senior Managing Editor: Pamela D. Bennett
Senior Project Manager: Linda Hillis Bayma
Production Coordination: Holly Henjum, GGS Book Services, Inc.
Design Coordinator: Diane C. Lorenzo

Photo Coordinator: Sandy Schaefer
Cover Designer: Jason Moore
Cover image: istock
Operations Specialist: Susan Hannahs
Electronic Composition: GGS Book Services, Inc.
Director of Marketing: Quinn Perkson
Marketing Manager: Darcy Betts Prybella
Marketing Coordinator: Brian Mounts

For related titles and support materials, visit our online catalog at www.pearsonhighered.com

Between the time website information is gathered and then published, it is not unusual for some sites to have closed. Also, the transcription of URLs can result in typographical errors. The publisher would appreciate notification where these errors occur so that they may be corrected in subsequent editions.

ISBN-10: 0-13-159181-9
ISBN-13: 978-0-13-159181-3

Library of Congress Cataloging in Publication Data

Beal, Candy.
  Teaching social studies in middle and secondary schools / Candy Beal, Cheryl Mason Bolick, Peter H. Martorella.—5th ed.
      p. cm.
  Fourth ed. entered under: Peter H. Martorella.
  ISBN 0-13-159181-9
  1. Social sciences—Study and teaching (Secondary)—United States.
I. Bolick, Cheryl Mason. II. Martorella, Peter H. III. Martorella, Peter H.
Teaching social studies in middle and secondary schools. IV. Title.

H62.5.U5M38 2009
300.71'273—dc22   2008005914

Printed in the United States of America

10 9 8 7 6 5 4 3 2 1   CMA 12 11 10 09 08 07

Photo Credits for Chapter Openers: Ch. 1, Anna Elias/Prentice Hall School Division; Ch. 2, Anthony Magnacca/Merrill; Ch. 3, Myrleen Ferguson/PhotoEdit Inc.; Ch. 4–5, Anne Vega/Merrill; Ch. 6–8, Scott Cunningham/Merrill; Ch. 9, Anthony Magnacca/Merrill; Ch. 10, Copyright 2001–2007 SMART Technologies Inc. All rights reserved; Ch. 11, KS Studios/Merrill; Ch. 12, Scott Cunningham/Merrill.

Allyn & Bacon
is an imprint of

PEARSON

Preface

Greetings! Welcome to the field of social studies education and to the fifth edition of the book that many continue to call the Martorella methods text. Peter Martorella made many exemplary contributions to the field of social studies education and we are honored to continue to revise and rewrite the book that was dear to his heart. If you used the fourth edition you know that we were both colleagues of Peter and share many of the same beliefs that he held regarding the teaching and learning of social studies. If you didn't have a chance to work with Peter, we hope that you will get to know him through his work, much of which lives on in this textbook and in the many books and articles he authored. His work demonstrates what a gifted and forward-thinking educator he was and is a testament to the enormous impact Peter had in the field of social studies education. He was a visionary who, among other things, predicted years before its time that technology would play an influential role in how we teach and learn in social studies. If only the technology superhighway could keep up with what Peter had envisioned for it!

Peter had a wealth of colleagues with whom he researched and presented and who shared his philosophy about teaching the social studies. The foundational beliefs about how to teach and develop outstanding social studies educators have remained intact through the fourth and now the fifth revision. We have merged some chapters and expanded others in order to be current in the field of social studies education as well as responsive to the suggestions of colleagues who have long used this textbook. In this text you will find classic Martorella as well as many new ideas for teaching in our 21st-century classrooms. Some research cited may appear old by date but was the foundational work on which we have all built, and we have chosen to continue to cite the original research source. When needed, we have updated and added new information to what we already know. It's a weighty responsibility to revise Martorella. We have done so staying true to his teachings, and we believe that he would be proud to know that both the colleagues who use his book and the current authors are carrying out the work he felt was so important.

The fifth edition taps three wellsprings of information: teacher craft wisdom, research findings relative to instruction, and well-grounded theories. We believe that, when blended, these streams give new and experienced educators insight into how effective social studies instruction can be nurtured and sustained. Research and theory, in turn, offer complementary insights into how teachers might most effectively teach social studies. These represent the accumulations of scholars' tested conclusions under controlled conditions and in varied settings over time. They also include scholars' hypotheses and reflective deductions supported by logic and evidence. Research and theory help to explain craft wisdom. They can also suggest other practical applications for instruction and identify areas that require attention in our social studies classes. Work done by researchers and theorists can aid us in designing and selecting materials and texts that engage students and stimulate reflection. In addition, they can provide us with models for analyzing our teaching behaviors and generating new instructional strategies.

Head, hand, and heart will always be identified with Peter Martorella's belief that a well-balanced social studies program consists of matters of the head, the hand, and the heart. He used this metaphor to illustrate that the fundamental purpose of social studies should be the development of reflective, competent, and concerned citizens. He believed that theory, research, and craft wisdom were the beacons for effective social studies teaching. His approach was constructivist, and he urged teachers to build and implement meaningful activities to engage students. We share this philosophy and draw on our research, theory, and university work as well as the craft wisdom honed through 55+ years of teaching experience. We hope those who did not know Peter will learn from the foundation he laid and that those who knew him will continue to carry on the important work of social studies education. It is an understatement to note that in the light of world events, our work is more important today than it has ever been.

Features of This Text

This book was designed to assist preservice and inservice middle and secondary teachers in becoming more effective teachers of social studies. Toward this end, several steps have been taken to make it readable and understandable to audiences with different levels and needs.

Each chapter has a detailed outline on the opening page to serve as an advance organizer. Also, throughout the text, key terms appear in **boldface** to alert the reader to their importance. At the end of each chapter are suggested activities that extend and apply learning. Technology applications and resources have been woven throughout the text. We have also included a list of Web-based resources at the conclusion of each chapter. We have checked each of the websites noted and have found them to be current and timely.

Numerous field-tested lessons and activities are given throughout the text. These were obtained from a variety of sources and reflect a combination of craft wisdom, research, and theory.

Text Organization

This book is divided into three major parts. In Part I, we examine the origins and evolving state of the social studies and citizenship education across the United States. This segment provides a window into the dynamics of the profession and a feel for the ferment, controversies, and challenges that characterize social studies teaching and learning in the middle and secondary grades. It also includes a discussion of ways to move the walls of the classroom beyond the school and incorporate the community into the social studies classroom. This part of the book also offers ideas on how to advance the professional growth of social studies teachers.

Part II focuses on the art, science, and craft of social studies teaching against the backdrop of engaging students in knowledge construction. This part of the text draws heavily on grounded theory, research, and practitioner wisdom in formulating instructional models, applications, and examples. Illustrations and strategies from a wide range of different social studies projects and materials developed over the past several decades are provided.

The final segment, Part III, examines approaches to analyzing and improving social studies instruction while incorporating emerging technologies. These approaches include ways to create a positive classroom environment and provide for students with special needs through individualizing instruction. In addition, this section of the text addresses the implications of the rich cultural diversity within our nation.

Global Perspective

We have continued to address the need to focus on helping students develop a global perspective. It is not just the websites that link us electronically, but a mind-set that moves us from an Americentric prejudice to an open-minded, reflective citizen-of-the-world view that appreciates and values other cultures for what they bring to the world community and what they can teach us. In the light of international events, we consider developing a deeper understanding of other nations as well as globalizing students' perspectives to be of paramount importance. We should note that the many references you will find to Russia are a result of the research work that Beal has done in the study of Russian history, culture, and education. We hope that you will find the information useful. All websites are active and many be used in your classroom. Although the Russia NC6 was a one-year project, all parts can be used, as well as the questions and answers posed for research on Russia. Your students may find they have the same interests. Beal can be reached at candy_beal@ncsu.edu and is happy to answer questions or brainstorm the use of the sites.

Reflections of Current Research

All chapters have undergone revision to make them current with changes in research and practice. Some chapters have been combined to merge related information.

Addressing the Issues Boxes

These boxes are informational in some cases, link theory to practice in others, and we hope are always thought provoking. New boxes have been added to this edition.

Web Resources

Website addresses continue to be woven throughout each chapter, with additional new resources now found at the end of every chapter for easy reference. All are up to date and timely.

Nothing is more frustrating than to be reading along and have pages of reference/resource examples interrupt your flow. By the time you flip past the good but lengthy examples, you cannot remember the beginning of the sentence you were reading. We have addressed that issue in this new edition. You'll find that the longer examples we reference have been moved to the back and put in a new Appendix C, Resource Examples Cited in Text.

Figures in the text have their own numbering and the moved figures are separately numbered in their own section. Examples that do not exceed a page, and those which do not interrupt the flow of your reading, have been retained in the text. We hope you will find this makes meaning making easier for you.

About Your Authors

Candy Beal is an Associate Professor and Advising Coordinator in the Middle Grades Language Arts and Social Studies Teacher Education Program at North Carolina State University. Dr. Beal was a colleague of Dr. Martorella's and coauthored the third edition of *Social Studies for the Elementary Classroom: Preparing Children to Be Global Citizens* with him. She is a development theorist and middle school curriculum specialist who helps student teachers understand how adolescents learn best and then aids them in designing and implementing effective teaching and learning programs for the classroom. Her research is in the area of curriculum integration and assessment. Her work on the Russia and Ghana projects is included in several chapters as examples of curriculum development that allow you to effectively reach and teach your students with a more global perspective.

Cheryl Mason Bolick is an Assistant Professor at the University of North Carolina at Chapel Hill. She earned her M.Ed. and Ph.D. under Peter Martorella at North Carolina State University. It was Peter's call to "awaken the sleeping giant" that slumbered in the field of technology integration in the social studies that led Dr. Bolick to become a researcher in the field of social studies and education technology. She currently teaches technology and social studies courses and conducts research in the field of technology and social studies teaching and learning. Dr. Bolick is the author of numerous technology and social studies articles and is the coeditor of *Social Education's* monthly technology column.

Acknowledgments

We thank all of the students and teachers with whom we have both worked for their ideas that are woven throughout this text. Our beliefs about teaching have been influenced through interactions with colleagues and students in our combined 55+ years of teaching. Thanks to the reviewers of the manuscript for their insights and comments: Penelope Fritzer, Florida Atlantic University; John Lee, Georgia State University; Kim Roberts, East Tennessee State University; Steven Thorpe, Southern Oregon University; and Stephanie Van Hover, University of Virginia. We are grateful to our editor, Meredith Fossel, and Pearson for their support and for their desire to continue to share Peter's fundamental beliefs about social studies teaching and learning. We hope that we have remained true to the Martorella spirit and tradition. We believe that his contributions to the field will continue to guide the work of all of us.

Our Personal Message

To Students

Putting together a methods textbook is a daunting task. We have worked to relate important information to sound research so that you will have a solid foundation on which to build your social studies teaching career. Occasionally, you will hear your authors' voices, but books of this nature are expected to be scholarly, so for the most part we have limited our personal asides to the *Addressing the Issues* boxes. For those boxes we have called on our colleagues' expertise as well as including information of our own.

We have been in the place you are in now, getting ready for student teaching. We have felt all of the feelings you are feeling now, too—eager anticipation and nervousness as you start a new Great Adventure. Both of us became teachers because we love people and want to help children of all ages grow and be the best they can be. Social studies is a passion for us. Unfortunately, too often social studies is maligned and discounted. It only takes walking down a school hallway and a little eavesdropping to understand why some students hate social studies. In too many school classrooms the environment is "old school," desks in straight rows, textbooks ready to open and be read following a lecture, and little posted on the walls to indicate awareness of events in the world outside. All of these elements do little to help students develop a passion for the subject whose understanding is critical to our nation's future. Now is the time to be teaching social studies as effectively as we possibly can because the needs around the world are so great. It's easy to give up in the face of today's educational challenges. There's no secret about what we face as educators—students who are behind (or ahead) and in need of differentiated instruction, a lack of adequate funding for education, a lack of recognition for our long hours and hard work, and the advent of No Child Left Behind legislation has made it even more difficult to fight for social studies instructional time. The mantra seems to be that if it is not tested, it is not important. In addition we are forced to defend how and what we teach. Standardized testing of discrete facts (spit back testing) does not lend itself to teaching for understanding or abstract learning. What you must realize is that there has always been a list like this, and individuals who are good enough to teach have always worked to change things for their students and for the profession.

As teachers, much is expected and much is given. On the plus side, there is no other job in the world that has as much variety and unpredictability as teaching. No day is ever like another. Thank goodness for that! Teachers must be risk takers and try everything they can think of to reach their students. Except in brain surgery, there is no other situation where one professional is trusted with the cognitive well-being of so many. Teachers face daily challenges and opportunities. Would a smaller class size enable us to reach students who need extra help? Yes, of course. Would being supplied with materials and equipment enable us to do a better job getting our students ready for a technology-driven world? Yes, of course. Would added funding help erase the learning gap in our classes? Yes, of course. Jonathan Kozol, humanitarian, educator, and gifted author, tells a story about his wealthy friends who have chosen not to send their children to inadequately funded inner-city schools. They pack them off to prep schools and then, with a straight face, challenge Kozol to defend his belief that more money is needed to solve our education problems. The scenario goes like this, "Jonathan, surely you can't tell us that the education problems can be solved by throwing money at them?" To which Jonathan answers, "Yes, that is exactly what's needed to address and solve education problems. That approach worked for you and your children, didn't it?" Trust Jonathan to cut to the chase and nail the answer.

We have many years of teaching experience between us, having both taught some challenging classes and laughed and cried (too many times to count) about some of our teaching adventures. We believe that it's important to celebrate your successes, acknowledge your shortcomings, and learn from your failures. Nothing is more dangerous for a teacher than becoming part of a frequently held pity party. It's important to remain positive and to put that positive energy toward finding solutions. Candy Beal offers the following "glass half full" way of thinking she used during her first year as a teacher:

> I started my teaching career in 1968 with seventh graders who could not read the social studies textbook. It never occurred to me to give up on these students. Nor did I treat them, and their shortcomings, differently than I did my average class. They knew they had reading problems. These children had been tracked into basic level classes. They had been told of their inadequacies often enough. So what do you do as a new seventh-grade social studies teacher with a class of low-level readers? Define the problem and work on a solution! I rewrote the book by taking out the big words. I added interesting historical stories to spice up the topics. Then, I read my text to them. The whole class worked on reading and writing skills by tweaking my version until it was on their reading level. Our new "edition" included all the facts students needed to know and many stories of famous people whose lives taught lessons and exhibited grit and character. We wrote, produced, and presented learning dramas. We composed stories based on historical facts. Everyone pitched in to help one another become successful learners.

> When some of the children missed the first few weeks of school for tobacco picking, and then later were out for other agricultural chores, the whole class helped to catch them up. The missing students were not suspended for excessive absences nor were they given a stack of assignments and a deadline for completion. Good sense, heart, and the willingness to go the extra mile for your children and their families make teaching a never-ending lifelong adventure in learning.

I like to think that in those early years I was the ultimate professional and caring teacher. Sometimes a few students would fail to learn the right answer, but they tried and often were awarded a point or two for creativity.

We often think that first-year teachers work the hardest and have the best attitudes about their jobs. First-year teachers have not become jaded by the process or succumbed to a negative pity party school culture. They believe they can do anything, including teach everything that's needed to every child in every class by the end of the year. Bravo! That attitude is a great example of the historically correct and spirited phrase, *"Damn the torpedoes and full speed ahead,"* and it's something everyone needs to do today. We know that you have done years of homework and gotten into the classrooms for observations and exchanges with good, positive practicing teachers. You are ready to go! So get in there! Be an advocate for students, teachers, and for the most exciting subject in the curriculum, social studies! We wish you enormous success!

Candy Beal and Cheryl Mason Bolick

Brief Contents

PART I
The State of Social Studies and Citizenship Education   1

CHAPTER 1 Alternative Perspectives on the Social Studies   2

CHAPTER 2 Contemporary Social Studies   22

CHAPTER 3 Teaching and Learning Social Studies   46

PART II
Developing Reflective, Competent, and Concerned Citizens   81

CHAPTER 4 Organizing and Planning for Teaching Social Studies   82

CHAPTER 5 Engaging Students in Learning Through Small Groups, Questions, Role Playing, and Simulations   124

CHAPTER 6 Promoting Reflective Inquiry: Developing and Applying Concepts, Generalizations, and Hypotheses   158

CHAPTER 7 Fostering Citizenship Competency   185

CHAPTER 8 Social Concern in a Globally and Culturally Diverse World   216

PART III
Analyzing and Improving Social Studies Teaching and Learning   247

CHAPTER 9 Comprehending, Communicating, and Remembering Subject Matter   248

CHAPTER 10 Using Technology to Enhance Social Studies Instruction   280

CHAPTER 11 Adapting Social Studies Instruction to Individual Needs   299

CHAPTER 12 Evaluating and Assessing Student Learning   333

APPENDIX A
NCSS Standards and Performance Expectations   361

APPENDIX B
Sample of a Social Studies Textbook Evaluation Form   371

APPENDIX C
Resource Examples Cited in Text   377

References   397

Index   409

Contents

PART I
The State of Social Studies and Citizenship Education   1

1   Alternative Perspectives on the Social Studies   2

The Origins and Evolution of the Social Studies   8
    The 1916 Report of the Committee on the Social Studies   9
    The New Social Studies   10
    Social Studies Past, Current, and Future   12
Alternative Definitions of the Social Studies   14
    A Working Definition of the Social Studies   15
The Contemporary Social Studies Teacher   15
    Certification of Social Studies Teachers   17
    Teaching Portfolios   18
    Lateral Entry Teachers   18
Summary   20
Activities   20
Web Resources   21

2   Contemporary Social Studies   22

Citizenship Education as the Purpose of the Social Studies   24
    The Context of Citizenship Education   25
Alternative Perspectives on a Curriculum for Effective Citizenship
    Education   26
The Enduring Goal of the Social Studies Curriculum: Reflective,
    Competent, and Concerned Citizens   29
    The Nature of the Effective Citizen   30
    Social Studies as a Matter of Head, Hand, and Heart   31
Existing Social Studies Scope and Sequence Patterns   33
    The Curriculum Pattern in the Elementary Grades   34
    The Curriculum Pattern in the Middle and Secondary Grades   34
    The Dominance of Traditional Scope and Sequence Patterns   35
National Standards   36
    Social Studies Standards   37
    Technology Standards   37

State Standards 37
Professional Standards for Teachers 37
Basal Textbooks and the Social Studies Curriculum 41
Use of Basal Textbooks in the Social Studies 42
Selection and Adoption of Basal Textbooks 42
Implications of State Adoption Policies 43
Summary 43
Activities 44
Web Resources 44

3 **Teaching and Learning Social Studies** **46**

Engaging Students in Constructing Knowledge 48
Schemata and Prior Knowledge in Social Studies Instruction 49
Sources of Subject Matter for the Social Studies 50
**The Social Sciences as Sources of Subject Matter for the
  Social Studies 51**
Geography 53
History 53
Economics 54
Political Science 55
Anthropology 55
Sociology 56
Psychology 56
Other Sources of Subject Matter for the Social Studies 57
*Multidisciplinary, Thematic, Interdisciplinary, and Integrative
  Approaches 57*
*The School and Community Help Students Establish
  Their Own Sense of Place 61*
Social Service Projects 63
The School and Community as Sources of Social Data 64
Using Community Resource Persons Effectively 65
Newspaper Articles and Editorials 67
Fieldwork in the Community 67
Collecting Oral Histories 71
Collecting Social Science Information Through Surveys 72
*Communicating with the Community About the Social Studies
  Program 73*
Alerting the Community to School Activities 74

Identifying Professional Resources   75
Organizational Resources   76
Professional Journals   77
Effective Citizenship as Professional Development   77
Professional Development Through the Internet   78
Summary   78
Activities   79
Web Resources   80

PART II
Developing Reflective, Competent, and Concerned Citizens   **81**

4   Organizing and Planning for Teaching Social Studies   **82**

Basic Issues in Planning Social Studies Instruction   85
Identifying a Purpose for Citizenship Education   86
Beginning the Planning Process   86
Social Studies Goals for Instruction   91
Identifying and Stating Goals   91
Social Studies Objectives for Instruction   91
Identifying and Stating Objectives   92
General Objectives, Behavioral Objectives, and Student Learning
  Outcomes   92
Objectives in the Cognitive and Affective Domains   93
Organizing Subject Matter into Units   94
Planning and Creating Units   94
Sources of Units   96
Resource Units and Teaching Units   99
Building Units Around Key Social Problems, Questions,
  and Themes   99
Incorporating Multiple Perspectives into Units   100
Using Concept Maps/Webs to Plan Units   101
Planning Units Using Interdisciplinary Teams   103
Formats for Unit Planning   104
Organizing Subject Matter into Lessons   105
Lesson Plans   105
Formats and Procedures for Lesson Planning   107

The Fundamental Elements of Lesson Planning   108
*Back Mapping Lessons and Using Various Types of
    Instruction*   110
Classrooms as Environments for Learning   111
The Uses of Space in Planning Social Studies Instruction   111
Allocation of Time in Lesson Plans   111
Creating and Managing the Classroom Environment   113
*Student Behavior in the Classroom and Teacher and Student
    Expectations*   114
Characteristics of Well-Managed Classrooms   116
Supportive Teacher Behaviors   116
**Balancing Goals and Objectives in the Curriculum: Linking the
    Head, the Hand, and the Heart**   118
Guidelines for Social Studies Program Development   118
Variety in Instructional Planning   121
Summary   121
Activities   122
Web Resources   123

**5   Engaging Students in Learning Through Small
    Groups, Questions, Role Playing, and Simulations   124**

Grouping Students for Learning   127
Planning for Small-Group Work   127
Small-Group Techniques   128
Cooperative Learning Group Techniques   130
The Jigsaw Technique   132
The Group Investigation Technique   137
*Curriculum Integration Approach to Teaching
    and Learning*   138
Using Structured Questions to Aid Learning   139
Patterns of Effective Questioning—Types   140
Effective Use of Time—Duration   140
Effective Selection and Ordering of Questions—Sequencing   142
*More About Using Questioning Strategies to Teach Your
    Lesson*   145
Engaging Students in Role Playing and Simulations   149
Managing Role-Playing Enactments   150
Managing Simulations   153
Sources of Simulations   153

Summary   154
Activities   156
Web Resources   157

6   **Promoting Reflective Inquiry: Developing and
Applying Concepts, Generalizations, and Hypotheses   158**

Learning and Teaching Concepts   160
   The Nature of Concepts   161
   The Science of Learning   162
   Misconceptions and Stereotypes   163
   The Process of Learning a Concept   163
   Concept Analyses   164
   Instructional Strategies That Promote Concept Learning   165
   Graphic Organizers   165
Learning and Teaching Facts and Generalizations   167
   The Nature of Facts   167
   The Nature of Generalizations   168
   The Value of Generalizations   169
   Generalizations, Facts, and Hypotheses   170
   *Instructional Strategies That Promote the
      Learning of Generalizations   171*
   *Using Data-Retrieval Charts in Developing
      Generalizations   171*
The Reflective Citizen and Problem Solving   172
   Uses of the Term Problem *in Instruction   176*
   Instructional Strategies for Problem Solving   176
Summary   182
Activities   183
Web Resources   184

7   **Fostering Citizenship Competency   185**

The Nature of Citizenship Skills   187
Social Skills   187
   Conflict Resolution Skills   188
Research and Analysis Skills   190
   Interpreting and Comparing Data   190
   Analyzing Arguments   197
   Processing Information from Pictures   201

Chronology Skills   203
  Comparative Conceptions of Time   204
  Recording Events on Time Lines   204
Spatial Skills   205
  The Impact of Spatial Perspectives   206
  Using and Creating Maps in Instruction   206
  *Integrating Maps and Globes into All Social Studies
    Instruction*   208
**Identifying and Using Reference Sources in
  Developing Skills**   209
  Sample Reference Works for Social Studies   209
Activities for Introducing Reference Materials   210
Summary   214
Activities   214
Web Resources   215

8   Social Concern in a Globally and Culturally Diverse World

216

Social Concern and Citizenship Education   218
  The Morally Mature Citizen   219
The Dimensions of Concern   219
  The Nature of Beliefs, Attitudes, and Values   220
**Instructional Strategies for Examining Beliefs, Attitudes,
  and Values**   220
  Self-Concept Activities   221
Social Issues as a Curricular Focus   224
  *Curricular Framework for Analyzing Social Issues
    in the Classroom*   225
  Global Education in an Interconnected World   226
  Peace Education   228
Multicultural Education   229
  Issues in Multicultural Education   231
  *Designing Strategies for Multicultural
    Education*   233
  *Guidelines for Selecting Appropriate Curriculum
    Materials for Multicultural Education*   235
  Gender Issues in Multicultural Education   235
Current Affairs   241
  Strategies for Analyzing Current Affairs   241
  Teacher Positions on Controversial Issues   244

Summary   244
Activities   245
Web Resources   246

PART III
Analyzing and Improving Social Studies Teaching and Learning   **247**

9   Comprehending, Communicating, and Remembering Subject Matter   **248**

Comprehending Social Studies Subject Matter   250
Building on Existing Knowledge in Reading   250
Strategies for Improving Reading Comprehension   251
Specific Strategies   252
Reading and Social Studies Text Materials   258
Using Adolescent Literature in Social Studies Instruction   259
Reading Newspapers and Periodicals   264
Visual Literacy   264
Communicating Social Studies Subject Matter   266
Listening and Speaking   266
Integrating Writing into the Social Studies Curriculum   268
Technology Tools in Writing   269
Remembering Social Studies Subject Matter   270
Imagery and Memory   271
Structured Mnemonic Techniques   271
Notetaking Techniques   272
English as a Second Language (ESL)   274
Summary   278
Activities   278
Web Resources   279

10   Using Technology to Enhance Social Studies Instruction   **280**

Integrating Technology into Today's Classrooms   282
Internet Applications for Social Studies Instruction   284
Media Literacy   284
Web-Based Resources for Teachers and Students   285
Telecollaboration   285

Software Applications for the Social Studies Classroom   290
Simulation Software   290
Database and Spreadsheet Software   291
Multimedia Editing Software   291
Mapping Software   293
Personal Digital Assistants in the Social Studies Classroom   293
Technology Challenges   294
Internet Safety   295
Copyright   295
Digital Divide   295
Emerging Technologies: Challenges of the Future   296
Summary   297
Activities   297
Web Resources   298

11 **Adapting Social Studies Instruction to Individual Needs   299**

Matching Social Studies Instruction to Students' Developing Capabilities   301
Symbolic, Enactive, and Iconic Social Studies Activities   302
Social Discourse in the Classroom   303
Social Studies for the Middle Years   303
Exemplary Middle-Grades Schools   304
Exemplary Middle Grades' Social Studies Programs and Teachers   305
High School Social Studies   306
Individualized Instruction and Individual Differences   307
Individual Differences Among Students   307
Individual Styles of Thinking and Learning   308
Thinking and Learning Styles   308
Matching Thinking Styles to Instruction   309
Matching Learning Styles to Instruction   309
Organizing the Classroom for Individualized Instruction   312
Computers   312
Multilevel Reading Materials   312
Learning Contracts   313
Using Jackdaws®, Artifact Kits, and Teacher-Made Materials for Individualizing Instruction   314
Instructional Resources for Individualizing Instruction   316

Equity for Those with Disabilities   318
*Individuals with Disabilities Education Improvement
Act of 2004 (IDEA 2004)   319*
Mainstreaming   322
*Strategies for Mainstreaming Students for Social Studies
Instruction   324*
Equity for the Gifted   326
Societal Perspectives on the Gifted   327
Identifying the Gifted   327
Approaches to Gifted Education   328
Gifted Students in Social Studies Classes   328
Summary   331
Activities   332
Web Resources   332

12 Evaluating and Assessing Student Learning 333

The Dimensions of Evaluation   335
Grades, Assessments, and Standards   336
The Use and Misuse of Tests   336
Norm-Referenced Tests   337
Criterion-Referenced Tests   338
The National Assessment of Educational Progress   338
National Standards and National Testing   339
Performance Assessments   341
Social Studies Performance Assessments and Portfolios   341
Teacher-Made Paper-and-Pencil Tests   343
Posttests and Pretests   343
Constructing Essay Test Items   343
Constructing Objective Test Items   345
Test Software   348
Evaluating Reflection, Competence, and Concern   349
Assessing Reflection   349
Assessing Competence   351
Assessing Concern   354
**A Framework for Evaluating the Outcomes of Social
Studies Instruction**   356
Matching Evaluation and Instructional Goals and Objectives   357
Summary   358
Activities   358
Web Resources   359

APPENDIX A
NCSS Standards and Performance Expectations   361

APPENDIX B
Sample of a Social Studies Textbook Evaluation Form   371

APPENDIX C
Resource Examples Cited in Text   377

References   397

Index   409

NOTE: Every effort has been made to provide accurate and current Internet information in this book. However, the Internet and information posted on it are constantly changing, and it is inevitable that some of the Internet addresses listed in this textbook will change.

Part I

The State of Social Studies and Citizenship Education

CHAPTER 1   Alternative Perspectives on the Social Studies
CHAPTER 2   Contemporary Social Studies
CHAPTER 3   Teaching and Learning Social Studies

1

Alternative Perspectives on the Social Studies

The Origins and Evolution of the Social Studies

    The 1916 Report of the Committee on the Social Studies

    The New Social Studies

    Social Studies Past, Current, and Future

Alternative Definitions of the Social Studies

    A Working Definition of the Social Studies

The Contemporary Social Studies Teacher

    Certification of Social Studies Teachers

    Teaching Portfolios

    Lateral Entry Teachers

Summary

Activities

Web Resources

Sal Margione decided it was time for a break. For much of the evening he had been busily planning "getting to know you" activities for his social studies classes. Tomorrow he would meet his students for the first time, and he was anxious to get off to a good start. In addition to making sure he was ready for tomorrow, he was also trying to do a little curriculum mapping, laying out how he would sequence the topics and themes he would teach throughout the year. He wanted to be sure that the interest he generated on the first day carried over and set the tone for the year's worth of exciting social studies' Great Adventures. He had read the stats that suggested that social studies is the least liked subject in the curriculum, but he was also current with his professional journals and had recently read an interesting piece in Social Education *by Mark Schug. Schug (2007) suggested that a teacher could pique students' curiosity in historical events by examining those events as "economic" mysteries. The article's title was a good example of a puzzling question that he thought his students might enjoy tackling, "Why Did the Colonists Fight When They Were Safe, Prosperous, and Free?" Why, indeed?*

Sal was constantly reading and searching for new teaching ideas. Studying historical events as economic mysteries sounded promising. A workshop opportunity about using original source documents for capturing eyewitness accounts to history had sent him to digital archives around the nation. What treasure troves!

Flipping the pages of that same issue of Social Education *brought Sal to Stacey Bredhoff's (2007) ideas for using Lincoln's doctor's account of the president's death as a way to teach history by using documents. Sal found he could actually hand his students copies of the doctor's handwritten account.*

3

This would fit beautifully with the idea he had gotten a couple of years before from a Hutchinson (2005) article that shared how to teach about the Civil War using soldiers' letters from the battlefield. Sal's mind was racing. If he used the Chism (2006) piece on the Freedmen's Bureau, which included land lease documents to study, he would have a series of fascinating resources that would take his students from the fighting on the battlefields to the death of a president, and finally, to new opportunities for formerly enslaved people. Sal raced on to an idea of sharing all of this activity and learning with the community. This could be done through digital videos that his students would make (Stoltz, Banister, Fischer, 2007). The idea for a Civil War Day community gathering was taking shape. Sal believed that original documents were the ultimate "bottom up" teaching source and this kind of resource kept everyone excited about learning "real" history (Hutchinson, 2005).

Sal loved teaching and was determined to show his students the excitement and fascination that comes with better understanding your own culture and peoples around the world. He knew that broadening one's global perspective was critical in today's world. To that end, his diningroom table was covered with a collection of textbooks, trade books, artifacts, 3 × 5 cards, URL addresses, and several software programs.

Sal had found it difficult that evening to concentrate solely on planning. A hundred issues and questions raced through his mind. His nonteaching workload had increased tremendously over the past few years. All of the extra office reports and administrative duties made him begin to question whether he had made the right decision in choosing teaching as a career. He liked working with adolescents and coaching the geography team, but his schedule was packed and he saw his time with his students being usurped. After all, working with the students was the reason he was teaching. Everyone commented on his natural teaching skills. Being a good listener and being able to explain things clearly were at the top of the list of his strengths.

His enthusiasm and high energy was a good match for the demands of teaching. As a single parent, he liked the idea of being on the same schedule as his children. Whether they opted for year-round or 10 months, they all could spend more time doing what they loved—traveling, reading, and canoeing.

While he was pondering the new school year and what the future would bring, Sal rose and accidentally knocked a book from the table. Several yellowed, neatly clipped newspaper articles slipped out, and one caught Sal's eye. He recovered it, and slowly began to read the article he had saved for many years, and had then forgotten (Figure 1.1).

Sal had read and clipped the article early in his teaching career. It had made a big impression on him. It still did, and rereading it energized him and dispelled any doubts he might have had about the wisdom of his career choice. Cyclone Sal was ready to go!

FIGURE 1.1
Alternative Perspectives on the Social Studies and Citizenship Education

Fred Murphy is a legend in Williamsville. Murphy taught history, but not the way most people remember it. He told stories. He brought historical figures to life, with anecdotes that revealed their foibles as well as their strengths. History is people, his students learned, and that is a lesson they will remember much longer than any date or historical fact.

Along the way—and rather painlessly—Murphy's students also learned an awful lot of history.

"There can't be many people in the country who do what Mr. Murphy does for high school students," Williamsville South parent Marjorie McNabb said. "He makes history come alive for these students, not only dramatically, but also accurately."

"I'm live and in color," Murphy explained. "I'm in show business. I've got to keep my audience. If I play to an empty house, (the students) may be here, but they're not with me. . . ."

Murphy leaves on top. "I'd have to say he's the best teacher I've ever had," 1983 graduate Marah Searle said. "The one word for him is dynamic. He's so interested in the material, he makes it interesting for us, and we get interested in it."

Murphy's favorite historical figure is Franklin D. Roosevelt: an FDR bust in his classroom is nicknamed St. Francis I. His favorite teaching topic is the Depression, which he taught partly through personal anecdotes. . . .

Murphy gave his students insights into the characters of historical figures such as Hamilton, Jackson, Marshall and FDR, with colorful and memorable anecdotes.

"I wanted them to know the truth about America," he said. "I know that sounds corny. I didn't make these people out to be saints. They weren't, but they were good people."

He hopes his students learned that no country was perfect. America's treatment of the Indians and slavery proved that here. "But there is no other country quite like ours," he added.

Murphy's recipe for teaching success is simple. He loves his subject—U.S. and European history and sociology—and he loves children. . . .

His advice for would-be teachers? "If you don't like kids, don't get into the profession. . . . The beauty of teaching is that you stay young. Young people are enthusiastic. They're not cynical yet."

Note. From "Murphy Taught History 30 Years, Became a Legend in Williamsville," by G. Warner, in *Buffalo News* (June 12, 1985, "second front page"). Reprinted with permission.

What made you decide to be a teacher? Was it an exceptional teacher who took the time to get to know you and your abilities, made learning exciting, and encouraged you to be better than you ever thought you could be? Maybe because of this you saw the potential to make a difference for others. At the same time, becoming a teacher gave you the chance to honor the teacher who showed you the way. On the other hand, it might have been a negative experience that made you want to teach. You vowed to make it better for students coming up, thus ensuring that they would not have the same awful experience you did.

Most teacher educators have heard many stories of their students' former school experiences and they fit into two categories, pleasure and pain. Interestingly, these kinds of experiences fit into Erik Erikson's theory of epigenesis (Erikson, 1968). Erikson, a developmental theorist who specialized in social and emotional development, saw life as an unfolding process, much like a flower going from seed to bloom. He believed that each of us grows and develops based on a series of stages we go through in our lives. Each stage offers a challenge. If you resolve that challenge positively, then you gain a positive personal quality that is part of your identity. That positive quality allows you to be more psychologically healthy and enables you to live a richer, happier life (Santrock, 2008). If the result is negative, then you fail to gain the positive trait and instead pick up a negative quality that influences your personality and all that you will do. All is not lost, however, because later in life you can revisit an earlier challenge/stage, work through it again, erase the negative result, and replace it with a positive one. As an example, early in life, babies cry for attention. Doting parents rush to the baby's side to give love and support. As young children, we trust that our caregivers will do that and we feel secure in knowing that they will be there for us. A neglected child will not have that same support and may not be able to trust that her needs will be met. Her inability to trust influences her as she grows up. She may find it difficult to trust people and depend on them to be supportive. Along the way, however, a close friendship with a teacher or peer might change her view about trusting, and she will go from being a person prone to mistrust to one who is trusting. This is the beauty of Erikson's theory; the "do-over." There is always hope that a negative character trait can be changed to a positive one. It should be noted that the sooner the positive resolution can be adopted and replace the negative one, the better. Negative resolutions can tend to influence other challenges yet to be resolved.

Dr. Sam Snyder, Associate Dean for Research and Engagement in the College of Education at North Carolina State University, has a unique way to explain the early stages of epigenesis. He likens the resolution of the stage challenges to gathering tools to fill one's personality toolbox. He suggests that as you grow and develop, you meet challenges that, if resolved positively, enable you to gather a positive personality trait tool for your toolbox. A negative resolution leaves you short a positive, helpful character-building tool for your personality. Students are especially heavy users of the toolbox when they reach middle grades and high school. During adolescence everyone is trying to build their identity, and they rely on the tools they have gathered to put that identity together. If your box is full of good-quality trait tools, you are on your way to constructing a well-rounded personality.

Erikson suggests that one of the stages following adolescence is generativity. Generativity can best be characterized as *giving back to make it better for those who come next*. Clearly, teachers are in perpetual generativity. If you studied Erikson's theory closely, you could probably trace your own pathway to teaching. You would recognize the tools you gathered and honed throughout your development and understand how they enabled you to have the personality and skills that make you a perfect candidate to be a teacher leader. Take heart! The final stage of epigenesis is when you look back to consider the worth of your life. Have you made a difference and do you feel your time on earth has mattered? Teachers can recite a host of stories told to them by former students or parents of former students that validate their life choice to teach (see Box 1.1).

BOX 1.1	Addressing the Issues: On Becoming a Memorable Master Teacher

There are many outstanding teachers across the world. One who is truly exceptional is Jackie Brooks, a Wake County Public Schools teacher who excites children about social studies. For countless eighth graders, she has become a legend in her own time.

I (Beal) began an inquiry Research Project 10 years ago that each semester brings together middle school students and my preservice teachers for an afternoon question-and-answer session. The college students interview the middle schoolers about their school life, relationships with peers and parents, and best and worst practices of the teachers with whom they work. The purpose is to help the preservice teachers stay informed about what makes early adolescents tick, learn about what works and doesn't work in the classroom (according to the students), and practice asking leading questions. One of the questions that is always asked is "Who was your best teacher and why?" And every semester the answer is always "Ms. Brooks." Students can tell you every story she ever told, the teaching and learning techniques that she uses to capture the class and infuse excitement into the lesson, and the projects that they worked on.

I mentioned to a colleague at NC State University, Ken Vickery, an African history professor and a favorite among my students for his fascinating classes, that there was a teacher at

Ligon Middle School whose reputation was as sterling as his own. "You must mean Jackie Brooks. I've heard about her from local NCSU kids who had her in middle school. She must be a great teacher!"

I had a chance to meet with Jackie Brooks at Ligon and told her about the impact she has had on her students and on the subject of social studies. I mentioned how they describe her lectures as spellbinding and have kept all the notebooks that they used to take down the facts and stories that she told. I'll never forget her quick response to me: "Lectures? Those weren't lectures. Those were dramatic narratives!" Later, I wondered if we haven't done a disservice to the lecture approach by always characterizing it as ineffective. Granted, if by lecture you mean droning on endlessly to feed students a notetaking marathon, then lecture is both inappropriate and ineffective. But if, instead, we mean sharing exciting stories, told with great pleasure while we make eye contact with individual students so that they feel that they alone are privy to a closely guarded secret, then lecture takes on a whole new meaning. It becomes never-to-be-forgotten dramatic narrative. Today, students are plugged in and turned on to so many impersonal forms of media that a connection made through an approach like dramatic narrative is unique and stands out for the students.

What made you decide to teach social studies? Sal knows that the subject most disliked by students is social studies. This viewpoint is puzzling, because how much more exciting can it be than to have the whole world as your curriculum? Change is the name of the game in social studies. It is a little like teaching. No day is the same as the next, just as global events are rarely predictable. Customs are fascinating, geography determines so much of the life and look of a country and region, and with a flick of a switch you can jump on the technology super highway and find up-to-date information and images from around the globe.

If you can agree that the subject is dynamic, then perhaps it is the way it is taught that does not translate to the students. Examining historical events as economic mysteries and using original source documents to recapture the past are only two teaching and learning approaches that can bring social studies to life for your students. Are you familiar with any others? There is also the possibility that you have a group of resistant students who have never been turned on by social studies. Now is your chance! Another factor that could be making for a ho-hum social studies experience is the current push to measure knowledge by the number of facts you know. Fact loading or memorization of country or state capitals, GNP, population, and so on, does not explain the heart and soul of a country. Good teachers know that facts are important to build a learning base, but it is the application of facts and their relation to one another that determine how much you know and truly understand. Teaching for understanding goes hand in glove with the gathering of facts. Dewey (1968) reminds us that it is the experience, the continuity of the authentic learning experience and how it relates to what we already know and understand, that draws us into the process and makes learning meaningful.

This textbook is your guide to teaching social studies. It will give you the tools you need to make your mark in the classroom, school, and field of social studies. Your journey in defining yourself and becoming a social studies practitioner is shared by many student teachers around the world. Throughout time, social studies educators have struggled to sharpen and clarify their professional identity. Three topics they frequently debate are:

1. The nature of the social studies
2. The purpose of the social studies
3. The source of subject matter for the field

We will examine these, and related issues, as they have been analyzed by social studies educators for a century.

The Origins and Evolution of the Social Studies

What are the origins of the social studies? In the early history of our nation, the social studies curriculum drew heavily on the areas of history, geography, and civics. The term *social studies*, Saxe (1991, 1992) has reported, became the official term used to designate the curriculum in the late 19th and early 20th centuries. He contended it came into use as an outgrowth of the writings of Sarah Bolton, Lady Jane Wilde, Heber Newton, and later, Thomas Jesse Jones. Saxe (1991) noted further: "From Newton and Jones we find that the initial use and sharpening of the term 'social studies' was directly tied to the utilization of social science data as a force in improvement of human welfare" (p. 17).

Jones later served as a member of a group known as the Committee on the Social Studies. The committee of 21 members representing different social science disciplines and different levels of professional education had been appointed by the National Education Association (NEA) in 1912. Its charge was to make recommendations concerning the reorganization of secondary curriculum.

The 1916 Report of the Committee on the Social Studies

The final report of the committee, issued in 1916, was called by Hertzberg (1981) "probably the most influential in the history of the social studies" (p. 2). One social studies educator, Engle (1976), credited the committee's report with setting the general direction of the field from that time forward.

The 1916 report defined the social studies as "those whose subject matter relates directly to the organization and development of human society, and to man as a member of social groups" (U.S. Bureau of Education, 1916, p. 9). It also laid out the broad aims or goals for the social studies, the cultivation of the "good citizen," a theme we will examine in detail in later chapters. In addition, the report sketched some guidelines for the curriculum and touched on a variety of other issues, including the preparation of teachers and text materials.

Although the report looked to the social sciences as the primary sources of enlightenment for the preparation of good citizens, the high ideals the report embodied clearly require a broader base of subject matter. For example, it asserted, "The social studies should cultivate a sense of membership in the 'world community,' with all the sympathies and sense of justice that this involves among the different divisions of human society" (U.S. Bureau of Education, 1916, p. 9).

Legacy of the 1916 Report. Among other features, the 1916 report reflected the diversity of disciplines that individuals on the committee represented, the dominant perspective being that of history. It also reflected the emergence of the behavioral sciences and the growth of professional associations. Additionally, it represented the flowering of progressivism and the apprehension of a nation on the brink of a world war (Hertzberg, 1981). The report became the touchstone for conceptions of what the social studies curriculum should be for the next eight decades, transcending the dramatic shifts in the nation and the world over that period.

The report also gave impetus to the rise, in 1921, of the first professional organization devoted to the concerns of social studies teachers, the National Council for the Social Studies (NCSS). Sixteen years later, the NCSS would publish the first professional journal for social studies teachers, *Social Education*. More than a half century later, in 1988, it would publish a second journal devoted to the elementary grades, *Social Studies and the Young Learner*.

A major legacy of the 1916 report has been a festering debate that continues to the present concerning both the nature of the social studies and the subject's relationship to the social sciences. The first sentence of the book *Defining the Social Studies*, written in 1977, captures the flavor of contemporary debates and analyzes: "The field of social studies is so caught up in ambiguity, inconsistency, and contradiction that it represents a complex educational enigma. It has also defied any final definition acceptable to all factions of the field" (Barr, Barth, & Shermis, 1977, p. 1). In exasperation, Barr et al. concluded, "If the social studies is what the scholars in the field say it is, it is a schizophrenic bastard child" (1977, p. 1).

The New Social Studies

All revolutions can be identified by some singular marker in time and space. For curriculum studies in the United States, the place of revolution was a quaint village along the eastern seaboard of Massachusetts. Its narrow strip of gray land, a mecca for tourists escaping the summer heat, also serves as a major research center for maritime studies. Tucked away, the tiny village of Woods Hole became the birthplace of what would later be known as the new social studies.

The impetus for the revolution was the Soviet launch of *Sputnik* in 1957 and the subsequent space race. For the Soviets to have beaten the United States into space, conventional wisdom said, meant that something must be wrong with our schools and their curricula. An intense and extensive reassessment of the American educational system was undertaken. In 1960, at the conference center in Woods Hole, some of the most prominent and recognized scholars in the social sciences gathered for the purpose of reconstructing curriculum. Their conference report, later published as *The Process of Education*, became the guidepost and rallying point in curriculum research. One key assertion of the report was the notion that every discipline is structured. From the rudimentary to the complex, effective teaching requires the discovery of structure. With this argument developed an understanding of curriculum as an upward spiral in which learning at higher levels builds upon and reinforces earlier, more basic teaching. Additionally, out of the conference at Woods Hole, there arose an awareness of the need to involve a whole range of professionals, teachers and practitioners alike, in the process of curriculum development. Mathematicians joined mathematics instructors and anthropologists joined social studies instructors in the search for the underlying structure of their respective disciplines in the hopes that education would be enhanced.

First, the science and mathematics, and later, the foreign language curriculum came under scrutiny. In response, the federal government sponsored a wave of reforms aimed at improving the curricula of schools. By the mid-1960s, the social studies were also drawn under the umbrella of reform. From that point forward through the early years of the 1970s, the social studies would witness an unprecedented period of innovation with respect to both the development of curricular materials and related teacher education efforts.

The fruits of this period became known as *the new social studies*. The efforts at innovation were fueled primarily with funds from the federal government and private foundations. Ultimately, commercial publishers would underwrite the final stages of development and publication of some of the curricular products.

Haas (1977), who was directly involved in the evolution of the new social studies, has written of this period, "If measured by the sheer output of the materials, the period 1964 to 1972 is unequaled in the history of social studies education in this country" (p. 61). Driving the new social studies were over 50 major projects (Fenton, 1967) and scores of minor ones touching every grade level (Haas, 1977). The projects were scattered throughout the nation in different centers. A first-hand observer of many of these projects and the director of a history project at Carnegie Mellon University, Fenton (1967), wrote of them:

> They are organized in a variety of ways: one or two professors in a university run most of them; organizations of scholars such as the American Anthropological Association administer a few; others are run by school systems, groups of schools or universities, or independent non-profit corporations … some projects aim to turn out a single course for a single discipline [sic], such as a course in tenth-grade geography; others are preparing units of material—anthropology, sociology, economics—which can fit into existing course structures; still others propose to develop entire curriculum sequences or to isolate the principles upon which curricula can be built. (p. 4)

Included in the new social studies were projects for the middle and secondary grades. The following five examples offer support of the complete project:

- Man: A Course of Study (MACOS)
- The University of Minnesota Project Social Studies, K–12
- The Anthropology Curriculum Study Project
- Sociological Resources for the Social Studies
- The High School Geography Project

A sample lesson from *Sociological Resources for the Social Studies* relating to poverty is shown in Appendix C, Resource Figure 1.1. The excerpted lesson is the first of a series of 12 that form a unit entitled, *The Incidence and Effects of Poverty in the United States.*

Many of the projects were based on the seminal ideas in psychologist Jerome Bruner's *The Process of Education* (1960), the slender conference report that summarized the discussion at Woods Hole. Particularly appealing to social studies educators were Bruner's ideas concerning the structure of the disciplines and discovery modes of learning. Bruner himself was extensively involved in MACOS, a middle-grade curriculum that integrated the disciplines of anthropology and biology to help students discover the similarities and differences between humans and animals.

Legacy of the New Social Studies. Despite the concerted efforts at curricular reform, the new social studies projects collectively failed to affect significantly the scope (list of topics and courses) and sequence (order of topics and courses) patterns of the social studies curriculum across the United States (Fancett & Hawke, 1982; Haas, 1977, 1986; Massialas, 1992). By some accounts, the projects had no significant impact on teaching practices, either (Shaver, Davis, & Hepburn,

1979; Superka, Hawke, & Morrissett, 1980). How can we account for this? Lockwood (1985) has suggested that the new social studies had limited lasting effects for three basic reasons: (1) teachers perceived that adoption of the innovations would have required major changes in the scope and sequence of existing curricula and teaching practices; (2) the reading levels of the new social studies materials were too advanced; and (3) students lacked the intellectual capacities required to use the materials. Massialas (1992) also argued that the new social studies lacked a research base and that projects failed to adequately address issues such as gender and ethnicity (see also Fenton, 1991; Rossi, 1992).

There is evidence, however, that the new social studies did have some significant sporadic effects. The new social studies, for example, gave rise to a larger role for the emerging social sciences. Similarly, although the new social studies failed to shake the dominance of the textbook as the primary instrument of instruction, it did stimulate the use of commercial and teacher-made supplementary materials. It also encouraged the use of media in teaching.

Although the new social studies did not substantially loosen the grip of teacher-centered approaches, it opened the door for a more active role for students and for greater consideration of their concerns in the curriculum. It also increased the use of instructional strategies that emphasized students' inquiry in the learning process, foreshadowing later constructivist arguments for greater engagement of students in the learning process. The new social studies also helped establish the principle that affective concerns relating to significant beliefs, attitudes, and values should have a place in social studies classes.

Social Studies Past, Current, and Future

In contrast to the excitement of the new social studies era, the 1980s were a period of reaction and soul searching for the social studies. One author summed up the decade with the following metaphor:

> It can be argued that the 1980s must be the adolescent period for social studies as social studies educators, through their journals and in dialogue at national and regional meetings, are diligently seeking consensus on definition and purpose, as well as agreement on scope and sequence. At this point it is unclear how long the adolescent period will last for social studies. (Atwood, 1982, p. 10)

At the beginning of the 1990s, the social studies were awash with alternative scope and sequence curriculum proposals. These offered new options for social studies educators and text publishers to consider the modification of programs and materials.

National Standards for the Social Studies Curriculum. By 1995, in addition to alternative scope and sequence models, several groups, including the NCSS, had either advanced proposals for national standards for the social studies or had projects in progress. Standards set out voluntary guidelines for what students in kindergarten through grade 12 should know and be able to do in subject areas such as civics, history, geography, and economics (U.S. Department of Education, 1994). The standards movement was propelled by the Goals 2000: Educate America Act, passed by Congress in 1992. Among other provisions, the act established the following goal:

> By the year 2000, all students will leave grades 4, 8, and 12 having demonstrated competency over challenging subject matter including English, mathematics, science, foreign languages, civics and government, economics, arts, history, and geography, and every school in America will ensure that all students learn to use their minds well, so they may be prepared for responsible citizenship, further learning, and productive employment in our Nation's modern economy. (The National Education Goals Panel, 1995, p. 11)

Since the introduction of social studies standards, and the Goals 2000 Act, school systems have taken a number of different actions in order to be more responsive to mandated expectations. O'Shea (2005) notes that systems have aligned their curricula with the scope and sequence of the standards, selected books and materials that were compatible with the standards, and held workshops to keep teachers current on standards and curricula. Signed into law on January 8, 2002, the No Child Left Behind (NCLB) legislation took this effort for ongoing readiness one step further. Since students needed to prove their competency through standardized tests, teachers were required to add test preparation to the curricula tested. In some cases, pacing guides and continuous assessment instruments were added (O'Shea, 2005). Tested or not, all curricula are affected by NCLB. Many teachers argue that the move to discrete fact testing has limited their teaching options, all the while imposing a strict monitoring of what they actually can do in their classrooms. Reflect on what you have heard from experienced teachers and discuss the issue of additional requirements being placed on education professionals. This issue is especially timely in light of the national teaching shortage, soon to be made that much more critical by the retirement of baby boomer teachers.

The 21st century is here and the need to understand the historic, economic, political, and social upheavals occurring daily in the world demands an increasingly important role for the social studies. In addition, the shift in our society from a national to a global economy and the emergence of new notions of what will be required of effective citizens in an increasingly interdependent and culturally diverse world demonstrates the need for more social studies work, not less. Unfortunately, our preoccupation with test scores in literacy, math, and science has reduced the time allotted for the study of social studies. The national conversation cannot seem to grasp the importance of broadening perspectives to achieve global understanding. Especially problematic with the emphasis on any drill and kill social studies fact-loading is that the memorization of discrete facts alone does not support students asking big questions about social studies issues that interest them. Answering one's own questions and issues and engaging in abstract thinking is motivational and stretches students to widen and deepen their understanding of complex matters. Searching for an answer using the disciplines as research tools allows for natural curriculum integration (Beane, 1997). James Beane has gone so far as to suggest that rigidly imposed standards bring us one step closer to a standardized curriculum and thus eliminates the ability of teachers to customize their lessons to address the context in which they are teaching (Beane, 2005).

Students must be social studies fluent so that we may address important democratic issues, such as the continuing erosion of individual rights and the decrease in voter participation in local, state, and national elections. Instead of addressing issues of democratic rights, the current national discussion centers around test scores that demonstrate the fact and skill loading accomplished by the other disciplines. There seems to be more interest in a numerical score as a measure of success than in how to stimulate students to become active rather than passive participants in the construction of knowledge. It is an uphill battle for the social studies, but one well worth waging and one that we must win.

Alternative Definitions of the Social Studies

Since the term *social studies* came into use as an outgrowth of the report of the Committee on the Social Studies in 1916 (U.S. Bureau of Education, 1916), through the era of the new social studies, and into the turn of a new century, many social studies educators have attempted, without success, to set out a definition of the field that would embrace all the disparate views. Consider the following examples:

> The social studies are the social sciences simplified for pedagogical purposes. (Wesley, 1950, p. 34)

> Social studies is the integrated study of the social sciences and humanities to promote civic competence. (National Council for the Social Studies, 1993, p. 3)

> The social studies are concerned exclusively with the education of citizens. In a democracy, citizenship education consists of two related but somewhat disparate parts: the first socialization, the second counter socialization. (Engle & Ochoa, 1988, p. 13)

> The social studies is an integration of experience and knowledge concerning human relations for the purpose of citizenship education. (Barr et al., 1977, p. 69)

> Social studies is a basic subject of the K–12 curriculum that (1) derives its goals from the nature of citizenship in a democratic society that is closely linked to other nations and peoples of the world; (2) draws its content primarily from history, the social sciences, and in some respects, from the humanities and science; and (3) is taught in ways that reflect an awareness of the personal, social, and cultural experiences and development levels of learners. (Task Force on Scope and Sequence, 1984, p. 251)

The diversity reflected in the proposed definitions reveals that the field reflects a lively and healthy controversy about what the social studies curriculum in middle and secondary schools should be. As Lybarger (1991) underscored: "One of the most remarkable aspects of the history of the social studies has been the ongoing debates over the nature, scope, and definition of the field"

(p. 9). In keeping with the ongoing debate, the NCSS definition has been expanded to include well-developed sections of explanation that emphasize the need for powerful social studies teaching and learning. Curricula are considered powerful when they are meaningful, integrative, value-based, challenging, and active.

A Working Definition of the Social Studies

As a point of reference, we will use throughout the textbook a working definition of the social studies.

The **social studies** are:

Selected information and modes of investigation from the social sciences

Selected information from any area that relates directly to an understanding of individuals, groups, and societies

Applications of the selected information to citizenship education

Now that we have looked at the history of the field and considered multiple definitions of social studies, let's briefly consider what it means to be a middle or high school teacher of social studies, typically including grades 6 through 12.

The Contemporary Social Studies Teacher

Each state sets its own requirements for certification for social studies teachers in the middle or secondary grades. Among subject-area teachers, social studies teachers may have the most diverse responsibilities in their assignments. Certification as a social studies teacher in most states permits you to teach courses in history, geography, sociology, anthropology, and psychology. It also typically authorizes you to teach economics, political science, civics, government, philosophy, consumer education, and numerous other courses with combinations of these titles.

In practice, of course, social studies teachers typically are called on to teach a small number of the possible options. Several examples of teaching configurations are shown in Figure 1.2. *True* middle schools are structured for two-teacher teams. This structure has several benefits for the student and the teacher. Each teacher on the two-teacher team usually teaches 60 students. The usual pairing of subjects is language arts/social studies and science/math. Benefits for teacher and students include the following:

- The team approach enables the teacher to better know students since they are fewer in number.
- The structure is ideal for curriculum integration of two well-matched subjects—language arts and social studies.

FIGURE 1.2
Schedule of Social Studies Teachers in Middle and Secondary Schools

---

Teacher: Susan Albright   **School:** Turner Middle School
          (member of two-teacher team)

	Teaching Assignment
Block 1	8th-grade Social Studies–American History (group 1) 8th-grade Language Arts (group 1)
Planning Block	2 periods—Team, individual
	Lunch period
Block 2	8th-grade Social Studies–American History (group 2) 8th-grade Language Arts (group 2)

Other Assignments: Hall duty one week each month during half of lunch period; advisor for Student Council.

Teacher: Jerry Koslowski   **School:** Cady High School

Period	*Teaching Assignment*
1	10th-grade World History
2	10th-grade World History
3	10th-grade World History
4	Lunch period
5	12th-grade Problems of Democracy
6	12th-grade Problems of Democracy
7	Planning period

Other Assignments: Bus duty in the morning one month during year; advisor for yearbook.

Block Schedule (90-minute classes)
Teacher: Libby Poppe   **School:** Southeast Raleigh High School

Period	*Teaching Assignment*
1	Planning
2	9th-grade Communications Technology (semester)
3	Lunch
4	9th-grade Honors Communications Technology (semester)
5	9th-grade American History 1400–1800 (semester)

Other Assignments: Lunch duty every fourth week; school improvement team.

- Curriculum integration is easier between two teachers who teach four subjects because fewer people are planning and making decisions.
- Classroom rules and practices are easier to determine since only two styles of teaching are being teamed.
- Coordinating meetings with one's teammate is easier with only two schedules to consider.

- Students have only two teachers to know and understand; that is, fewer rules to memorize and personalities to accommodate.
- Students also have fewer peers with whom to interact, a blessing for youngsters who feel lost in big middle schools.

Some former junior high schools are now calling themselves middle schools, but have kept the junior high schedule. Typically, these schools operate with four-teacher teams. This makes each teacher on the team responsible for one subject taught to 120 students a day. It is not difficult to understand why two-teacher teams, each teacher teaching 2 subjects to 60 students, have the advantage. Unfortunately, the teacher shortage is causing some true middle schools to abandon two-teacher teams for the four-teacher team approach. Principals find it easier to hire a teacher qualified to teach just one subject than to hire one who holds dual certification.

At the high school level, teachers have long followed the traditional teaching pattern: five classes, a planning period, and lunch break. Recently, some high schools have adopted block scheduling. This means each course is taught daily for a longer block of time, usually for 90 minutes. The course itself lasts for only one semester. How do high school teachers, students, and parents feel about this approach? Viewpoints are mixed. Some experienced teachers welcome the opportunity to teach the same course for longer periods each day. They believe that the extra time allows for (1) more in-depth study and discussion, (2) the possibility of using a more hands-on teaching approach, and (3) the chance to finish the day or lesson with a more comprehensive closure. Others argue that today's students have much shorter attention spans and that it's harder to keep students engaged for longer periods of time. Mainstreamed special needs students, especially, have a difficult time staying focused for 90 minutes. Those opposed to block scheduling also note the time-consuming process of revamping already prepared 45-minute lessons to 90 minutes. Perhaps you attended a high school that used block scheduling. What do you believe were the advantages and disadvantages of this teaching and learning approach for teachers, students, and parents? On the other hand, if you were taught using a traditional schedule, how do you think a switch to block scheduling would have been received? How would you represent the pros and cons of the traditional scheduling approach?

History and political science are the two primary disciplines represented in the middle and secondary social studies curriculum. The social studies staff in a typical middle or secondary school likely will contain a mix of teachers who have a primary core of course work in one or more of the discipline areas already mentioned.

Certification of Social Studies Teachers

In addition to completing a required number of courses in the social sciences and professional education, certified social studies teachers typically complete a supervised *student teaching* or *internship* experience in a middle or secondary school. States provide an *initial* or *provisional* certification upon successful completion of course work and the internship. Many states now offer separate certification authorizations for teaching in the middle grades (typically covering grades 6 through 9) or the secondary grades (typically grades 9 through 12). The traditional certification pattern has covered authorization for teaching grades 7 through 12. Once certified, states require their teachers to renew their certificates regularly. States specify how many courses or inservice hours are required for renewal and in which areas these offerings must be taken. Periods of time for renewal vary, but most states require renewal every 5 years.

Teaching Portfolios

As part of the certification and assessment process, teachers usually are asked to create portfolios of items such as philosophy of education, classroom management plan, sample lesson plans, examples of student work, and an electronic representation of teaching. They also may include observation notes by supervisors, mentors, or cooperating teachers and endorsement letters from students (see Figure 1.3). Some states require both a teaching and a technology portfolio. Colleges and universities align their requirements with those identified by the National Education Technology Standards (NETS). Students are required to demonstrate competence through the use of technology in the context of their student teaching experiences. The portfolio chronicles technology lessons and provides evidence and evaluation of their implementation. More and more colleges and universities are requiring their students to provide electronic portfolios. Colleges of education must validate completion and competency to state licensing agencies.

Lateral Entry Teachers

There are a number of different approaches that are being used to help individuals who wish to leave their chosen nonteaching occupation and enter the classroom. These teachers-to-be are classified as lateral entry (LE) and are needed to help alleviate the national teaching shortage. State assessment centers, community colleges, 4-year colleges, and universities are being asked to evaluate the transcripts of those seeking lateral entry status and determine what courses they must take for certification. Individuals who have been successful in other careers wish to enter teaching for any number of reasons. Some are in Erikson's generativity stage of development and wish to give back to education. Others hope their previous work success might be translated to meaningful classroom success, the kind that will help young people ready themselves for the real world. Still others may wish to look back at their final career choice as one that has made a difference

FIGURE 1.3
What Is a Teacher Portfolio?

A **teacher portfolio** is a compilation of items that a teacher has done, both in the classroom and elsewhere. It is designed to display that teacher's talents and proficiencies and to demonstrate that teacher's knowledge and skills. What the teacher includes is always a matter of intent. The question that should be asked is, "***What am I trying to tell the reader about myself?***"

Include a resumé with the portfolio and with any letter of application. If possible, bring your portfolio to the school where you are interviewing at least 3 days before your interview. This gives the committee time to review your work in advance. Have your portfolio well organized. This is a personal reflection. It should look very professional.

A Typical Portfolio Might Include the Following:

1. A brief yet interesting biographical sketch, not a lengthy resumé or a dissertation on education. Include a short essay that tells the reader about yourself and what you have done.
2. A description of the kinds of classes you have taught recently. Do not include everything. Review committee time is short. Do not bore them. Note the grade level, class content and describe your teaching style.
3. Copies of documents, licenses, tests, and so on. Include what graduate classes or inservice seminars you have recently attended. Demonstrate your continuing education and creativity.
4. A short essay about your teaching philosophy, how you teach, and why. Avoid any lengthy discourse.
5. Your classroom management and discipline plan.
6. Copies of recent lesson or unit plans you have used. Photos of the class engaged in these activities will help. (Photo permissions necessary.)
7. Creative handouts you have designed and student papers you have graded showing your comments, and so on.
8. If you have photographs of your classroom or an electronic representation of you in action, include it.

for themselves and others (Medford & Knorr, 2005). The No Child Left Behind (NCLB) legislation requires principals to hire highly qualified teachers and has made employing lateral entry teachers more difficult. LE teachers must have an ongoing work plan for certification and it must be completed in 3 years. Even with this plan LE teachers are not yet highly qualified and are the last to be hired. Lateral entry teachers who are hired receive full salary and benefits for the first 3 years. If they are not fully certified at the end of those 3 years they will begin to receive substitute salary. Currently, the NCTEACH program at North Carolina State University provides lateral entry teachers with a fast track to certification, thus helping to address the state's teaching shortage. Lateral entry teachers in

NCTEACH complete a rigorous summer of teacher education courses and attend after-school workshops twice a month for a year. At the end of the program, these teachers receive certification in their major field. Early data show that NCTEACH graduates exceed the national teacher retention averages.

SUMMARY

In this chapter we have discussed your "career" evolution. You seek to become an educator and, in particular, a teacher of social studies. Teaching is often referred to as a calling. Those who answer the call develop and hone the skills that enable them to meet the needs of students at a variety of levels. Most teachers will counsel you that patience and humor are needed for day-to-day interaction with coworkers, students, and parents. The first step in the traditional process to becoming a teacher is a rigorous college experience that provides you with depth of subject knowledge, a pedagogical framework, many and varied field opportunities, and a culminating student teaching experience. Portfolio completion and standardized test taking round out your college experience and are rapidly followed by hunting for the first job. Teacher performance assessment centers, as well as colleges and universities, help those seeking a nontraditional alternative approach to licensure, namely, lateral entry.

This chapter has also examined the subject of social studies and has traced the evolution of the social studies. Although social studies is often criticized as being "all things to all people," in a rapidly changing world it takes the diversity of many different areas of the social sciences to explain complicated issues. One of the greatest challenges for teachers of social studies, besides getting our share of instructional time, is to help students understand and appreciate our nation's diverse cultural heritage. As this is done and students become educated in the principles of a democratic society, they must understand their role in preserving our system of government and be ready to actively participate. Helping students move beyond strictly Americentric views will enable them to embrace and develop a global perspective. The saying, "No man (person) is an island," was never truer than it is today.

ACTIVITIES

1. Discuss your recollections of social studies when you were in the middle and secondary grades. Are they pleasant or unpleasant? Examine the teaching approaches used by your teachers. Which enabled meaningful learning experiences and which did not? How do you explain the failures and successes of these various approaches?

2. How much time should be devoted to teaching and learning social studies in the middle grades? In high school? What is the rationale you have taken?
3. Construct a time line indicating five or six key developments in the social studies over the last 100 years. Include all of the major events in world and U.S. history that you can remember.
4. Construct a personal teaching autobiography narrative. Include defining people or experiences that have influenced your desire to become a social studies teacher. Discuss the importance of social studies education and the goals you have for yourself as a teacher.
5. Visit different College of Education or State Departments of Education websites and explore how these programs and requirements are similar and different from your school.

WEB RESOURCES

National Council for the Social Studies: www.ncss.org

Kathy Schrock's Guide for Educators: www.school.discovery.com/schrockguide/

Eric Clearinghouse for Social Studies: www.education.indiana.edu/~ssdc/eric~_chess.htm

New York Times Learning Network: www.nytimes.com/learning

Connections: www.mcrel.com

National Middle School Association: www.nmsa.org

Chapter 2

Contemporary Social Studies

Citizenship Education as the Purpose of the Social Studies
  The Context of Citizenship Education
Alternative Perspectives on a Curriculum for Effective Citizenship Education
The Enduring Goal of the Social Studies Curriculum: Reflective, Competent, and Concerned Citizens
  The Nature of the Effective Citizen
  Social Studies as a Matter of Head, Hand, and Heart
Existing Social Studies Scope and Sequence Patterns
  The Curriculum Pattern in the Elementary Grades
  The Curriculum Pattern in the Middle and Secondary Grades
  The Dominance of Traditional Scope and Sequence Patterns
National Standards
  Social Studies Standards
  Technology Standards
  State Standards
  Professional Standards for Teachers
Basal Textbooks and the Social Studies Curriculum
  Use of Basal Textbooks in the Social Studies
  Selection and Adoption of Basal Textbooks
  Implications of State Adoption Policies
Summary
Activities
Web Resources

*Envision that you planned an e-Pals project for your eighth-grade students. e-Pals (**www.epals.com**) is an Internet project that links students and classrooms around the globe through e-mail. Suppose that each of your eighth-grade students was randomly linked with an eighth grader from another city and state. The purpose of the activity was for students to discuss the roles of local governments. Imagine your surprise when you realized that some of the other students knew very little about local governments, while other students were actively involved in local government activities. You quickly realized that some of the eighth graders were indeed studying civics, while other eighth graders were studying world history or U.S. history. Almost all of the students from across the country were studying different topics than you and your students were studying!*

What curriculum would you expect the other students to be following? What criteria would you surmise were used to establish the curriculum? Who or what agency has the primary responsibility for determining what students in these classes will study? What impact does this have on student learning and teacher autonomy?

The answers to these questions are rooted in our history and constitutional framework. Because the framers of the Constitution rejected a national system of education, the matter of schools and curriculum fell to the individual states. States, in turn, often granted considerable authority in these matters to local governments.

Consequently, we have no national control of curriculum. Rather, a collection of thousands of local school districts and governing boards exists, each with varying degrees of autonomy over its social studies curriculum.

Citizenship Education as the Purpose of the Social Studies

Defining the social studies can be problematic. Social studies encompasses history, geography, sociology, psychology, economics, archaeology, philosophy, political science, and law. The breadth of the field of social studies makes it difficult to define, but it also makes social studies such an essential component of the school curriculum. NCSS advocates that social studies is "the integrated study of the social sciences and humanities to promote civic competence." (National Council for the Social Studies, *Advocacy ToolKit*. Online serial: **www.ncss.org/ toolkit** accessed Dec 4, 2007.) Over time, the evolving definitions of the social studies have pointed toward citizenship education. Those entrusted with the formal responsibilities for the maintenance, defense, and improvement of the society depend on some degree of citizen participation so that social, political, and economic institutions can operate.

Citizenship provides individuals with a sense of identity and belonging. It also may bestow such benefits as the promise of a high standard of living, educational and health care benefits, opportunities for self-fulfillment, and a sense of belonging to a larger social group. In the global age of technology, the role of citizenship education is becoming increasingly significant.

The NCSS Task Force on Revitalizing Citizenship Education defines an effective citizen as "one who has the knowledge, skills, and attitudes required to assume the office of citizen in our democratic republic." The task force further promotes citizenship education by stating:

> To accomplish this goal, every student must participate in citizenship education activities each year. These activities should expand civic knowledge, develop participation skills, and support the belief that, in a democracy, the actions of each person make a difference. Throughout the curriculum and at every grade level, students should have opportunities to apply their civic knowledge, skills, and values as they work to solve

real problems in their school, the community, our nation, and the world. These opportunities should be part of a well-planned and organized citizenship education program.

Citizenship education is as important today as at any other time in our history. Citizens in the twenty-first century must be prepared to deal with rapid change, complex local, national, and global issues, cultural and religious conflicts, and the increasing interdependence of nations in a global economy. For our democracy to survive in this challenging environment, we must educate our students to understand, respect, and uphold the values enshrined in our founding documents. Our students should leave school with a clear sense of their rights and responsibilities as citizens. They should also be prepared to challenge injustice and to promote the common good. (NCSS, retrieved Dec. 4, 2007, from **www.socialstudies.org/positions/effectivecitizens**)

The Context of Citizenship Education

Citizenship education in our society occurs in many forms, both outside and inside of schools. Institutions external to the school, including those of the mass media, increasingly have assumed a larger role in the process. Advertisements (for example, on billboards and book covers) urge students to serve their country in the military, to use condoms to prevent social epidemics, and to protect the environment. Political action groups, representing every shade of the political spectrum and fueled by tax exemptions, now loom as a major force in the political process.

Citizenship education within the schools also takes place in many ways, both within the formal and the "hidden" curriculum, the policies, mores, activities, rules, norms, and models that the school provides outside of the classroom. Within the classroom, civic education has several dimensions, as Oppenheim and Torney (1974) have reminded us:

> Civic education does not merely consist in the transmission of a body of *knowledge*, . . . it aims at inculcating certain shared *attitudes* and values, such as a democratic outlook, political responsibility, the ideals of tolerance and social justice, respect for authority, and so on. . . . Indeed, the cognitive content of the curriculum is frequently used in order to highlight the underlying principles and ideology; thus, information about electoral systems could be utilized in order to bring out fundamental ideas about equality and majority rule. (p. 13)

The Civic Education Study (CivEd), sponsored by the International Association for the Evaluation of Educational Achievement (IEA), is a comprehensive study that examines civic education in the United States and 28 other countries. The results of the study reveal that U.S. ninth graders scored significantly above the international average on the total civic knowledge scale and that 55% of U.S. school principals reported that ninth-grade students are required to take five to six periods a week in civic-related subjects such as social studies, history, or civics. Additional findings from the report include:

- U.S. students were more likely to study domestic civic issues than international civic issues.
- U.S. students were more likely to report reading from a textbook or filling out worksheets when studying social studies than engaging in activities such as receiving visits from leaders or writing letters to give their opinion.
- Eighty-five percent of students reported being encouraged by teachers to make up their own minds about issues, and about two-thirds reported being encouraged by teachers to discuss political or social issues about which people have different opinions. (Baldi, Perie, Skidmore, Greenberg, & Hahn, 2001)

A look at the recently created NCSS Advocacy ToolKit (online serial) emphasizes the role citizenship education plays in the contemporary social studies classroom. The ToolKit has a series of materials to be used by parents, educators, and administrators to advocate for social studies education. One resource in the ToolKit is a series of sample letters to the editors. Figure 2.1 is one example of a sample letter to the editor that highlights the role of citizenship education.

Alternative Perspectives on a Curriculum for Effective Citizenship Education

As we have noted, social studies educators generally agree that citizenship education should be the major focus of the social studies curriculum. Beyond this basic statement of agreement, however, are disagreements regarding which specific purpose the curriculum should serve in promoting citizenship education. We will characterize these different views as alternative perspectives on citizenship education.

A related debate continues over the characteristics of the ideal or "good" citizen, who is the object of the social studies curriculum. In our discussions, we will use the term **effective citizen** to refer to this idealized type.

Over the past quarter of a century, a number of social studies educators have attempted to delineate the characteristics of effective citizenship in relation to our democratic society and the social studies curriculum. One NCSS standard is dedicated to civic ideals and practices:

Standard X: Social studies programs should include experiences that provide for the study of the ideals, principles, and practices of citizenship in a democratic republic.

This standard calls upon students to consider such questions as: What is civic participation and how can I be involved? How has the meaning of citizenship evolved? What is the balance between rights and responsibilities? What is the role

FIGURE 2.1
Sample Op-Ed Article

Op Ed on Value of Social Studies

By *Your Name*

Today's social studies is more important than ever before for students in kindergarten through high school. The vast array of courses under the social studies umbrella teaches students the skills they need to be effective citizens. Whether it's through a community service project where students learn to appreciate the value of "giving back" or a civic course where students learn how to influence a bill in the state legislature, what students learn in social studies will allow them to be responsible citizens in our modern society. Social studies education is the thread that holds our democracy together.

As our nation strives to promote citizen interest in voting and participation in the democratic process, social studies education delivers valuable lessons. Social studies teachers provide students first–hand experience in how the electoral process works, and not just by reading books. Mock elections are held in government classes where students play the role of delegates to political parties, nominate candidates and plan campaigns. In other settings candidates are encouraged to come to social studies classes to discuss the issues with students and aspects of campaigning such as debates and advertising. In such activities, students learn to listen critically to positions people state, evaluate those positions, and make decisions.

In still other schools, students are given the opportunity to shadow elected officials for a day to see what being mayor or a councilperson actually entails. All of these activities, and more that are being offered in our schools every day, expose youngsters to the workings of a democracy so that they can make intelligent decisions as adults.

Some schools even go further, offering 18-year-olds and members of the nearby community the chance to register to vote before elections. Working with such organizations as the League of Women Voters, students publicize the opportunity in a non-partisan manner working to generate greater participation. They learn to work with other people and develop pride in their contributions to the community.

Social studies educators often supervise extended programs to provide students with additional eye-opening experiences that set the foundation for participation in our democratic form of government. These include field trips to the state capitol or even Washington, D.C.

Some educational experiences, especially at the high school level, actually have students become involved in projects that have a positive impact on their community right now. Classes would study challenges that face their community, ranging from providing activities for the elderly to identifying the source of pollution in a local water supply to assuring that young children have a clean recreation area. They adopt one of those challenges, meet with community leaders to learn about the problem, discuss potential solutions, determine a strategy to solve the problem, and implement that strategy. Their work could include convincing the city council to allocate funding for a solution, seeking coverage of the issue in the local news media, mobilizing public opinion to become involved in the solution, and other strategies that are essential in a democracy.

Still other schools stress community service projects where students experience the positive feeling of helping other people. Activities range from collecting food for flood victims to serving food at a homeless shelter to meeting with the elderly in senior homes.

The opportunities that social studies provide students today are endless. Students are learning to listen critically, develop arguments to support their beliefs, evaluate what others say, think critically, and make informed decisions. What all social studies classes have in common is that they are all helping young people understand the value our democratic ideals. They are building effective citizens for the future.

of the citizen in the community and the nation, and as a member of the world community? How can I make a positive difference? In schools, this theme typically appears in units or courses dealing with history, political science, cultural anthropology, and fields such as global studies, law-related education, and the humanities (NCSS, **www.ncss.org**).

Some proponents of citizenship education have argued that it should consist of a core of basic civic competencies that all citizens acquire. The NCSS Task Force on Revitalizing Citizenship Education has prepared the following list of characteristics of an effective citizen:

- Embraces core democratic values and strives to live by them
- Accepts responsibility for the well-being of oneself, one's family, and the community
- Has knowledge of the people, history, and traditions that have shaped our local communities, our nation, and the world
- Has knowledge of our nation's founding documents, civic institutions, and political processes
- Is aware of issues and events that have an impact on people at local, state, national, and global levels
- Seeks information from varied sources and perspectives to develop informed opinions and creative solutions
- Asks meaningful questions and is able to analyze and evaluate information and ideas
- Uses effective decision-making and problem-solving skills in public and private life
- Has the ability to collaborate effectively as a member of a group
- Actively participates in civic and community life (NCSS, **www.ncss.org**)

Other advocates for civic education have incorporated citizenship competencies within a broader skeleton of goals. As an illustration, *CIVITAS* is a project that provides a K–12 framework for citizenship education that integrates the development of knowledge, skills, and social service (Center for Civic Education, 1991).

Barr, Barth, and Shermis (1977) analyzed and attempted to categorize the various statements of purpose related to citizenship education that various social studies educators have advanced in the 20th century. The authors created three categories into which they grouped all approaches to citizenship education—social studies taught as (1) *transmission of the cultural heritage,* (2) *the social sciences,* and (3) *reflective inquiry.*

We have extended their set of categories by drawing on the further analyses of Engle (1977) and Nelson and Michaelis (1980) to create two additional categories: social studies taught as *informed social criticism* and *personal development.* These five major perspectives on citizenship education and their respective emphases are summarized briefly in Figure 2.2.

FIGURE 2.2
Alternate Perspectives on Citizenship Education

Perspective Social studies should be taught as:	Description Citizenship education should consist of:
Transmission of the Cultural Heritage	Transmitting traditional knowledge and values as a framework for making decisions
Social Science	Mastering social science concepts, generalizations, and processes to build a knowledge base for later learning
Reflective Inquiry	Employing a process of thinking and learning in which knowledge is derived from what citizens need to know in order to make decisions and solve problems
Informed Social Criticism	Providing opportunities for an examination, critique, and revision of past traditions, existing social practices, and modes of problem solving
Personal Development	Developing a positive self-concept and a strong sense of personal efficacy

These five perspectives certainly do not exhaust all of the possible classifications. Furthermore, none of the alternative categories that have been outlined completely avoids overlap among the others. Often one category, when analyzed and discussed, appears to include all other categories of purposes. Teaching social studies as social criticism, for example, may at times include teaching for reflective inquiry.

Nevertheless, it may be helpful to clarify your own views by considering some of the different emphases or dominant perspectives that each statement of purpose reflects. As you do this, you may wish to borrow elements of several categories to create a new composite category of your own.

The Enduring Goal of the Social Studies Curriculum: Reflective, Competent, and Concerned Citizens

Frequently, arguments over the purpose of the social studies cannot be easily categorized into one of the five perspectives shown in Figure 2.2. For example, in 1993, the NCSS endorsed the view: "The primary purpose of social studies is to help young people develop the ability to make informed and reasoned decisions for the public good as citizens of a culturally diverse, democratic society in an interdependent world" (p. 2).

Barbara Schwartz/Merrill

The overarching goal of the social studies is to assist students in becoming effective citizens of today's global society.

Similarly, our position does not match neatly with any one of the five perspectives, although it draws on several of them. Our perspective borrows heavily from the tradition of *reflective inquiry,* as developed in the works of Dewey (1933), Engle (1977), Griffin (1992), Hullfish and Smith (1961), and Hunt and Metcalf (1968).

It also includes an emphasis on learning to be an informed and responsible social critic of society, as described by Engle and Ochoa (1988). Additionally, the perspective reflects the influence of recent research in the field of cognitive psychology that addresses how individuals construct, integrate, retrieve, and apply knowledge.

The Nature of the Effective Citizen

The effective young citizens that such a perspective seeks to develop require a three-dimensional social studies program, one that emphasizes rationality, skillful behavior, and social consciousness. Further, such a program must cast citizen roles within the framework of a democratic society and its corresponding continuing needs for maintenance, nurturance, and renewal.

Effective citizens in this vision have an informed view of their societal birthrights and the constitutional and legal bedrock that undergird them. They also accept a corresponding commitment to contribute to the sustenance and improvement of their society and the preservation of other citizens' rights.

Such citizens are *nationalistic,* because nationalism engenders a strong sense of community and identification with others who have similar characteristics, experiences, commitments, and aspirations. At the same time, effective citizens are also *global minded,* because all peoples of the world are passengers on the same spaceship earth. Their destinies are inextricably intertwined.

Reflective, Competent, and Concerned Citizens. We will characterize the young citizens who emerge from such a program as **reflective, competent,** and **concerned.** We propose that reflection, competence, and concern, in some form, can be nurtured at all levels, from the primary through the intermediate, middle, and secondary grades. Correspondingly, throughout the text we will argue that the basic purpose of the social studies curriculum across the grades is to develop reflective, competent, and concerned citizens.

Reflective individuals are critical thinkers who make decisions and solve problems on the basis of the best evidence available. Competent citizens possess a repertoire of skills to aid them in decision making and problem solving. Concerned citizens investigate their social world, address issues they identify as significant, exercise their rights, and carry out their responsibilities as members of a social community (see Box 2.1).

Social Studies as a Matter of Head, Hand, and Heart

We characterize social studies programs that seek to develop the three dimensions of the reflective, competent, and concerned citizen by way of a simple metaphor, **social studies as a matter of the head, the hand, and the heart.** The head represents reflection, the hand denotes competencies, and the heart symbolizes concern. The characteristics of the reflective, competent, and concerned citizen are summarized in Figure 2.3. Subsequent chapters will provide more detailed analyses about what each of these three dimensions of the effective citizen entails and will describe how they may be developed through social studies instruction.

The Interrelationship of Head, Hand, and Heart. Thinking, skillful action, and feeling are intertwined. No one of the three dimensions operates in isolation from the others. The head, the hand, and the heart are interrelated and work in concert.

The relationship among head, hand, and heart often is not systematic or linear. Juan, an 11th grader, may read an article about an issue—genetic cloning, for example. As a result, he begins to examine its dimensions rationally and systematically by employing his research skills. His level of social consciousness and concern then is aroused, and he is driven to investigate further. Finally, he may be moved to social protest and action to support his position on the issue. This cycle of events, however, just as easily might have begun more dramatically as a matter of the heart if one of Juan's family members was suffering from a disease that could benefit from genetic research.

Teachers and students at the Centennial Campus Middle School in Raleigh, North Carolina, and some North Carolina State University professors and their preservice teachers have chosen to join churches in the area as part of a Partners for Environmental Justice project, Wetlands 2000, to clean up and protect a wetland area. The area, located in a poor section of the capital city at a point where two creeks come together, had become a dumping ground for trash and large household items. It was also subject to flooding during rainy times, because a major highway built nearby covered the ground with miles of hard-surface asphalt. Rain, previously absorbed into the ground, now ran off the road and spilled into the creeks, increasing the flooding. Filthy, polluted water poured into the homes of neighbors located near the creeks. Area residents were forced to fight rats and bugs drawn by the food and debris carried into the area. Besides the flooding, trash was regularly dumped in the wetlands and into the creeks. The general deterioration made the neighborhood an eyesore and the wetlands a dangerous playground. This was no creekside adventureland reminiscent of Huck Finn and his friends.

Before the students could be part of a solution, they had to research the problem. They used all manner of materials. They consulted books, surfed the Internet, interviewed residents and city officials, and used GIS (global information systems) to plot the characteristics of the area: how much and what kinds of businesses were located there, types of zoning, median family income, and the like. They studied topography maps that showed the elevations in the area and made it easier to see which areas were subject to the worst flooding. They engaged in a hands-on workshop led by a preservice social studies teacher that introduced them to the flora of the area. Some participated in a Saturday clean-up which netted 60 tires, 500 bottles, refrigerators, bikes, barrels, and other refuse. A major part of their research was action oriented. They took a field trip to the site and walked along the creek, gathering data about the area. They sketched, learned about the history of the site, and planted 70 bald cypress trees and hundreds of wetland plants native to North Carolina.

To educate a citywide audience, this remarkable group of students prepared and presented their findings at the North Carolina State University Spell of the Land Symposium. They premiered a new song that they had composed about the wetlands, shared original poetry that spoke to the importance of this reclamation project, unveiled a 12-foot-long mural of the wetland area that they had sketched and painted, performed a question-and-answer news report skit that revealed facts that they had learned about the wetlands and, finally, showed a digital stream of images that they had taken on the field trip, complete with voice-over student reflections and classical music as background.

This was not a short-term project. Students plan to write letters to their city council representatives to inform them about the facts of the wetland area. They want measures taken to eliminate the flooding in the neighborhoods and patrols increased to catch the people who are illegally dumping. They support the Partners' plans to have an environmental education center built in the area so that citizens can visit the wetlands and realize how lucky they are to have this treasure in their capital city.

When asked how they felt about being involved in this wetlands service project, the students cited the chance to get involved and make a difference for their city and its residents. They saw themselves as proactive for people and animal rights and believed that as protectors they were also "keepers of the history." They acknowledged that they appreciated being valued for their contribution and felt that they had been changed by the experience. They now had a stronger sense of place because of their investment in their city.

Teachers and the university professors and their students upon whom the teaching and coordinating of this research project fell used their skills in preparing and teaching an integrated language arts, social studies, math, and science unit. Using a local problem as the vehicle for the unit gave purpose to the learning and empowered a school full of children to demonstrate citizenship education. A website entitled Curriculum Integration featuring this project can be found at **www.ncsu.edu/chass/extension/ci** (Click on Taking Theory to Practice, Follow their CI Unit, Chapter 10).

FIGURE 2.3
The Reflective, Competent, and Concerned Citizen

Social Studies as a Matter of the Head: Reflection

The *reflective* citizen has knowledge of a body of concepts, facts, and generalizations concerning the organization, understanding, and development of individuals, groups, and societies. Also, the reflective citizen can engage in hypothesis formation and testing, problem solving, and decision making.

Social Studies as a Matter of the Hand: Competence

The *competent* citizen has a repertoire of skills. These include social, research and analysis, chronology, and spatial skills.

Social Studies as a Matter of the Heart: Concern

The *concerned* citizen has an awareness of his or her rights and responsibilities in a democracy, a sense of social consciousness, and a well-grounded framework for deciding what is right and what is wrong and for acting on decisions. Additionally the concerned citizen has learned how to identify and analyze issues and to suspend judgment concerning alternative beliefs, attitudes, values, customs, and cultures.

Social studies programs designed within this framework should offer students a balance of activities and subject matter for growth in the areas of reflection, competence, and concern. The relative amounts of attention or proportions of time paid to matters of the head, the hand, or the heart may vary according to the grade level, the abilities and needs of students, and the current needs of society. The hand, for example, may receive more weight in the social studies curriculum in the lower grades and less in later years. Some attention to all three dimensions, however, is necessary for a balanced social studies program. We will explore the role of each of these aspects as they are woven throughout the social studies curriculum.

Existing Social Studies Scope and Sequence Patterns

Subject to general guidelines and standards for the social studies curriculum established by each state, a local school district often has considerable freedom in the development of its social studies program. Thus the potential for variety in the social studies curriculum scope and sequence patterns across the United States is great.

Although the principle of local control holds out the promise of diversity in curriculum offerings, in reality there is considerable homogeneity in the social studies programs in grades K through 12 across the 50 states. A review of state standards demonstrates that a spiraling scope and sequence pattern has changed relatively little over the past 30 years. The pattern seems to be based on the following sequence, with variation by state and local entities.

Grades K–1   Self, family, school

Grade 2   Neighborhood

Grade 3   Communities and local history

Grade 4   State history, geographic regions

Grade 5   U.S. history, culture, and geography

Grade 6   World cultures, history, and geography

Grade 7   Civics and economics

Grade 8   World geography

Grade 9   World history and geography

Grade 10   World history and geography

Grade 11   American history

Grade 12   American government

The Curriculum Pattern in the Elementary Grades

The existing organizational pattern of the social studies curriculum in grades K through 6 follows what has been characterized by Hanna (1963) as the **expanding-communities curriculum pattern.** This approach, which has dominated the elementary curriculum for several decades, is based on the notion that a student will be introduced during each year of school to an increasingly expanding social environment, moving from examining the self and the family in grades K through 1 to the world at large in grade 6. Hanna's model also identified nine categories of basic human activities that should be addressed during each year of the social studies curriculum: expressing, producing, transporting, communicating, educating, recreating, protecting, governing, and creating.

The Curriculum Pattern in the Middle and Secondary Grades

The long-term impact of the 1916 report of the Committee on Social Studies (see Chapter 1) ironically proved to be pervasive and enduring, extending into the 1990s. Note the close similarities between the typical national pattern described in the preceding section and the following general recommendations for grades 7 through 12 from the 1916 report of the Committee on Social Studies:

Grades 7–9   Geography, European history, American history, civics

Grade 10   European history

Grade 11   American history

Grade 12   Problems of democracy

Contrary to the intent of the committee, its report became a paradigm of what the scope and sequence of courses in the curriculum should be. The committee itself had refrained from offering detailed outlines of courses. It believed that the selection of topics and the organization of subject matter should be determined by the needs of each community.

A further irony spawned by the report was that its recommendations often were viewed as being literal, timeless, and universal, applicable in all particulars to all generations and communities. The committee's intent, however, had been to sketch only general principles on which different schools could build their curricula in concert with the changing character of each time period, community, and group of students.

The 1916 committee constructed its recommendations in the context of a school population vastly different from the one that exists today. It saw its immediate task as planning a social studies curriculum that emphasized citizenship education for a nation in which the majority of students completed their education without entering high school. This short educational period meant that all of the essential elements in the curriculum needed to be provided before the 10th grade.

Some might suggest that we have come full circle. Today, there is great concern for the need to reemphasize citizenship education. Proponents wish to build it into the curriculum to be sure that students who leave school early have had citizenship training.

Advocacy groups such as the National Alliance for Civic Education report that the majority of states require a set of topics associated with civic education be included in the curriculum, but leave the details of instructional implementation to local schools. Thirty-one states currently test students on topics related to civic education, but only three states have a separate standardized test based on civic education. Thirty-four states require high school students to take a civics or government course prior to graduation.

The Dominance of Traditional Scope and Sequence Patterns

Why has the dominant national scope and sequence pattern for the social studies curriculum endured so long? A major part of the answer lies, perhaps, in several inter-related factors: *tradition, accrediting agencies and professional organizations, preservice teacher education programs*, and *patterns of textbook selection and adoption*.

The weight of tradition bears down heavily on those who would challenge the conventional scope and sequence of the social studies curriculum. Parents and community members tend to encourage preservation of the status quo. Teachers themselves are often more comfortable with the known than the unknown.

Moreover, tradition influences the norms for accrediting agencies that examine the quality of our school districts across the country. It is also an important consideration for national organizations such as the National Council for the Social Studies (NCSS) and for state departments of education.

The enduring goal of the social studies curriculum is to develop reflective, competent, and concerned citizens.

National Standards

In recent years, the debate concerning what students should learn in the social studies and when they should learn it has shifted to the arena of national *standards*. Such standards can function as tools for individual teachers and instructional leaders to aid in designing K–12 programs, planning curricula, and engaging students in meaningful learning experiences. Standards, in effect, are extensive reference works or guidelines that social studies educators can consult to craft scope and sequence patterns.

A number of professional organizations have worked on standards related to the social studies curriculum. Their efforts are represented in the History Standards Project, the Geography Standards Project, the National Council on Economic Education Standards, National Standards for Civics and Government, and the NCSS Curriculum Standards for the Social Studies, addressing the social studies curriculum as a whole. The International Society for Technology in Education (ISTE) has published sets of technology standards for both students and teachers. Although the standards for students cross the different content areas, there are specific applications and examples for social studies.

Each set of recommendations from the various projects contains some type of *content standards* that indicate what subject-matter themes should be included at each level and *performance standards* that specify what students are expected to learn. The statements of performance standards for the social studies and civics and government standards are the most general, whereas the structure of the history standards recommendations is the most complex to understand. Figure 2.4 highlights each of these sets of standards and provides the URL for more information.

Social Studies Standards

The NCSS content standards consist of 10 themes that are to be included for each grade. They are Culture; Time, Continuity, and Change; People, Places, and Environments; Individual Development and Identity; Individuals, Groups, and Institutions; Power, Authority, and Governance; Production, Distribution, and Consumption; Science, Technology, and Society; Global Connections; and Civic Ideals and Practices. For a description of each theme, see Figure 2.5. Corresponding to each theme, grade-level–appropriate performance expectations provide a means for measuring student capabilities as they relate to established standards (see Appendix A).

Technology Standards

The International Society for Technology in Education (ISTE) developed technology standards for students and for teachers. The National Educational Technology Standards (NETS) for students are divided into six categories: basic operations and concepts; social, ethical, and human issues; technology productivity tools; technology communications tools; technology research tools; and technology problem-solving and decision-making tools. Performance indicators are then provided for clusters of grade levels and lesson plans are detailed for different content areas. Visit **cnets.iste.org** to view these indicators and sample lessons.

Just as national standards have emerged for students, they have also been developed for classroom teachers. The NETS for teachers are based on the student standards. The teacher standards are divided into the same six categories as the student standards; however, the performance indicators are different.

State Standards

In addition to the series of national standards, the majority of U.S. states have their own set of state social studies standards. Many states also require students to take an end-of-course exam that is based on the state standards. Education World is an online resource with information about state standards for each U.S. state. Visit **www.education-world.com/standards/state/index.shtml** to view your own state standards and contact your state department of education to learn more about them.

Professional Standards for Teachers

The National Board for Professional Teaching Standards (NBPTS) (**www.nbpts.org/**) developed a set of five core propositions and standards in over 27 fields for teachers. The standards are specific to the grade level and content area. For

FIGURE 2.4
Competing Social Studies Standards

Standards	Sponsor	Grade Levels	Organized Around	URL
Expectations of Excellence: Curriculum Standards for Social Studies	National Council for the Social Studies	K–12	thematic strands	www.ncss.org
National Standards for History (K–4)	National Center for History in the Schools	K–4	topics, eras	www.sscnet.ucla.edu/nchs
National Standards for United States and World History (5–12)	National Center for History in the Schools	5–12	topics, eras	www.sscnet.ucla.edu/nchs
National Standards for Civics and Government	Center for Civic Education	K–4, 5–8, 9–12	questions	www.civiced.org/stds.html
Geography for Life: National Geography Standards	National Council for Geographic Education	4, 8, 12	standards	www.ncge.org/tutorial
Voluntary National Content Standards in Economics	National Council on Economic Education	4, 8, 12	standards	www.economicsamerica.org/standards
National Standards for the Teaching of High School Psychology	American Psychological Association	high school	domains	www.apa.org/ed/natlstandards.html

Note. Reprinted by permission from *The Social Studies Curriculum: Purposes, Problems, and Possibilities*, Revised Edition, edited by E. Wayne Ross, the State University of New York Press © 2001, State University of New York. All rights reserved.

FIGURE 2.5

The Ten Social Studies Themes Underlying the NCSS Standards

The Ten Themes

The 10 themes that form the framework of the social studies standards are:

Culture. The study of culture prepares students to answer questions such as: What are the common characteristics of different cultures? How do belief systems, such as religion or political ideals, influence other parts of the culture? How does the culture change to accommodate different ideas and beliefs? What does language tell us about the culture? In schools, this theme typically appears in units and courses dealing with geography, history, sociology, and anthropology, as well as multicultural topics across the curriculum.

I

Time, Continuity, and Change. Human beings seek to understand their historical roots and to locate themselves in time. Knowing how to read and reconstruct the past allows one to develop a historical perspective and to answer questions such as: Who am I? What happened in the past? How am I connected to those in the past? How has the world changed, and how might it change in the future? Why does our personal sense of relatedness to the past change? This theme typically appears in courses in history and others that draw upon historical knowledge and habits.

II

People, Places, and Environments. The study of people, places, and human–environment interactions assists students as they create their spatial views and geographic perspectives of the world beyond their personal locations. Students need the knowledge, skills, and understanding to answer questions such as: Where are things located? Why are they located where they are? What do we mean by "region"? How do landforms change? What implications do these changes have for people? In schools, this theme typically appears in units and courses dealing with area studies and geography.

III

Individual Development and Identity. Personal identity is shaped by one's culture, by groups, and by institutional influences. Students should consider such questions as: How do people learn? Why do people behave as they do? What influences how people learn, perceive, and grow? How do people meet their basic needs in a variety of contexts? How do individuals develop from youth to adulthood? In schools, this theme typically appears in units and courses dealing with psychology and anthropology.

IV

Individuals, Groups, and Institutions. Institutions such as schools, churches, families, government agencies, and the courts play an integral role in people's lives. It is important that students learn how institutions are formed, what controls and influences them, how they influence individuals and culture, and how they are maintained or changed. Students may address questions such as: What is the role of institutions in this and other societies? How am I influenced by institutions? How do institutions change? What is my role in institutional change? In schools, this theme typically appears in units and courses dealing with sociology, anthropology, psychology, political science, and history.

V

Power, Authority, and Governance. Understanding the historical development of structures of power, authority, and governance and their evolving functions in contemporary U.S. society and other parts of the world is essential for developing civic competence. In exploring this theme, students confront questions such as: What is power? What forms does it take? Who holds it? How is it gained, used, and justified? What is legitimate authority? How are governments created, structured, maintained, and changed? How can individual rights be protected within the context of majority rule? In schools, this theme typically appears in units and courses dealing with government, politics, political science, history, law, and other social sciences.

VI

(continued)

FIGURE 2.5
continued

Production, Distribution, and Consumption. Because people have wants that often exceed the resources available to them, a variety of ways have evolved to answer such questions as: What is to be produced? How is production to be organized? How are goods and services to be distributed? What is the most effective allocation of the factors of production (land, labor, capital, and management)? In schools, this theme typically appears in units and courses dealing with economic concepts and issues.

Science, Technology, and Society. Modern life as we know it would be impossible without technology and the science that supports it. But technology brings with it many questions: Is new technology always better than old? What can we learn from the past about how new technologies result in broader social change, some of which is unanticipated? How can we cope with the ever-increasing pace of change? How can we manage technology so that the greatest number of people benefit from it? How can we preserve our fundamental values and beliefs in the midst of technological change? This theme draws upon the natural and physical sciences, social sciences, and the humanities, and appears in a variety of social studies courses, including history, geography, economics, civics, and government.

Global Connections. The realities of global interdependence require understanding the increasingly important and diverse global connections among world societies and the frequent tension between national interests and global priorities. Students will need to be able to address such international issues as health care, the environment, human rights, economic competition and interdependence, age-old ethnic enmities, and political and military alliances. This theme typically appears in units or courses dealing with geography, culture, and economics, but may also draw upon the natural and physical sciences and the humanities.

Civic Ideals and Practices. An understanding of civic ideals and practices of citizenship is critical to full participation in society and is a central purpose of the social studies. Students confront such questions as: What is civic participation, and how can I be involved? How has the meaning of citizenship evolved? What is the balance between rights and responsibilities? What is the role of the citizen in the community and the nation, and as a member of the world community? How can I make a positive difference? In schools, this theme typically appears in units or courses dealing with history, political science, cultural anthropology, and fields such as global studies, law-related education, and the humanities.

Note. From "Ten Themes from the Executive Summary" in *Expectations of Excellence: Curriculum Standards for Social Studies*, pp. x–xii, by National Council for the Social Studies, 1994, Washington, DC. © National Council for the Social Studies. Reprinted by permission.

example, a high school social studies teacher would apply to receive National Board Certification in the area of Adolescence and Young Adulthood/Social Studies-History. To apply for certification, teachers develop an extensive portfolio that demonstrates their competency as a teacher. Many states award supplemental pay for successful completion of the certification process. The certification process is extensive, but rewarding, as explained in Box 2.2.

BOX 2.2   Addressing the Issues: National Board Certification

Gail Barham
Sixth-grade National Board Certified social studies teacher in Wake County, North Carolina

The National Board Certification process consists of completing a portfolio and taking an assessment of content knowledge. In doing so, teachers show evidence that their teaching practices exemplify a set of standards. These standards describe what accomplished teachers should know and be able to do.

The portfolio consists of four entries, in which a teacher submits samples of students' work, videotapes of classroom teaching, and documentation of accomplishments outside the classroom. There are many areas in which to become nationally certified, and many middle school social studies teachers pursue an "Early Adolescence/Social Studies-History" certificate. In the first portfolio entry, titled "Teaching Reasoning through Writing," teachers demonstrate how to teach reasoning skills through three writing assignments. In the second portfolio entry, entitled "Fostering Civic Competence," teachers submit a 15-minute videotape showing how they use a whole-class lesson to strengthen student understanding of an important topic, concept, or theme. In the third portfolio entry, entitled, "Promoting Social Understanding," teachers submit a 15-minute videotape illustrating how they use small group interactions to examine an important topic. In the fourth portfolio entry, teachers submit and explain evidence that they have impacted student learning by working as a partner with students' families and the community, as a learner and as a leader and/or collaborator. In all four portfolio entries teachers write commentaries in which they describe, analyze, and reflect on their teaching practices.

In addition to completing a portfolio, teachers must demonstrate their content knowledge by completing six assessment center exercises. These exercises deal with topics in the areas of U.S. history, world history, political science, geography, and economics.

Going through National Board Certification was an incredibly rigorous but extremely rewarding experience. I had just completed a master's degree in middle grades education, and being a student had enabled me to better convey to my students that learning enriches our lives and is a never-ending process. Going back to school revealed to me how little I know and how important it is for teachers to be learners; it is indeed impossible to separate the two. Becoming nationally certified appeared to be a natural way to continue learning. I knew it was the right time for me when I read the five core propositions (written by the National Board for Professional Teaching Standards), which state what should be valued and respected in teaching. When I read through the 12 social studies–history standards, I was assured that this would be a worthwhile experience for me.

Going through the process was much more difficult and took a great deal more time than I had anticipated. It requires teachers to do something that few of us have time to do: to describe, analyze, and reflect on how we teach and how our students best learn. Becoming nationally certified made me a better teacher because it forced me to examine what I do in my classroom and to try new ways to help my students learn social studies. It forced me to make learning an integral part of teaching. Going through national certification is not something a teacher does for a year; it changes the way a teacher teaches.

Basal Textbooks and the Social Studies Curriculum

Perhaps the most significant factor that influences the standardization of the scope and sequence pattern of the social studies curriculum is the system of selecting and adopting **basal textbooks** that schools employ. The impact of textbooks on perpetuating the scope and sequence of the curriculum has been profound.

A basal textbook represents the major elements that the author or publisher regards as basic to provide an appropriate social studies curriculum for a particular grade or subject. Generally publishers of basal social studies texts build them around some model or notion of scope and sequence related to the grades for which the texts have been developed. Thus, adopting a basal text, in effect, means adopting the curricular pattern on which it is based.

Use of Basal Textbooks in the Social Studies

Teachers and schools often build on a basal text, using commercially produced and teacher-made supplementary materials, newspapers, articles, and trade books. Some teachers use no textbook at all, instead creating their own programs by following general scope and sequence guidelines. Other teachers use texts primarily as reference books. Still other teachers use a *multitext* approach, picking those units or chapters from each textbook that best meet their specific curricular needs. As we will consider in Chapter 11, textbook publishers may also offer supplementary books, such as adolescent literature, correlated to the basal text.

Surprisingly perhaps, basal textbook series available from major publishers display striking similarities with respect to the scope and sequence models they incorporate. Contrary to the canons of capitalism that we might expect to operate when major corporations are competing for large profits from widely distributed heterogeneous customers, basal texts reflect more homogeneity than diversity. Although individual basal texts differ considerably in the types of activities, pictorial content, and specific objectives they include, in the main they reflect the *dominant* curricular pattern that we considered earlier.

Typically, publishers provide few alternatives for educators who wish to experiment with different curriculum configurations or even vary the grade levels at which certain subjects—for example, world cultures—are studied (Parker, 1991).

Selection and Adoption of Basal Textbooks

Textbook adoption for books that appear in elementary, middle, and secondary classrooms occurs in two basic ways. One is through **local selection** in which local districts are free to adopt any texts they wish. The other is through **state selection** in which the state in some fashion selects and prescribes the books that local districts may use.

Currently, a majority of states permit local selections of basals. However, 21 states use state adoption procedures. Texts typically are adopted for a 5- or 6-year cycle. Adoption committees at the state level often include parents, teachers, college and university faculty, civic leaders, and organizational representatives.

Both the process of selecting members of textbook adoption committees, as well as the selection criteria they use and the recommendations they make, often are politically sensitive and controversial issues (Keith, 1981). A number of reviews have charged that the textbooks that emerge from the state adoption process are, among other things, bland, overburdened with factual context, overly sensitive to pressure groups, distorted, and watered down (e.g., Brophy, 1991; Nelson, 1992; People for the American Way, 1986, 1987; Sewall, 1987; Tyson-Bernstein, 1988).

Implications of State Adoption Policies

The implications of state adoption policies for the 29 states and the District of Columbia that do *not* have them and permit local selection are considerable. Since the costs of developing and producing major texts are extensive, publishers have been reluctant to produce more than one for each grade level. Their objective was to design their products for the greatest possible sales. This involved attending carefully to the adoption criteria formulated by the states with the largest student populations among the group of 21 having state adoption policies. The net effect of state adoption policies has been that a small minority of states have had a major impact on the textbooks that are available to all states.

The textbook adoption process is dominated by a highly political environment. Populous states such as California and Texas dominate the adoption process, leaving most other states to follow their leads. Many textbook publishers today publish online resources to accompany their traditional text. Emerging trends in technology may prompt textbook publishing companies to publish entire texts online, for a fee much like purchasing a textbook. This trend will provide publishers more flexibility with producing supplementary and specialized materials, it will allow authors to provide regular updates to the content, and it will provide teachers and students with more flexibility.

SUMMARY

We have explored the concept of citizenship education as the purpose of the social studies in this chapter. This perspective will serve as a framework as you continue to learn more about the middle and secondary social studies classroom.

The past few years have seen a renewed interest in civic education as the core of social studies education. Advocates of civic education are fighting with vigor for the increased role of civic education in state scopes and sequences. Programs that promote democratic ideals and instructional materials that encourage activities such as engaging with local governments, reading the newspaper, and holding mock debates and elections are becoming more and more prevalent throughout social studies classrooms.

Teachers are often surprised to learn that there is not one particular social studies scope and sequence that is nationally mandated. Although there is flexibility and opportunities for a school system to tweak the traditional model or adopt its own, most systems are careful to maintain the standard sequence to ensure that certain things are being taught at each grade level.

Some say that social studies is still in its adolescent stage. It is not as identity defined as other subjects, but then how many others are comprised of so many study areas? Social studies is still trying on different looks as it works to more clearly define itself. A focus on national and state standards combined with scope and sequence gives the teacher a picture of what needs to be taught and learned at the various grade levels. This is critical information for the planning process. Standards inform you about the content and performance objectives that your students need to meet. We will continue to explore these foundational concepts in the upcoming chapters.

ACTIVITIES

1. Select five individuals to interview. Ask them to list the characteristics of a good citizen. Summarize the similarities and differences in their responses. Compare your findings with others in the class.
2. Discuss which of the three dimensions—the head, the heart, or the hand—should receive the most emphasis in the social studies classroom. Explain your response with examples from the classroom.
3. Select a local school district and determine what the scope and sequence pattern is for social studies in grades K through 12. To what degree is it similar to or different from the dominant national pattern described in this chapter?
4. Locate a copy of your state's guidelines for teaching social studies. What role does citizenship education play in the guidelines?
5. Visit the websites listed in this chapter for the competing social studies standards (Figure 2.4). Review the standards and compare them to the standards for your state. What similarities and differences do you note? How will you address these differences in your own classroom?

WEB RESOURCES

NCSS Curriculum Standards: **www.ncss.org/standards/toc.html**
Learn NC: **www.learnnc.org/**
McRel: **www.mcrel.org/standards-benchmarks/**

Developing Educational Standards: **www.edstandards.org/Standards.html**

Center for Civic Education: **www.civiced.org/**

Street Law: **www.streetlaw.org/**

CivNet: **www.civnet.org/**

CloseUp Foundation: **www.closeup.org/**

Youth Leadership Initiative: **www9.youthleadership.net/youthleadership/**

Chapter 3

Teaching and Learning Social Studies

Engaging Students in Constructing Knowledge
  Schemata and Prior Knowledge in Social Studies Instruction
  Sources of Subject Matter for the Social Studies

The Social Sciences as Sources of Subject Matter for the Social Studies
  Geography
  History
  Economics
  Political Science
  Anthropology
  Sociology
  Psychology

Other Sources of Subject Matter for the Social Studies
  Multidisciplinary, Thematic, Interdisciplinary, and Integrative Approaches
  The School and Community Help Students Establish Their Own Sense of Place
  Social Service Projects

The School and Community as Sources of Social Data
  Using Community Resource Persons Effectively
  Newspaper Articles and Editorials
  Fieldwork in the Community
  Collecting Oral Histories
  Collecting Social Science Information Through Surveys
  Communicating with the Community About the Social Studies Program
  Alerting the Community to School Activities

Identifying Professional Resources
  Organizational Resources
  Professional Journals
  Effective Citizenship as Professional Development
  Professional Development Through the Internet

Summary

Activities

Web Resources

In the fifth-period social studies class at Apex Middle School, several groups of sixth graders are busily constructing large poster charts that reflect information gleaned from their examinations of Russian cities. Each group has selected a specific city and researched facts that will enable them to address quality-of-life issues in that city. The posters will be hung in the hallway for examination by other classes studying the same topic. Every group will also prepare a PowerPoint presentation about their city to share with the class. The PowerPoints will also be set up for parents to review when the class hosts an "All Things Russian" night, the culminating experience for their participation in the North Carolina Sixth Grade Goes to Russia project (www.ncsu.edu/chass/extension/russia-nc6). Posters, projects, PowerPoints, and food will round out the evening. Arrangements are also being made to podcast the event, something the TechnoWizards club is trying for the first time.

The students are clustered around tables analyzing data and consulting reference works the student teacher, Amy Beal, has identified. They are also examining their textbooks and recent articles pulled from the library.

Additionally, some students periodically refer to the large wall maps at the front of the class. To gather up-to-date unpublished information, several youngsters have exchanged e-mail with the Russian Embassy in Washington, D.C., and consulted with citizens who have recently emigrated from Russia. Before the students used both home and classroom computers to go online to question and collect data, Ms. Beal critiqued the questions that students were going to ask. Were they appropriate and sensitive to issues regarding international relations? Was the grammar used in the questions impeccable? She remembered her own trips to Russia and the excellent English grammar the Russian students used.

Ms. Beal circulates among the groups. She is monitoring student activities, offering additional information, and suggesting new sources to pursue to ensure accuracy and balance. She also illustrates how to document and summarize the information gathered from various sources. When the groups complete the charts, Ms. Beal will provide them with a set of questions to use in processing the data they have collected, summarized, and recorded. She will also help the students develop generalizations concerning the social, political, and economic conditions in Russia and in each group's specific city.

Eventually, when the groups present their PowerPoints and hang their posters, they will have an opportunity to compare and discuss their respective findings and any new questions they may have generated. They will also be able to suggest further indicators of quality of life that may enable them to better understand the Russian culture.

Engaging Students in Constructing Knowledge

From reflective encounters with social data, such as in the activity just outlined, students construct knowledge.

In the social studies, there are many sources from which information can be gathered. Gone are the days when what is presented by the teacher and what is found in the textbook as public and agreed-upon knowledge or beliefs are the only sources of information. Technology has opened new pathways for research that yield up-to-date information. Of course, the same concerns of accuracy and bias exist using Internet information as do using textbooks and newspapers. Whatever the means of securing information, that information is received by the student and given meaning in terms of his or her past experience and cognitive capabilities or structures (Piaget, 1972; Torney-Purta, 1991, p. 190).

Knowledge is the fabric of social studies instruction. Woven into it are the facts, generalizations, skills, hypotheses, beliefs, attitudes, values, and theories that students and teachers construct in social studies programs. The threads from which the rich and intricate patterns of learning are spun are concepts.

During knowledge construction, students activate both cognitive and affective processes. *Cognitive processes* refer generally to how individuals confront, encode, reflect on, transform, and store information. In turn, *affective processes* relate to the beliefs, attitudes, values, and ethical positions we bring to and derive from analyses. Both of these processes also shape the meanings we extract from information.

Schemata and Prior Knowledge in Social Studies Instruction

Our knowledge is organized into **schemata**, which are mental structures (pegs) that represent a set of related information (Howard, 1987). Schemata provide the basis for comprehending, remembering, and learning information. Schema theory posits that the form and content of all new knowledge is in some way shaped by our **prior knowledge** (i.e., existing knowledge).

We apply our individual collections of schemata to each new knowledge-acquisition task. Students, for example, bring their map schemata to the study of spatial issues. They have certain expectations concerning the kinds of information a map contains and the types of questions a map can answer.

Schemata are activated when our experiences elicit them. Perkins (1986) cited the example of how the date 1492 can serve as an important cognitive place holder for analysis of parallel historical events. (Dr. Candy Beal found the date 1865 to be a parallel historical time item for both the United States and Russia. Around this date both ended enslavement in their respective countries.) Perkins suggested that key dates in American history also provide a structure for placing intermediate events. In this way, dates become not merely facts but tools for collecting and remembering information. Construction of timelines help visual learners place and remember dates.

We may restructure schemata when our prior knowledge conflicts with new data. New schemata are formed when we make comparisons with prior ones and modify them to reflect our current experiences (Marzano et al., 1988).

Confused? Think of it this way: Knowledge acquisition may be likened to a coat rack analogy. If you imagine that you have a sorting and storing system in your head, like a coat rack, it is easy to see how you make sense of new facts. First, the main pegs on the rack are the general concepts with which you are familiar. As you gain new information, you try to associate the new facts with what you already know. You sort the new information to go on one peg or another. Sometimes information can fit into two categories and you find that you can make a pathway or connection between pegs or concepts. You are constructing knowledge as you relate the new information to what you already know. Lev Vygotsky (1978, 1986) believed that real learning was not the exchange of information between teacher and child, but what the child did with the information that was offered. He believed that *intermental* learning, that which occurred between individuals as they exchanged information, was taken one step further to *intramental*, internalized learning. In the intramental stage, the learner processed the information herself and sorted it to hang on her own coat rack. In this sense, knowledge does not exist independent of learning. It arises from students' interactions with texts, images, other people, and the larger culture in which they reside.

Sources of Subject Matter for the Social Studies

The process of knowledge acquisition cuts across the disciplinary boundaries established by social scientists and other scholars. Further, disciplines themselves are in a constant state of flux, with shifting parameters. This begs the question of why some teachers are so rigid in their belief in the separation of the disciplines. Curriculum integration sees the disciplines as tools to be used to address larger questions and issues that cross individual areas of study (Beane, 1997, 2005). This explains why in solving a problem, a student is less likely to be concerned about whether the relevant data are drawn, let us say, from the discipline of history, than whether they contribute to a solution, whatever the source. See, for example, the middle grades activity in Appendix C, Figure 3.1, which involves students in problem-solving activities that draw on geography, history, math, English, art, and current events. In addition to materials noted for use in the Chunnel Vision activity (Appendix C, Resource Figure 3.1), we suggest using online encyclopedias as well as providing students with preidentified appropriate website URLs to research the topic. Surfing the Internet is time consuming and may lead students to sites that are inappropriate. Often teachers and students are limited in their time on computers, and by prescreening and identifying good websites the teacher can make the best use of class time.

In unusually harsh and strident terms, over a half-century ago John Dewey (1933) attacked the dualism that isolates the concerns of scholars for their disciplines from the cognitive and affective needs of learners:

> The gullibility of specialized scholars when out of their own lines, their extravagant habits of inference and speech, their ineptness in reaching conclusions in practical

matters, their egotistical engrossments in their own subjects, are extreme examples of the bad effects of severing studies completely from their ordinary connections in life. (p. 62)

Hunt and Metcalf (1968) have also argued: "Content assumes an emergent character. From the standpoint of the learner, it comes into existence as it is needed, it does not have a life independent of his own" (pp. 281–282). Their observation suggests that teaching simply by fact loading is pointless. The result is only a "spit-back" exchange, student to teacher. Although facts may be critical parts of concepts, students must see how facts relate to concepts. In identifying subject matter for the social studies curriculum, teachers must search for information that will enable students to construct knowledge that will be useful in their current and future roles as citizens (Beane, 2005). It is the teachers' job to establish the pathway that relates new information to what students already know (Dewey, 1968). Piaget calls this "assimilation and accommodation." Teachers who only offer up information and do not help students connect it to their individual schemata cannot be sure that the information becomes the student's own. The information may be assimilated for a short time and then be lost. When the teacher lays the proper foundation for new information, the student can establish a connection, accommodate the new information, and relate it to what was previously known (Piaget, 1972). This explains why cramming for a test does not work in the long term. Students who are cramming do not make meaningful, personal connections to the material and that material then fails to become part of their schemata. *In one ear and out the other* is certainly an appropriate description for that which is gained and then soon lost in last-minute cramming.

The subject matter that fuels functional knowledge in social studies classes must be drawn from a number of sources, including the social sciences, other disciplines, and interdisciplinary areas. It must also embrace the school and the community. Together, these resources constitute a reservoir of information for the social studies curriculum.

The Social Sciences as Sources of Subject Matter for the Social Studies

The academic disciplines of the social sciences are the touchstones of the social studies (Gross & Dynneson, 1991). Most social studies educators would concede that the field of social studies gains a significant portion of its identity from a core of disciplines: history, political science, geography, economics, sociology, anthropology, and psychology (Figure 3.1). We will consider history, which arguably may be regarded as a discipline from either the humanities or the social sciences or both, as one of the social sciences throughout our discussion. Among all the social sciences, history and geography particularly have nourished the social studies curriculum throughout its history. In the last few decades geography study

FIGURE 3.1
Contributions of the Social Sciences to the Social Studies Curriculum

has fallen off. Americans' lack of geography knowledge and skills is the present-day result.

The *methods of inquiry* used in the social sciences, such as the formulation and testing of hypotheses, are also important sources of social studies' subject matter. To function effectively in their daily lives, citizens often need the same skills as social scientists. Citizens, for example, must frequently locate data or verify information.

The social sciences share certain commonalities—their use of the scientific method, focus on understanding and explaining human behavior, and systematic collection and application of data. Their methods are both quantitative and qualitative. Social scientists measure phenomena and draw inferences from observations. They also share an interest in predicting patterns of behavior, a concern for verification of information, and a desire for objectivity.

Hartoonian (1994) has observed:

Like students and citizens, scholars attempt to find out not only what happened but also why it happened, what trends can be suggested, and how humans behave in certain social settings. Some of the most important questions they consider include:

- How can a topic, issue, theme, or event best be conceptualized?
- What defines a historical period? What defines a theme? What defines an issue?
- What constitutes primary and secondary evidence? How can evidence be evaluated and used?
- How are cause and effect relationships explained and discussed? (pp. 2–3)

Each social science discipline, however, claims special insights and character-istics that provide its distinct identification. In the sections that follow, the nature and scope of each of the social sciences are outlined.

Geography

Geographers sometimes organize their discipline in terms of five central themes: location, place, relationships within place, movement, and region. *Location* is the description of the positions of people and places on the earth's surface in either absolute or relative terms. *Place* is seen as detailing the human or physical char-acteristics of places on the earth. *Relationships within place* refer to cultural and physical relationships of human settlements. The theme of *movement* describes relationships between and among places. *Region* is viewed in terms of the various ways that areas may be identified, such as governmental units, language, religious or ethnic groups, and landform characteristics.

The concept of place is central to the discipline of geography. Geographers are concerned with the location and character of places on the earth's surface. They have an abiding interest in how places affect the people who live there. Foremost is their interest in why people and things are located in particular places. They attempt to relate these places to events and explain how goods, events, and people pass from place to place. They also try to ascertain the factors that have shaped these places.

Geographers attempt to accurately describe, from many perspectives, loca-tions on the earth's surface. They examine, for example, what is below ground in the form of rocks and mineral deposits and what is above in the form of climate.

Maps and globes of all types are geographers' basic tools. These geographic representations have become more sophisticated with the development of advanced spatial technologies, such as geographic information systems (GIS) and global positioning satellites (GPS). Technology enables greater up-to-date geography research opportunities of multifaceted global issues. The ability to use geospatial technologies is important for citizens who must understand ever-changing chal-lenges and opportunities in the world (Bednarz, Acheson, & Bednarz, 2006). For example, the ability of GIS to layer and show land use studies over time may help communities and countries better understand their changing demographics, a key to issues of sustainability. Other major concepts that are addressed by geographers include *population distribution, spatial interaction, environment,* and *boundaries,* all made clearer through the use of GIS technology.

History

History includes chronicles, interpretations, syntheses, explanations, and cause–effect relationships. In essence, history is always a selective representation of reality. It is one or more individual's chronicles or recollections of what occurred using his or her frame of reference. Such chronicles may be oral, visual, or written, and they may relate to oneself, others, events, nations, social groups, and the like. As chroniclers, historians are concerned with constructing a coherent, accurate, and representative narrative of phenomena over time.

Although absolute objectivity—the search for truth regardless of personal preferences or objectives—is unachievable, some historians in the tradition of Otto von Ranke regard it as their methodological goal. Others, in the spirit of James Harvey Robinson and Carl Becker, consider such a goal "history without an objective" and urge historians to state explicitly the frames of reference that they bring to their analyses.

Since it is impossible to record everything about any event or individual, and since all records are colored to some extent by our attitudes and frame of reference, history is a selective *interpretation* of what occurred. Often the task of recording and interpreting an event also involves investigating and reconciling alternative accounts and incorporating documents into a pattern of verified evidence. Hence, history is also a synthesis and explanation of many different facts concerning the past. For this reason it is critical that students use multiple and varied sources to construct a balanced view of a historical event.

Historians search for the *causes* of events, as well as the *effects*. Where the relationships between the two are ambiguous, historians construct hypotheses about causal relationships. Over time, as new evidence is uncovered, hypotheses are tested and determined, tentatively, to be facts or are rejected.

In addition to the ones mentioned, major concepts that are addressed by historians include *change, the past, nationalism,* and *conflict*.

Economics

Economics is concerned with relationships that people form to satisfy material needs. More specifically, the discipline deals with production, consumption, and exchange. The objects of these three activities are some set of goods (e.g., cars) or services (e.g., lawn cutting).

Since countries often differ in their systems for organizing production, consumption, and exchange, economists compare their applications. Economists also examine comparatively specific economic institutions within a nation, such as banks and small businesses. Similarly, they examine the international patterns of exchange or currencies and how these affect economic behavior among countries.

Within the framework of production, consumption, and exchange, economists also study, document, and attempt to predict patterns of human behavior. Other issues that they consider include job specialization, incentives, markets and prices, productivity, and benefits to be derived in relation to the costs incurred. Economists also examine the surplus or scarcity of goods and services in relationship to people's needs and wants.

Since these issues arise at all levels and on all scales—an international conglomerate (macrolevel) or a local lawn-cutter (microlevel)—economists often examine them according to the scope of their impact. They also consider patterns of interdependence among nations and the relative levels of their imports and exports.

In addition to the ones mentioned, major concepts that are addressed by economists include *cost, division of labor, standard of living*, and *balance of payments*.

Political Science

The discipline of political science has its roots in philosophy and history. Works such as Plato's *Republic* and Aristotle's *Politics*, for example, are used today in college classes both in philosophy and political science. Broadly speaking, political science is concerned with an analysis of power and the processes by which individuals and groups control and manage one another. Power may be applied at the governmental level through the ballot box and political parties, but it is also exercised in many social settings. Power, in some form, is exercised by all individuals throughout society.

Above all, political science is concerned with the organization and governance of nations and other social units. Political scientists, for example, are interested in political interaction among institutions and the competing demands of various groups in our society as they affect governmental institutions. They analyze how different constituencies or interest groups influence and shape public policy. Such analyses include polls of public opinion and investigations of the impact of the mass media.

At the international level, political scientists are concerned with the relationships among nations, including the ways in which cooperation and ties develop and the ways in which conflicts emerge and are resolved. Political scientists trace patterns of interdependence and compare and contrast political systems. They also examine national and international legal systems and agreements between nations.

Other major concepts that are addressed by political scientists include *rules, citizenship, justice*, and *political systems*.

Anthropology

Closely aligned with the discipline of sociology is anthropology. Anthropologists, speaking in a broad sense, like to say that their discipline is the study of humankind. They are interested in both the biological and the environmental determinants of human behavior. Since its scope is far ranging and the discipline has a number of major subdivisions, anthropology is perhaps the most difficult subject to define.

Culture is a central concept in anthropology, much like the concept of *place* in geography. Culture refers to the entire way of life of a society, especially shared ideas and language. Culture is unique to humans, and it is learned rather than inherited. The totality of how individuals use their genetic inheritance to adapt to and shape their environment makes up the major framework of what most anthropologists consider culture.

Cultural anthropologists are interested in how cultures evolve, change over time, and are modified through interaction with other cultures. These scholars study cultural or subcultural groups to ascertain common patterns of behavior. They live among the groups, functioning as participant observers (recording observational data). Another group of anthropologists, *archaeologists,* unearth the past through excavations (digs) of artifacts from past generations and carbon-dating techniques. *Physical anthropologists* share many interests with natural scientists such as biologists, including the study of nonhuman primates and animal fossils.

Other major concepts that are addressed by anthropologists include *enculturation, cultural diffusion, cultural change,* and *traditions.*

Sociology

Sociology is the study of human interactions within groups. Sociologists study people in social settings, sometimes called *social systems.* They exercise wide latitude in their fields of investigation. For example, within various community settings, they examine behavior in basic social units such as the family, ethnic groupings, social classes, organizations, and clubs.

Sociologists are interested in how the basic types of institutions—for example, social, religious, economic, political, and legal institutions—affect our daily lives. Other areas that sociologists examine include how the actions of individuals in groups preserve or change social systems, such as worker behavior in plants or teacher activities in schools.

Sociologists attempt to abstract patterns from cumulative individual studies. From the study of different cases of specific social systems, such as the various families within a small community, sociologists try to derive general principles that can be applied to all similar groups.

Since the scope of sociology includes some analysis of behavior in every major institution within society, it often overlaps with the other social sciences. For example, the work of a sociologist studying the political behavior of various groups during a national election and that of a political scientist analyzing voting patterns may intersect.

Other major concepts that are addressed by sociologists include *norms, status, socialization,* and *roles.*

Psychology

A discipline with many subdivisions, psychology focuses on understanding individual mental processes and behaviors. Modern psychology derives from earlier religious and philosophical studies into the nature of humans and the reasons for their behavior. The question of whether an individual has a free will, for example, was merely shifted into a scientific arena as psychology developed.

The boundaries of psychology are often difficult to determine, since its investigations spill over into the areas of biology, medicine, and physics, as well as into the other social sciences. Psychologists study animal as well as human behavior. Like anthropologists, they are interested in both the genetic and learned aspects of behavior. The major branches of the discipline concentrate on investigating the learning process, which psychologists regard as a major determinant of human behavior.

Psychology has both an applied and an experimental side. Some branches, such as counseling psychology, apply knowledge directly to the solution of human problems in clinical settings similar to a doctor–patient relationship. Other psychologists function in laboratory environments conducting controlled experiments, which may not have any short-term applications to human behavior.

In addition to the ones mentioned, major concepts that are addressed by psychologists include *values, self, motivation,* and *learning.*

Other Sources of Subject Matter for the Social Studies

Besides the findings and methods of inquiry of the social sciences, the social studies curriculum has and will continue to draw on many other areas for data. The social studies are concerned with the application of social knowledge to citizenship education. Many sources of information beyond the social sciences can aid in this task.

The arts and sciences, the law, religion, popular culture and music, data from students' daily lives, the social life within the school, and the mass media are but a sample of the possible sources of subject matter that are outside the framework of the social sciences, but that bear on the human condition (Figure 3.2). Subject matter within these areas that relates to the organization, understanding, and development of individuals, groups, and societies has considerable relevancy for the social studies curriculum.

Multidisciplinary, Thematic, Interdisciplinary, and Integrative Approaches

In teaching social studies, we may draw primarily on the subject matter of a particular social science discipline, such as when we look to history for an account of the Persian Gulf War, 1991. On other occasions, we may wish to link the perspectives of multiple disciplines, wherein several of the social sciences are tapped to solve a problem or analyze an issue. This would be the case when we used the combined insights of economists, sociologists, anthropologists, and geographers to help explain why some areas of the United States are growing more rapidly than others.

FIGURE 3.2
Other Sources of the Social Studies Curriculum

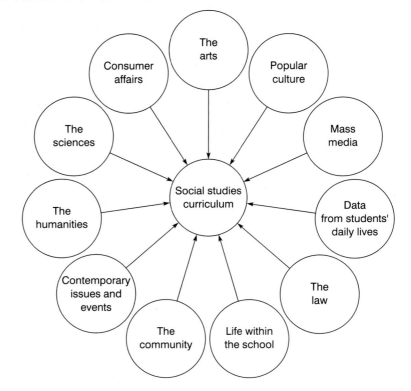

An example of interrelating the perspectives of disciplines in media occurs in the DVD series for middle and secondary students, *Geography in U.S. History* (Backler, Patrick, & Stoltman, 1992) available through the Agency for Instructional Technology (AIT). The programs link key geographic themes with historic contexts in addressing issues. Figure 3.3 illustrates the linkages in a sample of five of the video programs.

Although the traditional social science disciplines are important structured sources of systematically analyzed data for students' knowledge construction, insightful and creative contributions of scholars do not always fit neatly into any existing or single discipline. Most areas of study within the middle and secondary grades can be enriched by combining subject matter that is drawn from a variety of sources and related to a central theme (Jenkins & Tanner, 1992; Beane, 2005; Virtue, 2007). Some examples well suited for themed investigation are poverty, homelessness, AIDS, destruction of the ozone layer, natural disasters, imbalance of resources and wealth among nations of the world, proliferation of nuclear arms, illegal trafficking in arts, and conflicts among peoples.

FIGURE 3.3
Program Outline

Program Outline	Historical Topic	Geographic Theme	Cognitive Skill
North vs. South in the Founding of the USA 1787–1796	Establishing constitutional government; growth of political democracy	Regions	Interpreting geographic information
Jefferson Decides to Purchase Louisiana 1801–1813	Territorial expansion/westward movement	Location	Organizing and presenting information
Clash of Cultures on the Great Plains 1865–1890	Settlement of the frontier	Human/environment relationships	Formulating and testing generalizations
An Industrial Revolution in Pittsburgh 1865–1900	Industrial development	Place	Making evaluations
A Nation of Immigrants: The Chinese-American Experience 1850–1990	Immigration	Movement	Interpreting geographic information

Note. From "Geography in U.S. History: A Video Project," by A. L. Backler, J. P. Patrick, and J. P. Stoltman, 1992, *The Social Studies*, p. 60. Reprinted with permission of the Helen Dwight Reid Educational Foundation. Published by Heldref Publications, 1319 Eighteenth St., NW, Washington, DC, 20036-1802. Copyright © 1992.

Shapiro and Merryfield (1995) have described how one high school used interdisciplinary themes and teacher teams in a global-conflict course. In addition to a social studies team member, English, science, and mathematics teachers were involved in planning units that had global connections and curricula from each discipline. For example, the biology teacher engaged students to consider genetic engineering and its global moral implications.

At a middle school in Raleigh, North Carolina, an eighth-grade team of 100 students took on the study of a local wetland. Failure by the City Council to address persistent rain-related flooding of a modest housing area that was sandwiched between high waters in the wetlands and runoff from a new hard-surface highway was cause for alarm by the students. As the students worked with their team of teachers, they found that the theme of the wetlands cut across all of their subjects. In *science*, they investigated what constituted a wetland and studied its systems. Students planted native shrubs and trees to help address erosion near the houses. For *geography* students used GIS to study the changing land use of this particular area over time. During *language arts* they recorded oral histories of area residents and wrote musings about the wetlands themselves. For *social studies* they wrote letters to the City Council asking for redress of grievances. In *math* students developed spreadsheets to show the nature and amount of the trash taken from the wetland. For the *arts* students painted a large mural of the wetlands and prepared a wetlands digital photography show with classical and rock music accompaniment. Finally, all of the learning activities were used to construct a 60-minute interactive town and gown presentation, *Spell of the Land: Sense of Place, Use of Space,* hosted by North Carolina State University and attended by former mayors, the Chancellor, professors, college students, and local residents. The issues the students raised found a platform and voice, and students realized that they had developed skills for civic participation and practiced citizenship, firsthand (Wade, 2007). (Go to **www.ncsu.edu/chass/extension/ci** and click on Theory to Practice, Pam's Story, Chapter 9, to read the full wetlands story that has been fictionalized for the website.)

Tackling big questions and big issues that are important to students is the foundation of teaching and learning using the curriculum integration approach. James Beane (1997, 2005), the architect and leading proponent of curriculum integration, has done extensive research that has shown curriculum integration to be very successful for teaching and learning. Curriculum integration is a simple concept. Students ask questions or bring up issues of interest regarding the topic to be studied. They research those questions or issues using the disciplines as the tools for research. This research may be done individually, partnered, or in groups. Teachers, using differentiated instruction, help facilitate the students' research and keep them on task. The students are actually "postholing" or digging deeply into one issue of the topic the whole class is studying. The teacher continues to teach the general unit, which provides the context into which these deeper issues fit. Students present their research projects and their findings to their classmates either at the end of the unit or throughout the unit. The 2001 North Carolina's Sixth Grades Go to Russia project at North Carolina State University (**www.ncsu.edu/chass/extension/russia-nc6**) is a good example of a curriculum integration project taught in a technology-enabled environment (Beal, 2002). The project contains a fully integrated teaching unit built around students' big questions. Examination of that tailored unit shows that all of the social studies requirements of the sixth-grade standard course of study are addressed. This is further proof that teaching to answer students' big questions does address the standards we must teach.

Another example of a program that addresses important issues relating to ethnicity, peace, gender, race, and morality was developed at Brown University. It was organized around two questions: Why does world hunger persist in a world of plenty? What can be done to reduce or prevent hunger now and in the future? (Kates, 1989). The program brought together, from many different disciplines in both the arts and sciences, scholars and professionals who were committed to the pursuit of answers to those questions.

The School and Community Help Students Establish Their Own Sense of Place

In this fast-paced world where students and teachers move frequently, experience loss of extended family, and seem to be losing touch with one another, it is important to establish a personal connection to one's environment and work in order to establish a grounding in the school and in the community. Garbarino's (1985) ecology of adolescent development theorizes that the lives of children are segmented into four spheres of influence: home, peers, community, and school. The number and quality of connections among the spheres indicate the strength of the child's support systems. For example, if the parents consistently ask the youngster about daily school activity and scan the middle school assignment notebook for homework assignments, and the teachers contact the parents when they see the student's work slacking off, a safety net is put into place to support the child. If the parents are well informed about the child's whereabouts and friends with whom that child is spending time, then negative issues about hanging out after school or on the weekends are greatly diminished. Staying connected to adolescents today is no easy task, especially for parents of high school students. The need for independence is strong for adolescents, as is their desire for peer input and approval. Parents may come to you for advice about how to reconnect with their children. Parents must be told that, just as in your classroom, they must set fair rules for which there are consistently applied reasonable consequences. While experts know that negative behavior can only be changed when the individual wishes to do so, the rules must remain in place and with them the consequences. Eyes in the back of the head, "with-it-ness" (being aware of the teen scene), and active listening are often cited as a few of the things that new teachers (and parents) need to be successful. Experienced teachers and parents will add that a sense of humor helps ensure survival and ongoing teen connectivity.

When something goes amiss regarding youngsters, the first groups to be investigated and often blamed are the parents, the peers, and/or the school. Rarely is the community held responsible for "minding" the child. While some cultures observe the custom that "it takes a whole village to rear a child," American culture has drifted away from this practice. It is no wonder that children who are overextended with part-time jobs and after-school activities, or who are often left home alone, feel disconnected and adrift from responsible adults and family. They are left without an anchor or a sense of being grounded.

Community can provide a rich foundation for a child's development. The more you know about where you are living, the more you feel as though you belong. The more the community knows about what is going on in the schools, the more invested it will be in getting involved to create learning opportunities and support school needs, such as passing bond issues. Students who grow up learning about their city or town are usually the first to become involved in community service projects that promote active citizenship.

Dr. Billy O'Steen, Queens College, New Zealand, is a proponent of the importance of experiential learning. He is known for participating in Outward Bound experiences with teachers and students, leading groups of students planning a nature trail or coaching student teachers through a hands-on, pencils ready language arts activity. Highly sought after for his "out of the box" successful approach to working with students, he shares his thoughts about service-learning in Box 3.1.

BOX 3.1   Addressing the Issues: Service-Learning

Dr. Billy O'Steen
Queens College, New Zealand

Service-learning can be a powerful learning experience particularly suited for the middle and high school classroom. By utilizing the inherent desire of many adolescents to make a difference in their communities, educators can use this researched and well-developed strategy to integrate academic content, real-life service experience, and personal reflection. In so doing, a classroom community can be established that is founded on collaborative inquiry, engagement with the needs and issues of contemporary society, and reflection on the connections between personal and civic lives. These outcomes align with Benjamin Barber's (1992) belief that "community service can only be an instrument of education when it is connected to an academic learning experience in a classroom setting." Further, the service-learning approach addresses James Beane's (1990, 1997, 2005) suggestion that meaningful curriculum must be integrative and address real-world issues.

Components of Service-Learning (How to Do It)

Educator works with students to select a local issue to address (e.g., environment, affordable housing, treatment of animals, school grounds).

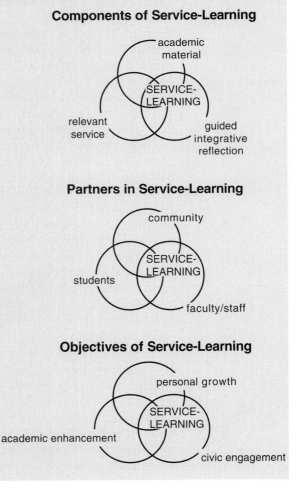

Components of Service-Learning

academic material

SERVICE-LEARNING

relevant service

guided integrative reflection

Partners in Service-Learning

community

SERVICE-LEARNING

students

faculty/staff

Objectives of Service-Learning

personal growth

SERVICE-LEARNING

academic enhancement

civic engagement

BOX 3.1	Addressing the Issues: Service-Learning

Educator and students determine a course of action to contact an organization about providing service at a site.

Educator selects academic content thematically or specifically related to the issue (can be used or adapted from existing curricular materials).

Educator and students use academic content for preservice reflections and discussions.

Students and educators render meaningful service at a site either on a one-time basis or in a sustained manner.

After each service experience, educators and students engage in reflection discussions regarding their perceptions and ideas about their service, their roles as community members, and their learning outcomes.

The following reflection is from a college student after participating in a service-learning experience:

I feel that what we did could easily be used in a classroom! This experience would be an excellent opportunity for students to learn about environmental ethics and the difference one person can make. Many people in our society, including myself, often feel that one person cannot make a difference in society. It would be a good experience for students to go out and work for a special cause so they realize exactly what one person can do.

Resources

National Service-Learning Partnership: **www.service-learningpartnership.org**

Learning In Deed: **www.learningindeed.org**

Social Service Projects

An illustration of what an individual school can do to promote social consciousness and responsibility is a program implemented by the Ravenscroft School in Raleigh, North Carolina. Ravenscroft has made social service part of the required curriculum.

Each month, students in the middle grades engage in **social service projects**. These include activities such as recycling, making sandwiches for a local soup kitchen, visiting the elderly, collecting toys and clothes for those in need, and spending time with disabled students from other schools. Teachers then build on the experiences and reflections of students and encourage them to do follow-up research on subjects such as the causes of poverty.

Other schools and consortia of schools across the United States are engaged in similar curricular efforts to encourage the development of social responsibility (Arnold & Beal, 1995). In 1992, Maryland became the first state to mandate community service by all students as part of graduation requirements. The law requires that all students in the middle and secondary school grades perform 75 hours of service in their communities.

The School and Community as Sources of Social Data

Middle and secondary level students also need to be guided in systematically using their schools and communities as laboratories for social data. To this end, they require assignments and activities that encourage them to view data from their daily life experiences as relevant and legitimate subject matter for analysis in the classroom. For example, a unit on crime might begin with students collecting objective data concerning the occurrence of crime in their school, neighborhoods, and communities. Often, weekly hometown sections of the newspaper will provide a map with notations indicating where and when criminal activities have happened. As another example, the study of contemporary bureaucracies (state and local government) might begin with an analysis of the school as a bureaucratic system.

The wealth of material that generally is available in every community is probably one of the least tapped resources for social studies teaching (see Box 3.2). Local organizations and businesses, for example, often cooperate with teachers in arranging for field trips, guest speakers, information, and assistance. Public agencies such as police and fire departments sometimes have special programs and speakers that they will provide to schools. Other sources of speakers include colleges and universities (organizations for international students), the chambers of

---

BOX 3.2 Addressing the Issues: Using Your City as Your Classroom

An example of getting to know your community through fieldwork is the Great Raleigh Trolley Adventure, which takes place in the capital of North Carolina. As part of special service learning projects, classes of students travel around the city in a trolley and make stops at historic sites. They learn about history through interesting stories told by their tour-guide teacher. Some of the children have never been downtown, and others who live downtown have never explored the city's rich history. Dramatic narrative holds students' interest and allows the teacher to pass on important historical information. Digital cameras record the sites for later use. Students do further research when they return to the classroom. They use their research and digital pictures to construct a virtual field trip of the city, complete with click-ons that highlight more facts and pictures. Oral histories can also be included. Students pride themselves in becoming experts about their city and, as "keepers of the history," are tuned into what is going on all around their town. (See **www.ced.ncsu.edu/2/adventure/** for one such service learning project.)

This activity does not require high-tech application. Regular cameras or even student drawings of the historic sites can be used to make an interesting "Album of Our City," mural of the trip, tourist brochure, or the like. By getting local people involved, you showcase your school and class and make the important community–school connection. Parents who serve as chaperones enjoy the trip and have an opportunity to observe their own children in action. In this activity all spheres of the Garbarino model are interacting and provide benefits for everyone.

commerce, the League of Women Voters, and museums. Individuals in the community are generally eager to offer their assistance to local schools. It is always a good idea to have heard the speaker first so you can determine that the topic and presentation style is appropriate for your class. Preparing a suggested list of things for the speaker to address and stressing that a storytelling format is more popular than a straight lecture will not guarantee success but will take you one step closer to it.

Using Community Resource Persons Effectively

Typical uses of community resource persons include having individuals who represent different career areas report on what they do, serve as mentors, or share specialized advice concerning selected topics.

The South Carolina Department of Education (1987) has prepared a useful set of general guidelines for using resource speakers. The agency's suggestions appear in Figure 3.4.

Fernekes (1988) described how speakers were used in a secondary social studies class to better understand the Vietnam War. Three veterans of the war were invited to be interviewed and recorded by the class. Questions ranged from subjects such as daily schedules to specific duties that veterans were expected to fulfill. Matters such as death, feelings, and fears were discussed. The following list describes good practices for hosting a classroom speaking event.

1. In-class brainstorming of question topics
2. Development of sample questions
3. Review of student questions by the teacher
4. Debriefing of sample interview to assist in improvement of student questioning techniques
5. Personal contact with informants [speakers] to explain purposes of visit and clarification of procedures for use of recording
6. Visit of informant for recorded interview
7. Evaluation of completed interview in terms of course learning objectives
8. Thank-you letter to the informant
9. Copying of tape (video, CD); depositing of original and copy in school library (p. 53)

The following is the process one teacher used to host a speaker: Lamm (1989) prepared her middle school class for a speaker's visit by involving the class in a related activity prior to the speaker's arrival. The speaker, from Children's Services, a local social service agency, was to serve the class as a resource on the problem of child abuse. The day before the speaker arrived, the teacher gave each member of the class a card that contained one piece of information concerning a fictitious case of an abused child. Several cases were part of the activity. Students were asked to seek out and form a group with other class members who had

FIGURE 3.4
Guide for Using Resource Speakers

Locating Resources

Community/school contacts may be made through:

> Partnership coordinator in the school district
> Businesses (domestic or foreign owned)
> Local Chamber of Commerce
> College or university
> Technical education center
> Parent interest survey
> Identification of students for peer teaching
> Local speakers bureau
> School volunteer coordinator
> Clubs
> Museums

Contacting Community Resources

How?

> Personal contact
> Phone call
> Written request stating exact need
> Combination of the above

Through whom?

> Partnership coordinator in the school district
> Public relations or community relations executive (business)
> Survey information (parents)
> Local Chamber of Commerce

Preparing Students

Please remember: The purpose is to enrich and enhance, not to teach the unit!

Let the students help with preparations whenever possible. A feeling of responsibility helps ensure interest.

Students will profit from understanding of some kind of expected measurable results. They should know what will be expected from them prior to the visit. The results may take the form of one or more of the following:

> Quiz
> Puzzle or "treasure hunt"
> Identification list
> Report or summary
> Problem solving
> Model or project
> Interview results
> Letter

Secure materials and biographical information from the speaker in advance. These materials may include:

> Posters or brochures
> Background of speaker
> History of the company
> Photographs
> Audiovisual aids to be shown in advance

Note. From *Guide for Using Guest Speakers and Field Trips* (pp. 8–9), by South Carolina Department of Education. Copyright 1987 by South Carolina Department of Education. Reprinted with permission.

related information on the same child. Once the groups were formed, students were to discuss what they believed would be an appropriate remedy to their particular child's case of abuse.

When the speaker arrived the following day, she spent the session comparing each group's recommendations with what the services bureau typically would do in cases similar to the ones the groups considered. A follow-up discussion brought out the key issues involved in child abuse cases and detailed the scope of the problem nationally and locally.

Newspaper Articles and Editorials

The newspaper is a useful tool for linking the classroom to the community. Articles on current events as well as letters to the editor provide social studies students the opportunity to engage with their communities at local, state, national, and global levels.

Fieldwork in the Community

In addition to bringing the community to the school to enrich lessons, students can go into the field and conduct action research, either independently or under teacher supervision. Social scientists refer to the process of gathering information directly on-site, rather than secondhand through texts and other such materials, as engaging in fieldwork. **Fieldwork** is often used to generate or test hypotheses in problem solving or to provide clear examples in concept learning.

Fieldwork should be a well planned change-of-pace activity for students and not merely a diversion. In fieldwork, students act on what they observe or experience. They do this by relating their field experiences to other information they have studied or are studying, and then reflecting on the connections. It is important that a trip to the field be an *integral* part of school instruction. Excellent examples of how this can occur appear in *Ralph Nader Presents: Civics for Democracy: A Journey for Teachers and Students* (Isaac, 1997). The book provides guidelines for community action projects, as well as case studies of successful student activities. One such project is highlighted in Figure 3.5.

Often it may be appropriate to have individual students or small groups working in the field, either during or after school hours. These activities can involve mentoring, service activities, and a host of data-collection projects. A premier example of a community service action research project can be found in the Ligon History Project (**www2.ncsu.edu/ncsu/cep/ligon/about/history/intro.html**). In 1999, Dr. Marsha Alibrandi, associate professor and program chairperson of Secondary Social Studies Teacher Education at North Carolina State University, led a diverse team of university and public school researchers in a joint community, university, and middle school history recovery project (Alibrandi et al., 2001). Alibrandi knew from previous experience that involving middle schoolers in social studies original historical research was the best way for them to live and learn social studies. The Ligon History Project helped students at Ligon Middle School, once the premier black high school in Raleigh, North Carolina, recapture their school's rich history. Students used investigatory tools to uncover Ligon's high school past. GIS technology enabled them to peel back layers of city and community growth and change. In addition, students learned about the history of Raleigh through the Great Raleigh Trolley Adventure, plotted growth rings on an ancient felled campus tree and timelined historic events that paralleled the life of the tree, recorded oral histories from community leaders, and accessed archives

FIGURE 3.5
Profiles of Students in Action

Saving What's Left of Florida

It all started in 1987, when Charles DeVeney, a teacher at Coral Springs High School in Florida, was biking to work and saw that land near the school was slated to be cleared for development. He spoke to his outdoor education class about the rapid rate of deforestation in southern Florida and of his desire to preserve some of the area's nature for future generations. The students wanted to know what they could do.

So DeVeney and his students formed a club, called Save What's Left, to try to save the 68 acres of dense wetlands, including a large stand of cypress trees, that were to be cut down to build soccer fields. The students began by writing letters to anyone they could think of who might be able to stop the destruction of the trees.

At first, no one in the community listened. So Save What's Left students began to gather signatures on petitions to protest the development. Standing on the sidewalk in front of their school, they held signs asking drivers passing by in their cars to stop to sign the students' petition. The response was so overwhelming that on the second day of petitioning, the highway patrol had to direct traffic. Save What's Left eventually gathered 3,500 signatures from community residents concerned about the rapid rate of development....

The students spoke at city and county council meetings and gathered petitions to convince the City and County Commissions to ask residents to vote to buy the land. After two years, the issue was put on the ballot for the voters to decide. In March of 1989, Broward County voters approved a $75 million bond issue to buy the 68 acres of Coral Springs trees as well as 13 other sites in the county. The 68 acres turned out to be the largest cypress tree stand left in Broward County. County Commissioner John Hart said, "It was because of people like these kids in Save What's Left that this got done."

The city of Coral Springs and Save What's Left have since begun a project to completely restore the land over the next few years. Eventually it will be used as an outdoor classroom in which to teach environmental appreciation and to inspire other environmentalists to use their power to "save what's left."

Note. From *Ralph Nader Presents: Civics for Democracy: A Journey for Teachers and Students* by Katherine Isaac, 1992, Washington, DC: Center for Study of Responsive Law. Reprinted with permission from Essential Information.

to learn the origin of neighborhood buildings. Facts and stories emerged about the life of the black community during the days of Jim Crow. Students were empowered by what they learned and appalled that much of it was not written down. They recorded and transcribed hours of video interviews intent on telling the story before those who lived it were gone. Many of the project's products can be found on the website.

Research into social studies education and GIS is Dr. Shannon White's focus. White is a gifted curriculum developer, teacher, and program administrator, and is highly sought after for her expertise in teaching using GIS technology. In Box 3.3

BOX 3.3	Addressing the Issues: GIS—Using Technology to Bring the World to the Classroom

Dr. Shannon White
Program Administrator, Florida Center for Instructional Technology, University of South Florida

Geographic Information Systems, or GIS, allow students to explore the world with technology. This analytical mapping software enables students to explore locations from a local to a global level. Data that may be used in GIS maps include aerial photographs, robust databases that can be queried, and digital images. The layers that are added to a map are decided by the user and could include demographics, voting precincts, transportation data, hydrography, elevations, buildings, and more. GIS maps are dynamic. GIS software allows the students to view different layers of a map and different approaches to a problem from multiple perspectives. They are able to turn on and off the layered themes of the map as needed. The student can change the way in which data are displayed by changing the colors and symbols of the map and the legend. The student can zoom in on the playground of the school or out to the continent of Africa with a click of a button. While one student may need the streets, lakes, and rivers for investigation of a historic, social, economic, legal, or geographic problem, another student

may only need transportation and population data. With GIS software each student can present an individual analysis and perspective with professional maps.

Students can create maps from their own data or explore problems from existing data. GIS data can be created from almost any source—texts, Internet research, existing data that have been queried, student-collected data, GPS data, and so on. There are many sources of free existing data from federal, state, county, city, and other local sources. The U.S. Geologic Survey (**www.usgs.gov/**) is an example of a federal source for GIS information. Environmental Systems Research Institute (ESRI) is a private company that has free downloadable data, lesson plans, and web-based GIS data that teachers may use (**www.esri.com/industries/k–12/index.html**).

What is needed? A computer, GIS software, GIS data, other geo-referenced information (known locations on the earth), and a geographic question are all that is necessary. Most topics have a geographic tie. Whether students are exploring war and famine and their effect on global populations or economics, or a community-based problem, there is a geo reference that can tie GIS maps to the curriculum. What geographic questions can be explored in your curriculum?

White shares her view on how to use GIS technology to bring the affairs of the globe into the classroom.

The Ligon History Project demonstrates the power of active citizenship. Students reunited Ligon High School classmates who were long forgotten. The middle schoolers' research showcased important community leaders who were all but overlooked during the years of segregation. More importantly, the words of community elders allowed the students to better understand national and state social history from the perspective of those who lived it. GIS technology had shown them how the living and working patterns of their capital city, specifically in the black community, had altered over the years. As the stories of living history unfolded, the students came to see the injustices of the Jim Crow era as real. Transcribing the stories into a booklet allowed rich history to be told and preserved. The students were empowered and transformed into "keepers of their history." Social studies would never be just a subject to them again.

When an entire class is to be engaged in fieldwork during normal school hours, a great deal of teacher planning is involved to ensure a successful and productive experience. The planning process may be viewed in three stages—before the trip, during the trip, and after the trip—as the following guidelines suggest.

Before the Trip

1. Establish clear and specific goals and objectives for the trip. Plan to share these with the students either before or after the trip, as appropriate to your instructional strategy.
2. View the trip as a *means* rather than an end. Consider such issues as how time will be used and how variety in experiences will be provided.
3. Familiarize yourself with the major features of the site you will visit. Identify those features of the visit that will interest students and reflect *action* (i.e., people doing things). (Note: If you are having a guided tour be sure to have heard the presentation first. Tour guides welcome input **before** the field trip. This helps them tailor the presentation to match the level and attention span of your students.)
4. Make a list of those features of the site you plan to discuss and emphasize during the trip. Then make some notes on the types of comments and questions you plan to raise concerning them.
5. If possible, obtain pictures, written information, slides, and the like to introduce the site to be visited. In preparing for the visit, focus on special features you wish students to notice.
6. If appropriate, provide students with a sheet of points to consider and data to collect during the visit. If students are to engage in an activity, be sure to indicate what they are expected to do and not to do.
7. Develop a checklist of all the procedural, administrative details that need to be arranged, such as confirmation of visitation date, bus plans, parental permissions, provisions for meals or snacks (if any), restroom facilities, safety precautions (if necessary), and special student dress (if needed).
8. Organize a simple file system for collecting all forms or funds required from students and parents.

During the Trip

1. Focus students' attention on those features of the trip that are most important. Have them observe and record, where appropriate, answers to questions such as (a) What things did I see? (b) Which people did I see, and what were they doing? (c) How did _____ get done? (d) Which people were involved? (e) What materials were used?

2. Where possible, engage students in some activity during the visit. Where this is not possible, raise related questions and provide relevant information.
3. Take pictures or videotape to use in discussing important aspects of the trip during the follow-up.
4. Make brief notes on what seemed to interest and bore students and on the more important questions that were asked. Note also those points you would like to call attention to during the follow-up discussion.

After the Trip

1. Ask students to offer their open-ended impressions of what they learned from the trip and what they enjoyed most from it and why.
2. Review your notes from the trip and discuss important points, referring to the data students collected.
3. Review (or identify) the objectives for the trip and relate the experiences to previous learning.
4. Engage the students in additional related follow-up activities.
5. While the procedural and substantive features of the trip are still fresh in your mind, construct a file card of notes for future reference. Be sure to note what worked and what did not.

Collecting Oral Histories

A data-collection project that lends itself well to individual and small group field-work is recording oral histories (Mehaffy, Sitton, & Davis Jr., 1979). An **oral history** may be defined as any record of "reminiscences about which the narrator can speak from first-hand knowledge" (Baum, 1977, p. 1). One of the best series of books that describes the actual process of oral history taking is the Foxfire books (Wigginton, 1985). Written by students in Rabun County, Georgia, who discovered their region's heritage through oral histories, the books inspire teachers to engage in their own oral history projects. The Southern Oral History Program provides a comprehensive guide to designing and implementing an oral history project (**www.sohp.org/howto/guide/index.html**).

As fieldwork, recording oral histories provides students with a sense of personal engagement in a stream of events (Totten, 1989). Students are elevated to the important role of "keepers of the history." The activity, a "bottom up" approach to grass roots local research, helps relate specific historical events to a real person who was affected by them (Hutchinson, 2005). Because the narrator is a local person, the oral history may help to tie the local community into the national history being examined in the classroom.

Procedures for Collecting Oral Histories. In fieldwork, the emphasis is on students *recording* oral histories. Totten (1989) suggested that a teacher introduce students to the procedures involved in recording oral histories by modeling one in

Collecting oral histories is one way to extend social studies learning beyond the school.

class. He recommended that, prior to the recording, students be involved in developing the set of questions to be asked.

Foci for oral histories include themes, events, issues, recollections of individuals, periods and places, and biographies. Each focus requires different types of questions to bring out relevant data. Open-ended questions enable the person to respond with answers that may offer unexpected information. Zimmerman (1981) suggests that the following questions be included when compiling detailed, open-ended questions:

- What have been the major accomplishments in your life?
- What have been the biggest problems, mistakes, or adversities in your life?

Collecting Social Science Information Through Surveys

Closely related to oral histories are surveys. Surveys, which may include interviews, allow students to transform the school and community into a laboratory for gathering social data. Surveys can help answer questions such as:

- What do you think is the most important invention of the past 100 years, and why? (Downs, 1993, p. 104; see Figure 3.6 for a sample activity)
- How do people on my block feel about the idea of raising taxes to create a new park in the community?

FIGURE 3.6
Using Survey and Interview Techniques

Student Surveys

After a unit on the industrial revolution and inventions, I sent every student home with a neon yellow sheet of paper with the question: What do you think is the most important invention of the past 100 years, and why? Students had brainstormed aloud in class and had come up with inventions such as plastic, microwaves, vaccinations, rocket engines, television, and a few inventions such as the telephone, which is actually slightly older than one hundred years.

For this assignment, students asked the survey question of a parent, a teacher, and a friend who did not attend the school. Students were instructed to record and paraphrase respondents' answers and to return the survey within one week....

My seventh graders liked the assignment because it was easily achievable, involved outside interaction, and stimulated their thinking. We tabulated the results from all six of my classes and found that the most frequently given response was "vaccinations," followed closely by "the electric light bulb."

For a school-wide project, several teachers might poll their classes and compare responses across classes or grade levels. Other possible survey questions for students to field test include:

1. What would you most like to see invented that has not been invented yet, and why?
2. If you could travel back in time to any year or period in history, what would it be, and why?
3. Which historical figure would you like to be, and why?
4. If you could invite any historical figure to dinner, who would it be, and why?
5. If you could have been the first person to discover something or some place, what would it be, and why?

Teachers might also introduce students to the notion of Delphic polling, in which they show survey responses to participants, and then ask new questions incorporating the first survey responses. This involves the theory that people are usually influenced by others' responses. For example, students tell participants that in the first survey, 60 percent of respondents wanted to be George Washington, 30 percent Abe Lincoln, and 10 percent Betsy Ross. The participants then rank their choices, and a new perspective is added to the primary study. Even younger students can handle comparative data when the concept is clearly explained to them. Moreover, they are taking a hands-on approach to public opinion and survey methods.

Note. From *The Social Studies*, "Getting parents and students involved using survey and interview techniques" (pp.104–106). Reprinted with permission of the Helen Dwight Reid Educational Foundation. Published by Heldref Publications, 1319 Eighteenth St., NW, Washington, DC 20036-1802. Copyright © 1993.

Communicating with the Community About the Social Studies Program

"Whatever happened to history and geography?" someone in the school community is likely to ask. "Why don't the kids know all of the names of the states and capitals anymore?" another may wonder. Since many aspects of the social studies program that students in the middle and secondary grades study today will differ considerably from the programs their parents and other members of the community have experienced, teachers should anticipate community questions such as these. When the school curriculum does not reflect people's recollections of their own school experiences, it is not unusual to find that they are puzzled or apprehensive about the changes. Questions about current students' lack of skills and knowledge in social studies, especially regarding their ability to "spit back" discrete facts, offer you the chance to speak out not only for the importance of teaching social studies, but for teaching to develop depth of knowledge in social studies and the ability to apply what is learned. In an effort to target specific subjects for test score improvement, some school systems have instructed middle school teachers to drop social studies instruction or "teach" social studies solely through young adult literature in language arts. Just because a story is set in a particular historic period does not mean that important social studies concepts and vocabulary have been identified and are being learned. Jeff Passe, former president of the National Council of the Social Studies, cites a case in point. In New York in 2004, students' scores dropped on a particular reading comprehension test. Upon further examination, it was found that one passage alone was responsible for the lower score. That passage used the term *wagon trains*. Unfortunately, wagon train was not a reading vocabulary term, but certainly would have been taught in the social studies curriculum. Language arts and social studies can certainly support one another, but not if social studies is only being "taught" through the literature of language arts (Passe, 2006).

One of the important roles that a contemporary social studies teacher plays is communicating with parents and parent surrogates about students' progress in class and the nature and importance of the social studies program. As funding and test scores have become more of an issue, members of the extended school community have become increasingly involved with school boards and schools and they too wish to be well informed.

The net effect is that teachers need to interact on an ongoing basis with various sectors of the community to better achieve their classroom objectives and promote the welfare of their students. This process often involves publicizing the activities and goals of the school and the social studies program and preparing informational materials, websites, and programs. It may also include engaging in public dialogue and inviting parents and others to aid and observe in classrooms and examine curriculum materials and policy statements of the school. Additionally, it will involve soliciting parents and surrogates to cooperate in encouraging students to work toward program objectives and to maintain appropriate standards of conduct in the classroom.

Alerting the Community to School Activities

Local school board meetings provide one forum to publicize school and classroom activities. Another way to keep the public informed is through building your own class website. In smaller communities where board agendas are not overfilled, opportunities exist for students, as well as teachers, to participate in programs.

Some social studies teachers use the local newspaper as a vehicle to reach out to the community. In some cases, students themselves have been encouraged to contribute articles, even on a regular basis, reporting on matters such as school life, student achievements, academic programs, emerging issues, and important events. In other cases, teachers and administrators regularly contact the local press to publicize school matters that they feel are important to share with the community.

Events such as "Back to School Night" are also an important way of both involving families and others in the life of the school and communicating the nature of the educational program. It is especially important that new teachers develop a well-thought-out program for such occasions. The impressions of the teachers, classroom, and school that individuals receive during that event often stay with them throughout the year. Be friendly, forthcoming, well informed, and well organized. Remember you only have one chance to make a first impression.

Types of activities that teachers have used for such meetings are as follows:

1. Use pictures, PowerPoints, and/or podcasts to share typical classroom scenes, activities, or special class events. (Remember to get a signed release from parents for anything containing an image of their children.)
2. Provide a graphic organizer to show what the year's social studies work will be. Follow it with a question-and-answer period and make a point of emphasizing the importance of social studies education and in-depth learning.
3. Have members of one or more classes report on different phases of the social studies program. Involving the students in the program ensures parental participation.
4. Involve parents themselves in some sample activities similar to the ones that the students have done in class.
5. Collect questions from parents in advance of the night and organize discussions around them, or that night distribute cards for quick notation of questions, collect them, and reserve time at the end to respond.
6. Introduce and explain new programs, materials, units, activities, or procedures.
7. Share specific expectations for homework and class work, and clearly explain your testing and grading policies.

Identifying Professional Resources

Today's social studies teacher in the middle and secondary grades has access to a wealth of sources for professional development. Not the least of these is the extensive network across the United States of colleges and universities; teacher centers; local, state, and national professional organizations; various governmental agencies; and websites.

Teachers should identify those resources that will enable them to grow as professionals and enrich their instruction. This process includes locating individuals, agencies, centers, and organizations that help keep teachers abreast of new developments, issues, and trends within their field.

Organizational Resources

To aid them in their search, teachers can look especially to professional organizations that focus exclusively on the social studies. The following list identifies some major institutions that meet this criterion:

American Anthropological Association	www.aaanet.org/resinet.htm
American Bar Association	www.abanet.org/home.html
American Economic Association	www.vanderbilt.edu/AEA/org.htm
American Historical Association	www.historians.org
American Political Science Association	www.apsanet.org/about/
American Psychological Association	www.apa.org/about
American Sociological Association	www.asanet.org/
Association of American Geographers	www.aag.org/Info/info.html
*Educational Resources Information Center (ERIC)	www.skeric.org
Joint Council on Economic Education	www.ncee.net/about/
National Council for Geographic Education	www.ncge.org/ncge
National Council for the Social Studies	www.ncss.org
National Middle School Association	www.nmsa.org
Organization of American Historians	www.oah.org

*Outstanding, teacher-friendly site with many social studies sites noted, lesson plans, and activities.

These organizations produce a number of materials, including guidelines and policy statements. Their periodical publications include newsletters and journals. They also sponsor annual regional and national conferences for teachers of social studies on topics covering a range of issues in the field. The National Middle School Association (NMSA) represents the needs and interests of middle-level educators and their students. Although NMSA does not solely deal with social studies, teaching and learning approaches in middle school classrooms directly relate to teaching social studies are the subject of journal articles and conference presentations.

Some of these organizations also represent the interests of social studies teachers before state and federal legislative bodies. The National Council for the Social Studies (NCSS), the National Council for Geographic Education (NCGE), and the National Middle School Association (NMSA) also elect representatives from their membership to serve as officers and committee members. This provides classroom teachers with an opportunity to participate in establishing policies and practices for the organizations.

In addition to these national organizations, affiliate units in many states provide similar services. Regional social studies organizations and middle school associations cover several states. The national organizations listed can provide information on the affiliates.

Professional Journals

A number of specialized professional periodicals are available for social studies teachers. Some of the periodicals are sponsored by the organizations cited. They include:

American Political Science	**www.apsanet.org/pubs/**
Journal of Economic Education	**www.indiana.edu/~econed/tocindex.htm**
Journal of Geography	**www.ncge.org/publications/journal**
Middle Ground	**www.nmsa.org**
Middle School Journal	**www.nmsa.org**
Perspectives in Politics	**www.apsanet.org/pubs/**
PS: Political Science and Politics	**www.apsanet.org/pubs/**
Social Education	**www.ncss.org**
Teaching Sociology	**www.lemoyne.edu/ts/tsmain.html**
The History Teacher	**www.thehistoryteacher.org**

Effective Citizenship as Professional Development

Due to the unique relationship of the social studies to citizenship education, social studies teachers carry a special professional responsibility. If they are to promote with any credibility the development of reflective, competent, and concerned citizens, they must model and practice responsible citizenship. Simply put, they must walk the talk.

Each individual professional must determine what is required to fulfill this responsibility. Engle and Ochoa (1988) have laid out seven questions they suggested might be used to survey students who had graduated as a way of inferring the impact of the social studies curriculum on their lives. Social studies teachers, by turning the questions on themselves, may gauge their own stage of citizenship development. How well would you do?

- Do you keep up with community and national issues?
- Are you active in community affairs?
- Do you subscribe to news magazines (or on-line news sources)?
- Are you registered to vote?
- Did you vote in the last election?
- Have you followed current global and political issues such as protectionism, the national debt?
- Do you belong to any civic groups? (Engle & Ochoa, 1988, p. 191)

Burgeoning technology offerings enable all citizens to keep up with national and international news. Websites for TV news shows, as well as for newspapers at home and abroad, give us up-to-the-minute regional, national, and international news (e.g., **www.thenytimes.com** and **www.thewallstreetjournal.com**).

Professional Development Through the Internet

Social studies teachers increasingly rely on technology to supply ongoing professional development. The Internet is a major source of information on current developments, as well as an important medium for teachers to share ideas, seek assistance, solve problems, and acquire inservice training. A growing number of institutions also offer courses over the Internet and through distance education.

SUMMARY

Engaging students in constructing knowledge is not as simple as most people may think. Students are reading less and watching more, and often at home there is not supervision and the commitment to learning. Some think that going back to the *read the chapter, answer the questions at the end* teaching approach of the 1950s is the solution. "Just go back to the basics and put some rigor into it while you are at it," would sum up their charge. But this is a different day and time and that edict misses the whole point of how knowledge is built. You build the knowledge wall brick by brick, each brick placed squarely straddling and connecting those underneath it. Remember, learning is not just memorizing discrete facts for spit back. Application is the key to knowledge. Can you apply what you know?

In this chapter we looked at knowledge construction. To really understand and own the learning, you must have related what is new to that which the student already knows. Sorting information into concept groups and adding onto the schema already in place enables students to deepen their understanding and form new connections to what was previously learned.

Teaching and learning are not isolated events. Students who are heard to ask, "When am I ever going to use this information?" clearly have not seen the connection of what they are learning to real life. Teaching students using the curriculum integration teaching approach helps students see how knowledge can be built using the disciplines as tools to address a concept, idea, issue, or question. Studies have shown that curriculum integration promotes reflective learning, motivates both teacher and student, and provides for differentiated instruction.

Using the community as your resource makes teaching social studies real for both you and your students. It promotes active citizenship and, when combined with service projects that support community endeavors, enables students to become "keepers of the history." Not only does that role demonstrate to them that they are worthy, but it also shows the community that the negative stereotypes often attributed to adolescents are false. Connecting students to the community, giving them a vested interest in their past while enabling them to play a part in their future, provides all-important grounding.

There is never a reason to feel isolated when you are teaching. Help can be right next door or just a mouse click away. Surfing the Internet will acquaint you with the plethora of resources that are available at your fingertips. Professional organizations welcome new members and provide excellent magazine and online resources. Their conferences, local and national, network you with your colleagues, and the organization journals provide valuable advice and research about what is going on in the field. Unfortunately, new educators often feel that they cannot take the time or money to attend conferences. They are reluctant to ask for support or may feel it is a perk for more experienced teachers. Express your interest in representing your school at a conference. Apply to present a project or idea that you have developed. Offer to bring back a report to your faculty regarding the conference sessions you attended. Schools and school systems that do not support and encourage teachers to join professional organizations and attend conferences have only their bottom line, and not teacher excellence, as their agenda.

In the next chapter we will begin the planning process that will help you see how the standards are the foundation on which we build. It is important to realize that the standards are meant to serve as a springboard to effective teaching. Remembering this, you will begin to design lessons that employ standards as a guide for creative and meaningful instruction.

ACTIVITIES

1. Which of the social sciences do you think should receive the most emphasis in the middle grades? In the secondary grades? What are the reasons for your answers? Discuss these among your group members.
2. Start your own community resource file. Make a list of the community resources on which a social studies teacher could draw. Go online and see if any have websites. Download the information on each of the sites that you feel would be important to have in a resource file. Compare your list with those of others in the group.

3. Select some of the websites noted in this chapter and have each member go online to investigate what the site has to offer. Critique the site and suggest how you might use the site as a teacher.
4. Two websites that will enable you to see the wealth of information and the help available for teaching social studies are **www.askeric.org** and **www .socialstudiesforkids. com.** Access each of them and navigate around the sites for teaching and learning ideas. Share these ideas with your classmates.

WEB RESOURCES

TechLINK

Virtual Field Trips: **www.ibiblio.org/cisco/trips.html**

Newslink: **www.newslink.org/**

Newsday Project: **www.gsn.org/project/newsday/index.html**

Online NewsHour: **www.pbs.org/newshour**

Current Events in the Social Studies Classroom: **www.eduplace.com/ss/current/index.html**

Designing School Websites: **www.fno.org/webdesign.html**

Museum Management Program: **www.nps.gov/history/museum/index.htm**

Online Tools for Schools: **www.ced.ncsu.edu/onlinetools/**

Part **II**

Developing Reflective, Competent, and Concerned Citizens

CHAPTER 4   Organizing and Planning for Teaching
             Social Studies

CHAPTER 5   Engaging Students in Learning Through
             Small Groups, Questions, Role Playing,
             and Simulations

CHAPTER 6   Promoting Reflective Inquiry: Developing
             and Applying Concepts, Generalizations,
             and Hypotheses

CHAPTER 7   Fostering Citizenship Competency

CHAPTER 8   Social Concern in a Globally and Culturally
             Diverse World

Organizing and Planning for Teaching Social Studies

Basic Issues in Planning Social Studies Instruction

    Identifying a Purpose for Citizenship Education

    Beginning the Planning Process

Social Studies Goals for Instruction

    Identifying and Stating Goals

Social Studies Objectives for Instruction

    Identifying and Stating Objectives

    General Objectives, Behavioral Objectives, and Student Learning Outcomes

    Objectives in the Cognitive and Affective Domains

Organizing Subject Matter into Units

    Planning and Creating Units

    Sources of Units

    Resource Units and Teaching Units

    Building Units Around Key Social Problems, Questions, and Themes

    Incorporating Multiple Perspectives into Units

    Using Concept Maps/Webs to Plan Units

    Planning Units Using Interdisciplinary Teams

    Formats for Unit Planning

Organizing Subject Matter into Lessons

    Lesson Plans

    Formats and Procedures for Lesson Planning

    The Fundamental Elements of Lesson Planning

    Back Mapping Lessons and Using Various Types of Instruction

Classrooms as Environments for Learning

    The Uses of Space in Planning Social Studies Instruction

    Allocation of Time in Lesson Plans

Creating and Managing the Classroom Environment

    Student Behavior in the Classroom and Teacher and Student Expectations

    Characteristics of Well-Managed Classrooms

    Supportive Teacher Behaviors

Balancing Goals and Objectives in the Curriculum: Linking the Head, the Hand, and the Heart

Guidelines for Social Studies Program Development

Variety in Instructional Planning

Summary

Activities

Web Resources

Consider a teacher, Mr. Olerud, who has traveled throughout Russia over the summer. He wishes to share his experiences and insights with his sixth-grade classes. Further, he hopes to provide them with a perspective and level of in-depth current information that their social studies text cannot.

The idea for a unit entitled "Russia: From Czars to Presidents and Back Again" begins to take shape. Gone are the days when he opened the text and taught it page by page. He has already consulted the national social studies standards available at www.ncss.org and is also familiar with the standard course of study for his education district. These two sources alone have given him a wealth of information and helped him answer two basic questions:

- *How would this unit fit in with my overall purpose in teaching social studies?*
- *Why should my students be asked to learn about this topic?*

From these initial questions, a basic goal emerges that offers an important rationale for the unit, other than that of merely sharing the teacher's interesting experiences or "covering" the material because it is part of the sixth-grade curriculum. No, his own professional judgment tells him that the key to the process is finding the answer to the following question:

- *What specifically should my class of culturally diverse students gain from the study of the unit?*

Mr. Olerud ponders important issues he hopes the unit will address. He brainstorms and makes a list of his ideas. Later, after he has given the unit more thought, he will review and revise them.

- *Which instructional techniques would be the most effective with the students?*

Mr. Olerud has a few ideas but later he will more fully flesh out the answers to this question. This will occur as he gets to know his students better and is able to learn their interests, needs, learning styles, and capabilities.

- *What resources already exist to help create the unit?*

By front loading the Russia study, he knows that the school resources will be plentiful. Because Russia appears at the end of the social studies book, most teachers teach it in the spring, if they get to it at all. He's done some background reading augmented by the travel guides that he purchased for his trip and examined the school's and local library's holdings, as well as found Internet sites that contain a wealth of recent information and resources. His research also revealed some dated political maps that nevertheless will be useful for then-and-now comparisons.

Several telephone calls establish that various community agencies can help provide guest experts. The local university's international student organization scored a big hit. Two students from Russia are visiting for the semester.

The local paper featured a professor doing research in Russian education. Her websites will be invaluable.

- *What are the most appropriate ways to determine the quality and quantity of what my students learn from the unit?*

Mr. Olerud browses through his professional library to gather some initial ideas. Since the school district is sponsoring an in-depth workshop on authentic assessment techniques during the preschool period, he also will have some concrete models available to guide him.

- *How much time can be devoted to such a unit?*

The answer to this question helps to determine the scope of the unit. Time is always a limited resource in the curriculum. Further, the amount of time required for a unit often is difficult to estimate accurately, especially for beginning teachers. If the teacher is block scheduled, then the unit can take on a new dimension and become a collaborative effort among colleagues teaching language arts, science, math, and social studies (see **www.ncsu.edu/chass/extension/russia-nc6** *and click on the Russia unit).*

From the teacher's informed questions, reflections, and initial investigations flow a rationale, goals, specific objectives, related teaching strategies, and authentic assessment procedures. The planning process also identifies student activities, resource materials and speakers, and a schedule appropriate for the unit. A new social studies unit is born!

Basic Issues in Planning Social Studies Instruction

One of the major challenges that new social studies teachers face is instructional planning. Carefully prepared, well-designed plans are a key ingredient in all successful teaching. Experienced teachers often make effective teaching look effortless or spontaneous to an untrained observer. Such teachers even may tell you they have done no immediate or sustained planning for their lessons. In reality, through trial and error over the years, seasoned social studies teachers gradually build on their collection of successful planning experiences. However, it is important to realize that no matter how experienced the teacher or how well planned the previously used unit, each and every unit is "new" in light of the new and different needs of each class of students. **Failure to make allowances for student needs spells doom for even the most gifted teacher with a can't-fail unit.**

Planning involves having a clear rationale for why we are teaching the topic, an idea of what we specifically hope to accomplish, how we intend to proceed, and how we will know if our instruction has been successful. Planning also requires attention to the wise use of the limited instructional time available to us during the school day (Borich, 1996).

Planning for social studies instruction may occur at the classroom, departmental, local, or state levels for a day, extended period, or school year. In every case, planning involves thoughtful consideration of the nature of what students are to learn and why they are to learn it.

Identifying a Purpose for Citizenship Education

All social studies planning begins with some *explicit* (conscious or stated) or *implicit* (unconscious or unstated) notion of the purpose of the social studies. As a quick review, we have examined seven alternative perspectives concerning the major purpose of citizenship education—namely, that the emphasis in citizenship education might be placed on:

- Transmission of the cultural heritage
- Concepts and methods of inquiry from the social sciences
- Reflective inquiry
- Informed social criticism
- Personal development
- Development of reflection, competence, and concern
- Development of a global perspective

The process of planning social studies instruction should begin with the teacher's adoption of any or all of these seven perspectives. When you are constructing your rationale or purpose, you may find that the seven purposes listed are *all* a part of the unit. One might predominate, but the others support it. If *transmission of the cultural heritage* is your main goal, it is logical for you to have students investigate aspects of the culture (concepts and methods of inquiry from the social studies), consider different sides of an issue relating to the culture (informed social criticism), and reflect about their own personal views about culture (reflective inquiry). All of these would be part of your effort to aid in student development of reflection, competence, and concern for the cultural heritage under study, your originally selected purpose for the unit. The statement of purpose then becomes a rudder that guides the remainder of the planning decisions. There should be a clear connection between the teacher's statement of purpose and the individual lessons, activities, and total curriculum developed for students.

Beginning the Planning Process

Before you open your textbook and lay out your teaching year, you have another important step to complete. You must have an understanding of what material you are to teach and what concepts and skills should be developed. To do this, you must be familiar with the national, state, and district standards and the local course of study. For example, if Russia is a focus for part of the year, you must know what it is about Russia that your students must know and understand.

Russia is a vast country with a long and varied history. How will you teach for *both* facts and understanding? They must go hand in hand. Just memorizing the czars and the countries that now make up the CIS (Commonwealth of Independent States) will not help students understand why Russia moved through three different forms of government in less than 100 years. How did czarist rule bring on communism and what was the tipping point that led to the downfall of the Soviet Union? Finally, what's happening today to all the freedoms gained in 1991? You and your students must engage in a discovery process that is much like unwrapping a package. One fact leads to another until you have built a framework for understanding. Piaget (1972) would say that the facts are all part of the schema and as each new piece of information is added, it is categorized and placed into a grouping that already exists. Consideration of a new concept would necessitate a new grouping or perhaps the information might provide the connector that helps link concepts together. You use what you unwrap to rewrap as you build a new and revised version of the original information. The process of unwrapping and rewrapping the package is what teaching is all about. Remember, Vygotsky (1986) reminds us that information exchanged among learners (intermental) is preliminary to the actual learning that takes place within the student. The student processes the shared learning within herself (intramental). It becomes her own when she relates it to her own unique schema.

Once you have studied the standards and course of study, it is time to open your plan book and begin to lay out the school year. The process of determining when you will teach each topic or concept is called *curriculum mapping*. Laying out your yearlong plan for teaching your curriculum has several benefits. Determining how much time you can devote to each topic is critical to deciding what can be taught in the time allowed (see Box 4.1). The simple act of placing your topics in a well-thought-out sequence helps you to feel organized and more confident about starting your year. A more subtle benefit of curriculum mapping is the opportunity to compare your map with those of others on your team or in your school to determine when and where collaborations might occur.

Trying to position topics so that when you teach them they will match up with a related topic that a colleague is teaching allows you to do either interdisciplinary or integrative teaching. If you teach in a middle school and your school has block scheduling, that is, scheduling that allows for longer periods of teaching time and the integration of other disciplines, your teaching team has an excellent opportunity to plan together for collaborative teaching. For example, you teach on a middle school two-teacher team (60 students) and your responsibility is for the language arts and social studies. Both you and your teammate have separate double periods in which to teach one set of 30 children, you with group A and your teammate with group B. After the first double period grouping, you exchange groups for another double period, you with group B and your teammate with group A. If the theme you are teaching is one that lends itself to incorporating all four subjects (your two and your teammate's two), and if you have a large enough space, you both can teach all 60 students together, showing the interrelatedness of the disciplines, making entirely

BOX 4.1	Addressing the Issues: Determining What Is Important to Teach

We are so caught up in national standards, local courses of study, textbook overviews, reviews, and curricula in general that we sometimes overlook the importance of asking ourselves just what is important for our students to know. Too often teachers are tempted to just open the book and begin to jot down important facts that they want their students to learn. Although the textbook is a tool for teaching, it does not always have the most current information. A lot can change in the 5 years that it takes for textbooks to be revised. It is our job to keep current in our field, gather the most timely information, and relate it to the topics taught at our grade level. This does not mean that we do not address issues and countries taught at other grade levels if they are current in the news. Nor does it mean that if we travel to a country that is not part of our grade-level study we do not share the richness of this adventure with our students. Yes, we do have an obligation to work within the curriculum, but this does not mean that we must feel boxed in and unable to enrich our teaching and learning with what we feel is important for our students to know. You are a professional. Presumably, you have skills in planning, teaching, and evaluation, as well as a good understanding of the age group with whom you are working. As a professional, it is your job to increase your knowledge base in all areas of your profession.

It is our obligation to make judgments about what children need to know and understand. Vygotsky's (1986) cognitive socialization recognizes the importance of our role as teacher–mentors. We operate in the zone of proximal development, scaffolding students from where they are currently achieving to higher levels of achievement and understanding. At the same time, we pass on the expectations and traditions of our society. Teaching is never just teaching. It is so much more. We have limited time with our students and so much to do. For these reasons, it is critical that we examine what we will teach and how we will teach it.

How will you determine what is important for your students to know?

new combinations of student groupings, and stretching your time to allow greater project work. This is rarely done on a day-to-day basis, but can be used for integrative project development time. It becomes a little more difficult if you are on a four-teacher team (120 students) and your responsibility is for a single subject. It is not suggested that you try to make a 120-person group learning experience work on a daily basis, but it is possible for teachers to adopt the same theme and teach their material in a parallel fashion. Language arts teaches the novel *Johnny Tremain*, social studies focuses on the politics and geography of the American Revolution, science talks about the discovery of gunpowder, and math calculates the troop and supply numbers and movements during the war. Presenting final projects, such as showing the digital timeline that has been developed to include all of the learning discoveries (Peirano, Wilson, & Wright, 2007), and engaging in culminating team activities both provide opportunities for large groups to come together. Interdisciplinary and integrative teaching is a little more difficult for high school teachers whose discipline is usually seen as being "stand alone." Of course, it is always possible to do integrative and interdisciplinary teaching within your own discipline; that is, teachers can answer students' topic questions that do not appear to be social studies in nature or offer asides that refer to information that comes from other subject areas. Colleagues on the high school level are willing to share subject-specific information that might pertain to your social studies topic of study.

If the high school has gone to block scheduling so that the class formerly taught throughout the year moves to double the time for one semester, the social studies teacher faces two immediate issues:

1. Redesigning the course for longer periods of teaching and activity, but with only one semester to complete the course of study.
2. Understanding that learning taught in the fall semester must be retained for spring AP testing. Students must be helped to understand how to review after an absence of one semester.

It is important to understand the difference between interdisciplinary and integrative teaching. Many educators use the terms interchangeably, even though there are significant differences between the two. Interdisciplinary can be parallel topic teaching among teachers who also provide opportunities for students and subjects to come together when appropriate or possible. This can involve any number of teachers on a team. If you are on a two-teacher team and you are the language arts and social studies teacher, you have the flexibility of interweaving the two subjects as you teach for mastery in both. Or, you can pair up with your teammate and address all of the subjects in a common theme you have both identified in your respective curricula. If you are teaching a single subject and have no opportunity to plan and teach with your teammates, you can still teach using an interdisciplinary approach. For example, you teach social studies and in your Russia study you discuss the nuclear meltdown at the Chernobyl nuclear power plant. You would be remiss if you did not address the science of how this meltdown occurred, the speed and dispersal range of the particulate matter, the health issues that resulted from the disaster, and the political fallout that accompanied the tragedy. Fictitious journal accounts of victims, as well as reactionary letters from citizens around the world, could be composed. Teaching in a way that shows the interdisciplinary nature of learning demonstrates the real world. Students will not question how they will use a piece of information they are asked to learn. Rather they will see the fact in light of the full picture needed for understanding.

Integrative teaching also blends the disciplines, but begins with a belief that the students' need to find answers to big questions and issues that are of interest to them should be part of the development of the curriculum. The topic of study can spring from a local issue, such as a social injustice built around the wetlands project noted previously, or the teacher can introduce a topic and solicit a list of big questions that the students want to explore. Big questions are grouped around common themes. Students may investigate a big question independently or form groups to do research. Teachers continue to provide general lessons from the unit while the students do in-depth research on a particular question or issue. Rubrics (guidelines that spell out what is to be included in the study and how the study is to be evaluated) are developed in concert with the students so expectations for the learning products are clear. Because there is great flexibility in research methods, and rubrics are tailored to the research study and the assessments, it is possible to differentiate the instruction, assignments, and evaluations to meet the needs of all students. Students' work centers around a theme and they use the disciplines as tools for their research. A website devoted to curriculum integration (**www.ncsu.edu/chass/extension/ci**) provides a great deal of information on the curriculum integration approach to teaching and learning.

When doing curriculum mapping and laying out your teaching year, it is important to note all of the holidays, teacher work days, dates that grades must be turned in, and when report cards go out. A yearlong instructional plan must work around all the things that interrupt your teaching. Timing is everything. You will want to consider where to place your high-interest units. Think about what both you and the students might consider to be of high interest. For example, after winter holidays it is more of a challenge to get students refocused. Your hands-on newspaper unit that incorporates global issues, weather, geography, maps, and editorial and news writing might be just the thing to jumpstart the new year. Attention lags in mid-December and a few weeks before school is out, so extra care must be used to tailor shorter, high-interest units for those times.

Another consideration to keep in mind when you are planning your curriculum for the year is the number of teachers sharing the resources for each topic of study. Altering the sequence of the topics as they appear in the textbook may enable greater availability of resources. Of course, this is not possible if chronology is essential to understanding and one topic builds upon another, but when studying separate regions or countries it is entirely possible to deviate from the order of the book. This is especially beneficial if a country or region is experiencing radical change. A good example was the breakup of the Soviet Union in 1991. Consider this social studies teacher's attitude regarding the Soviet unrest. She offered the comment that she didn't care what was happening in the Soviet Union. She had always taught England first and would not alter her plan just because the largest country in the world was breaking up. Her rigidity was the reason 120 children missed studying a monumental event *while* it was happening. The teacher would have found that resources were plentiful and interest was high. This is not to suggest that once you are well into teaching a topic that you drop it and move your focus to a hot spot in the news, but you cannot ignore current events. Often there are worldwide connections that one country has with another, for example, trade. Showing how current events can influence what you are studying allows you to show global interconnectedness and keeps your students on top of world happenings. Flexibility enables you to take advantage of the teachable moment and is the hallmark of good teaching (Virtue, 2007).

Planning can be overwhelming, and teachers who wait until Sunday to get ready for the new week's worth of lessons often find that day to be their least favorite of the week. Granted, you do have to make daily corrections and adjustments to your day-to-day plans, but switching your overall planning to Wednesday and formulating a Wednesday to Wednesday planning schedule will leave your weekends free for recharging your batteries and making a life for yourself outside of school.

Social Studies Goals for Instruction

The *general* expectations for what educators plan to accomplish in the social studies curriculum over the course of the year or a shorter unit of time constitute **curricular goals**. Establishing goals is an important step toward creating a basic framework for a course of study and for leading the way to more specific curriculum expectations. Brophy and Alleman (1993) have suggested that all aspects of the curriculum should be driven by goals, including questions, subject matter, and evaluation items. Your statement of purpose will guide your year's program and be supported by several goals that are designed to achieve the purpose. Goal statements may be different for each level of the social studies curriculum, or they may remain the same across the grades.

Identifying and Stating Goals

Goal statements are distinguished by their *level of generality*. For example, consider the following goals. The course of study for the **year** will help students:

1. Prepare to be technology literate in the workplace
2. Acquire the necessary skills for effective interpersonal relationships
3. Understand and appreciate cultures round the world
4. Develop an understanding of and tolerance for different values and lifestyles
5. Exercise their rights and responsibilities as citizens of a democracy

The preceding goals are important statements of broad concerns that teachers may wish to address in the social studies curriculum, but they require further elaboration and detail if they are to be helpful in crafting individual lessons. For example, the second goal statement does not indicate the specific skills that will be addressed.

Goals may be related to a particular discipline, such as history. For example, teachers may wish to have their students develop an appreciation of the roles political dissenters and minorities have played over time in changing the laws and policies of our nation. Whether they are related to one discipline or are multidisciplinary in their scope, goal statements are distinguished by their level of generality.

Social Studies Objectives for Instruction

Related to goals are the more specific **objectives** that the curriculum is designed to achieve over a school year, single period, or some other unit of time. Whereas goals communicate what the broad general framework for the curriculum will be, objectives identify the learning needed to take place to accomplish those goals. Objectives are *specific* statements of what students are expected to learn and/or do as the outcome of some measure of instruction. It is important to look back at your goals and determine what level of learning the students must be able to demonstrate to show that they have actually achieved the goals. Objectives are like stair steps or the scaffolding you put in place that helps students climb to the goal. Objectives may be stated for individual lessons, for a unit of study, or for the entire year's course of study. The same objective also may be included in more than one lesson.

Identifying and Stating Objectives

Consider the following sample objectives, and then contrast them with the five year-long goal statements listed earlier. As a result of the lesson (activity), the *student will be able to (SWBAT)*:

- Identify correctly at least five of the countries of Africa by writing in their names on an outline map
- Create and describe in a well-developed paragraph a hypothetical solution to one of the community problems from the list provided that meets 75% of the criteria required
- Present in writing three causes of World War II, specifying in the answer key actors, roles, places, or events
- Define orally the terms *natural resources, ozone layer, smog, radon,* and *global warming*
- Identify five examples of the concept "refugee" from an unlabeled set of examples and nonexamples provided
- Using a timeline you have constructed, place with 80% accuracy a set of 10 events and their corresponding dates
- Construct and explain at least three hypotheses that examine why the American Revolution occurred when it did
- Identify in writing two groups of American citizens who originally were not protected by the Constitution
- Construct a chart summarizing the data that compares and contrasts the positions on five major issues that have been taken by the major candidates for president

Note how much more specific and measurable these statements are than the goals statements made previously.

General Objectives, Behavioral Objectives, and Student Learning Outcomes

All of the sample objectives provided indicate some clear and specific student learning outcomes, but some are more precise than others. The first one, for example, is an illustration of a highly specific objective. It states exclusive *criteria* or standards, such as the number of items expected. It also specifies the *conditions* for demonstrating achievement of the objective, such as through writing.

Objectives that provide this degree of specificity and describe clearly the expected behavior of the student are characterized as **behavioral** or **performance objectives**. Generally, discrete facts lend themselves more to the use of behavioral or performance objectives than others, such as locating on a U.S. map and labeling with correct spelling the location of states and their corresponding capitals.

Writing Statements of Objectives. Sources such as curriculum guides and basal texts often contain examples of types of social studies goals and objectives for various grade levels and subjects. Typically, statements of objectives begin with the headings similar to the following: "The student will be able to. . . ." In other cases, the introductory phrase is assumed, and the objective is stated in a briefer form similar to the following: "To [write] [draw] [point to]. . . ."

Many lists of verbs have been identified to aid teachers in writing objectives. A sample list is provided here to suggest the range of possibilities that can be considered. As a result of the lesson (activity), the student will be able to:

rank	identify	defend
estimate	assemble	sort
predict	match	summarize
rate	point to	explain
select	organize	demonstrate
role-play	classify	locate
construct	define	draw
write	diagram	modify
state	create	criticize
justify	judge	support
listen	share	hypothesize
debate	convince	map
formulate	theorize	internalize
conduct	use	argue
display	resolve	exhibit

Objectives in the Cognitive and Affective Domains

Curriculum planners often classify goals and objectives as being within the cognitive or affective domains. The **cognitive domain** emphasizes thinking processes, and the **affective domain** emphasizes feelings and emotions. Systems for creating and classifying goals and objectives within these domains were developed by Bloom and his associates more than five decades ago (Bloom, 1956; Krathwohl, Bloom, & Masia, 1969).

Some goals and objectives indicate directly which of the domains they highlight. Many goals and objectives, however, are not so easily classified and require reference to the context in which they arise.

Summing up, thus far we have looked at laying out your social studies program for the year. First, begin with a *statement of purpose* that will guide your year's program. Second, determine *statements of curricular goals*. These note what you want your students to accomplish by the end of the year. For example, use such phrases as the following: prepare to be . . . , acquire the necessary skills for . . . , understand (something specific), develop an understanding of (something general), exercise their rights to (do something). Third, write *objectives* that describe what the students must do to demonstrate that they have mastered learning that will lead to achieving the goals. *Behavioral objectives* describe how they will behave and what they will do to show you their learning level, *cognitive objectives* emphasize the thinking process, and *affective objectives* emphasize the development of feelings and emotions. In light of the national focus on assessment, it is important to be sure that your objectives are measurable. Now, you are ready to divide your year into *units*.

Organizing Subject Matter into Units

Years ago teachers were typically assigned only the general framework for the subject matter of a course (for example, "world history"). Today that flexibility is likely gone and the complete course of study for the entire year will be laid out, because a district, school, or department has adopted a standard course of study that spells out a scope (what is taught and how deeply) and sequence (in what order) pattern. That having been said, you must remember that you are a professional and that you must do what is in the best interest of your students. In planning, you will always need to consider the background, interests, capabilities, and learning styles of your students. Teachers should always augment the existing course outline with supplementary lessons on timely topics, such as local elections or current events. Further, individual teachers have the opportunity to infuse their own sense of purpose, goals, and objectives into existing curriculum outlines and guidelines.

One way to determine student interests and concerns as a basis for preparation of a new unit is to use a survey or questionnaire. An example of how this might be done is given in Figure 4.1. You can always prepare your own student interest inventory or simply ask the students what questions they have about the upcoming topic or unit. Involving the students and their questions in your planning process helps to ensure that the students will be motivated to participate and stay involved in the learning (Beane, 2005).

Planning and Creating Units

The subject matter of a course is divided into **units** of study. A unit is organized around a topic, theme, issue, or problem. The unit subject is studied through a series of sequenced and related learning activities that are directly related to the

FIGURE 4.1
Assessing Students' Special Needs

YOUR ROLE: Teacher _____ Student_____ Parent_____

We are interested in getting your opinion about what special topics might be added to the school's curriculum. We want to be sure that the curriculum includes topics that are important to our students. Listed below are some topics that have been suggested. Consider each one. Then tell us your opinion about whether these topics should be added to the curriculum. Circle one of these answers:

Definitely: This topic should *definitely* be added to the curriculum.
Maybe: This topic *maybe* should be added, if there is time.
Not: This topic should *not* be added to the curriculum.

At the bottom of the page you may list any other topics that you think should definitely be added.

As you answer, keep in mind that if topics are added, then some present topics will have to be dropped or given less time.

The results of the survey will be used by the faculty in determining which changes, if any, should be proposed to the superintendent and the school board.

Topic	Your Opinion		
1. Avoiding alcohol and drug abuse.	Definitely	Maybe	Not
2. Learning how to be a good citizen.	Definitely	Maybe	Not
3. Making good moral choices.	Definitely	Maybe	Not
4. Learning about careers.	Definitely	Maybe	Not
5. Understanding how families are changing.	Definitely	Maybe	Not
6. Making wise decisions about sex.	Definitely	Maybe	Not
7. Learning how to be a smart consumer.	Definitely	Maybe	Not
8. Knowing how to prevent suicide.	Definitely	Maybe	Not
9. Protecting the environment.	Definitely	Maybe	Not
10. Preparing for college entrance tests.	Definitely	Maybe	Not
11. Improving our community.	Definitely	Maybe	Not
12. Making good use of leisure time.	Definitely	Maybe	Not
13. Understanding the future.	Definitely	Maybe	Not
14. Living in a nuclear age.	Definitely	Maybe	Not
15. Understanding the world's religions.	Definitely	Maybe	Not
16. Learning about world population control.	Definitely	Maybe	Not
17. Valuing our own and others' ethnic heritage.	Definitely	Maybe	Not
18. Reducing conflict between groups.	Definitely	Maybe	Not
19. Selecting and getting into the right college.	Definitely	Maybe	Not
20. Living in peace with other countries.	Definitely	Maybe	Not

If there are any other topics not listed above that you think should definitely be added, list them here:

21._____

22._____

23._____

Note. From *Curriculum Renewa* (p. 60) by Allan A. Glatthorn, Alexandria, VA: Association for Supervision and Curriculum Development. © 1987 ASCD. Used with permission. Learn more about ASCD at www.ascd.org.

goals, objectives, resources for learning, and procedures for evaluation that you have developed.

Resources identified within units frequently include primary source materials, computer software, textbooks, artifacts, maps, periodicals, websites, and readings. They may also include posters, worksheets, simulation games, transparencies, and drawings. Further, resources may encompass guest speakers, field trips, films, videotapes, DVDs, audiotape/CD recordings, and assorted other media.

Units may be designed for any length of time. Typically, however, they require from 2 to 6 weeks to complete.

Sample Unit Topics. Some illustrations of unit titles are:

- "The Environmental Crisis in the World"
- "The Causes of the American Revolution"
- "The Role of Women in Developing Nations"
- "International Terrorism"
- "Homelessness in America"
- "China's Emergence as an Economic Super Power"

Sources of Units

Units are available through any number of sources. Professional organizations and local school districts have developed collections of units for different grade levels on a variety of topics. Many can be found online at the organization's website.

Surfing the Web will give you many complete units and a wealth of good ideas. You have only to identify a search engine, type in as completely as you can what you are looking for, and wait for the results. One very useful site is World History for Us All (**http://worldhistoryforusall.sdsu.edu/**). This site provides a model curriculum of world history from ancient to present day. The curriculum is the result of a multiyear effort between classroom teachers and scholars of world history. The underpinning of the curriculum's focus lies in developing essential questions. Two of the three essential questions include: How has the changing relationship between human beings and the physical and natural environment affected human life from early times to present? Why have relations among humans become so complex since early times?

"Slavery in the Nineteenth Century" is an example of a unit designed for grades 5 through 8 that is available from a professional organization, the National Center for History in the Schools (**www.sscnet.ucla.edu/nchs**). The basic *goal of the unit* is to "make slavery comprehensible to students, showing its oppressiveness and yet explaining how white Southern culture rationalized and sustained it" (Pearson & Robertson, 1991, p. 9). Note, as developed below, the unit goal would also be the goal of each lesson in the unit.

Anne Vega/Merrill

Units should include a mix of activities, especially ones that connect to "real world" learning.

The *unit goal* and six lessons of varying length with corresponding *objectives* are as follows:

Unit Goal and Lesson Goal: To make slavery comprehensible to students, showing its oppressiveness and yet explaining how white Southern culture rationalized and sustained it.

Lesson 1 Objectives:

1. To list at least three justifications of slavery used by whites
2. To speculate on the validity of the justifications of slavery
3. To explain ways in which white Southerners were legally required to support slavery (Pearson & Robertson, 1991, p. 15)

Lesson 2 Objectives:

1. To study part of a slave inventory
2. To comprehend how slaves were treated as both people and property
3. To understand that slaves had various occupations requiring various skills
4. To compare various forms of slave labor (Pearson & Robertson, 1991, p. 27)

Lesson 3 Objectives:

1. To appreciate African American culture as reflected in stories and crafts
2. To demonstrate in discussion an understanding of the ways in which African American culture helped give slaves the skills and strength to endure slavery
3. To identify some aspects of American culture that have African American origins (Pearson & Robertson, 1991, p. 39)

Lesson 4 Objectives:

1. To understand why open rebellion was rarely undertaken
2. To list different ways slaves resisted their condition
3. To enact through the *Readers' Theatre* an example of the minor resistance which pervaded slaves' interactions with masters (Pearson & Robertson, 1991, p. 51)

Lesson 5 Objectives:

1. To understand that not everyone accepted slavery
2. To learn the names and accomplishments of three abolitionists
3. To explore the diverse arguments for abolition
4. To appreciate the moral and physical courage of the abolitionists (Pearson & Robertson, 1991, p. 61)

Lesson 6 Objectives:

1. To understand that black and white women were prominent in the struggle for abolition
2. To express the connection between abolition and the women's rights movement
3. To list some of the prominent women involved with both abolition and women's rights (Pearson & Robertson, 1991, p. 75)

Look back at the lesson objectives and consider how you would classify each of them: cognitive, affective, and behavioral. Now look at each objective again and determine what you might require the students to do (behavioral) to demonstrate their learning so that you can determine if they have successfully achieved that objective. A portion of the text of Lesson 4 from the unit is shown in Appendix C, Resource Figure 4.1.

Teachers, themselves, are the major developers of individual units. Many of these are shared within a school or district and often are published in curriculum guides and professional texts and journals. An illustration of this is the set of teacher-generated global studies units detailed in the text *Teaching about International Conflict and Peace* (Shapiro & Merryfield, 1995).

In developing units, teachers build on their special interests, expertise, or experiences, such as travel. Teacher-created units often begin with a general set of ideas or questions that address topics required by the standard course of study and that the teachers regard as important (and, hopefully, mirror questions students would ask and want to answer). From this base of ideas, the other specific details are fleshed out to give the unit shape and focus.

Student textbooks are organized into units that are frequently arranged in chronological order. The text is usually divided into 10 units that normally would be spread over the 36 weeks of the school year. The subject matter of each unit is organized into three to four subtopics or chapters. Each chapter, in turn, is organized into two or more related lessons. Resource materials, follow-up activities, and evaluation measures are provided in each unit. Because of block scheduling, the cost of textbooks, and a plethora of Web resources, textbooks have taken on a new look. Some publishers use a mini-book format and divide their larger books into smaller segmented booklets for ease of reading and carrying. This format also gives school systems some flexibility in what they wish to purchase.

Resource Units and Teaching Units

Units are sometimes classified as either **resource units** or **teaching units**. Although the two types share many of the same elements, resource units generally are more extensive and detailed than teaching units. Also, they often are designed as multipurpose collections of multileveled material to be used by many different teachers for a variety of students. A resource unit typically would list more subtopics, objectives, teaching strategies and activities, resources, and evaluation procedures than an individual teacher needs to use for a topic. Drawing on a resource unit, a teacher can create a teaching unit that is tailored for a specific population of students and for a given length of time.

Building Units Around Key Social Problems, Questions, and Themes

Along with using students' and teachers' immediate interests as the basis for creating units, key social problems, questions, and themes may serve as the foundation for a unit. Using the Revolutionary War period in an American history class as an example, Engle and Ochoa (1988) have provided questions that teachers might raise to shape the design of a unit (see also Onosko, 1992; Shapiro & Merryfield, 1995):

> Under what conditions is a revolution justified? Did conditions in America in the late eighteenth century fulfill those conditions? Are there better ways than revolution for bringing about social change in society? Under what conditions, if any, should people disobey the law? Is it equally right or wrong for governments to break the law than for individuals to break the law? (p. 156)

Years ago, sensitive issues, such as sex, religion, race and ethnicity, and politics were avoided in the classroom. Today, these topics are freely discussed in our culture, but teachers still must exercise caution when addressing them in the classroom. Because these are sensitive issues, they require much advance planning, parent contact and explanation, and anticipation of a variety of questions and stands that students will take. You should remember that often the student's belief is her parent's belief. Tact is important when dealing with any sensitive issues. Class ground rules must be established for discussion of sensitive topics. One must use care when dealing with the person whose views are being expressed and also be sensitive to the students who may be offended by those views. It is extremely important to be aware of the policies that exist in your school system for teaching sensitive issues. Principals want to be informed whenever a sensitive issue is planned for discussion. Remember, principals are often the first to be contacted by a disgruntled citizen.

Oliver and Shaver (1966) and Newmann (1970) advocated building units around enduring value issues that recur throughout history. For example, a unit might be shaped around the value issue: "When, if ever, should the value of the public's health override personal freedom?" (Oliver, Newmann, & Singleton, 1992, p. 101). This question surfaces in general issues such as prohibiting smoking in public places, or preventing those with highly communicable diseases from traveling on public transportation. Teachers must consider how their approach to social issues, sometimes called the **jurisprudential approach,** can be evenhanded when they develop units of study.

Incorporating Multiple Perspectives into Units

Units may also be constructed around multiple perspectives—that is, different views or interpretations of the same set of events. Almost two decades ago Noddings (1991), for example, urged that feminist perspectives be included throughout the curriculum to provide a contextually richer analysis. Woyshner (2006) agrees, but notes that the emphasis on NCLB testing of discrete facts does not support rich contextual analyses and thus voices that provide gender equity are less prevalent. Banks (1993) suggested the study of topics might be advanced and enriched by including the following five perspectives: personal/cultural (students' personal and cultural experiences), popular (mass media, pop culture, and films), mainstream academic (research from mainstream scholars), transformative academic (research that challenges mainstream findings or methodologies), and school (information in school texts and related media).

He illustrated how these five perspectives might be integrated in a unit on the Westward Movement:

> When beginning the unit, teachers can draw upon the students' personal and cultural knowledge about the Westward Movement. They can ask the students to make a list of ideas that come to mind when they think of "The West." It is possible to construct a KWL chart. What do we know (K), what do we want to know (W) and what have we learned (L). Some teachers add another segment, what more can we

learn? To enable the students to determine how the popular culture depicts the West, teachers can ask the students to view and analyze . . . *How the West Was Won.* They can also ask them to view videos of older westerns and more recently made films about the West and to make a list of its major themes and images, as well as noting how views have changed over time. Teachers can summarize Turner's frontier theory to give students an idea of how an influential mainstream historian described and interpreted the West in the late 19th century and how this theory influenced generations of historians.

Teachers can present a transformative perspective on the West by showing the students the film, *How the West Was Won and Honor Lost.* Teachers may also ask the students to view segments of the popular film *Dances with Wolves* and to discuss how the depiction of Native Americans in the film reflects both mainstream and transformative perspectives on Native Americans in U.S. history and culture. Teachers can present the textbook account of the Westward Movement in the final part of the unit. (Banks, 1993, pp. 11–12)

Apart from providing an in-depth examination of a topic and promoting multicultural education, this approach introduces students to the value of different types of knowledge and perspectives and enables them to better understand the complexity of determining what actually occurred during an event.

Using Concept Maps/Webs to Plan Units

One way for the teacher to sketch out the general structure of a unit is through the use of a concept map (Novak, 1998). A **concept map** is a listing and an ordering of all of the major concepts to be discussed within a unit. Related concepts are joined in the map, along with a brief statement that explains how they are linked. Concept maps have a number of applications in teaching. Our focus in this section is on their application to *unit planning.* Concept maps are often called webs. In building a web, concepts are connected and related to one another. They are a quick way for teachers and students to demonstrate a visual representation of work done brainstorming a topic.

Concept maps offer teachers a planning tool for thinking about all of the important topics they wish to include and connections they wish to make among them in a unit. They provide a comprehensive graphic representation of the unit. Teachers must use their own judgments about how many concepts to address. Students' abilities, length of time to teach the material, and requirements of the standard course of study help to determine the breadth and depth of the unit. A map that represents one instructor's plan for a unit of study on Roman history is shown in Figure 4.2.

To show the evolution of a concept map, a partially completed one depicting initial ideas for a unit on Russia has been included. It is shown in Figure 4.3. As the unit evolves, a teacher would fill in key nodes of the map. For example, the teacher would list more specific elements of general geography, actual location, relative location and physical features, along with specific objectives and activities to teach each geographic element.

FIGURE 4.2
Concept Map for Planning a Course of Study

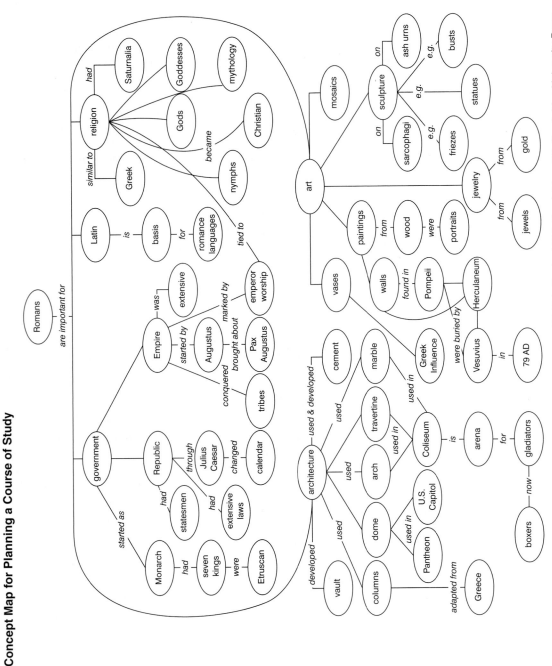

Note. From *Learning How to Learn* (pp. 84–85) by Joseph D. Novak and D. Bob Gowin, 1984, Cambridge, UK: Cambridge University Press. Copyright 1984 by Cambridge University Press. Reprinted with permission of Cambridge University Press.

FIGURE 4.3
Instructor's Concept Map for a Unit on Russia

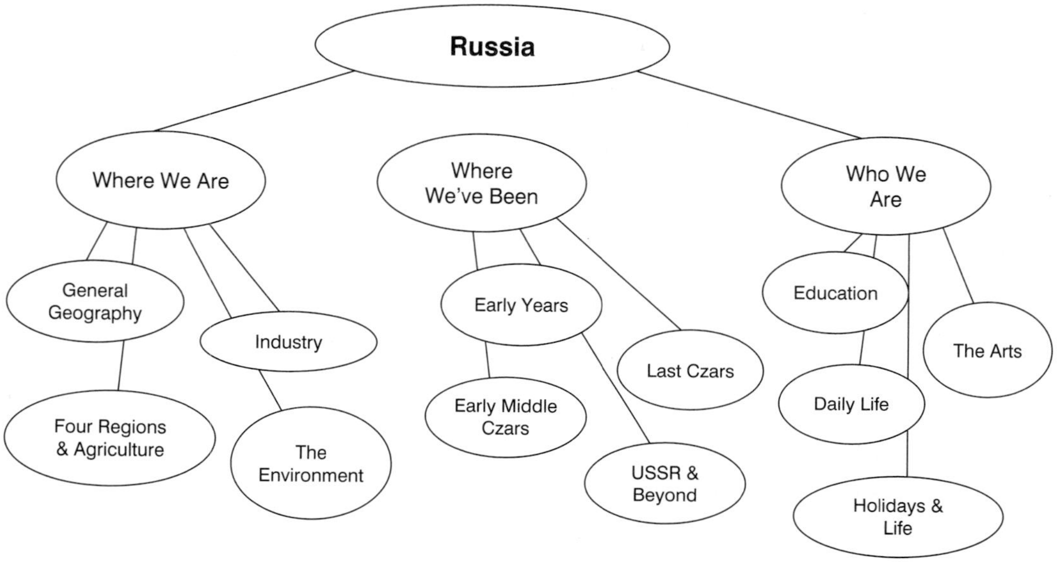

Planning Units Using Interdisciplinary Teams

"A problem inherent in the structure of the American high school," Merryfield and Remy (1995) have concluded, "is fragmentation of the curriculum" (p. 48). They explain:

> For example, students rarely have the opportunity to connect their study of Thoreau's Civil Disobedience in English class in November with their study of the passive resistance tactics of the civil rights movement in U.S. history in March. In most American high schools students are not taught to appreciate important relationships across different academic disciplines or to examine issues holistically. Through the development of interdisciplinary teams such relationships and connections become part of course planning, unit construction, and student thinking. (Merryfield & Remy, 1995, pp. 48–49)

Interdisciplinary teaming encourages teacher collaboration and sharing, and provides greater opportunities for experimentation. Teachers are less isolated and more willing to take an instructional risk when there is another teacher with whom to brainstorm and who can offer a reality check to out-of-the-box ideas. In addition, teaming also permits more efficient use of instructional time, since redundancy in topics can be avoided.

Formats for Unit Planning

There are a variety of different unit **formats**, or ways of organizing and presenting the information in a unit. A sample format for developing a unit plan is given in Figure 4.4. The choice of a format to use in unit planning, however, is largely a matter of personal preference. The most practical course of action for teachers is to identify a format in an existing unit that they find easy to follow, and to adopt it.

In summary, the general process for creating one of the units in your yearlong study of social studies can be outlined as follows:

1. Develop an idea or adopt a chapter topic for study and translate it into a brief, clear statement of your theme or problem focus. (Unit title) Can this be curriculum mapped onto teammates' plans?
2. Determine approximately how much time can be spent on the unit. (Time required)

FIGURE 4.4
Sample Format for Unit Planning

Unit Plan Format

I. Descriptive Characteristics
   Title:
   Student Target Population/Grade Level:
   Estimated Time Required:
   Rationale and Overview:

II. Goals and Objectives *(Number each for easy referral in constructing lesson plans.)*

   Goals:

   Specific Objectives:

III. Teaching Strategies and Activities *(Briefly describe the list of possibilities and number them for later reference.)*

IV. List of Resources *(List each item and subdivide by type—e.g., textbooks, speakers, field trips, reference works, various media. Number each for easy reference.)*

V. Evaluation Procedures *(Relate each item to the goals and objectives stated earlier.)*

---

3. Brainstorm and break the big idea or theme for the unit into a set of more specific ideas and smaller subtopics. (List of topics/Concept mapping)
4. Indicate for which group of students or grade levels the unit is intended and include them in the planning by allowing them to identify big questions and issues of interest to them. (Target and involve student population)
5. Construct a brief overview of what the unit is to be about and why it is important and useful for the intended class to learn it. (Rationale)
6. Identify a goal or set of basic goals that the unit will be designed to accomplish. (Goals)
7. Outline the specific objectives that enable the goals to be accomplished and arrange them in sequential order. (Objectives) Remember that they must be directly related to achieving the goals.
8. Identify and develop related significant teaching strategies and activities. (Teaching strategies and activities)
9. Identify, locate, and organize all the individuals and the instructional resources that are available and will be needed. (Resources)
10. Develop a plan to evaluate the effectiveness of the unit. Include formal and informal assessment. (Evaluation procedures)

In addition to planning a curriculum around units, some programs are structured more flexibly. The Paideia Program shown in Figure 4.5 is such a case.

Organizing Subject Matter into Lessons

Congratulations, you have considered your yearlong study of social studies and the units into which that year will be broken up. You have followed a specific layout and building format that is becoming very familiar (i.e., rationale, goals, objectives, materials, procedure, and assessment). The next important element that follows your work thus far is developing **lessons**. They are the heart and soul of your day-to-day work. Lessons are part of the process that supports unit learning and understanding, thus securing your students' yearlong achievement and success in social studies. A lesson may last for a single class period or extend over several days.

Lesson Plans

Lesson planning includes taking into account what has come *before* the lesson and what is to *follow* it, as well as what happens *during* the lesson. Lesson planning requires careful attention to the conditions under which learning is to occur. This includes an awareness of the prior knowledge and special needs of individual students within a class.

Developing effective lessons also requires teachers to give careful thought to the specifics of what is to be achieved. Additionally, it involves consideration of how instructional activities can accomplish objectives in an interesting and

FIGURE 4.5
The Paideia Program

The goal of the Paideia Program is to provide a rigorous, liberal arts education in grades K–12 which will allow all graduates to have the skills necessary to earn a living, to think and act critically as responsible citizens, to continue educating themselves as responsible citizens, and to continue educating themselves as lifelong learners. The Program supports block scheduling, integration of learning styles, cooperative learning, and interdisciplinary unit planning. The Program promotes the following teaching techniques to ensure both educational quality and equality. The Paideia Program advocates three modes of teaching:

- The didactic mode is the acquisition of organized knowledge through means such as textbooks, lectures, and videos. John Goodlad has estimated that roughly 85% of our classroom instruction time in the U.S. is currently spent this way. While necessary, this portion of learning should be more interactive and should monopolize much less of the school day.
- The coaching aspect of the program is the way students actively gain the intellectual skills that are necessary for further learning. Coaching is the core of the Paideia Program and requires practice, mastery, and learning by doing. The amount of time given to this activity should be greatly expanded, and a wide array of methods and approaches should be used in the classroom (e.g., labs, cooperative learning techniques, project-centered/product-oriented learning).
- The seminar component is a way for students to deepen their understanding of the ideas they have been studying, and apply them to their own lives and values. Seminars should be used as a regular instructional method in all grades, K–12. The seminar process, with the teacher facilitating an open exploration of the ideas in a work, has the greatest capacity to transform the nature of school for students and teachers.

The National Paideia Center was established in the School of Education at The University of North Carolina at Chapel Hill in 1988. Its mission is to:

Act as an information clearinghouse for schools nationwide that are establishing Paideia programs

Provide training in Paideia methods and technical assistance to interested schools and educators

Create a group of Paideia schools to serve as national demonstration sites for implementation; continue research on and evaluation of the results of Paideia methods

Because the Paideia reform agenda is the most comprehensive of those currently on the educational horizon, it is being endorsed across the country by those educators most interested in systemic, whole-school reform.

Note. Reprinted by permission of The National Paideia Center, The University of North Carolina.

meaningful way for a particular group of students. Above all, in planning lessons, the teacher should have an informed grasp of the subject matter under investigation. In Dewey's (1961) words:

> When engaged in the direct act of teaching, the instructor needs to have subject matter at his fingers' ends; his attention should be upon the attitude and response of the pupil . . . the teacher should be occupied not with the subject matter itself but in its interaction with the pupils' present needs and capacities. (p. 183)

Formats and Procedures for Lesson Planning

Lesson plan formats and what they include may vary in structure, terminology, degree of detail, and the number of elements. The two different types of lesson plans presented in Appendix C, Resource Figures 4.2 and 4.3, illustrate this point. Take a moment to turn to Appendix C and study these plans.

Selecting a format and procedures for lesson planning is largely a matter of a teacher's professional judgment or school requirements. Some schools, for example, request that teachers employ a format and set of procedures that have been standardized in the school or district.

An example of a standardized approach to lesson planning that was adopted by schools across the United States in the 1980s is a seven-step plan developed by and popularized by Madeline Hunter (1984). Her plan, or some form of it, is still in use today. Sometimes called the **Theory and Practice (TAP) Model,** it provides for the following elements:

1. Establish anticipatory set. (Hook—to get students' attention)
2. Explain the objective of the lesson. (Purpose—students will be able to . . . .)
3. Provide instructional input. (Teach)
4. Model the desired student behavior. (Show students how to do it)
5. Check for understanding. (Informal assessment—get feedback)
6. Provide for guided practice. (Supervised practice)
7. Provide for independent practice. (Students try it on their own)

Hunter's model (lacking only a formal final assessment stage) is similar to the seven-step instructional model developed earlier by Gagné and Briggs (1979):

1. Gain attention. (Hook)
2. Inform the learner of the objective. (Purpose)
3. Stimulate recall of prerequisite learning. (Bridge to previous learning)
4. Present the stimulus material. (Teach)
5. Elicit desired behavior. (Students practice and learn)
6. Provide feedback. (Teacher responds to needs)
7. Assess behavior. (Formal and informal)

(The sample lesson plan seen in Appendix C, Resource Figure 4.3, follows the Gagné and Briggs seven-step format.)

The issue of mandated lesson plan formats and procedures has become controversial among teachers and professional groups. Some of the reasons schools have given for instituting such policies are to establish minimal teaching standards and to expedite communication among teachers, supervisors, and administrators. For some teachers, however, such a requirement presents a serious constraint. They regard such formats as overly restrictive and inflexible, inappropriate for many types of significant learning activities, and in general an infringement on their professional prerogatives. Generally, it is thought that the need for lesson planning falls somewhere between mandated format and the laissez faire approach. Planning for your daily lessons can be thought of as taking a trip. When much of the journey is over familiar territory, only significant routes need be noted; however, when new area is covered it is important to have detailed plans for the journey as well as notations suggesting alternate routes. You might look at it as an evaluation question. If you do not know where you are going, how will you know if and when you arrive?

Don't fall into the trap of thinking that you can be more responsive and timely if you do minimum planning. Rather, you need a good plan to be responsive and timely when events dictate that you make a sudden lesson plan change. Being clear about what your lesson was trying to achieve will allow you to know how to relate the unexpected adjustments to the objectives and goals you had planned. Being unprepared encourages spur of the moment choices that may not be in the best interest of maintaining discipline. Stringing several days of laissez faire planning together may result in loss of control of the classroom. This is also a cautionary note for teaching absences. Preparing fully developed, easy to follow, tightly crafted lesson plans for your substitute is a must. Sketchy plans are not fair to the substitute or your students and may leave your classroom much harder to reorganize and manage when you return.

The Fundamental Elements of Lesson Planning

Some fundamental elements to consider in developing a lesson plan structure and format include the following items:

- Lesson title and rationale
- Goals and objectives
- Initiatory activity (Hook and students' questions and issues)
- Teaching strategies
- Resources
- Transition/assessment

To help illustrate the lesson planning process, for each item, we have included an example taken from the elements of a lesson plan developed by the National Geographic Society (1988, pp. 14–15). Though written in the late 1980s, this plan about a worldwide energy resource, petroleum, is as timely today as it was then, perhaps more so.

1. *Title and rationale.* Giving each lesson a title communicates its focus. Example: "The Geography of Petroleum." Follow it with a rationale to indicate why it is important to teach this lesson.

2. *Goals and objectives.* The goals of the lesson should be broad and general. Example: "Students will know the major areas of world petroleum production and consumption." The objectives are designed to build an information base and the skills needed to meet the goals. The objectives should be stated in behavioral terms and be as clear and specific as possible. Tell students what the lesson will teach them and what learning behavior is expected of them. If they know where they are going, they will know when they have arrived or be able to judge how much longer it will take to get there. Example: "Students will be able to (SWBAT) use maps and graphs to identify and label the major areas of world petroleum production and consumption."

3. *Initiatory activity.* A lesson plan should begin with some brief initiatory activity that arouses curiosity, puzzles the students, or somehow focuses attention on what is to be learned. This is often called "the hook." Example: "Ask students to imagine an end to all international sales of petroleum tomorrow. What would be the impact on the United States? How would students' lives change? What would happen to countries that consume major amounts of petroleum but produce little or none? Use Japan as an example." Ask students to share their questions and issues regarding the hot topic of the production and worldwide sales of petroleum resources.

4. *Teaching strategies.* Teaching strategies and activities refer generally to the set of procedures that teachers employ to achieve their instructional objectives. Different types of strategies exist for different objectives. Strategies incorporate questions, statements, directions, actions, and the sequence in which they are to occur. Strategies also deal with how the teacher plans to structure and present new subject matter and relate it to students' prior knowledge. They also indicate teacher and student roles in the lesson. Example: "Direct students to examine maps in an atlas or online to identify major petroleum-producing countries. (See Goode's *World Atlas* or URLs you provide.) Post the findings. Have students shade and label these countries on their world outline maps."

5. *Resources.* Somewhere within the lesson you should clearly note a list of the resources that you will be using and the order in which you will use them. As you use and reuse this lesson you will add to your list of resources. Be sure to keep them updated.

6. *Transition/assessment.* Transition occurs within the lesson as well as at the end of the lesson. We cannot emphasize enough how critical it is to make swift transitions within your lesson. Do not allow the lesson to drag as the students slowly get out new material or shift places. Keeping students at the ready keeps them focused and moving forward, making a

world of difference for classroom management. Time on task means less time needed to reengage and refocus. Finally, the end of each complete lesson should include some transition to the next one. This may consist merely of a summary of the day's activities, with some "hook" for what is to follow and an explanation of how the two lessons are related. It might also consist of some assessment of a phase of learning that has just been completed.

You might provide opportunities for students to apply, extend, or experiment with what they have learned. Example: "Have students research the much talked about environmental implications of the widespread use of petroleum as an energy source. (Examples include air pollution, global warming, oil spills.) Use the exit card strategy and ask students to write a question that they would like answered which the lesson did not address, or indicate some point of clarification that needs to be provided. Have the students hand the 3x5 card to you as they leave the class. This helps you assess the overall understanding of the lesson and provides a place to start the next day."

Back Mapping Lessons and Using Various Types of Instruction

Back mapping is another way to plan lessons. It is the reverse of what we have already considered. Here's how it works: When you have determined the topic for the lesson, you consider what you want the end learning result to be for your students. What attitude, skills, and knowledge should your assessment indicate they possess? Once that outcome is decided, then the lesson can be crafted so that students can learn the material and can demonstrate the skills needed (objectives). Those skills and that specific learning should support the more general overall goal or goals of the lesson. Consider this example: Deciding on a vacation spot. You pick the place and then determine what it will take to get there as well as how you will benefit from visiting that location.

The teaching approach involving a large percentage of "teacher talk" is called **teacher directed**. Some might call it lecture, but if you remember the comments of Jackie Brooks in the Addressing the Issues Box 1.1 *On Becoming a Memorable Master Teacher,* you'll recall that she made a distinction between the lecture/storytelling approach that she uses, dramatic narrative, and straight-up, teacher-only talk, lecture. Brooks's approach resonates with the students because she skillfully makes a personal contact with each listener. To watch her move around the room pausing at desks and looking directly into the eyes of her students to make a point is pure magic. As the lesson flows, she skillfully moves from teacher-directed dramatic narrative to student-directed interactive group work. As you can imagine, at that point enthusiasm for the lesson has been made infectious and groups launch into their assignments. It is no surprise that studies have long shown that students respond positively to the opportunity to interact with one another. Ask the students and they will tell you that school is "all about social." Educators must factor in the joy of learning to ensure teaching success.

Lessons that allow students to research and draw conclusions based on supporting contextual information (specific facts and examples) use **inductive learning**. Example: Students are on the Great Raleigh Trolley Adventure and have the opportunity to explore Haywood Hall (**www.ced.ncsu.edu/2/adventure/**). They are trying to determine the use of some of the unique antique implements that are in the Hall and its barn. The teacher has placed numbered cards next to each mystery item and has asked that the students to use the context in which they find the item to help them determine what it is. The location of the item and its proximity to other things may give clues to the possible use of the implement. Students use inductive thinking to speculate about the item. Can you think of a lesson you were taught that used the inductive approach to learning? Did this type of learning resonate with you?

Classrooms as Environments for Learning

Although teachers often have limited control over many of the physical features of a classroom, they generally have some freedom, even in the case of shared rooms, to transform their classroom in ways that facilitate the achievement of their objectives.

The Uses of Space in Planning Social Studies Instruction

Space in a classroom is an important instructional resource. By carefully determining how your classroom space is organized, you may predetermine the success or failure of your lessons. How individuals are located within the space can determine whether productive collaboration and learning, or misbehavior, occurs. For example, the dynamics of a class likely will be different if a room is filled with tables and chairs rather than desks. Can you explain the reasons for this?

Allocation of Time in Lesson Plans

Today, attention is paid to how instructional time in classrooms is used by teachers and students. Time, like texts and other instructional materials, represents an important resource for social studies teachers. In planning and executing lessons, teachers need to watch carefully how time is distributed across various activities.

How do you determine where to spend your instructional time? This has become a very sensitive issue. The move to increase standardized testing to measure knowledge of discrete facts means that more instructional time must be devoted to drill and memorization. What, then, happens to the time for discussion, brainstorming, and application of those facts? Discrete fact testing does not usually support the application aspect of learning. How is a teacher able to prepare her students for their roles in a democratic society if application of knowledge is not an important part of a democratic curriculum?

The sample teacher schedules in Chapter 1 illustrate a conventional approach to organizing class periods. Such traditional school schedules require that a teacher typically monitor how approximately 45 to 50 minutes of total class contact time is used. For example, in the lesson shown in Figure 4.8 in Appendix C designed for a 50-minute period, Borich (1996) recommends that the following distribution of time be used for each of the seven steps in the lesson:

Step 1: Gaining attention: 1 to 5 minutes

Step 2: Stating objective: 1 to 3 minutes

Step 3: Stimulating recall: 5 to 10 minutes

Step 4: Presenting stimulus material: 10 to 20 minutes

Step 5: Eliciting desired behavior: 10 to 20 minutes

Step 6: Providing feedback: 5 to 10 minutes

Step 7: Assessing behavior: Zero to 10 minutes*

*Your authors note that the increased importance of assessment requires you do informal assessment throughout the lesson and have some means of judging the effectiveness of the overall lesson before you move on to additional learning.

Scheduling Alternatives. Block scheduling, as noted in a previous chapter, lengthens teaching time and allows you to revamp the time you can spend at all points in your lesson. It also affords you the luxury of teaching several mini lessons within that block of time. Students with reduced attention spans are often unable to focus for long blocks of time and multiple mini lessons help to keep their interest.

Scheduling options, and there are many formats, afford teachers, students, and administrators opportunities to experiment with different instructional models and to integrate curriculum such as English and social studies. They also permit activities that are not easily compressed into a traditional class period, such as simulations and debates, to be initiated and completed without interruption.

Whatever scheduling options are available to teachers, as they become more skilled in organizing resources, in brainstorming, and in planning lessons and units, there will be increased opportunities to focus on the needs, interests, and progress of individual students. Keep in mind that the latter is your number one job.

Creating and Managing the Classroom Environment

Apart from the issue of how time should be allocated, perhaps one of the most common concerns of beginning teachers is that they will be unable to manage their classes effectively. They often are frightened that their classes will "get out of control." Clearly established classroom rules and procedures are essential. Quick transitions as you move from one area of study to another are critical to retaining student focus and teacher control. Tight planning and engaging students by using a teaching approach that enables them to actively participate makes the students partners in the learning success of the class. Enabling students to investigate their own interests and concerns about a topic motivates them to find the answers. Students who are at risk of failure must be drawn into the process. Establishing a risk-free environment where students' views can be heard enables everyone to contribute.

An individual or group of students bent on antisocial, violent, or destructive behavior can be frightening for the teacher who is responsible for redirecting the individual or group into constructive learning activities. When a teacher is unsuccessful in doing this, the feeling may be one of complete powerlessness and incompetence. Seek help sooner rather than later from your mentor or administration.

No effective instruction can occur in the midst of a maelstrom. Communication in a classroom out of control is garbled and coated with tension. Students and teacher lack the sense of security and stability that is necessary for effective teaching and learning to transpire. In schools where teachers operate in teams, team teachers may have an understanding among themselves to place a student who is experiencing behavior problems in another teammate's classroom for a period of time or the full day. Simply a change of scene may help the student settle in and cope. Seated at the back of the classroom, the student may work on the class work that is going on in that class or homework from the previous class.

The administration has the power to reconfigure student assignments in order to separate troublemakers. You must not remain silent if you are put in an untenable situation. Remember you are not responsible for making that class configuration. It is a sad commentary on school politics when new, inexperienced teachers are given the most difficult classes to teach.

A number of comprehensive texts address fears and real problems regarding disruptive classes, as well as the general mechanics of classroom management (e.g., Charles & Charles, 2004; Glasser, 1998; Good & Brophy, 2004; Manning & Bucher, 2007; Nissman, 2006). A full and adequate discussion of the issues they cover is beyond the scope of this text. Because a successfully managed classroom environment is central to all effective social studies instruction, however, the subject merits at least brief attention in our discussion.

Student Behavior in the Classroom and Teacher and Student Expectations

Gottfredson, Gottfredson, and Hybl (1993) note: "Disruptive behavior in school harms both the misbehaving individual and the school community" (p. 180). There may be many reasons for a student's misconduct. Discipline may be lax at home and the student is used to getting away with disrespectful behavior. The student may be placed at the wrong level and has become frustrated and is unable to cope. Perhaps the student is bored and feels negative attention is better than no attention at all. Peer groups, class placement in the daylong schedule, the added pressure of standardized test performance, events at home, and any number of other things may be responsible for student misconduct. Jonathan Kozol in his 1967 book, *Death at an Early Age*, describes a girl walking to school. She passes burned out cars, ruined old buildings, and gangs of youth hanging out on street corners beckoning to her to join them. By the time she reaches the school building, she has no more coping power to enable her to handle the stresses of her school day. It is important for us as teachers to remember that many of our children today face harried, hectic, and less than ideal lifestyles. Stress at home may not leave them with much coping power by the time they reach your classroom. You may be the one bright spot in their lives.

Each teacher has expectations regarding how students are to behave in the classroom and those expectations influence the management plan you develop. Some teachers, for example, will accept the noise and student movement within the classroom that accompanies cooperative learning. Others require students to request permission to speak or move about. Students often have to make quick adjustments from period to period, from one teacher's set of expectations to another's. At best, these adjustments are often just another challenge that students associate with schooling. At worst, they represent for some students a continuing source of confusion and eventual conflict.

Students have very real expectations for the behavior of their teachers. Polls conducted among students indicate that they tend to respond better to teachers who are good listeners, have a sense of humor, can empathize with the adolescent's world, are flexible and understanding when dealing with student concerns, and are structured in their teaching approach as well as in establishing and maintaining rules and policies that have consistent consequences. Reread the list of teacher characteristics and think about your own views about the teacher/student relationship. How well do you think your style will resonate with students?

Often beginning teachers receive countless well-intentioned suggestions from their more experienced colleagues on how to be successful in managing a classroom. These range from maxims such as "Don't smile before Christmas" to lists of specific teacher behaviors to model. The difficulty for the beginning teacher in trying to implement well-intended suggestions is lack of an underlying framework or set of principles that can provide a rationale for that behavior. The absence of such a framework ultimately creates problems when a specific behavior that normally is effective proves to be ineffective. At that point, a teacher is at a loss as to what went wrong and which adjustments should be made.

One central element of a classroom management framework is the teacher's expectations concerning what is appropriate student behavior in a classroom. Because teachers' expectations of student behavior may vary within a given school, it is important to make explicit at the beginning of the year the rules, policies, and procedures students are to follow within a given class. Posting positively worded classroom procedures spells out a teacher's or team's expectations for learning. These may cover many different areas as the list in Figure 4.6 illustrates. The process of underscoring expectations can also be accomplished through brief statements on assignment sheets, or verbal reminders. In all cases, the teacher should ensure that all students, even chronic absentees, have been briefed about school and classroom rules and procedures.

FIGURE 4.6
Classroom Rules Related to Conduct and Work

	Rules related to classroom conduct	Rules related to academic work
Rules that need to be communicated first day	1. where to sit 2. how seats are assigned 3. what to do before the bell rings 4. responding, speaking out 5. leaving at the bell 6. drinks, food, and gum 7. washroom and drinking privileges	8. materials required for class 9. homework completion 10. make-up work 11. incomplete work 12. missed quizzes and examinations 13. determining grades 14. violation of rules
Rules that can be communicated later	15. tardiness/absences 16. coming up to desk 17. when a visitor comes to the door 18. leaving the classroom 19. consequences of rule violation	20. notebook completion 21. obtaining help 22. notetaking 23. sharing work with others 24. use of learning center and/or reference works 25. communication during group work 26. neatness 27. lab safety

In middle school, team teachers should meet to decide general classroom and assignment procedures and expectations as well as overall classroom and team rules. This practice eliminates the ever-shifting instructional playing field and means fewer adjustments must be made by students as they move between class blocks.

Characteristics of Well-Managed Classrooms

What do teachers who have well-managed classrooms do to achieve their results? The answers can be complex and varied, depending on the criteria used for successful management, the subject area, and the ages and personalities of the students. Consequently, answers often appear more in the form of hypotheses that have been partially tested, rather than as definitive prescriptions. Much of the evidence, however, suggests that managerial success involves preventing behavioral problems *before* they occur through the use of specific teacher behaviors (Good & Brophy, 2004).

Kounin's (1970) work remains timely on the subject of classroom management. His research found that it was possible to isolate specific teacher behaviors that led to managerial success in the classroom. His findings were that teachers who had a *high* degree of work involvement and a *low* degree of misbehavior in their classrooms consistently demonstrated certain behaviors. Some of those were the following:

1. *Withitness.* Communicating that one knows what is going on in the classroom at all times. (Also may be applied to a teacher's understanding of the life and times of adolescent "society.")
2. *Overlapping.* Being able to attend to two issues simultaneously.
3. *Smoothness.* Managing physical movement from one activity to another without jerkiness, distractions, or halts. (Speaks to quick transitions.)
4. *Momentum.* Keeping physical activities moving at an appropriate pace.
5. *Group alerting.* Attempting to involve nonparticipating students in discussions.
6. *Accountability.* Holding students responsible for their tasks.
7. *Valence.* Pointing out that an activity has something special about it.
8. *Challenge.* Providing intellectual challenges in work.
9. *Lesson variety.* Planning varied activities both interactive and solitary.

Supportive Teacher Behaviors

In 1995, Beal (1996) conducted a yearlong study of at-risk students who were placed in heterogeneously grouped middle grades classrooms. She found that teachers who *set up their students for success* were the least likely to experience discipline problems. Providing props that enabled a student's success was important for all students, but especially for those at risk of school failure. Supportive teacher behaviors included:

- *Prop 1: Providing props that allowed students to get and remain on track.* These were having each student set and keep track of *individual* quarterly learning goals (in addition to mandated systemwide goals); posting and giving reminders about short- and long-term work assignments, behavior expectations, overdue assignments, and upcoming events; and providing organizational physical structures, such as baskets to store journals and folders for writing.
- *Prop 2: Setting high and **realistic** expectations for all students.* This was evident when the teacher provided positive reinforcement to individuals and groups through comments and actions; established a *sense of group* that fostered interactive support by and for all members; publicly and privately valued the individual student and what she or he brought to class; and provided physical (high fives), emotional (risk-free learning environment, advisor–advisee relationship), and intellectual (appropriately leveled material, opportunities for second chances to improve one's work) support.
- *Prop 3: Establishing rubrics that clearly spelled out the expectations for learning at each of the assessment levels.* The teacher modeled each level of assessment and showed examples of what that level of work looked like as well as providing continuous assessment to keep students on task and moving forward.
- *Prop 4: Modeling and instructing students in social/cultural skills and values, and setting expectations for student follow-through.* Teacher set expectations for positive, supportive behavior, modeled that behavior, and recognized and reinforced positive student efforts to achieve that behavior. She set up role-playing scenarios that highlight appropriate social interactions and enabled students to discuss social and moral issues.
- *Prop 5: Providing cooperative learning and peer mentoring opportunities that enabled socialization and peer acceptance.* Teacher conducted a total group activity to demonstrate how to achieve support within the group and establish a supportive group identity. She suggested well-matched student work partnerships that were mutually beneficial and supportive of each of the members.

Beal found that the support for learning given by the teacher was the single most important factor in the students' efforts to try and to achieve. Students believed they could not fail. Both the process and the teacher provided their incentive to learn. In such an environment where hope, promise, and supports are present, discipline becomes a minor issue.

Balancing Goals and Objectives in the Curriculum: Linking the Head, the Hand, and the Heart

In earlier chapters, it was suggested that the purpose of citizenship education was the development of the reflective, competent, and concerned citizen. Further, it was stated that the social studies curriculum should incorporate at each grade level some balance among lessons that seek to develop reflection, competence, and concern. Although individual lessons may not include objectives that address all three dimensions, each unit should include some balance that the teacher considers appropriate. Additionally, it was proposed that the year's program should contain a mix of objectives that reflects the curricular priorities the teacher has established.

The *reflective* citizen was characterized as having knowledge of a body of concepts, facts, and generalizations concerning the organization, understanding, and development of individuals, groups, and societies. Also, the reflective citizen was viewed as being knowledgeable of the processes of hypothesis formation and testing, problem solving, and decision making.

The *competent* citizen was seen as having a repertoire of social, research and analysis, chronology, and spatial skills. The *concerned* citizen was characterized as one who has an awareness of his or her rights and responsibilities, a sense of social consciousness, and a well-grounded framework for deciding what is right and wrong. In addition, the concerned citizen was seen as having learned how to identify and analyze issues and to suspend judgment concerning alternate beliefs, attitudes, values, customs, and cultures.

To illustrate, if a teacher decides that it is most important to emphasize the dimension of competence and is less important to emphasize the dimension of concern during the school year, her distribution of objectives should reflect this fact. That is, *over* one-third of them should deal with competence, and the smallest percentage with concern.

Both units and the total curriculum can be analyzed for balance. Figure 4.7 shows a sample of objectives that might be used to frame a 10th-grade unit related to the lesson developed by the National Geographic Society that we considered earlier in this chapter. The theme for the unit would be "The Power of Oil."

In Figure 4.7, note that although all three dimensions are included in the example, one receives greater emphasis (i.e., the reflective dimension).

Guidelines for Social Studies Program Development

Apart from guides for units and lessons, a number of guidelines for developing complete social studies *programs* at the state and local levels have been developed (e.g., Glatthorn, 1987; Parker, 1991). You should consult the guidelines your state

FIGURE 4.7
Tenth-Grade Unit: The Power of Oil

Sample Unit Objectives That Emphasize the Reflective Citizen Dimension
Students should be able to:
1. Identify the top 10 nations with respect to concentrations of oil.
2. Rank the top 10 oil-consuming countries.
3. Identify the major uses of oil in the United States.
4. State two ways in which countries that contain large concentrations of oil have exercised power over those who need oil.
5. Predict what would happen if other nations cut off the supply of oil to the United States.

Sample Unit Objectives That Emphasize the Competent Citizen Dimension
1. Conduct a cooperative learning activity (see Chapter 6) that reveals the social and economic consequences of discoveries of large oil reserves.
2. Locate on a map the top 10 oil-producing and consuming nations.
3. Construct a chart that shows the average cost of gasoline, excluding state and federal taxes, in the United States over the past 20 years.
4. Identify and use appropriate reference sources, such as *Goode's World Atlas.*

Sample Unit Objectives That Emphasize the Concerned Citizen Dimension
1. Take a position on a moral dilemma involving an issue of whether one nation is justified in violating the sovereignty of another to obtain a vital natural resource.
2. Argue either pro or con that the wealthier nations have a moral obligation to help those that are developing nations.
3. Formulate a position on the question: Assuming the United States should continue to give foreign aid, to which nations should it be directed?
4. Judge whether U.S. conservation policies should be directed primarily toward conserving natural resources or making agreements with other nations to secure the resources that we will need in the future.

has established regarding the social studies requirements and recommendations for each grade level. These should be available online at your state's Department of Public Instruction.

Organizations such as the NCSS periodically issue general guidelines for curriculum planning that cover a range of issues and provide checklists of practical considerations and suggestions. One illustration is the *Curriculum Standards for Social Studies, Expectations of Excellence* (NCSS, 1994). You'll remember from a previous chapter that the NCSS curriculum standards provide 10 themes that are basic guidelines for developing a social studies program. Each of the 10 themes is clearly spelled out and has a related set of more specific questions that address subthemes. Briefly again, the 10 themes are Culture; Time, Continuity, and Change; People, Places, and Environments; Individual Development and Identity; Individuals, Groups, and Institutions; Power, Authority, and Governance; Production, Distribution, and Consumption; Science, Technology, and Society; Global Connections; and Civic Ideals and Practices. Information is available at the NCSS website (**www.ncss.org**). Current social studies national standards are more theme specific than the previous guidelines. The NCSS (1979) guidelines listed next are instructive as general characteristics of a good social studies program and have been included, although they have been superceded by the 1994 curricular themes and the focus on powerful learning:

1. The social studies program should be directly related to the age, maturity, and concerns of students.
2. The social studies program should deal with the real social world.
3. The social studies program should draw from currently valid knowledge representative of human experience, culture, and beliefs.
4. Objectives should be thoughtfully selected and clearly stated in such a form as to provide direction to the program.
5. Learning activities should engage the student directly and actively in the learning process.
6. Strategies of instruction and learning activities should rely on a broad range of learning resources.
7. The social studies program must facilitate the organization of experience.
8. Evaluation should be useful, systematic, comprehensive, and valid for the objectives of the program.
9. Social studies education should receive vigorous support as a vital and responsible part of the school program.

A similar set of seven guidelines for program development was created by Engle and Ochoa (1988):

1. The curriculum should have a relatively small number of topics.
2. The topics selected should be those with the greatest potential for stimulating thought or controversy.
3. Students should continually be asked to make value judgments about factual claims and to generate hypotheses.
4. The social science disciplines should be treated as sources of information that can help answer questions rather than truth to be learned.
5. Information from areas other than the social sciences, such as from the humanities, should be used.

6. The curriculum should use varied sources to study in depth a relatively small number of topics.
7. The curriculum should draw on students' experiences to help answer questions.

Variety in Instructional Planning

Subsequent chapters will offer a variety of different instructional strategies, activities, and materials to engage students and foster exemplary social studies teaching. We will examine how the group activities and types of questions we employ affect the quality of our instruction, as well as how simulations and role-playing techniques can be used effectively to achieve certain objectives.

In applying these strategies in their planning, teachers need to guard against overreliance on any one approach, however successful it may be. They need to ensure that their lesson and unit plans incorporate variety, as well as qualitatively significant activities.

SUMMARY

This chapter provides a good start in learning how to prepare lessons for students. Social studies teachers have a lot to think about when they lesson plan. The journey from August to June, or year-round with intervening breaks, needs careful mapping so that everything can be studied and understood. This is how knowledge is built. There is much to be considered, from national standards to local curricula. Above all, you must determine what is important for your students to know. This is not just opening the book, jotting down the most important facts, and figuring out some activities to hold the students' interests. Your professional judgment is needed here.

When you set goals and objectives, you are saying that you have determined what is truly important for the students to know and understand. This is your map and target wrapped into one. Have you treated discrete facts as building blocks to a fuller understanding of the subject? If so, you have taken the students beyond the fact-building level to thinking about how they might use these facts to better understand a problem in their city, state, nation, or world.

It takes organization to fit all of the parts of the social studies puzzle together. The more you front-load into your planning, the more comfortable you will be when you conduct your class. You can never be too well prepared. Be ready to hear your colleagues' "first-year teacher stories." Some teachers will reminisce about the early days when they taught the lesson that was intended to last a day in just 15 minutes. Conversely, some can remember planning for one day and having enough material to last the entire week. Getting your lessons to work out as you planned comes with time and experience. The variable of the students makes strict adherence to a plan all but impossible. This is especially true if you believe that students need input into the process. Framing a unit around students' big questions and issues is highly motivational and helps to diminish behavioral problems.

Making decisions about what to teach, when, and how to teach it is where your profession becomes your craft. Teachers "work" the material and the students. Subtle and not-so-subtle cues will tell you if you are reaching your students. Make as many observations as you can of experienced teachers. Look for the way that they introduce the lesson and the different ways that they present the material. Gardner's (1983) multiple intelligences tells us that not all students learn the same way, so we must teach using different styles and approaches. If possible, meet the teachers whom you are observing before and after the lesson. Knowing what to look for and what the teacher is trying to accomplish will make the observation more instructive for you. Debriefing with them will illustrate the ongoing crafting and recrafting teaching process that lesson presentation involves.

It is the many variables that make teaching a dynamic, exciting adventure. Teaching is for lifelong learners who like to mix it up and exchange ideas with learners. Next we will discuss grouping, cooperative learning, questioning techniques, and role playing. You will use these tools to help you to prepare and teach lessons that meet your students' needs.

ACTIVITIES

1. After consulting several sources, identify a format for a lesson plan that you prefer. Discuss the features of the format that you consider to be desirable and explain why.
2. For each of the middle grades and secondary levels, locate online either a social studies resource unit or a teaching unit on any topic. Discuss what you consider to be the strengths and weaknesses of the units.
3. Consult Figure 4.9 and develop two additional objectives relating to the unit theme for each of the three dimensions.
4. Examine the objectives for the six lessons in the unit, "Slavery in the Nineteenth Century," presented in the chapter. Which ones do you consider to be specific and which ones general? How could the general ones be made more specific?
5. Prepare a stand-alone lesson plan on something about which you know a great deal. Use this as your emergency plan for a teaching day when you need a substitute but are unable to prepare a lesson for that substitute to follow. Keep it simple and include the handouts and worksheets that should be used.

WEB RESOURCES

Howard Gardner: **www.pz.harvard.edu/**
Bilingual Resources: **www.eduplace.com/bil/index.html**
Phi Delta Kappa (PDK): **www.pdkintl.org**
Meridian: **www.ncsu.edu/meridian**

Chapter 5

Engaging Students in Learning Through Small Groups, Questions, Role Playing, and Simulations

Grouping Students for Learning

    Planning for Small-Group Work

    Small-Group Techniques

    Cooperative Learning Group Techniques

    The Jigsaw Technique

    The Group Investigation Technique

    Curriculum Integration Approach to Teaching and Learning

Using Structured Questions to Aid Learning

    Patterns of Effective Questioning—Types

    Effective Use of Time—Duration

    Effective Selection and Ordering of Questions—Sequencing

    More About Using Questioning Strategies to Teach Your Lesson

Engaging Students in Role Playing and Simulations

    Managing Role-Playing Enactments

    Managing Simulations

    Sources of Simulations

Summary

Activities

Web Resources

*It was late January and Mrs. Bates was knee deep in the Russia Project (**www. ncsu.edu/chass/extension/russia-nc6**). Her classes had been part of a North Carolina State University College of Education Russia project since September when she registered online and the students received the first of the Postcards From Russia. The students had been excited about the cards and all of the interesting facts they had learned about a country that was formerly shrouded in mystery. In December, the students had formulated their big questions for Russia and sent them to the NC State research team. The plan was for Dr. Beal and her team to take the questions to Russia in February when they visited and taught in Russian schools. The team would send back answers from the Russian people, as well as pictures and journal accounts of the trip. While the traveling team was actually in Russia, the middle school students, who were members of the Russia Project home base research team, would do in-depth research on the questions or issues they had posed. Each student could select either a partner or team with whom to work. Some of the students were content to be single researchers. The plan was for Mrs. Bates to teach a unit on Russia that Dr. Beal had developed. Mrs. Bates had also had a hand in the unit, generously adding* *map and study guide activities. The unit was designed around many of the big questions that the students had asked and wanted answered, so the middle schoolers were motivated to pay attention and participate when Mrs. Bates taught the unit. Mrs. Bates's teaching would parallel the students' research into their big questions. The unit would establish the context into which all of the big questions would fit.*

As she looked around she was pleased to see everyone deeply engrossed in research. Rubrics helped the students determine the level of responsibility each had for the chosen project. Many had gone far above the expectations, so empowered by the exciting things they were learning. Who knew that tactics in the World War II Battle for Stalingrad were so like the Battle of Vicksburg that took place during America's Civil War? Imagine being under siege for 300 days in Stalingrad or 1,000 days in St. Petersburg! Students could hardly imagine missing lunch or the weekly pizza, but to starve to death was unimaginable. Perhaps overcoming these hardships explained the citizens' fierce loyalty to Mother Russia and the respect the Russians have for their veterans who served during World War II. The students grappled with these more reflective questions and observations as they worked cooperatively to build their fact base about Russia.

This was Mrs. Bates's finest hour and most enjoyable teaching experience. The research was coming along nicely and all of the projects would be done for the Global Connections Conference that she would host later in the year. The students' journals suggested how much they were benefiting from researching with their classmates. Each student could use her or his own approach to learning and sharing the information gained. This was the perfect example of differentiated instruction, using varied teaching approaches when she taught the unit, varying the research assignments, and providing a plethora of ways to demonstrate learning.

Mrs. Bates jotted down some materials she needed to pick up for tomorrow's activity. She had planned a special treat. All of the classes would make valentines to send over to Russia with the team. Each card would have the big question for Russia that the student had asked, and the American answer to that question. The Russian children would enjoy receiving greetings from Mrs. Bates's class and the added cultural information just as much as her students would enjoy sending them. What a great adventure! She wouldn't trade teaching for anything!

As the previous chapter revealed, in planning exciting and challenging social studies lessons and units, teachers have an assortment of effective tools at their disposal. In this chapter, we consider three sets of instructional strategies that may be used to enrich social studies lessons and activities: the use of *small structured groups, structured questions*, and *role-playing enactments and simulations*.

Chapters that follow will identify other specific instructional strategies that focus on developing objectives related to social studies as a matter of "the head, the hand, and the heart." These comprise the three dimensions of the effective citizen that were outlined in earlier chapters: reflection, competence, and concern.

Grouping Students for Learning

Groups, such as committees, teams, and social organizations, play a major role in our society. In schools, placing students into groups for instructional purposes has a long history (Vygotsky, 1978, 1986; Schmuck & Schmuck, 1983). Traditionally, teachers and administrators have assigned students of all ages to groups to achieve a variety of cognitive and affective objectives. These include completing tasks efficiently, encouraging tolerance and appreciation of diversity, enabling interest exploration, and providing greater opportunities for in-depth discussions (Beal, 1996).

Structured group settings that include diversity also afford students an opportunity for social dialogues that can stimulate cognitive growth. They offer the promise of environments where youngsters can explore alternative perspectives, develop new insights, and modify prior knowledge. As Newman, Griffin, and Cole (1989) noted: "When people with different goals, roles, and resources interact, the differences in interpretation provide occasions for the construction of new knowledge" (p. 2).

Planning for Small-Group Work

Before organizing students into small groups, teachers should consider a number of basic issues. These include having adequate space and sound control and avoiding potential distractions. Teachers should also vary grouping techniques to prevent boredom. As a further critical consideration, they need to determine the optimal size of a group in relation to the objective of an activity.

Groups may be as small as two members or as large as the whole class. There is no magic number in determining the optimal size of a "small" group, although four to six students is a good general rule of thumb for many social studies activities. Groups of three should be avoided since this configuration always makes possible two against one or an "odd person out" scenario. As we shall see, certain group techniques specify the number of students required and the procedures they must follow.

Members of a group must also be capable of assuming or experimenting with the *roles* they are to play within the group if the group is to function effectively. A simple example is the role of *recorder* or *scribe* in a group, which requires some basic writing, organizing, and reading skills. Students need to practice and experiment with different types of groups and alternate roles within them. In addition to recorder/scribe, roles such as time keeper, encourager, and daily leader are needed. Be sure to do the following: Teachers should set up scenarios that model the behavior expectations for each of the specific roles before students are asked to work in groups. This allows students to understand the expectations for each "job" within a group and more easily perform up to expectations.

Effective group activities also require as a prerequisite that students possess a number of basic social skills. These include:

- Listening and paying attention
- Taking turns and sharing participation time
- Working quietly
- Sharing ideas
- Asking for information and explanations
- Being polite, accepting and valuing others' ideas
- Sharing roles and responsibilities

Identifying Group Members. Among the many possible ways of identifying the members for a group are:

- Student self-selection
- Random assignment
- Assignment by backgrounds
- Assignment by special abilities or skills
- Assignment by behavioral characteristics
- Assignment by special interest

Aside from student self-selection, the remaining procedures involve some teacher decisions. You must assess how certain student characteristics are related to the task and effective operation of the group. Although there is no one best way to identify group members, there are better ways for different objectives.

For instance, consider an activity in which one of the objectives is to improve the level of multicultural understanding within a classroom. Assignment by general background to include a mix of racial or ethnic representatives within each group is likely to be a better choice than student self-selection of groups. Similarly, consider a class where a number of behavioral problems exist at the beginning of a school year. An important grouping consideration for some tasks may be to ensure that potentially disruptive students are not grouped together.

Small-Group Techniques

Aside from size and composition of the membership, there are other considerations in using small groups for social studies instruction. Certain group techniques can have multipurpose applications since they have flexible designs and are not tied to any particular set of objectives or type of subject matter. Others, such as cooperative learning techniques, are designed to promote specific instructional objectives, such as improving test scores or facilitating interpersonal relationships. We first consider three multipurpose techniques that frequently are used to facilitate decision making: brainstorming, consensus decision making, and decision making by ratings. Then we examine two cooperative learning techniques that have been designed to promote both cooperative behavior and achievement: Jigsaw and Group Investigation.

Brainstorming. Brainstorming is an effective technique when the objective of a group is to generate as many different solutions to a problem as possible for consideration (Osborn, 1963). The main ingredient for a brainstorming session is a potentially solvable problem, such as How can we get rid of the national debt? or How can we diminish global warming? A brainstorming session requires a leader to guide the discussion. A recorder is also needed to list on a large sheet of paper or on the board the possible solutions that the group members generate. The ground rules are that all ideas must be accepted and recorded *without* evaluation. Once all ideas have been recorded quickly without comment, they can be discussed. As a final step, the group members can try to agree which are the most useful solutions.

Consensus Decision Making. Consensus decision making requires *all* members of a group to agree to support the final solution. The group technique of majority rule with which students are more familiar encourages coalition building and produces temporary subgroups of "winners" and "losers." In contrast, consensus decision making, such as in jury decisions, is a useful technique for ensuring that *all* members' views are considered, since all must agree on the final results.

Decision Making by Ratings. The technique of decision making by ratings requires that various choices of individuals within a group be weighted and averaged through ratings. The approach commits a group to accept the decision that receives the best average rating from all members. It is an especially appropriate technique for resolving issues where several attractive alternatives exist, none of which has attracted support of a majority.

Consider the situation in which a group of seven students in a 12th-grade class is trying to decide which actions the federal government should take to reduce the national debt. Through research, the students have identified and listed five major types of possible actions the government may take. Then they individually rate each of the five actions in order of their first through fifth choices (Figure 5.1).

Each student's first choice is given a 1, the second a 2, and so on, to their last choice. The individual ratings then are totaled; the action with the *lowest* total score becomes the group's choice. An optional final step in the rating technique is to permit the members to discuss their ratings further and then to conduct a second round of ratings to arrive at the final decision. The illustration also indicates how the rating technique can produce a *group* position that represents some compromise for everyone. In Figure 5.1, the group's selection through rating (i.e., Freeze all domestic spending), was *not* the first choice of any single member. Further, it was only the third choice of a majority of the members.

FIGURE 5.1
Example of Decision Making by Ratings

Issue: How the Federal Government Can Help Reduce National Debt								
Possible Actions Identified from Research	**Individual Ratings of Group Members**							
	Tad	Terry	Ali	Rex	Cy	Peg	Kea	Totals
Cut foreign aid	4	1	2	5	1	5	2	20
Increase taxes on poor and middle class	1	5	1	4	3	1	5	20
Cut defense spending	2	4	4	3	5	3	1	22
Freeze all domestic spending	3	3	3	2	2	2	3	18
Reduce all entitlements	5	2	5	1	4	4	4	25

Cooperative Learning Group Techniques

A special class of small-group techniques that have been designed to achieve both cognitive and affective objectives under certain conditions is called **cooperative** (or **collaborative**) **learning**. The term refers generally to grouping techniques in which students work toward some common learning goal in small heterogeneous groups of usually four or five students. Heterogeneity typically includes characteristics such as gender, race, ethnicity, and ability. To be effective, cooperative learning requires that students have been shown how to cooperate (Cohen, 1990). In addition, each member of the group must understand the role she/he is to play.

Advocates of cooperative learning techniques assert that those techniques motivate students to do their best, help one another, and organize their thinking through dialogue and elaboration (Newmann & Thompson, 1987; Slavin, 1990; Vansickle, 1992). Johnson and Johnson (1986) have summarized what they perceive to be the major differences between traditional and cooperative learning grouping techniques. They note that cooperative groups improve team-building skills, foster interdependence (all for one and one for all), nurture individual accountability, and support group processing of information, whereas traditional types do not.

Cooperative Learning and Student Achievement. Cooperative learning models that include two critical characteristics—interdependency among group members and individual accountability—were shown in Slavin's 1996 review of literature to be the main factors in students' improved academic and social success (Walters, 2000).

This supports Slavin's earlier work (1990) in which he had concluded that "cooperative methods can and usually do have a positive effect on student achievement" (p. 6). It is important to note that Slavin also believes group rewards to be an essential element necessary for cooperative learning techniques to be effective: (1) There must

Anthony Magnacca/Merrill

Cooperative learning activities stimulate both cognitive and affective growth.

be a group goal that can result in some form of recognition (e.g., class newspaper, certificate, bulletin board, grades, rewards). Walters emphasizes that it is important to keep rewards separate from grades and cites Slavin's comment, "The grading system should be completely based on your (the student's) own personal performance, whereas the group recognition or rewards can be parallel to that" (p. 4).

Although group work appears to be one of the answers to fostering cooperation among students, it can present some challenges. The workloads must be evenly assigned and each student must be held responsible for the completion of his or her part. That having been said, however, no person's part for the group effort should be so critical as to be indispensable. If it is and the student is unable or unwilling to perform, the group feels obligated to complete that person's work so the group will not fail. This situation is unfair. Having to shoulder someone else's work is the most common complaint heard among members of a heterogeneous group, especially by above-average students and their parents (Robinson, 1990). This problem can be solved if rubrics for extensive group projects, such as developing a group newspaper, contain requirements for both group and individual work. This enables each student to play a dual role, group member and individual worker. The teacher is able to reward the group effort for those who contributed and grade the individual for his or her work. No one feels responsible to do someone else's work.

For example: The group is composing a newspaper. As a group job, Sue is responsible for one editorial letter and a profile of a national leader. Tamika writes another editorial and draws the editorial cartoon. Charlie writes a bio piece and compiles the weather forecast. Elizabeth contributes a review of the student play and a local newsmaker profile. These responsibilities are equal and are special pieces done for the good of the group paper. Each student also has to submit a common group of items: three want ads, a news story, a family recipe, a biography of a teacher, an interview with a student, and so on. No one's special piece for the group product (editorial, review, etc.) is so critical that the paper will fail if it is not done. Nor will the individual pieces required of each student (want ads, news stories) make or break the effort. Of course, everyone would like to have every piece done that has been assigned, but when a group member is slack, no one should have to take on extra work to satisfactorily complete the group project.

"Structuring activities" help students who are unfamiliar with cooperative learning become more at ease with the process. One popular activity that supports student interaction is Think, Pair, Share. Teachers pair up students for a time-limited discussion of an issue. Student A shares with her partner for 2 minutes and Student B then does the same. Everyone has a voice and what would have taken 60 minutes for a whole-class round-robin discussion is done in less than 5 minutes. It is important that teachers monitor cooperative learning activities. Some students may hang back and allow others to do the work and "hitchhike" on the group's efforts (Johnson & Johnson, 1986). Holding students accountable for their own learning guarantees that both individual and group will be successful.

Cooperative Learning and Affective Outcomes. In addition to achievement outcomes, researchers have discovered that cooperative learning techniques can promote positive intergroup relations and self-esteem. They can also improve attendance and promote positive attitudes toward school and the subjects being studied (Slavin, 1990, 1991). For example, "When students of different racial or ethnic backgrounds work together toward a common goal, they gain in liking and respect for one another. Cooperative learning also improves the social acceptance of mainstreamed academically handicapped students by their classmates . . ." (Slavin, 1990, p. 54). In sum, it appears that cooperative learning techniques that meet the criteria outlined by Slavin can produce both positive cognitive and affective outcomes.

Let us now examine in some detail one specific approach that has wide applicability to all types of social studies subject matter. This cooperative learning strategy, the **Jigsaw technique**, is especially effective with subject matter that has a high degree of factual detail.

The Jigsaw Technique

Educators and psychologists working in the Austin, Texas, schools in the post-integration 1970s to improve relationships among white, Hispanic, and black students devised a cooperative learning technique to reduce racial tensions (Aronson, Blaney, Stephan, Sikes, & Snapp, 1978). The objective of the technique was to encourage children to cooperate, share, and work together effectively, and, in the process, begin to break down interpersonal barriers. It was called *Jigsaw* because it resembled the structure of a jigsaw puzzle.

Jigsaw required students to work in small interracial groups and share parts of a solution to a common challenge. The challenge generally was successful performance on a quiz or assignment given by the teacher. Each member of the group was given only some of the "pieces of a puzzle" (i.e., part of the social studies information that the quiz would address). No single member of the group was supplied with enough information to solve the problem alone. Only through sharing and relying on all the others in the group could each member succeed. At the conclusion of the exercise, all the group members took *individual* tests covering *all* of the collective subject matter that had been shared.

Aronson and his associates (1978) offered a brief example of how they developed their technique:

> For example, in the first classroom we studied, the next lesson happened to be on Joseph Pulitzer. We wrote a six-paragraph biography of the man, such that each paragraph contained a major aspect of Pulitzer's life. . . .Next we cut up the biography into sections and gave each (of the six) child(ren) in a learning group one (of the six) paragraph(s). Thus every learning group had within it the entire life story of Joseph Pulitzer, but each child had no more than one sixth of the story and was dependent on all the others to complete the big picture. (p. 47)

After the completion of the experimental program that used Jigsaw, the investigators reported that, in integrated schools, whites learned equally well in both Jigsaw and competitive classes. However, blacks and Hispanics performed *better* in Jigsaw classes than in non-Jigsaw ones. Delpit's (1988) studies of black learners found the importance of the social context for learning to be a key factor for black students. These students began the learning process by making a connection to colleagues. Jigsaw's group learning approach thrives on students caring that *all* members of the group learn and perform with excellence (interdependency and accountability). Further, it was found that at the conclusion of the Aronson study, students liked both groupmates and others in their class better than when the study began. In sum, Jigsaw produced both positive achievement and attitudinal outcomes (Aronson et al., 1978).

Variations of the Jigsaw Technique. The original Jigsaw technique can be used for any social studies activity where a body of subject matter can be divided easily into four or five pieces for individuals (see Stahl, 1994a). For example, in studying about the Great Depression in the United States, information might be organized into the following categories: causes, solutions, political effects, economic impact, and social consequences, and each student might be given the information for one category. Students are expected to become "expert" on the information they are given. They are responsible not only for mastering the assigned content, but also for teaching it to their peers and ensuring their peers understand the information.

Often, however, this technique requires extra effort on the part of the teacher to reorganize or rewrite material. Some subject matter cannot be organized to stand alone without reference to other sections. Additionally, the original Jigsaw was found by researchers to be not as effective as some other alternative cooperative learning techniques (Newmann & Thompson, 1987).

One variation on the original Jigsaw that often is easier to implement in social studies instruction was developed at Johns Hopkins (Slavin, 1986). Called the **Jigsaw II technique**, it can also be used with any subject matter, including conventional textbook passages, with little or no modifications. Further, it provides more structured group roles and places more emphasis on the achievement of group goals than the original Jigsaw. Other variations exist as well (see Mattingly & Vansickle, 1991). The Jigsaw II scoring approach has been amended by your authors to reflect sensitivity for teacher workload and use of teacher instructional time. Jigsaw II requires a group of four or five students selected in the following fashion: one high-ability student, one low-ability student, and two or three average-ability students. Further, to the extent possible, the makeup of the group should reflect the racial, ethnic, and gender composition of the class as a whole.

There are two alternate scoring approaches. In the first approach, each student takes a pretest of the subject matter to be studied by the group. After the Jigsaw II learning activity in which material is split up, learned individually, and shared back with the group, the teacher gives a posttest and adds the individual posttest grades to get a group score. In the second approach, a pre- and posttest are given and each individual's difference in scores is calculated. (Both approaches have the advantage of pretesting the students, thus alerting them to the important facts to be learned. Those facts will stand out as they read the material. Learning should never be a game where students try to guess what the teacher wants them to know or what the teacher expects when they write a paper. Teachers must set students up for success by giving them as much information as possible about performance expectations and learning achievements.) After calculating the difference between the pre- and posttest scores for each member of the group, the teacher adds the individuals' scores together. This is the improvement score for the group. Both approaches are offered by your authors. You must select which better fits your needs and that of your students.

Let us illustrate an application for Jigsaw II. Our example involves a quiz and a basal text chapter that deals with the development of the New England colonies. Because this involves topics, themes, or issues, it is not possible to get a pretest score. Scores will be based on a posttest that reflects individual learning scores.

1. Select a chapter within the text and identify four basic topics, themes, or issues that the chapter encompasses.
2. Organize four-member teams according to the group selection criteria given earlier (i.e., ability, ethnicity, gender). Then, allow them to establish their identity and name (e.g., "The Dudes," "Cool Lightning").
3. Distribute to each team a copy of an Expert Sheet that contains a list of the four topics, themes, or issues that have been identified as focusing on some

FIGURE 5.2

Sample Expert Sheet for a Jigsaw II Activity on a Chapter Dealing with the New England Colonies

---

Expert Sheet
The Development of the New England Colonies

Topics:

I. Who were the pilgrims?

II. How did the Indians and the colonists get along with each other?

III. How did the colonists get along with one another?

IV. How did the Massachusetts Bay Colony develop?

---

important aspect of the chapter material. (See the example in Figure 5.2.) Each topic should be presented in the form of a question.

4. Assign a topic on the Expert Sheet to each member of each team. Designate these individuals as "experts" on their topics. Where there are more than four team members, assign one of the topics to two members.

5. Have all students read the chapter selected in class or for homework, focusing on his or her topic on the Expert Sheet.

6. Once students have read the chapter, allow experts from different teams who have the same topic to meet and discuss their topic. It may be helpful to provide a discussion sheet similar to the one shown in Figure 5.3 for each expert group.

FIGURE 5.3

Sample Discussion Sheet for Jigsaw II Expert Groups

Discussion Group for Expert Group I

Topic: Who were the pilgrims?

Points to consider in your discussion:

1. What is a pilgrim?

2. Why did the pilgrims come to America?

3. When did they leave England for America?

4. Where did they settle in America?

5. Why did they settle at the places they did?

6. What was the Mayflower Compact?

7. What was the significance of the Mayflower Compact?

---

7. Once the expert group discussions are concluded, have the experts return to their teams. They should take turns teaching the information related to their topics to the other members.
8. When the teaching has concluded, have each student take an individual quiz covering all the topics. All students are to answer all questions. If there are individual scores that need improvement, individuals can be retested after they have further studied the material.

The previous approach can also be used when you need to have the whole class read a chapter, but cannot be sure it will be read if you assign it as homework. First, form heterogeneous groups and have each group focus on one part of the chapter. (Example: Cool Lightning group is responsible for pages 23–27.) Students within each group may decide how they want to cover the material. They may choose to have one student read the material aloud. They may have several volunteers read the material or they may all read the material silently. Students who are good readers and who volunteer to read aloud provide poorer readers with the exposure they need to the material. Prior to the groups' reading activity, the students should go over the guiding questions you have prepared so that they can be alert to recognize the answers when they are read. A poorer reader may be asked to be responsible for listening for an answer to a particular question. This way the student attends to the task and is valued for his or her contribution, but does not have to reveal inadequate reading skills by stumbling aloud through a passage. Each group discusses the material read. At this point each expert group may report to the entire class, with a discussion, study session, and test to follow. On the other hand, the teacher may ask the expert groups to regroup, with one expert from each group joining one expert from each of the other groups. The new groups each have one expert from each of the first groups. They can now assemble the chapter readings to make a whole. Each expert teaches her part to her new group. Each new group can demonstrate its overall knowledge of the material through traditional assessment, such as a quiz or by some alternative means of evaluation—project, reflection paper, group game, or the like. The teacher can discuss the material after the activity is finished because everyone has read the chapter and is now capable of following and joining the discussion.

With this simple Jigsaw approach the parts again become a whole through group sharing, the reading assignment work is completed, and the important points have been addressed. This is one approach to make sure that all students have the chance to learn the information. This approach answers the problem of failing to do assigned reading homework, while allowing the teacher continuous evaluation opportunities to ensure that all students are making the connection to learning.

To sum up: Jigsaws work in many different ways, but key to the process is that the student is committed to the interdependency with the group and accepts individual accountability for her or his part in the group process and outcome. Group processes:

1. Teachers may, or may not, pretest the material. Original groups read together, or separately, and then divide the material among the members (by theme, pages, etc.) so that each becomes an expert about his or her

part. Group members teach one another their parts. Teachers posttest for individual's improvement or total group improvement.

2. Teacher may, or may not, pretest the material. Original groups split to form new "expert" groups. Expert groups are responsible for one part of the lesson and members in diverse expert groups become experts in that one area. The expert groups split and original group members, each formerly in a different expert groups, come back together to share the total lesson. Teachers may posttest for group performance, individual improvement or total group improvement.

It is easy to see that when expert learning and teaching is necessary for individual and group success, it is critical for each class member to understand and value group interdependency and her or his own individual accountability in the process.

The Group Investigation Technique

Another cooperative learning strategy that has wide applicability in social studies instruction is the **Group Investigation Technique** (Sharan & Sharan, 1994). In comparison to Jigsaw techniques, the Group Investigation strategy is more open ended and permits in-depth study of complex problems and issues. It affords groups considerable latitude in how they define and study a topic and report their findings. To achieve its ends, the investigation technique requires students who already have learned to work effectively in groups. (Your authors have noted similarity to Beane's Curriculum Integration approach to teaching and learning that appears in the next section [Beane, 1990, 1997, 2005].)

Leighton (1990) has outlined six steps that Group Investigation involves:

1. Identification of topics and choices by teacher and students (asking big questions)
2. Formation of learning teams based on interests (themes, issues, big questions)
3. Investigation of topics selected with teacher assistance (differentiated instruction, informal assessment)
4. Preparation of presentations for class with teacher assistance (differentiated instruction, assignment)
5. Presentations to whole class (public demonstration of learning)
6. Evaluation of the work based on predetermined criteria (differentiated instruction, formal assessment)

An example of how the strategy might be implemented in a social studies class inquiring into the causes of the American Revolution has been provided by Leighton (1990):

First, students would be divided into temporary brainstorming groups of three or four, each charged with generating a list of questions one might ask in relation to study of the Revolution. The whole class would compile a composite list of questions, which would be sorted into categories. Learning teams would include those who are particularly interested in investigating each category of questions. The teacher's role is to guide the formation of teams so that, to the extent possible, each team includes a fair sampling of students.

The learning teams review the questions in their category and pull together those questions most amenable to the investigation. They set the goals for the work and divide the tasks among themselves. Then they begin to study the topic they have chosen. When their studies are complete, they present their findings to the class. A representative from each learning team is delegated to a central coordinating committee to ensure that team reports are presented in orderly fashion and work is equitably distributed within each team.

Evaluation may be designed by the teacher alone or in collaboration with a representative student group. The content on which students are evaluated must reflect the priorities established by the original choice of inquiry topics and by the presentations themselves. Students may be assessed individually on the basis of either the sum of the whole class presentations or the particular material developed within each group. (p. 326)

Sharan and Sharan (1990) offered an illustration of how a research project might proceed using the group investigation technique with a group of five and the topic: How did the different Native American tribes adapt their dwellings to their environment? Each student in the group assumes one of the following roles: coordinator, resource person (two), steering committee person, or recorder.

The specific questions to be answered are as follows:

- How did the nomadic Apaches design their shelters?
- In what way did hogans suit the Navajo way of life?
- What kind of dwelling did the ancient Native American design?

Resources for the group included a collection of books and reference materials, URLs, a group of people to be interviewed, and a list of sites to be visited (see also Sharan & Sharan, 1994).

Curriculum Integration Approach to Teaching and Learning

The Curriculum Integration approach to teaching and learning is similar to the Group Investigation technique. The chief proponent of curriculum integration is James Beane. Beane approaches learning as an exercise of democracy in the classroom. His research (1990, 1997, 2005) found that students are motivated to study the questions and issues that most interest and relate to them. Units are developed and studied based on big questions and issues that resonate with students. This is not to say that students have carte blanche when it comes to curriculum development, but they do have considerable input to the curriculum through the questions and issues that they find interesting concerning a topic.

Curriculum integration is based on three principles: (1) student input through big questions and issues that interest them; (2) differentiated instruction—the use of different teaching styles, the option for students to select among several research activities, and choice of a variety of final products that students may complete to demonstrate their learning; and (3) public presentation of research. The latter enables all students to learn from one another.

Curriculum integration allows students to see that learning is not discipline specific, but that the disciplines are interwoven as they help to inform the topic chosen. In fact, the disciplines act as the tools used in research to examine the topic. When using the curriculum integration approach to teaching and learning it is important for the teacher to know the standard course of study requirements. As students research the big questions, it is then possible for the teacher to connect the students' work to the information they are required to learn. For this reason, curriculum integration is not something a first-year teacher might start to implement day in and day out. It is an approach that can be adopted slowly, one special topic project at a time. (See, for example, **www.ncsu.edu/chass/extension/ci.**)

Using Structured Questions to Aid Learning

Questions are an excellent motivational tool. If generated by the students, they are particularly powerful because they address something of special interest to the students. Dr. John Arnold, emeritus professor, NCSU, warns us to be mindful about the types of questions asked. It has been his experience that teachers often ask too many questions for which students do not want to know the answers. Drawing students into the learning process requires interesting, reflective, meaningful questions. Teachers have a number of choices with respect to how they use questions to stimulate learning. Questions are the triggers of reflection. The *type, duration*, and the *sequencing* of questions can significantly affect the level of interaction and learning that results from instruction.

Evidence suggests that a great number of the communications between teacher and students consist of questions and answers. More often than not, teachers initiate the questions, read them from texts, or assign them in writing to students (Wilen & White, 1991). Questions are used extensively in both large- and small-group instruction, as well as with individual students.

Effective questions can focus attention on the important objectives of a lesson or activity. They can also encourage students to participate in discussions and move thinking along in a systematic fashion. Questions can also open new avenues of exploration for teacher and students alike.

Questions that originate from students during instruction, in addition to being vehicles for research, would appear to be especially helpful for identifying areas that are unclear, need amplification, or were neglected in the teacher's planning. Their spontaneous occurrence in middle and secondary classrooms, however, appears to be rare. This is troubling and requires teachers to ask themselves if they have (1) set up a risk-free environment in their classrooms, one that encourages free exchange of ideas and inquiry, and (2) taught an interesting and engaging lesson.

Perhaps the reason for few student questions is a function of the increased prevalence of the strict use of instructional time. "Less is more" might mean less student talk means more teacher talk and thus more material covered. To perform well on standardized tests, questions, especially reflective ones that involve discussion and contemplation, may be sensed by the students to be too time consuming to be heard. Restricting students to questions that require short answers or only deal with discrete facts is hardly supportive of good teaching and does not foster reflection and discussion.

Patterns of Effective Questioning—Types

What types of questions do teachers typically ask or assign to students? Borich (1996) has suggested that questions can be organized into seven general categories, those that:

1. Provoke interest or gain attention
2. Assess state of students' knowledge
3. Trigger recall of subject matter
4. Manage instruction
5. Encourage more advanced levels of thinking
6. Redirect attention
7. Elicit feelings (p. 344)

Just as with the use of grouping techniques, teachers have a number of decisions to make regarding the use of questions in instruction. The *type, duration,* and the *sequencing* of questions can significantly affect the level of interaction, thinking, and learning that results from instruction. Effective questioning techniques can focus attention on the important objectives of a lesson or activity. They can also encourage students to participate in discussions and move thinking along in a systematic fashion. Teachers can draw on a store of tested principles and strategies in these areas (e.g., Wilen & White, 1991) for sharpening the questioning skills they use in social studies instruction.

Some techniques associated with effective questioning apply to all questions, such as the efficient *use of time* and the appropriate *selection* and *sequencing* of questions. Teachers can draw on a store of tested principles and strategies in these areas for sharpening the questioning skills they use in social studies instruction.

Effective Use of Time—Duration

Ask a friend a question and time how long you have to wait before he or she begins to answer you. A critical element of effective questioning is known as **wait time**. Wait time is the length of time between the teacher's asking of a question and the point at which an answer is expected.

When wait time is short, teachers ask a question and expect an answer immediately. If one is not forthcoming, teachers tend to restate the question, rephrase it, ask a new one, or provide the answers themselves. When wait time is long, teachers ask the question and wait 3 seconds or longer for an answer. In Tobin's studies (1987), most teachers maintained an average wait time between 0.2 and 0.9 second.

Consider the following vignette from a social studies class studying the American Revolution that is taken from a text on questioning by Dillon (1988).

Teacher: OK, so we've kind of covered leadership and some of the things that Washington brought with it. Why else did they win? Leadership is important, that's one.

Student: France gave 'em help.

T: OK, so France giving aid is an example of what? France is an example of it, obviously.

S: Aid from allies.

T: Aid from allies, very good. Were there any other allies who gave aid to us?

S: Spain.

T: Spain. Now, when you say aid, can you define that?

S: Help.

T: Define "help." Spell it out for me.

S: Assistance.

T: Spell it out for me.

S: They taught the men how to fight the right way.

T: Who taught?

S: The allies.

T: Where? When?

S: In the battlefield.

T: In the battlefield? (pp. 87–88)

Dillon (1988) noted that the discussion in the transcript lasted approximately 30 seconds. The teacher asks a total of nine questions, and the student responses last about 1 second. Given the time required for the teacher to state the question and the students to formulate their responses, we can infer that the wait time in the episode given is quite short. It may also be observed that little wait time was necessary since the questions were simple, factual ones and not ones requiring reflective thought. Short wait times may often be justified when they are needed to keep the class moving and the students focused and on task (Stahl, 1994b). A steady diet of rapid fire questions and answers, however, does little for developing students' reflective thinking skills. Kay Toliver, a noted educator and consultant, makes a point of always asking her students who reply to short-answer questions to do so using complete sentences. This allows them to expand on their answers and gives others more time to think of information to add.

The Effects of Increasing Wait Time. The pioneering research of Rowe (1969) demonstrated the powerful effects of extending wait time. She found that, if a teacher prolonged the average time waited after a question was asked to 5 seconds or longer, the length of students' responses increased. Conversely, she found that short wait time produced short answers. A review of subsequent studies suggests that at least 3 seconds is an average threshold of wait time for teachers to attempt to establish (Tobin, 1987).

Rowe also discovered that teachers who learned to use silence found that children who ordinarily said little began to start talking and to offer new ideas. Teachers, themselves, as they extended their waiting time, also began to include more variety in their questions.

Further studies by others have shown that, depending on the type of questions used, extended wait time is associated with longer student responses (e.g., Honea, 1982; Swift & Gooding, 1983; Tobin, 1986; Stahl, 1990) and increased student-to-student interaction. Extended wait time was also found to be associated with greater achievement (e.g., Riley, 1986; Tobin, 1986; Stahl, 1990). Tobin's (1987) analysis of the related research has suggested that teachers can learn to increase their wait time through feedback and analysis of their questioning patterns.

Effective Selection and Ordering of Questions—Sequencing

Another important consideration in effective questioning is selecting questions that are *clear, specific*, and *focused*. These types of questions expedite communication, probe for details, keep a discussion on target, and foster sustained critical thinking. They also encourage students to make comparisons, identify causal relationships, see linkages to their own lives, and establish factual claims. Coming up with really good questions takes thought, time, and practice. Questions that are improperly worded are a major source of problems both for teachers and students. They frustrate teachers and keep them from accomplishing their objectives and are a source of confusion for students. Types of questions that teachers should avoid include those that are ambiguous, call for a yes or no answer, are slanted, parrot back the information the teacher has just given (spit back answers), or require students to try to guess what the teacher wants for an answer. Some examples of appropriate and inappropriate ways to phrase questions are illustrated in Figures 5.4 and 5.5.

Another useful questioning technique is learning to order questions in a sequence that stimulates the development of students' thinking. A logical sequence ensures that there is a rationale for the order in which the questions are asked. Brown and Edmondson (1984) have identified a number of questioning sequences that teachers may employ in instruction.

Sequencing is part of the process of developing a set or *script* of questions in advance of teaching a lesson. A **question script** is a basic set of questions that have been constructed, rehearsed, and logically sequenced prior to their use in a

FIGURE 5.4
Desirable Types of Questions

These are examples of desirable types of questions:
- Why do you agree with the candidate's position?
- What would happen if the world's supplies of oil and natural gas were used up?
- What were some major causes of the Civil War?
- What are some ways neighborhoods change over time?
- What are some ways cities, suburbs, and rural areas are alike and different?
- Suppose you were in Rosa Parks's place. What would you have done?
- What evidence do you have that auto emissions are bad for the environment?

FIGURE 5.5
Type of Questions to Avoid

Teachers should be sensitive to the types of questions that generally are *ineffective* in social studies instruction. These types of questions include those that are *ambiguous, require only a yes or no answer,* or are *slanted.* Such questions limit or stifle thinking and often are a source of frustration and confusion for students. The following are examples of the types of questions to avoid:
- What happened in the American Revolution?
- Was George Washington our first president?
- What makes our community the best in the state?
- Where do families live?
- How did Sojourner Truth live her life?
- What does our flag mean?
- What was the first Thanksgiving about?

lesson or activity. *Rehearsal* refers to the process whereby a teacher reflects on exactly how the questions will be phrased. They are then put in the correct order in the lesson or activity. The function of a question script is to ask appropriate questions that move students from more concrete to more abstract, lower to higher, levels of thinking. (Remember your Piaget!)

The presence of a questioning script ensures that several well-thought-out and carefully phrased questions will be used to guide students' thinking, as well as the development of a lesson or activity. Unlike spontaneous questions, which teachers develop as instruction unfolds, a script encompasses a small number of questions, usually three to five, that relate to the subject matter under investigation and that shape the lesson. Scripts, however, may be supplemented by other questions that are needed during a lesson, such as clarification or summarization questions (e.g., What do you mean by "the lunatic fringe"? or Could you sum up your point of view in a single sentence?).

The Taxonomy of Educational Objectives. An example of sequencing questions according to the levels of thinking they require is found in the **taxonomies of objectives** developed by Bloom and his associates. The most widely used taxonomy as a guide for framing questions is Bloom's taxonomy for the cognitive domain (Bloom, 1956). It identifies six levels of thinking, simple (knowledge) to complex (evaluation). The levels, along with an example of a question dealing with the American flag that is matched with them, follows.

Level of Thinking	Sample Questions
Knowledge	How many stars does our flag have?
Comprehension	Can you explain why our flag has 50 stars?
Application	To what extent does the First Amendment apply to those who burn the American flag?
Analysis	In what ways are the arguments of those who burn the flag different from those who support it?
Synthesis	Under what conditions, if any, would you support an individual's right to burn the flag and why?
Evaluation	Assessing the Supreme Court arguments and rulings in flag-burning cases, to what extent are they consistent with or opposed to your position on the issue?

Although it is desirable to have all students ultimately thinking at the highest level possible, most individuals need to move gradually from a lower to a higher level. Vygotsky (1986) referred to this as learning in the zone of proximal development. Mentors bring students from lower to higher levels of learning by scaffolding them through the zone with material or questions that are of ever increasing levels of difficulty. Getting students to reach a higher level of thinking becomes a matter of asking questions that call for progressively more complex cognitive tasks and allowing sufficient time for reflection.

For example, suppose you and I have just viewed the film *War and Peace* together. As we leave the theater, we begin to discuss the film. My initial question is, "Do you remember the names of the major characters?"

From that conversational opener, we progress to "Which parts did you enjoy the most? Why?" Toward the middle of the discussion, I inquire, "Did this film remind you of any others you have ever seen? In which ways?" We conclude our discussion by entertaining the final question, "What was the meaning of that film?"

Compare that sequence of questions with a second discussion. In this scenario, as you and I emerge from the film, I inquire concerning this stirring 3-hour epic, "How would you sum up the meaning of the film in a sentence?"

In the first case, the sequence of questions has helped me organize my thoughts in a way that prepares me for the final complex question. The very same type of question that occurs at the *beginning* of the second discussion, however, is likely to be difficult to tackle at first. Furthermore, even if I could respond to it at the outset, my answer is likely to be less thoughtful and complete than if I had the opportunity to order and build my thinking on a foundation of more concrete and specific details.

Similarly, in unstructured classroom questioning, it is important to engage students in discussions at the appropriate level of questioning. This sometimes requires trial and error, where a teacher discovers that he or she needs to lower the level of questions after drawing a blank from students. Consider the following exchange in which the teacher, Ms. Peterson, drops back to a lower level after her students fail to respond to the initial question. Later, she begins to work her way back to the original question.

Ms. Peterson: What was the significance of the New Deal?

Class: [Silence]

Ms. Peterson: What were some of the federal programs that were created during the period of the New Deal?

Roger: The WPA was started to put people to work on public jobs.

Julia: The banks were reformed. I can't remember the name of the program.

Laronda: Farmers got loans at low interest.

Merv: So did individuals for homes.

Ms. Peterson: [After 15 minutes of discussion about the nature and impact of the various New Deal programs] How might our lives be different if the New Deal had never happened?

More About Using Questioning Strategies to Teach Your Lesson

When you are preparing your lesson it is critical to think about how you will actually teach the lesson. Does that sound like an obvious statement? Of course it does, but you would be surprised how many beginning teachers plan a great lesson, replete with activities, without figuring how to get from the information to be learned to the activity stage. As we have already noted, there is a lot in between, such as how to guide students' learning through well-developed and appropriately sequenced questions. Planning how you will build from one fact or issue to another and give the students an opportunity to be part of a thoughtful process comes down to your plan to use questions to inform the process. We've pointed out that educators develop questioning scripts that are useful for achieving specific instructional objectives. Taba (1969) and associates developed a series of questioning scripts that are applicable for all topics within the social studies curriculum. Two of the strategies are considered here.

The first Taba strategy may be used when you want to (1) diagnose what students know and do not know about a topic prior to studying it; (2) determine what they have learned as a result of studying a topic or experiencing an event; or (3) encourage all students in the class to participate in a discussion of a topic. It uses a simple questioning script consisting of an *opening* question, a *grouping* question, and a *labeling* question. Ask them in the order indicated, starting with brainstorming the opening question:

Examples	Function of Question
Opening Question	
What comes to mind when you hear the word *apartheid*?	Calls for recollection of information. Allows all students to participate in the discussion on an equal footing.
What did you see in the film? What do you think of when Adolph Hitler is mentioned?	
Grouping Question	
Look over our list of items. Are there any that could be grouped together? Why did you group them in that way?	Requires students to organize information on the basis of similarities and differences that they have learned and to provide a rationale for their classification.
Are there any things on the board that could be grouped together? Why did you put those items together?	
Labeling Question	
Let's look at group A. Can you think of a one- or two-word label or name for it?	Requires students to summarize and further refine thinking. No set answer allows all to contribute.

Remember, you are trying to find out what your students know, what they have learned, and at the same time you are focused on encouraging everyone to participate in the process. Throughout your investigation, questions and statements such as the following types would be helpful to use to get the information you seek:

Clarifying Question. (More specificity needed.) Examples: What sort of strange clothing? Can you give an example of what you mean by liberal?

Refocusing Statement/Question. (Getting back on track.) Examples: Let me repeat the original question. Remember what I asked?

Using Structured Questions to Aid Learning **147**

Summarizing Question. (Putting it all together.) Examples: How could we put that in this space on the board? Could you put that in a single sentence?

When you are asking your students to brainstorm, such as you are doing in the listing type question, it is important to record all students' responses on the board or a chart *without* evaluation. In addition, class members are not permitted to challenge other students' responses. Students' comments are listed verbatim or with minor modifications. When comments are lengthy, students are asked to summarize them. The teacher should accept any rationale that a student provides for grouping items together.

Consider an illustration of how a discussion using this strategy might unfold in a secondary class. At the appropriate times in the discussion, as outlined earlier, the teacher asks the following *listing*, *grouping*, and *labeling* questions.

Listing Question. Example: What comes to mind when you hear the word *abortion*? (Be sure *your* question is age- and situation-appropriate.)

Grouping Question. Examples: Are there any things on the board that could be grouped together? (After the student suggests a grouping, ask the question that calls for a rationale.) Why did you put those items together?

Labeling Question. Example: Could you suggest a one- or two-word label for each of the groupings?

The students' responses to each question are shown in Figure 5.6.

The second Taba questioning script strategy has as its objective that students will be able to summarize data and draw conclusions and generalizations from subject matter examined or from experiences (Taba, 1969). The first Taba starts you off with a fact finding (i.e., what do students know and what specifically have they learned).The second Taba requires more abstract thinking using comprehension skills (i.e., drawing conclusions and making generalizations). The second Taba, like the first, employs a strategy that uses a simple script of three questions: an *opening* question, an *interpretive* question, and a *capstone* question as follows:

Examples	Function of Question
Opening Question	
What did you see on the trip?	Calls for recollections of information. Allows all students to participate in the discussion on an equal footing.
What did we learn about the Russian people?	
Interpretive Question	
What differences did you notice between the two countries?	Gets students to draw relationships between data being considered and to compare and contrast information.

How were Roosevelt's feelings
about the issue different from
Hoover's feelings?

Capstone Question

What conclusion could we draw
from our investigation?
From our study, what generalizations
can you make about institutions?

Asks students to form a conclusion,
a summary, or a generalization.

FIGURE 5.6
Illustration of a Classroom Discussion Using the Taba Strategy

> **Listing Question:** What comes to mind when you hear the word *abortion?*
>
> *Student Responses Are Listed on Chalkboard as Follows:*
>
> 1. Destroying human life
> 2. Unwanted pregnancy
> 3. Committing a sin
> 4. Population control
> 5. Rape
> 6. Abortion referral service
> 7. Future health and happiness of *all* concerned (mother and child)
> 8. Mental anguish
> 9. Father's rights
> 10. Complications
> 11. Quacks
> 12. Costs
> 13. Self-abortion
> 14. German measles
> 15. Why?
> 16. Why not?
> 17. Responsibility
> 18. Misery and depression
> 19. Women's rights
> 20. Morning-after pill
> 21. Contraception
> 22. Ignorance (not being careful)
> 23. Sex
> 24. Methods (vacuum, etc.)
> 25. The doctor
> 26. Sterilization
>
> **Grouping Question:** Are there any things on the board that could be grouped together? (After the student suggests a grouping, the teacher asks the next question, which calls for a rationale.) Why did you put those items together? (All rationales are accepted, and are *not* recorded.)
>
> *Student Responses Are Listed on Chalkboard as Follows:*
>
> | | | | |
> |---|---|---|---|
> | E | 1. Destroying human life | E | 3. Committing a sin |
> | DH | 2. Unwanted pregnancy | E | 4. Population control |

To help students recall, summarize, and draw conclusions and make generalizations from subject matter or experiences, the following types of questions and statements can be useful:

Mapping-the-Field Question. (Checking to be sure we got it all.) Examples: Have we left out anything? Are there any points that we missed?

Focusing Question. (Specificity needed.) Examples: What types of clothing did they wear? How many people actually were affected?

Substantiating Question. (Why do you say that?) Examples: What did you see in the film that leads you to believe that?

PNI Question. (Your input needed.) Examples: What did you find positive (plus), negative (minus), or interesting in the reading? Film?

Questioning is a teaching strategy that is complex in its use. Skillful teachers know how to use it effectively to involve students in the learning loop and stay informed about their progress. After all, when you fail to use guided questioning in teaching and activities, students are often left to pages of silent reading or long interludes of teacher talk to secure the information. Think back to middle and high school. Did either of those approaches work for you? To be an effective teacher you want to involve the students and be able to informally assess how the lesson is going. Depending on what a teacher is trying to achieve, specific questions can be devised and ordered to accomplish lesson objectives and achieve learning goals. What you ask, when you ask it, how long you allow for the answer, and how you respond to your students is no simple matter.

Engaging Students in Role Playing and Simulations

We turn now to two other complementary instructional techniques that can be applied across social studies topics: **role playing** and **simulations**. Although they can be used for many types of objectives, role-playing and simulation techniques are especially useful tools for examining issues that are abstract. They also facilitate consideration of affective matters that entail beliefs, attitudes, values, and moral choices. They do this by allowing students to "take on a role," step outside of their usual perspective on issues, and explore alternatives.

Often in social studies classes, we find it necessary to engage students in subject matter that is potentially complex or emotion laden. For example, we may wish to have students understand how supply and demand affect the market price of goods in a capitalist economy; or we might need to have our students develop more sensitivity to all forms of diversity. Role playing and simulations are excellent approaches to use when examining more sensitive situations.

Obviously, the use of high-interest, labor-intensive activities necessitates consideration of two issues: the additional instructional time needed to complete them and the close attention to classroom management that must be paid for the activities to be successfully implemented. Keeping in mind your lesson's goals and objectives will enable you to build activities that will keep your students focused and moving forward. Your focus drives their focus.

Managing Role-Playing Enactments

Successful role-playing activities require planning and careful attention to the details of how the steps are to unfold. Teachers need to be prepared for the honest emotions that may emerge when students become immersed in a role. Beyond the dramatic enactment of the role playing itself also lie the important stages of setting up, discussing, and internalizing the insights gained during the enactments (Shaftel & Shaftel, 1982).

Introducing role playing in a nonthreatening way is critical to its success as a technique. One approach that Merryfield and Remy (1995) suggest is to

seize an opportunity when there is heated discussion over a topic that involves several points of view. Ask Joe, who is strenuously arguing that the U.S. should have bombed the U.S.S.R. during the Cuban Missile Crisis, to take on the role of a Russian missile technician in Cuba. Then call for volunteers who will take roles of other people he might encounter such as a Cuban nurse or a Russian soldier. What would they think about the situation? What would they want to say to the Americans or the Soviet leaders? (p. 25)

Role-playing activities can be broken into five stages:

1. Initiation and direction
2. Describing the scenario
3. Assigning roles
4. Enactment
5. Debriefing

Initiation and Direction. Every role-play activity begins with some problem that the class or teacher has identified. Teachers should choose topics of a less controversial or sensitive nature until students become accustomed to the procedures. As students become experienced and comfortable with the technique, they can move on to more urgent concerns.

Describing the Scenario. The problem to be discussed should have some clear relevance to a social issue. The actual problem episode that is to trigger the role playing may be presented orally, pictorially, or in writing. A simple story problem may be some reenactment of a historical event, such as Truman's decision to drop the atomic bomb on Japan. It may also center on a contemporary issue, such as a young unwed couple telling one set of parents they are pregnant. (Again, be sure *your* issue is age- and situation-appropriate.)

Assigning Roles. Role assignment needs to be approached cautiously to avoid both the appearance of any possible typecasting and the inclusion of any reluctant actors. It is important to understand that some students are unable to risk taking on a controversial stance. They are yet too immature to divorce the "pretend" position from how they think others will perceive them. A teacher *must* be sensitive to this and use good judgment when assigning roles. Do not tolerate any comments that suggest that the actor is that character in real life. Students need to understand that they must immerse themselves in their portrayal, but that that portrayal is simply another character. Using volunteers or drawing by lots eliminates the suggestion of typecasting. At the same time, it has the disadvantage of possibly involving students who cannot function effectively in the roles to be assigned. Often it may be desirable to select certain students who are most likely to give the greatest validity to the roles identified and hence present the problem/ solution alternatives most effectively. In any case, assignment requires sensitivity and some experimentation to ensure a productive enactment.

Once assigned, all participants, as well as the rest of the class members (the audience), should be briefed on each of the roles. In most cases, this can be an oral briefing. In others, it is important to keep individual roles hidden. Role situation/profile cards may be supplied to the actors and referred to during the role play if necessary.

The students in the audience may also play a role. The teacher may ask them to watch for and list three items on a note card that concern the performance. They can list one thing they learned, one positive thing about the performance, and one question they would like to ask the actors. By having students complete this brief writing assignment while the performance is going on, students are quiet, engaged, and at the end, responsive to their fellow actors. Of course, the same can be accomplished at the end of the performance when students are given the opportunity to suggest alternative ways of playing the roles. They may also be asked to focus on a specific actor and identify vicariously with him or her. The advantage of the written approach is that it keeps the audience focused, attentive, and respectful of the actors. Written notes can be passed on to the actors as a way to positively reinforce their efforts.

Before moving on to the enactment, the class should be "warmed up" for dramatic activity. Simple pantomime scenes or one-sentence scenarios (e.g., you

> You work at a large grocery store. After school there is an influx of students purchasing snacks and sodas. For several days you have watched a group of three students. They come in, cluster around the candy section, and take their backpacks off and on. You suspect they are shoplifting snacks and when you check their backpacks you find you are correct. What do you do? Call the parents, police?

have just dropped your notebook in a puddle of water) for the students to act out can serve this purpose. Once the class is psychologically prepared, the role play itself can actually be enacted.

Enactment. A briefing with the characters individually before the role-play event begins can help to establish how they plan to enact their roles. You might consider providing characterization cards (different from situation profile cards) for each of the actors. These will help them know/feel their characters. These cards can be reused year after year. Although enactments may be modified during the actual event, rehearsal helps students clarify their roles.

It is important to remind students that during the enactment they should use the names of the characters. This procedure reinforces the fact that individual class members themselves are not the objects of analysis. Similarly, it often is necessary to remind players to *stay in character/role*—that is, deal with events as their characters actually might. In humorous or anxiety-producing situations, some individuals tend to stop the role-play enactment and respond as an observer.

Debriefing. The debriefing phase is a crucial and integral part of role playing. It requires the greatest attention and guidance on the teacher's part to ensure productive and meaningful results. The debriefing period should immediately follow the enactment. The characters should be allowed to share any feelings they had while they were playing their roles and possibly to entertain questions from the audience. At some point, an exploration of alternative ways of handling the characters' roles should occur. If participants are willing, they can be asked to reenact the event in different ways, possibly switching roles.

The debriefing session may take many forms depending on the issue, the maturity of the group, and its experience with role playing. At some point, the issue embedded in the role-play event should be abstracted and clearly addressed so that attention shifts to real experiences, individuals, and places. The teacher then can help students draw parallels between the role-play enactment and real events.

Mock trials are an effective technique for studying some issues. See a sample exercise in Appendix C, Resource Figure 5.1.

Managing Simulations

Closely related to role playing is simulation, any activity designed to provide life-like problem-solving experiences in the form of a "game." Simulations provide a representation of some phenomenon, event, or issue that actually exists or existed in the real world. Today's digital natives are very familiar with marketplace simulations. Games that are available commercially often have a very high level of violence. For that reason, care in selection must be made of any simulations, commercial marketplace or educationally prepared, that are considered for classroom use. In addition, teachers must evaluate simulations for character stereotyping.

A major asset of educational simulations is they enable many students to relate easily to and become highly interested in a problem that they might not otherwise take seriously. Furthermore, they allow students to assume some control over their own learning and to be less dependent on the teacher. However, less dependent does not mean that teachers should not be involved in the simulation's activities. By addressing the issues raised in the simulations, teachers can help students elevate their level of critical thinking and moral responses given to the difficult problems. Many commercial war game simulations that your students may be familiar with depend on a Kolhberg stage 1 solution, shoot and take no prisoners, so teachers must encourage use of simulations that offer solutions that take a higher moral ground. Often the suggestion of an "eye for an eye, tooth for a tooth" student response enables teachers to help their students move to solutions that involve higher stages of moral development.

Both a strength and a limitation of simulations is that they permit study of a *simplified* representation of some reality. All simulations limit the number of variables they present to players; otherwise they would be too complicated. In a simulation of Congress, for example, not all of the actual considerations that weigh on lawmakers in their deliberations could be included and weighed.

Sources of Simulations

In addition to developing their own simulations, teachers have access to a variety of ever changing commercial simulations on which to draw. Professional journals publish simulations that can be used in a variety of different courses and for a variety of grade levels. The National Council for the Social Studies publishes each spring an issue of *Social Education* that is devoted to teaching with technology. An illustration in one such issue is the money and banking simulation developed by Caldwell and Highsmith (1994) for use in a U.S. history course. Another issue offered an in-depth discussion of agent-based models to simulate the relationship between individuals and social phenomenon (Berson & Berson, 2007).

Simulations for social studies instruction fall into two broad categories: *computerized* formats for one or more people and *noncomputerized* formats for small groups that employ board games or role-play activities. Computers, especially handheld, provide the capacity for quickly handling many variables and give opportunities for an assortment of complex simulations. These often allow students to more closely approximate real events than noncomputerized media. Digital natives have grown up with the computerized format and therefore may be less than thrilled with noncomputerized simulations.

Tom Snyder Productions (**www.tomsnyder.com**) has long been a leader in the software that provides role plays and simulations for grades 5 through 10. Figure 5.7 shows Decisions, Decisions 5.0.

Guidelines for Conducting Simulations. A summary of the main steps in developing a simulation follows.

1. Define the problem or issue that the simulation is to represent.
2. State the objectives of the simulation as narrowly and clearly as possible.
3. Specify the actors or parts that are to be played.
4. Spell out in some detail the roles that the players are to assume or what they are to achieve.
5. Indicate the resources and the constraints or rules that exist for the players.
6. Specify clearly the decision-making mechanisms or how the simulation is to operate.
7. Develop a trial version of the simulation and field-test it.
8. On the basis of the field test, modify the simulation and retest it until all "bugs" have been eliminated.

To employ simulations effectively in instruction, one can follow the same set of guidelines suggested earlier for role playing. Again, the *debriefing* period is a critical and integral phase of a simulation activity. In establishing a time frame for the use of simulations, a teacher must set aside a sufficient block of time to discuss students' insights and reactions. It is also important in this discussion period to relate the simulated events to ones within students' experiences.

SUMMARY

The most impressive symphony conductor in the world has nothing on a good classroom teacher. This chapter introduced you to the many facets of orchestrating your classroom for effective teaching and maximum learning. Planning for small-group work is not as easy as it sounds, especially since many students have never had instruction in the various roles that they are asked to play as a member of a cooperative learning group. Assigning roles, modeling and

FIGURE 5.7
Decisions, Decisions

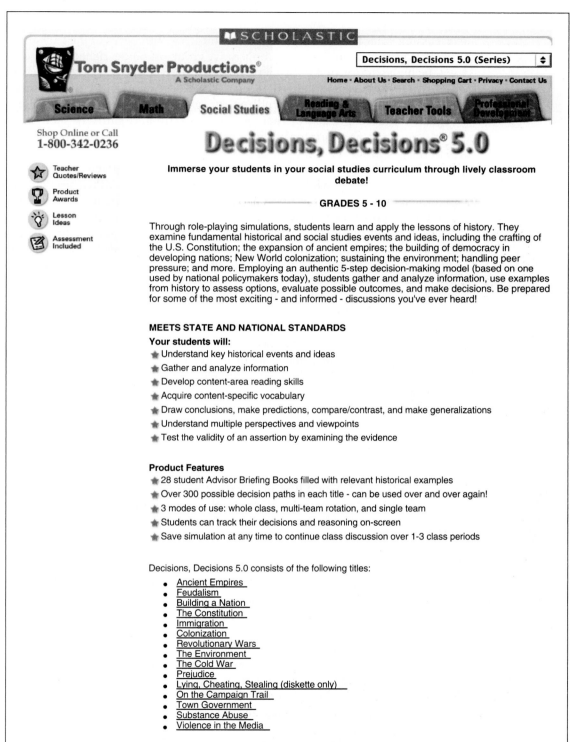

discussing what is expected, and then monitoring with "eyes in the back of your head" is usually enough to get a cooperative group off on the right track. Students will be highly motivated if they have a role in suggesting and selecting questions and issues they want answered. They will do best when their assignments are clearly spelled out with personalized rubrics and they are provided ways to organize and keep track of their progress. Graphic organizers such as data retrieval charts are an informal way for students to assess their progress and plan their next move.

Cooperative learning techniques such as Jigsaw are effective ways to promote subject mastery while empowering students to practice their teaching techniques on one another. It is also a good way to break reading material into manageable proportions and facilitate each group's study with guiding questions. Wait time and sequencing of questions come as second nature to you when you have been teaching for a while; but initially, when students fail to respond, there is the temptation to rush in to fill the void. Patience is a virtue, especially here. The answer is probably there; just give it some time to surface. Role playing and simulations are useful in helping students examine and understand complex issues, but care must be taken when using these teaching and learning approaches.

In the next chapter we will take your students one step further as we discuss how to help them in concept development and application. Our goal is to scaffold them in the zone of proximal development from facts to concepts and from knowing to applying.

ACTIVITIES

1. Work in a group of four or five students and select a film that is appropriate for use in a middle grades social studies class. View it and *individually* develop a brief questioning script consisting of four or five questions. Sequence the questions from simple to complex ones. In your group, compare the different scripts and the rationale for them. Repeat the process with a film for a secondary grade class.
2. Arrange to observe a teacher in a middle grades or a secondary school class during a social studies lesson. In one column on a sheet of paper, list verbatim all the questions that the teacher asks during the class. Also note the teacher's *wait time*, especially with regards to gender. Are boys given more time and more help as studies indicate?
3. Repeat activity 1 with the following changes: Identify a class from grades 9 through 12 and develop a set of questions applying the second Taba strategy.
4. Using any issue or topic, create a role-playing activity for a middle grade class.
5. Using any issue or topic, create a role-playing activity for a secondary grade class.

WEB RESOURCES

TechLINK

Cooperative Learning Center: **www.co-operation.org/**

Mr. Donn's Ancient History: **www.members.aol.com/donnandlee/**

George Lucas Education Foundation: **www.glef.org/**

Teacher Talk: **www.education.indiana.edu/cas/tt/tthmpg.html**

NEA Teaching Tips: **www.nea.org/tips/library.html**

A to Z Teacher Stuff: **www.atozteacherstuff.com/**

Teaching Best Practices: **www.agpa.uakron.edu/k12/best_practices/**

6

Promoting Reflective Inquiry: Developing and Applying Concepts, Generalizations, and Hypotheses

Learning and Teaching Concepts

The Nature of Concepts

The Science of Learning

Misconceptions and Stereotypes

The Process of Learning a Concept

Concept Analyses

Instructional Strategies That Promote Concept Learning

Graphic Organizers

Learning and Teaching Facts and Generalizations

The Nature of Facts

The Nature of Generalizations

The Value of Generalizations

Generalizations, Facts, and Hypotheses

Instructional Strategies That Promote the Learning of Generalizations

Using Data-Retrieval Charts in Developing Generalizations

The Reflective Citizen and Problem Solving

Uses of the Term *Problem* in Instruction

Instructional Strategies for Problem Solving

Summary

Activities

Web Resources

Social studies textbooks are filled with facts and disjointed information that students are often required to memorize. For example, when studying the American Civil War, students may be required to remember the dates of and main figures involved in the firing on Fort Sumter, the Battle of Gettysburg, the signing of the Emancipation Proclamation, and the surrender at Appomattox. Facts that are associated with each of these events are important, but what is most important is not the disconnected facts that surround each of these, rather it is the knowledge centered around important concepts that best support student learning.

*The students in Mr. Bull's U.S. History class are studying the American Civil War. The significance of the Emancipation Proclamation is one piece of information that is included in the unit. Mr. Bull has designed a lesson for his students to engage in historical inquiry. The students are using an online historical archive, such as the Virginia Center for Digital History (**www.vcdh.virginia .edu**) to investigate different aspects of the Proclamation. He has divided the students into different groups: newspaper archive, photograph collection, letters* *and diaries, maps, and official records. As a class, they discuss the steps of historical inquiry and develop an investigation plan. Each group of students gathers around a computer to learn as much as they can about the Emancipation Proclamation. The students dive into their research!*

Within moments a high-energy buzz develops throughout the classroom. The letters group is reading letters written by a soldier before and after the Battle of Gettysburg. He describes the scene and the soldier's sentiments prior to Lincoln's arrival. The newspaper archive group is reading Northern and Southern newspapers to compare the different accounts of the Battle of Gettysburg and the Emancipation. They also find out it was a really hot summer in Pennsylvania during this time. The photograph team begins to print out images of the people and land.

After allowing the students to conduct their research, Mr. Bull brings the students back together. He asks each group to report on their findings. The students are amazed at the different perspectives they found by researching different primary sources. Mr. Bull guides the students to weave together the multiple perspectives of the Battle of Gettysburg and the Emancipation. Together, they have made sense of these important events in a much more meaningful way than simply memorizing dates, names, and places as is done in some traditional social studies classrooms.

To function effectively and advance, a democratic society requires reflective citizens who have a well-grounded body of concepts, facts, and generalizations concerning human behavior, their nation, and the world. In applying such knowledge to civic affairs, citizens must be able to develop and test hypotheses and engage in problem solving using factual data and well-formed concepts. These reflective abilities are acquired cumulatively; they begin early in the home, become more formalized with the onset of kindergarten and schooling, and may develop throughout life.

In an earlier chapter, we discussed Piaget and noted that individuals organized knowledge into structures known as *schemata*. The elements of these schemata include a complex, interrelated web or network of concepts, facts, generalizations, and hypotheses. We now will consider teaching strategies and learning environments that provide students with subject matter and experiences that stimulate the development of such knowledge structures.

Learning and Teaching Concepts

All learning, thinking, and action involve concepts. They broaden and enrich our lives and make it possible for us to communicate easily with others. Because individuals share many similar concepts, they can exchange information rapidly and efficiently without any need for explaining in detail each item discussed. Similarly, when a communication breakdown occurs, it often is because one of the parties lacks the necessary concepts embedded in the conversation. Not infrequently, this happens in social studies textbooks when the author assumes certain knowledge that the student does not actually have.

Concepts are hooks on which we can hang new information. They are not a list of names, places, or dates. When we encounter new subject matter that does not appear to fit on any existing conceptual hook, we may broaden our idea of what some existing hook can hold or create a new one. These conceptual hangers allow us to tidy up our knowledge structure. They also make it easier to learn and to remember information.

It is the social studies teachers' responsibility to identify the essential concepts, or hooks, upon which to base instruction. Once these are identified, teachers should acknowledge students' prior knowledge related to the concept and use instructional strategies to help students broaden the knowledge and skills that surround the concept, or hook. By doing this, teachers emphasize the importance of *learning with understanding*.

The Nature of Concepts

In their simplest form, **concepts** may be regarded as categories into which we group phenomena within our experience. Concepts make it easier to sort out large numbers of living beings, objects, and events into a smaller number of usable categories of experience, such as cars, plants, nations, and heroes. As phenomena are sorted into concept categories, we discern their basic or distinguishing characteristics. We may check these characteristics against our memories of past examples or *prototypes* that represent our notion of a typical case of the concept.

Concepts, however, are more than just categories. They have personal as well as public dimensions. The **personal dimensions** consist of the unique individual associations we have accumulated in relation to the concept. People's concepts of money, as an illustration, are attached to their economic goals, perceptions of financial issues, and many other personal associations with money that make their concepts unique.

In contrast to the set of unique personal associations that each of our concepts incorporates, some defining properties are shared in common: the **public dimensions** of the concept. The public characteristics distinguish one concept from another and permit easy exchanges of information and experiences. This means that although a professional banker and I, for example, have had different levels of experiences with *money*, we can easily communicate with one another concerning checks, bank drafts, currency, travelers checks, and credit cards.

Substantive concepts are concepts that deal with the substance of history (Donovan & Bransford, 2005). Substantive concepts such as election, constitution, war, treaty, law, and election transcend time and place. The conceptions of kings, laws, presidents, or slavery vary throughout history. It can be complicated to teach substantive concepts, especially when we remember that the way students make sense of these concepts is heavily influenced by the prior knowledge.

The Science of Learning

The National Research Council (Bransford, Brown, & Cocking, 1999, pp. 14–21) has identified three primary findings that help us better understand how students learn and understand concepts. Each of these findings has important implications for classroom instruction.

Finding	Instructional Implications
"Students come to the classroom with preconceptions about how the world works. If their initial understanding is not engaged, they may fail to grasp the new concepts and information that are taught, or they may learn them for the purpose of a test but revert to their preconceptions outside the classroom."	Teachers must tap into students' prior knowledge. By understanding students' initial conceptions, teachers can expand and build on them.
"To develop competence in an area of inquiry, students must: a. have a deep foundation of factual knowledge, b. understand facts and ideas in the context of a conceptual framework, and c. organize knowledge in ways that facilitate retrieval of an application."	Teachers must lead students through in-depth exploration of limited topics, rather than covering many topics at a superficial level.
"A metacognitive approach to instruction can help students learn to take control of their own learning by defining learning goals and monitoring their progress in achieving them."	Teachers must integrate metacognitive strategies into classroom learning. For example, when analyzing a primary source, students should consider who wrote it, when it was written, why it was written, how it was received.

Misconceptions and Stereotypes

Much of the formal learning of concepts in schools often consists of correcting **misconceptions** (that is, incorrect or incomplete concepts), as well as forming new ones. When students focus on the *noncritical* properties of concepts and begin to treat them as defining ones, they often develop **stereotypes**. As an illustration, on the basis of a limited range of experiences with Americans classified as *American of Asian heritage*, a youngster may have developed the stereotype that Americans of Asian heritage are "people who are shy, hard-working, wear glasses, and are smart." From these limited and isolated experiences, the individual has overgeneralized to *all* Asian Americans.

The Process of Learning a Concept

It would be difficult for you to recall vividly the experiences that were involved in learning many of the concepts you already possess. Take as an example the three interview excerpts below. These students were asked about the concept of a king. The three examples vividly demonstrate how three students in one classroom have distinctly different perceptions on the concept of "king." These different perceptions are based on students' preconceptions and experiences.

Interview with Hosea (7th grade)

Interviewer: What is a king?

Hosea: Someone who makes laws, goes to war, and rules the country.

Interviewer: Do we have a king?

Hosea: Yes.

Interviewer: Can you tell me about our king?

Hosea: George Bush. He has us in a war. My dad is a soldier who went to Iraq.

Interview with Celia (7th grade)

Interviewer: What is a king?

Celia: A king has a castle. He has lots of money, horses, and jewels. A king is famous.

Interviewer: Do we have a king?

Celia: Well, we don't. But, England has King Charles. He has two sons who are princes. He used to be married to Princess Diana.

Interview with Mary (7th grade)

Interviewer: What is a king?

FIGURE 6.1
Fish Is Fish

Fish Is Fish (Lionni, 1970) describes a fish who is keenly interested in learning about what happens on land, but the fish cannot explore land because it can only breathe in water. It befriends a tadpole who grows into a frog and eventually goes out onto the land. The frog returns to the pond a few weeks later and reports on what he has seen. The frog describes all kinds of things like birds, cows, and people. The book shows pictures of the fish's representations of each of these descriptions: each is a fish-like form that is slightly adapted to accommodate the frog's descriptions—people are imagined to be fish who walk on their tailfins, birds are fish with wings, cows are fish with udders. This tale illustrates both the creative opportunities and dangers inherent in the fact that people construct new knowledge based on their current knowledge.

Mary: A king is a ruler. A king rules the people.

Interviewer: Do we have a king?

Mary: Yes.

Interviewer: Can you tell me about our king?

Mary: Our king is Martin Luther King. He fights for black people.

Similarly, the case presented in Figure 6.1 pertains to learners of all ages and the role preconceptions play in learning. It highlights the science of learning that emphasizes the importance of teachers understanding and calling upon students' prior knowledge and initial conceptions. Vosniadou and Brewer (1989) studied young children learning about the earth. Even when instructed that the earth was round, the students pictured the earth flat as a pancake. Their research highlights the importance of acknowledging students' prior knowledge and that didactic instruction is not always satisfactory.

Concept Analyses

A **concept analysis** involves identifying the **name** most commonly associated with the concept; a simplified **rule** or definition that specifies clearly what the concept is; the **attributes** that make up the defining characteristics of the concept; and some other attributes that are characteristics often associated with the concept but nevertheless are nonessential.

An analysis also involves selecting or creating some different **examples** of the concept, including a **best example** or clearest case of the concept, and some related **nonexamples** of the concept. These provide contrast by showing what the concept is not.

Instructional Strategies That Promote Concept Learning

In considering how to teach social studies concepts, Stanley and Mathews (1985) have pointed out that the defining features for most concepts are complex. Further, they observed that category boundaries often are not clear-cut (e.g., Was U.S. involvement in Korea a *war* or a police *action?*). They also noted that individuals tend to create concept categories based on "best examples," or "prototypes," especially where the concepts have fuzzy boundaries. Concept learning from this perspective is a search for central tendencies of patterns rather than just isolating specific exclusive properties of a concept (Medin & Smith, 1984; Smith & Medin, 1981).

Overall, research concerning how individuals learn concepts has provided a sophisticated, empirically based set of instructional guidelines for aiding students in learning concepts (Howard, 1987; Martorella, 1991; Medin & Smith, 1984; Tennyson & Cocchiarella, 1986). From the extensive body of research on concept learning, we can abstract a basic instructional model that consists of the following eight steps:

1. Identify the set of examples and nonexamples you plan to use and place them in some logical order for presentation. Include at least one example that best or most clearly illustrates an ideal type of the concept.
2. Include in the materials or oral instructions several cues, directions, questions, and student activities that draw students' attention to the critical attributes and to the similarities and differences in the examples and nonexamples used.
3. Direct students to compare all illustrations with the best example and provide feedback on the adequacy of their comparisons.
4. If critical attributes cannot be clearly identified or are ambiguous, focus attention on the salient features of the best example.
5. Where a clear definition of a concept exists, elicit or state it at some point in the instruction in terms that are meaningful to the students.
6. Through discussion, place the concept in context with other related concepts that are part of the students' prior knowledge.
7. Assess concept mastery at a minimal level—namely, whether students can correctly discriminate between new examples and nonexamples.
8. Assess concept mastery at a more advanced level; for example, ask students to generate new exemplars or apply the concept to new situations.

Graphic Organizers

Graphic organizers are essential tools for the teaching and learning of social studies concepts. Graphic, or visual, organizers assist students in classifying or organizing information. In other words, they help students make sense of disjointed facts and information. Graphic organizers can be used to assess students' prior knowledge and conceptions, to engage students in active learning, and to involve students in metacognitive strategies. Visual organizers can also be used to help students learn facts and generalizations. The examples in Figure 6.2 illustrate different visual organizers.

Examples of graphic organizers and templates for student use are available online at different websites (e.g., North Central Regional Laboratory, **www.ncrel.org/sdrs/areas/issues/students/learning/lr1grorg.htm**).

Software, such as Inspiration, has also been developed that allows teachers and students to create visual organizers. This software program is an excellent tool to assist students in the organization of information around various

FIGURE 6.2
Venn Diagram and Spider Map

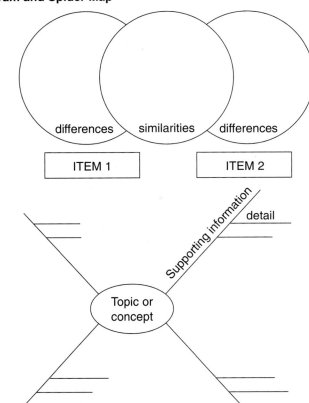

Note. Venn diagram from Raymond C. Jones, ReadingQuest.org. **http://www.readingquest.org.** Reprinted with permission. Spider map Copyright © 1988 North Central Regional Educational Laboratory. All rights reserved. Reprinted with permission of Learning Point Associates.

concepts. Teachers and students can enter information into a variety of graphic organizers. Graphic organizers can be manipulated in interactive formats such as flow charts or concept maps. Students can drag and click the organizers as information is added to reflect the process of building information around a concept. For more information about Inspiration, visit **www.inspiration.com.**

Learning and Teaching Facts and Generalizations

In what ways are facts and generalizations distinguished from concepts? As we have seen, concepts are the building blocks of knowledge. They are part of every fact and generalization that we know. If our concepts are ill formed or incomplete, so will the ideas we build from them be improperly shaped. When we think, make a decision, or act, we draw on a network of schemata that includes concepts, facts, and generalizations, the major elements of reflection.

The Nature of Facts

Citizens are bombarded daily with facts and assertions that appear to be *facts*. In our society, facts are valued. Individuals often go to great lengths, spending much time and even money, to get them. People who have knowledge of facts or have access to such knowledge often have considerable power and status; witness heads of countries, inventors, and columnists.

A **fact** is a statement about concepts that is true or verified for a particular case on the basis of the best evidence available. To illustrate, consider a concept cluster that includes *law, court trial,* and *drunken driving.* An example of a fact statement that relates these concepts would be that: In 1988, the North Carolina state courts conducted 132 trials involving drunken driving charges.

Some examples of facts are:

- The Carolina Panthers are a professional football team.
- President Bill Clinton served two terms.
- The largest state in the United States is Alaska.
- The Supreme Court interprets our Constitution.
- Slavery once was legal in the United States.

Assertions of fact are often accepted on the basis of the best evidence available at one point, only to be proven false later. The notion that atoms were the smallest particles in existence, for example, was long held in the field of science until later discoveries proved it false. Often an assertion will be accepted as a fact by an individual, even though it may not be supported by evidence or may be considered by most people to be false.

Learning Facts in Meaningful Contexts. All students need to have experiences in locating, identifying, organizing, and verifying significant facts. The facts they are asked to remember should also have practical meaning. A student can learn two lists of 50 pairs of names—one with capitals and states and the other with nonsense words—in the same way. Neither list has any real immediate functional value beyond gaining recognition or success, unless some meaningful context is provided.

Facts learned outside of some meaningful context are often quickly forgotten long before they can be put to any functional use. More importantly, they are not integrated into students' schemata of previously acquired knowledge. Remember, the importance of this was discussed earlier in the text with Piaget's concept of assimilation. This last point is illustrated by the student who had memorized all of the names of American presidents in the correct order, but who could not give the names of any three presidents who had served during the last half of the 20th century.

Teaching students techniques for more efficiently retrieving meaningful facts from memory is a worthy instructional objective. Citizens frequently need to remember a great number of names, places, events, dates, and general descriptive information to clarify and link new knowledge in functionally meaningful ways. In Chapter 9, we consider some of the general techniques that are useful for helping students to comprehend, communicate, remember, and access factual data acquired in social studies instruction.

The Nature of Generalizations

From an instructional perspective, a **generalization** is a statement about concepts that is true or verified for all cases on the basis of the best evidence available. Generalizations are similar to facts in that they are also true statements about relationships between or among concepts. However, generalizations summarize and organize a great deal of information obtained from analyses of many sets of facts. The summary results in a single broad, wide-reaching assertion that applies to the past, present, and even future. In contrast, facts assert claims about specific instances.

Consider the assertion of fact from a text:

- Franklin Roosevelt, who in 1932 campaigned for a balanced budget, as president initiated deficit spending to combat the economic crises facing the nation.

Compare it with this generalization:

- Economic well-being is a goal of all nations.

Further, consider each of the generalizations stated in Figure 6.3 with the corresponding factual statement that is related to the generalization.

FIGURE 6.3

Sample Social Studies Generalizations and Related Facts

Generalization	Example of a Related Fact
In the southern coastal states, climate is a big factor in determining agriculture choices.	Higher temperatures and lack of rainfall have forced North Carolina, South Carolina, and Georgia to consider switching to crops that require less water.
The specter of terrorism has influenced government funding.	Greater governmental funds have been allocated to Homeland Security and are being given to the states to increase their local safety measures.
Technology continues to change countries and cultures.	Third world nations without telecommunications infrastructure have found that cellular advances have allowed them to connect their citizens with others in the country and throughout the world in a fraction of the time and cost of years ago.
Citizens of the world are interdependent.	With the advent of international travel and trading, nations all over the world can import goods needed and export goods in surplus.
In the nineteenth century, immigrants struggled to assimilate.	At the turn of the century, new citizens sought to adopt the culture and ways of their new country, often losing the cultural characteristics that made them unique. America became known as a "melting pot."

The Value of Generalizations

Unlike facts, generalizations have the capacity to *predict* when they appear in the form of "If . . . then" statements. For example: "*If* there is a national election, *then* the turnout of white collar, professional, and businesspeople likely will be greater than that of semiskilled and unskilled workers." The statement predicts that "If certain conditions are present [national elections], a second set of consequences will follow [a pattern of voter turnout]."

As students examine and analyze data for patterns and then summarize their conclusions, they are progressing toward deriving significant generalizations. From the learner's perspective, the understanding that results from the analysis and that is represented by the statement of a generalization is significant.

The synthesis represented by a generalization provides the student with a broad, wide-reaching statement that applies to the past and the present and to all cases everywhere, such as: "Families vary in size and structure." A generalization may also apply to some more limited context, such as: "The nature of democracy in the United States continually evolves as the society grows and changes."

Generalizations, Facts, and Hypotheses

Unlike facts and generalizations, which are verified assertions, **hypotheses** are untested ideas or guesses. They are potential facts or generalizations, subject to verification. Hypotheses arise when we confront something we wish to explain. They are our attempts to provide plausible explanations for questions such as: What are the causes of poverty? Why does the government subsidize the tobacco industry at the same time that it requires health warnings on cigarette packs? Why do some people get more upset at burnings of the flag than instances of social injustice?

The process of forming a hypothesis begins when we try to resolve or answer such questions. Hypotheses formed are *tested* through the gathering and comparing of evidence that supports or refutes them. An original hypothesis may be revised or even discarded since some types of evidence are often conflicting and inconclusive. They may also be based on certain unproven assumptions, and as a result, never develop further. The hypotheses to explain why and by whom President Kennedy was assassinated are examples.

Some hypotheses can never be verified or refuted, since all of the necessary evidence is impossible to obtain. Speculations about "what might have happened" had certain events in history been altered fall into this category. An example would be the hypothesis that "The United States would be far different today had Jefferson not approved the Louisiana Purchase."

Many hypotheses can be tested in social studies classes by gathering and comparing data. When a hypothesis appears to "hold up" or seems to be true in the light of evidence gathered, it tentatively can be regarded as either a fact or a generalization.

Students engaged in developing and testing hypotheses need practice and assistance at each grade level. This includes help with generating plausible hypotheses to explain and answer simple but interesting problems and questions. It also implies assistance with gathering and comparing data to test them.

As they progress in developing and testing hypotheses, students can be introduced to the concept of **multiple causality,** which is crucial to the analysis of many issues in the social studies. Understanding multiple causality requires that students recognize and accept that more than one hypothesis may be correct—often several causes explain or account for an event. This relates to events rooted in history (e.g., What caused the American Revolution?), as well as everyday social phenomena (e.g., What causes gang violence?).

Instructional Strategies That Promote the Learning of Generalizations

As in teaching concepts, strategies that help students develop and test generalizations may employ either *discovery* or *expository* approaches. We have seen the two approaches differ chiefly in the degree to which they place the responsibility on students to identify relationships among cases and to derive the actual generalization. Both approaches involve students in thinking, doing, and learning. Each also guides students in understanding the necessary relationships among items. To provide variety, instruction should include some mix of both discovery and expository approaches.

Discovery Approaches. When a discovery approach is used, the teacher withholds the generalization from students. Instructional materials and procedures are structured in such a way that students will infer or discover a generalization from their investigations.

Through a variety of methods, teachers engage and help students in the process of examining sets of data and materials. Additionally, through questioning and explaining, teachers aid students in identifying similarities and differences, patterns, and trends in the data analyzed. Also, teachers assist students in summarizing their conclusions and in discovering or inferring the unstated generalization.

Using Data-Retrieval Charts in Developing Generalizations

Data-retrieval charts are an effective tool to help students develop generalizations. These charts consist of rows and columns of categories and cells of related data. For example, along the left side (rows) of a chart could be listed the names of cities: Pittsburgh, San Francisco, Vancouver, Paris, and Tokyo. Across the top (columns) of the chart could be listed selected characteristics of the cities, such as size, climate, cost of living, and major ethnic groups. In the related cells would be the corresponding data for each city.

To provide the structure for the data-retrieval chart (the categories of items that will be used for the rows and columns), a teacher first needs to identify the generalization to be taught. To construct the shell of the chart, we need to identify what the two sets of categories, our row and column indicators, will be. In examining the generalization, we can see that we will require data on some

FIGURE 6.4
Sample Shell of a Data-Retrieval Chart

Families Around the World					
Indicators of Lifestyles	China	United States	Argentina	Algeria	Poland
Life Expectancy					
Number of Children					
Per Capita Income					
Number of Rooms per Dwelling					

Note. Adapted from "Two Ways to Cope," 1988, *National Geographic*, December, pp. 942–943. Courtesy of National Geographic.

representative families and some *indicators of lifestyles*. Let us say that we assign the data on families to columns, and that we pick five diverse families from different countries: China, United States, Argentina, Algeria, and Poland.

To the rows we assign four indicators of lifestyle: life expectancy, number of children, per capita income, and number of rooms per dwelling. Our chart shell, with cells to be filled in with data, is shown in Figure 6.4.

The cells of information can be filled in by either the teacher or students or both. The teacher, for example, could begin by partially completing a chart to model for students how data are to be recorded in the cells. Data-retrieval charts are particularly appropriate group projects, since tasks can be easily divided, with each member taking responsibility for either a row or a column of data.

The Reflective Citizen and Problem Solving

The terms *inquiry, critical thinking, the scientific method, reflective thinking*, and *problem solving* have been used at one time or another to refer to the *process* by which individuals find solutions to problems through reflection. In the process of problem solving, students activate prior schema that include related facts, concepts, and generalizations, and they integrate new subject matter into meaningful knowledge structures.

Thus, problem solving is both a way to better organize and interrelate existing knowledge, as well as acquire new information. The elements of reflection are not learned as isolated bits of information, but as part of a pattern of psychologically meaningful knowledge. Students do not first learn facts, for example, *then* engage in problem solving. They use knowledge already acquired and add new elements, such as facts, concepts, and generalizations, *as* they engage in problem solving.

Most discussions of reflective thinking or problem solving derive from the work and writings of the American philosopher and educator John Dewey. His ideas on reflective thinking are laid out in detail in two books, *How We Think* (1933) and *Democracy and Education* (1916). In these works, especially the first, Dewey develops clearly the nature of a problem and its relationship to reflective thinking. Since Dewey's first investigations into how people learn, educators have been exploring how people learn through making their own journey. These forays themselves have become reflective tools over time. Dewey's ideas have been applied to the teaching of social studies by a number of prominent social studies educators, including Griffin (1992), Engle (1976), Hunt and Metcalf (1968), and Levstik and Barton (2005).

Levstik and Barton (2005) describe a classroom in which students are "doing history" as one in which students regularly and actively "frame questions, gather data from primary and secondary sources, organize and interpret the data, and share their work with different audiences" (p. xi). Lessons in which students engage in inquiry-based investigations arm students not only for learning content knowledge, but also for developing reflective tools that will assist them in their own metacognition. Inquiry is the act of developing questions, gathering data from multiple sources, and reflecting on the findings. The National Center for History in the Schools (NCHS) provides standards challenging teachers to design experiences that require students:

- to raise questions and to marshal solid evidence in support of their answers
- to go beyond the facts presented in their textbooks and examine the historical record for themselves
- to consult documents, journals, diaries, artifacts, historic sites, works of art, quantitative data, and other evidence from the past, and to do so imaginatively—taking into account the historical context in which these records were created and comparing the multiple points of view of those on the scene at the time. (National Center for History in the Schools, 1996, p. 14).

The purpose of teaching and learning is to "get students thinking." According to Gerwin and Zevin (2003), "we want to hear their ideas; we want to see evidence; and above all, we want to hear reasons, hypotheses, interpretations, and theories that analyze and explain events" (p. 13). Hicks and Doolittle have developed the SCIM-C model as a strategy to guide students through the inquiry process (**http://historicalinquiry.com**). Figure 6.5 describes this strategy.

FIGURE 6.5
SCIM-C Explanation: A Strategy for Interpreting History

Summarizing

Summarizing is the first phase of the SCIM-C strategy and begins with having students quickly examine the documentary aspects of the text, in order to find any information or evidence that is explicitly available from the source. Within this phase students should attempt to identify the source's subject, author, purpose, and audience, as well as the type of historical source (e.g., letter, photograph, cartoon). In addition, the student should look for key facts, dates, ideas, opinions, and perspectives that appear to be immediately apparent within the source. The four analyzing questions associated with the summarizing phase include:

1. What type of historical document is the source?
2. What specific information, details and/or perspectives does the source provide?
3. What is the subject and/or purpose of the source?
4. Who was the author and/or audience of the source?

Contextualizing

Contextualizing begins the process of having students spend more time with the source in order to explore the authentic aspects of the source in terms of locating the source within time and space. The teacher needs to emphasize that it is important to recognize and understand that archaic words and/or images from the period may be in a source. These words and/or images may no longer be used today or they may be used differently, and these differences should be noted and defined. In addition, the meanings, values, habits, and/or customs of the period may be very different from those today. Ultimately, students and teachers must be careful to avoid treating the source as a product of today as they pursue their guiding historical question. The four analyzing questions associated with the contextualizing phase include:

1. When and where was the source produced?
2. Why was the source produced?
3. What was happening within the immediate and broader context at the time the source was produced?
4. What summarizing information can place the source in time and place?

Inferring

Inferring is designed to provide students with the opportunity to revisit initial facts gleaned from the source and to begin to read subtexts and make inferences based upon a developing understanding of the context and continued examination of the source. In answering an historical question and working with the primary source, sometimes the evidence is not explicitly stated or obvious in the source, but rather, the evidence is hinted at within the source and needs to be drawn out. The inferring stage provides room for students to explore the source and examine the source's perspective in the light of the historical questions being asked. The four analyzing questions associated with the inferring phase include:

1. What is suggested by the source?
2. What interpretations may be drawn from the source?
3. What perspectives or points of view are indicated in the source?
4. What inferences may be drawn from absences or omissions in the source?

FIGURE 6.5
continued

Monitoring

Monitoring is the capstone stage in examining individual sources. Here students are expected to question and reflect upon their initial assumptions in terms of the overall focus on the historical questions being studied. This reflective monitoring is essential in making sure that students have asked the key questions from each of the previous phases. Such a process requires students to examine the credibility and usefulness or significance of the source in answering the historical questions at hand.

Ultimately, monitoring is about reflection, reflection upon the use of the SCIM-C strategy and reflection upon the source itself. The SCIM-C strategy is recursive in nature and thus revisiting phases and questions is essential as one begins to create an historical interpretation of a source in light of one's historical questions. The four analyzing questions associated with the monitoring phase include:

1. What additional evidence beyond the source is necessary to answer the historical question?
2. What ideas, images, or terms need further defining from the source?
3. How useful or significant is the source for its intended purpose in answering the historical question?
4. What questions from the previous stages need to be revisited in order to analyze the source satisfactorily?

Corroborating

Corroborating only starts when students have analyzed a series of sources, and are ready to extend and deepen their analysis through comparing the evidence gleaned from each source in light of the guiding historical questions. What similarities and differences in ideas, information, and perspectives exist between the analyzed sources? Students should also look for gaps in their evidence that may hinder their interpretations and the answering of their guiding historical questions. When they find contradictions between sources, they must investigate further, including the checking of the credibility of the source. Once the sources have been compared the student then begins to draw conclusions based upon the synthesis of the evidence, and can begin to develop their own conclusions and historical interpretation. The four analyzing questions associated with the corroborating phase include:

1. What similarities and differences between the sources exist?
2. What factors could account for these similarities and differences?
3. What conclusions can be drawn from the accumulated interpretations?
4. What additional information or sources are necessary to answer more fully the guiding historical question?

Students who engage in historical inquiry develop a more advanced understanding of the interconnectedness of history and causation. Most middle and secondary school students don't enter the social studies classroom prepared with the skills needed to gain in inquiry activities. Unfortunately, for most of their school experiences teachers have transmitted knowledge to students, rather than engaging students in active learning experiences in which students investigate and make sense of new knowledge. It then becomes the teacher's responsibility to scaffold students' learning, or to guide students through the inquiry process.

An exemplar of historical inquiry is Historical Scene Investigation (HSI), an online collection of inquiry-based cases for teachers and students. HSI has a series of Web-based cases that guide students through the inquiry process. Cases include titles such as: Children in the Civil War, The Case of Sam Smiley, Jamestown Starving Time, The Boston "Massacre," and School Desegregation. Each case has the four H.S.I. essential elements: becoming a detective, investigating the evidence, searching for clues, and cracking the case. Teachers and students can engage in these activities online at **www.hsionline.org**.

Uses of the Term *Problem* in Instruction

The term **problem**, as it occurs in discussions of problem solving, generally is used in three different ways. It refers to *personal* problems that individuals experience, such as how to become more popular, get along with others, or cope when you lose your job.

The term is also used to refer to significant *social* problems faced by our society or the world. These might be issues such as poverty, inequality of opportunity, crime, or unemployment.

A third usage relates to conditions in which individuals experience a *psychological* state of doubt. The classic example of this usage was provided by Dewey, who cited the case of an individual who comes to a fork in a road and has no sign to guide his direction.

Instructional Strategies for Problem Solving

Problem-solving instructional approaches may be based on one or more meanings of the term *problem*. One application is to focus on topics that intersect with personal and social problems, such as abortion rights or how wealth should be distributed in a society. This approach, relating to issues dealing with areas such as sex, religion, and economics, that are normally closed to discussion in the classroom, was advocated by Hunt and Metcalf (1968) (see also discussions in Chapters 3, 4, and 8).

The broadest application of problem solving, however, involves the third meaning of *problem*, creating a state of psychological doubt. It allows the teacher to use *any* subject matter in a problem-solving approach. The teacher's role is to create, in Griffin's (1992) words, "a problematic atmosphere—a set of conditions likely to render the beliefs of students in some degree doubtful" (p. 56).

A psychological problem is created when the teacher succeeds in structuring, displaying, and sequencing subject matter in a special way that casts doubt on students' convictions or conventional wisdom. It is not the subject matter itself, but the way in which it is presented that makes it psychologically problematical. The power of the approach derives from the natural tendency of individuals to

Well-designed computer software can engage students in problem solving.

want to relieve the psychological disequilibrium they experience by solving the problem or finding explanations to account for it.

Any subject matter can be used for problem solving in this sense if a teacher is able to pose the problem and then help resolve an interesting and intriguing question. Not every lesson or topic, however, lends itself easily to developing problem-solving strategies, since it is often difficult to create a sharp, relevant problem focus for students.

Problem-solving strategies require that teachers create a psychological state of **disequilibrium** in students. A state of disequilibrium is one in which a student perceives that something is peculiar, frustrating, irritating, puzzling, disturbing, contrary to what is expected, or incongruous. Disequilibrium is induced to cause them to attend to the subject matter being taught, regardless of its topical con-tent or their relative degree of interest in it. Students are asked to resolve the basic issue that puzzles them: Why is this so? or How can this be? or What is the cause of this?

One of the teacher's major roles in creating problem-solving activities is to ascertain what is likely to appear problematical to students in the context of the subject matter to be studied. Unless a teacher has organized material in a way that arouses students' initial curiosity concerning the problem, they are not likely to attend to the problem. If students do not perceive that there is any psychological problem that requires a solution, no real problem solving will occur.

A basic five-step model for problem solving, adapted from Dewey (1933), is presented in Figure 6.6. It outlines the basic sequence of activities that a teacher should follow in engaging students in problem solving. The general problem-solving instructional model outlined in this figure provides only a basic road map.

FIGURE 6.6
General Problem-Solving Instructional Model

1. Structure some aspect of the subject matter students are to learn to create a puzzle, dilemma, discrepancy, or doubt.

2. Have the students internalize the problem by asking them to verbalize it. Clarify the problem if necessary.

3. Solicit some hypotheses from the students that might explain or account for the problem. Clarify terminology where necessary, and allow sufficient time for student reflection.

4. Assist students in testing the validity of the hypotheses generated and in examining the implications of the results. Where necessary, assist in providing reference materials, background information relevant to the subject matter, and keeping students on the topic.

5. Aid students in deciding on a tentative conclusion that seems to be the most plausible explanation for the problem, based on the best evidence available at the time. Stress the tentative nature of the conclusion, because future studies and further evidence may lead to a different conclusion.

Note. From John Dewey, *How We Think.* Copyright © 1993 by D.C. Health and Company. Adapted with permission of Houghton Mifflin Company.

Dewey himself suggested that problem solving as it occurs in natural settings does not always follow through steps in a set order. In solving problems, individuals often "jump ahead," temporarily skipping steps, and at other times, may return to a step already passed.

Problem-based learning can also take the form of "problematizing" historical accounts. That is, students evaluate what they know and how they know it in seeking to better understand the past. Consider the example from Ms. Peabody's classroom.

Ms. Peabody asked her 11th-grade students what they knew about slavery. The students recorded their individual thoughts in a 3-minute free write. Ms. Peabody then asked the students to share what they had written down. Not surprisingly, the students reported a very traditional notion of American slavery prior to the U.S. Civil War. The students talked about large plantations in which hundreds of slaves worked in tobacco fields. They described horrid relationships between master and slave. They reported that slaves could not read. The students cited the Civil War as the end of slavery in this country.

Ms. Peabody then asked her students where they had learned about slavery and what evidence they had to support their knowledge. A few students reported watching movies such as *Beloved* or *Glory*. However, the majority of students said that was just what everyone knew. She asked the students to turn to their textbooks to see what else they could learn about slavery in the United States prior to the Civil War. Again, the students mostly reported back a generalized, shallow account of the institution of slavery. She led the students through a discussion that eventually helped students to see that they had questions about slavery, that they wanted to know more about the concept of slavery in the United States prior to the Civil War. The students began to understand that the traditional myths and stories weren't the complete account of this period in history. They also began to see that their textbooks did not have all of the information they needed.

Ms. Peabody then passed out excerpts from slave narratives to small groups of students. Each narrative was 2 to 3 pages long and provided a different perspective on slave life. Samples of the text the students received are below.

George Moses Horton (a poet)

I was early fond of music, with an extraordinary appetite for singing lively tunes, for which I was a little remarkable. In the course of a few years after my birth, from the sterility of his land, my old master assumed the notion to move into Chatham, a more fertile and fresh part of country recently settled, and whose waters were far more healthy and agreeable. I here become a cow-boy, which I followed for perhaps ten years in succession, or more. In the course of this disagreeable occupation, I became fond of hearing people read; but being nothing but a poor cow-boy, I had but little or no thought of ever being able to read or spell one word or sentence in any book whatever. My mother discovered my anxiety for books, and strove to encourage my plan; but she, having left her husband behind, was so hard run to make a little shift for herself, that she could give me no assistance in that case. At length I took resolution to learn the alphabet at all events; and lighting by chance at times with some opportunities of being in the presence of school children, I learnt the letters by heart; and fortunately afterwards got hold of some old parts of spelling books abounding with these elements, which I learnt with but little difficulty. (**http://docsouth.unc.edu/fpn/hortonlife/horton.html**)

William Brown (well-known abolitionist and author)

Most planters in our section cared but little about the religious training of their slaves, regarding them as they did their cattle,—an investment, the return of which was only to be considered in dollars and cents. Not so, however, with Dr. John Gaines, for he took special pride in looking after the spiritual welfare of his slaves, having them all in the "great house," at family worship, night and morning.

On Sabbath mornings, reading of the Scriptures, and explaining the same, generally occupied from one to two hours, and often till half of the negroes present were fast asleep. The white members of the family did not take as kindly to the religious teaching of the doctor, as did the blacks. (**http://docsouth.unc.edu/neh/brown80/brown80.html**)

Solomon Northrup (a slave who was once a freeman)

It was but a short time I closed my eyes that night. Thought was busy in my brain. Could it be possible that I was thousands of miles from home—that I had been driven through the streets like a dumb beast—that I had been chained and beaten without mercy—that I was even then herded with a drove of slaves, a slave myself? Were the events of the last few weeks realities indeed?—or was I passing only through the dismal phases of a long, protracted dream? It was no illusion. My cup of sorrow was full to overflowing. Then I lifted up my hands to God, and in the still watches of the night, surrounded by the sleeping forms of my companions, begged for mercy on the poor, forsaken captive. To the Almighty Father of us all—the freeman and the slave—I poured forth the supplications of a broken spirit, imploring strength from on high to bear up against the burden of my troubles, until the morning light aroused the slumberers, ushering in another day of bondage. (**http://docsouth.unc.edu/fpn/ northup/northup.html**)

Ms. Peabody then asked each group to summarize what they learned about their individual slave and what they now knew about slavery. She guided the students through an interactive discussion in which the students soon began to recognize the value of interpreting multiple sources to reveal multiple perspectives. She asked the students what else they wanted to know about slavery. Together, she and her students generated a series of questions. As a class, they discussed how they could research these questions. The class made a research plan that involved different groups of students using a variety of resources to deepen student understanding of slavery.

Another example of problem-based learning is project based and calls on students to grapple with real-world problems. Problem-based learning is touted as hands-on learning in which students engage in solving authentic problems. Sample classroom problems are:

A state has money to purchase land for the state forest. What land should the state purchase?

The government needs to build a new nuclear power plant. Where should they build the plant?

The school system is going to build a new school. Where should they build the school and how should the students be redistricted?

More and more local farmers are leaving the farming business. What can be done to support local farmers?

How can the local government best improve its public transportation?

Authentic questions such as the ones above may be posed to the students or the students may develop their own problem-based question. Either way, the teacher and students engage in a high level of investigation that is interdisciplinary in nature. This real-world learning is often motivating to students and fosters a deeper understanding of conceptual learning.

Using Case Study Approaches. Often effective teaching involves creating totally new instructional materials rather than modifying or restructuring existing texts. This creative process includes adapting relevant materials, such as advertisements or articles, and creating new instructional materials that incorporate media and primary source data. One such type of instructional material is case studies.

Case studies are brief sets of data that present a single idea, issue, event, document, or problem in some detail. They attempt to present in-depth coverage of a narrow topic. Further, through concrete examples, they seek to make vivid some general or abstract issue. For example, a case study might include an article examining how an individual was stalked and attacked as a way to begin examining the problem of violent crime in the United States. Or it might incorporate a video episode of a news program that recounts how an innocent victim was able to obtain release from prison to dramatize one dimension of injustices in our criminal justice system.

Types of Case Studies. Case studies may be presented through many different forms of media: transparencies, teacher-made sheets, records, video and audio cassettes, films, and various print materials. Four basic types of case studies are

1. *Stories and vignettes.* These are dramatized accounts of either authentic or fictitious events.
2. *Journalistic historical events.* These include original newspaper accounts, recordings, or video records of historical events, eyewitness accounts, and the like.
3. *Research reports.* These include materials such as the results of studies, statistical tables, and census reports that have been organized and summarized.
4. *Documents.* This category includes a range of different items such as speeches, diaries, laws, and records (Newmann, 1970).

An illustration of a simple case study is presented in Figure 6.7. It uses excerpts from various texts to examine an issue that has intrigued historians for over two centuries: Who actually fired the first shot in what became the American Revolution?

The confrontation between the militiamen and the British at Lexington Green on the morning of 1775 is generally credited as the first battle of the war. What is unclear is which side was responsible for first engaging the battle.

FIGURE 6.7
Date Sheet for Case Study

Issue: Who fired the first shot in the Revolutionary War?

Questions to answer in examining different accounts:

1. How many militiamen were involved in the battle?
2. What role did Captain Parker play in the battle?
3. How many militiamen were killed?
4. Who fired the first shot?
5. What was the significance of claiming who fired the first shot?

Account 1
About 70 minutemen were ready to dispute the passage of the British soldiers. They did not withdraw until they were fired upon and 8 of their number killed. Thus began the War of American independence.

Account 2
At daybreak of April 19 the British reached Lexington, where they were confronted by about 60 minutemen. Their commander, Captain Parker, told his men: "Don't fire unless you are fired upon; but if they want a war, let

---

(continued)

it begin here."A shot was fired, but from which side is not certain; t hen came a volley from the British soldiers which killed 8 men andwounded many others. U nable to oppose a force that outnumbered them ten to one, the minutemen fell back in confusion.

Account 3

Pitcairn reached Lexington at sunrise and found himself confronted by some 40 minute-men under Captain John Parker. With an oath he called on them to disperse, but they stood as motionless as a wall, and he ordered his men to fire. (Note: there are different state-ments as to the opening shots.) The volley laid 7 of the patriots dead and 10 wounded on the village green. Parker was greatly outnumbered, and, after making a feeble resistance, ordered his men to retire.

Account 4

At Lexington, 6 miles below Concord, a com-pany of militia, of about 100 men, mustered near the Meeting-House; the Troops came in sight of them just before sunrise; and running within a few rods of them, the Commanding Officer accosted the Militia in words to this effect: "Disperse, you rebels—throw down your arms and disperse"; upon which the Troops huz-zaed, and immediately one or two officers dis-charged their pistols, which were instanta-

neously followed by the firing of 4 or 5 of the soldiers, and then there seemed to be a general discharge from the whole body; 8 of our men were killed and 9 wounded. . . .

Account 5

I, John Parker, of lawful age, and commander of the Militia in Lexington, do testify and declare, that on the 19th [of April], being informed . . . that a number of regular troops were on their march from Boston . . . ordered our Militia to meet on the Common in said Lexington, to consult what to do, and con-cluded not to . . . meddle or make with the said regular troops [if they should approach] unless they should insult us; and upon their sudden approach, I immediately ordered our Militia to disperse and not to fire. Immediately said troops made their appearance, and rushed furiously, fired upon and killed 8 of our party, without receiving any provocation therefore from us.

Account 6

Captain Parker's Company being drawn upon the green before sunrise, and I being in the front rank, there suddenly appeared a number of the King's Troops, about a thousand, as I thought, at the distance of about 60 or 70 yards from us, huzzaing and on a quick pace toward us. . . .

Note. From "The Evaluation of Propaganda by the Historical Method," by E. Eills (Ed.), 1937, in *Education Against Propaganda*, pp. 134–146. Copyright 1937 by National Council for the Social Studies. Reprinted by permission.

SUMMARY

All learning, thinking, and action involve concepts. Concept development is critical to achieving in-depth understanding. This chapter has carefully built an instruc-tional model for teaching concepts and taken you through both the discovery and the expository approaches. Concept hierarchies, minitexts, folders, and bulletin boards are concrete activities that result in tangible examples of concept development. They are helpful to all learners, but especially to the visual learner.

Facts help to form the foundation for our learning. To be true building blocks, they must be learned in meaningful contexts. Generalizations can be made from sets of facts if the information has been carefully organized and analyzed. Students use facts and generalizations when they address a problem or an issue. One tool to help students organize facts is a data-retrieval chart. Students may use data-retrieval charts to help organize new subject matter as it relates to prior schemata. Often, they are asked to form a hypothesis as part of the reflective thinking process. Teachers regularly engage students in problem solving by setting conditions for student disequilibrium. While students are problem solving, they rely heavily on facts and generalizations to form hypotheses. These skill processes are needed to help students to develop citizenship competencies. As citizens of a complex world, students must be open to building accurate concepts of world neighbors, not fall back on old stereotypes that obscure truth and understanding. In Chapter 7 we will discuss specific skills needed to help students to develop effective citizenship competencies and build a global perspective.

ACTIVITIES

1. As discussed in this chapter, it is important to understand students' prior knowledge and misconceptions. List strategies you could use to better learn what knowledge and experiences your students bring to the classroom.
2. Use Inspiration or one of the Web resources mentioned in this chapter to generate a graphic organizer that you could use to help students understand a concept. Describe how you would integrate the organizer into a classroom lesson.
3. Visit the SCIM-C or History Online sites featured in this chapter. What did you learn from working through the activities? How could you use resources such as these in the classroom?
4. Identify a unit of study (e.g., World War I or Age of Exploration) that you could potentially teach. Review a social studies textbook to learn how the textbook presents the information for this unit. How could you problematize this unit for your students? Consider multiple perspectives you could share with your students and questions you will pose to your students.
5. Select one of the types of case studies described in the text. Develop a case study on a social studies topic and discuss how you would use the case as a springboard to a problem-solving activity.

WEB RESOURCES

Education Place's Graphic Organizers: **www.eduplace.com/graphicorganizer/**
Venn diagram information: **www.venndiagram.com/**
Reading Quest: **www.readingquest.org/**
Inspiration: **www.inspiration.com**

Chapter 7

Fostering Citizenship Competency

The Nature of Citizenship Skills

Social Skills

Conflict Resolution Skills

Research and Analysis Skills

Interpreting and Comparing Data

Analyzing Arguments

Processing Information from Pictures

Chronology Skills

Comparative Conceptions of Time

Recording Events on Time Lines

Spatial Skills

The Impact of Spatial Perspectives

Using and Creating Maps in Instruction

Integrating Maps and Globes into All Social Studies Instruction

Identifying and Using Reference Sources in Developing Skills

Sample Reference Works for Social Studies

Activities for Introducing Reference Materials

Summary

Activities

Web Resources

In Ms. Colazzo's seventh-grade world cultures class, students are working in small groups. Each group has computers that they are using to find up-to-the-minute statistics on world hunger. In the context of a unit on world hunger and poverty, the students' objectives are to determine which 15 countries in the world had the (1) highest infant mortality rate, (2) the highest population growth rates, (3) the lowest per capita GNP, and (4) the lowest life expectancy. Further, the students are to test the hypothesis that a relationship among these four categories exists (i.e., the same countries appear on each list).

The students shift from computer screens with stats to another site with an outline of a world map. Each of the four categories—highest infant mortality, highest population growth, lowest per capita GNP, and lowest life expectancy— are color coded and the students mark the 15 countries that fit into each category. By color coding the countries on the computer map, students can immediately see and analyze the relationships among the variables and determine whether the hypothesis is supported. After a discussion among the group members, the recorder in each group will summarize the conclusions. When all of the groups are finished, the entire class will discuss the results.

To determine whether there has been a pattern over time, Ms. Colazzo will instruct the groups to identify which 15 countries made the four lists a decade ago. Eventually, individual members of the groups will examine in more depth and report on the countries identified.

J ust as Ms. Colazzo's students, citizens acquire and use skills most effectively in the context of solving meaningful problems and performing tasks that they regard as interesting, functional, or important. Skills facilitate knowledge construction by enabling us to locate, analyze, validate, and apply information efficiently. Effective social studies instruction encourages students to both develop and apply skills. It also provides guidelines for when and why it is appropriate to employ the skills (Brophy, 1992).

The Nature of Citizenship Skills

Citizens require a repertoire of competencies (skills) to function effectively in our complex society. Over the years, numerous lists of such skills have been advanced for development throughout the social studies curriculum. For example, all basal social studies textbook programs enumerate the various skills that are embedded in the materials. Typically, such lists sequence the skills in the order they are to be taught in kindergarten through grade 12. They also suggest the relative degrees of emphasis that each type of skill should receive (Jarolimek & Parker, 1993). Equally important to a listing of citizenship skills is the very nature of how those skills are taught. Does the classroom itself provide an example of democracy in action? Are students' voices being heard? How can students learn the skills needed for participating in a democracy if they are not practicing those skills in your classroom (Beane, 1997, 2005)?

Social Skills

Whether one is at home, at school, on the job, or at a party, having good relationships or "getting along" with others requires social skills. Social skills are the glue that binds groups and society harmoniously and productively together as a whole. In whatever we hope to accomplish cooperatively with other individuals, social skills are instrumental in achieving our goals. The recent trend to situation comedies and reality television which embarrass and humiliate participants makes a teacher's efforts to foster good social skills in students all the more important, and difficult. *In-your-face behavior* is unacceptable and teachers must clearly establish what they will and will not accept in the classroom (see Box 7.1).

BOX 7.1   Addressing the Issues: Meeting the Needs of the Reluctant Learners

Beaver Cleaver, a 1950s TV character who was a sincere and model student (though prone to get into scrapes), no longer characterizes the majority of students in our classrooms. Rather, too often we are asked to teach the gang from *South Park*. Little teaching and learning can go on in a disruptive classroom. Clearly, some students choose not to behave or do their work, but others simply do not know how they should act. Many parents spend less and less time with their children. This has resulted in more children being reared by MTV, video games, and sitcoms. Our "in your face" and increasingly violent culture portrayed in the mass media is not what you want brought to your classroom.

Children from unstructured home environments seem to respond best to a highly organized classroom. This is one in which teachers provide specific tasks that carry fairly administered consistent consequences if those tasks are not completed. Instructors are careful to keep transitions short and move the class along at a quick pace. Expectations are high and individual goals that may reasonably be achieved are set for all students. Often individual goal setting is also done between the student and teacher. When students are to begin something new and unfamiliar, the teacher discusses and models behavior that is acceptable for the task. This must be done in a firm manner that leaves no doubt in the students' minds as to what is expected from them. While socially competent students are no longer a given, all students can be instructed how to behave if the classroom is structured, procedures are clear, and the teacher firm, patient, caring, and well organized.

Some teachers find it useful to post one "golden rule" over their doorways. The rule reads: *Each student has the right and responsibility to study and learn without the interference of others.*

If our social environment is rich in positive models and experiences as we mature, we continuously acquire and integrate sets of valuable social skills. Once mastered, such skills are often applied to settings different from the ones in which they were learned. In this fashion, over time, many people manage to assimilate naturally the basic social competencies necessary to navigate successfully through life.

Conflict Resolution Skills

Arguably, one of the most important skills that socially competent citizens in a democratic society have is the ability to resolve conflicts in a nonviolent and socially acceptable manner. Conflicts surround us. In all regions of our nation, youngsters of every age and from every social strata are exposed to conflict in a variety of forms.

Nightly on television, adolescents can view episodes of conflict between parents and among other adults, between ethnic groups or countries, among politicians, and between neighborhood gangs. The alarming national statistics on child abuse and gang deaths also suggest that many students often experience violent conflict firsthand and are themselves the victims of conflict and misplaced aggression. It is the teacher's responsibility to talk about conflict and help students understand that how we respond to conflict is a function of our stage of moral development. Knowing the work of moral development theorists Kohlberg and Gilligan, among others, and being able to share your knowledge of moral development stages with your students helps them better understand how to judge their own views and actions regarding moral dilemmas they may face.

Classroom activities that encourage students to experiment with alternative peaceful ways of resolving conflicts can help prepare them to cope with the larger conflicts that reside within our society. These include helping them to understand the sources of disagreements and confrontations and to work out constructive solutions to their own conflicts. It also includes aiding them in developing, applying, and observing rules.

Approaches to teaching conflict resolution skills should communicate to students that the presence of some conflict is a normal everyday occurrence in a complex, interdependent society and world. Conflicts arise when the goals of individuals or groups clash. The resolution of conflict can be destructive (e.g., a fight or battle) or constructive (e.g., a compromise or a treaty). It is helpful if students can suggest a conflict scenario that might occur in their own school. As they work through the conflict it is important for them to recognize when the conflict is escalating. Discussing how to diffuse the situation is one way to arrive at a solution to the problem.

FIGURE 7.1
Basic Negotiating Skills

- Check whether you understand the other person correctly and whether he or she understands you.

- Tell the other person what you think; don't try to read another's mind or tell others what you think they think.

- Talk about needs, feelings, and interests, instead of restating opposing positions.

- Recognize negotiable conflicts and avoid nonnegotiable ones.

- Know how you tend to deal with most conflicts and recognize others' styles.

- Put yourself in the other's shoes.

- Understand how anger affects your ability to handle conflict and learn how to avoid violence even when you're angry.

- Reframe the issues; talk about them in other ways to find more common ground between yourself and the other person.

- Criticize what people say, rather than who or what they are.

- Seek win-win solutions, not compromises; find solutions where all parties get what they need, rather than solutions where all get some of what they need.

Note. From "Solving Conflicts: Not Just for Children," by Marge Scherer, 1992, *Educational Leadership, 50,* p. 17. Copyright 1992 by Association for Supervision and Curriculum Development. Used with permission. Learn more about ASCD at www.ascd.org.

There are any number of practical programs, guidelines, and strategies to help teachers address conflict resolution. Scherer (1992) has outlined 10 basic negotiating skills that teachers can help students to develop, as shown in Figure 7.1. Another example of an excellent resource is *Teacher, They Called Me a _____!* (Byrnes, 1995). It includes activities appropriate for students that involve conflict themes. *Common Bonds: Anti-Bias Teaching in a Diverse Society* (Byrnes & Kiger, 1996) is instructive in ways to support commonalities among diverse student populations and lessen conflicts. With our nation's tremendous growth in population of culturally diverse individuals it is very important for teachers to address the need for groups to get along and value one another's heritage. Several websites are noted at the end of the chapter. Each is rich in ways to address the issue of conflict resolution. Many schools have instituted peer mediation programs, wherein students are trained to serve as mediators in conflicts.

Research and Analysis Skills

Research and analysis skills are interrelated and often are inseparable in applications. **Research** can be viewed as the process of both locating and finding information in response to some question. It often includes the identification, isolation, and recording of data, consistent with some agreed upon conventions.

Analysis, on the other hand, may be regarded as chiefly the process of examining, verifying, and comparing data to arrive at some conclusion. Analysis also includes reaching a conclusion.

The ability to select appropriate information, record it accurately, and organize it in some accessible fashion constitutes one of the social scientist's most important sets of skills. This ability is also a vital competency for effective citizens, since we all occasionally need to have a complete, correct, and easily accessible account of some event.

For these reasons, social scientists and others often develop common systems for categorizing and reporting information. Some of these are quite elaborate and complicated. Still others may seem strange to students initially, such as the procedures for citing footnotes and bibliographic references. Students should have opportunities to experiment with different conventions used by social scientists for categorizing, recording, and sharing data.

Three subcategories of research and analysis skills that we will examine in more detail are *interpreting and comparing data, analyzing arguments,* and *processing information from pictures.*

Interpreting and Comparing Data

A key aspect of research and analysis is interpreting and comparing data accurately and meaningfully. This skill requires paying careful attention to what is heard, seen, felt, and even tasted or smelled. Data are encountered through all of our senses. We may process these data firsthand through personal encounters, such as attending a concert or a meeting, and also indirectly, as when we read a book that describes a person, place, or event or watch a television show such as *CSI: Crime Scene Investigation.*

Cultural Filters in Interpreting and Comparing Data. Effective processing and interpreting of data requires recognition that each of us also filters what we experience through our individual "lenses," which in turn have been shaped by our experiences and culture, including our gender. We all are familiar with the phenomenon that different individuals processing the same data often focus on different aspects, and as a result, report different accounts of what was experienced. The theories of Kohlberg, authoritarian based, and of Gilligan, authoritative based, are an excellent example of this.

An activity from a social studies text illustrates how students can be helped to develop this recognition of the biases that observers bring to any event they view. As part of tracing the events leading to the end of the Revolutionary War, the authors of the text *The American Nation* (Davidson & Stoff, 1986, p. E8) asked students to compare the views of Washington and Cornwallis concerning the Battle of Yorktown. Through the activity, the students acquire both a skill and further insights into how the long and debilitating war was viewed by both sides.

Students using the text are provided with the excerpts shown in Figure 7.2. They are also given guidelines for comparing points of view and a set of questions that include these:

- What is Cornwallis's view of the events at Yorktown?
- What reason or reasons does Cornwallis give for surrendering?
- What is Washington's view of the events at Yorktown?
- Why did Cornwallis and Washington have different points of view?

The different accounts of the same event by Cornwallis and Washington may be reasonably accurate reports of what each person actually experienced, but they are clearly different. Students should learn to recognize that any single account is not necessarily more accurate, representative, or factual than another. Taken as a whole, however, collective accounts may present a more complete account than any single report.

Interpreting and Comparing Written Materials. In our roles as citizens, we often must process and interpret information from sources such as texts and books, articles, charts, graphs, tables, and pictures. In the social studies, it is especially important that students early on begin to develop the skills to carefully interpret and compare a variety of written materials reflecting different perspectives. It is especially important to identify the perspective of the author. Care must be taken by the teacher when presenting materials that reflect "other" voices in history (Chandler, 2006). Revisionist versions of the norm should be carefully considered.

FIGURE 7.2
Comparing Two Points of View

These two excerpts are from reports on the Battle of Yorktown. Read them carefully. Then, using the guidelines for comparing two points of view in Skill Lesson 8, answer the questions that follow.

Report of Cornwallis to the commander of British forces in America, October 19, 1781.

I have the shameful task to inform your Excellency that I have been forced to surrender the troops under my command to the combined forces of America and France. . . . [Cornwallis then describes how his outnumbered forces were surrounded and attacked by the American and French forces.]

Our numbers had been reduced by the enemy's fire, but particularly by sickness and by the fatigue of constant watching and duty. Under these circumstances, I thought it would have been inhuman to sacrifice the lives of this small body of gallant soldiers by exposing them to an assault [by the enemy] which could not fail to succeed. I therefore proposed to surrender. I enclose the terms of the surrender. I sincerely regret that better could not be obtained, but I have neglected nothing in my power to lessen the misfortune and distress of both officers and soldiers.

Report of Washington to the President of Congress, October 19, 1781.

I have the honor to inform Congress that the defeat of the British army under the command of Lord Cornwallis is most happily achieved. The tireless devotion which moved every officer and soldier in the combined army on this occasion has led to this important event sooner than I had hoped. . . .

I should be lacking in gratitude if I did not mention the very able help of his Excellency the Count de Rochambeau [a French commander] and all his officers. I also feel myself indebted to the Count de Grasse [the French admiral] and the officers of the fleet under his command.

Note. From *The American Nation* by J. Davidson and M. Stoff. © 1986 by Prentice-Hall, Inc. Used by permission. From *The American Nation Teacher's Resource Guide* by J. Davidson and M. Stoff. © 1986 by Prentice-Hall, Inc. Used by permission.

You may want to speak with your mentor, curriculum resource person, or principal to determine how best to introduce and use alternate historical views. These can quickly become flashpoints if your intentions are misinterpreted.

As competent citizens, students need to be able to practice reflective thinking and thereby distinguish fact from opinion, bias from objectivity, reality from fiction, and extraneous from essential information. Students also must be able to differentiate neutral from emotion-laden terms and to consider what is excluded, as well as included, in written material.

Written material often presents students with special problems in making interpretations and comparisons. Frequently this is because they have difficulties with reading in general, an issue previously discussed (Morrell & Rogers, 2006).

Critical interpretation skills are needed when analyzing biographical accounts. Students cannot possibly avoid reading biographies that suffer from flaws, nor should teachers try to prevent them. To attempt to shield students completely from inaccurate or distorted biographical accounts would be both undesirable and unrealistic. Doing so would cut them off from dealing with the same kind of deficiencies that are prevalent in mass media and in everyday experiences they encounter.

As an alternative, teachers can engage students in exercises that involve comparative analyses of biographical accounts. For example, students can be asked to read several biographical accounts of the same person and compare the discrepancies. This can be followed with discussion of questions such as these:

1. What did each of the books say about _____ with respect to the nature of his or her childhood and teenage years, important people in his or her life, educational background, interests and aspirations, and major accomplishments?
2. What things were similar in the books you read?
3. What things were different in the books you read?
4. How would you sum up what you have learned from reading all of the books about _____ 's life?

Interpreting and Comparing Charts, Graphs, and Tables. In our society, much of the information we share with one another is communicated through charts, graphs, and tables. These graphic organizers are plentiful in newspapers and periodicals such as *The New York Times, USA Today, Time, Newsweek*, and *U.S. News & World Report,* as well as student editions of these materials. They also appear in televised newscasts and on news stations' websites. Citizens, journalists, newscasters, and social scientists alike use charts, graphs, and tables to summarize information or to simplify communication. For example, the teacher's lesson may be to have students examine the relationship of gender, education, and earnings over time. One group may be studying the precursor to the boom era of the 1990s, the 1980s. Their group's task is to review the census published in 1991 to chart trends occurring in the 1980s regarding mean money earnings as related to educational attainment and gender. The chart noted in Figure 7.3 is a useful tool to help the group complete the task.

However, for students, extracting facts, generalizations, and hypotheses from charts, graphs, and tables frequently is a difficult task. This is particularly the case when the chart, graph, or table contains many details. It is also problematic if the students are operating on a concrete cognitive level and struggle with abstract reasoning. If abstract reasoning is weak, teachers need to provide direct instruction to guide students in making the connections necessary to fully understand the implication of factual data sets.

In addition to assistance in skillfully interpreting the data of others, students need guidance when they represent their own analyses in the form of charts,

FIGURE 7.3
Mean Money Earnings, by Educational Attainment and Sex, 1990

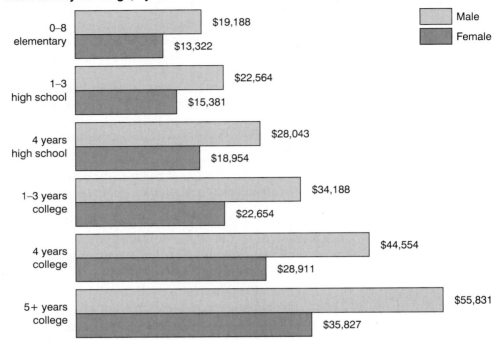

Note. From *Statistical Abstract of the United States: 1992,* (112th edition), (table 713), by U.S. Bureau of the Census, 1991, Washington, DC: Author. Reprinted with permission.

graphs, and tables. They need first to gain competency in handling small, simple sets of data rather than being overwhelmed at the outset. Teachers can help provide natural experiences by incorporating charts, graphs, and tables into all of their lessons and current affairs discussions to help explain a point, answer a question, or frame a problem. Students may also experiment with computer tools to help them represent data in the form of charts, graphs, and tables. An example is the student-constructed pie chart in Figure 7.4.

Using Charts, Tables, and Graphs in Instruction. Charts, graphs, and tables, when accompanied by probing questions and teacher-guided analysis, can serve as springboards to reflective thinking within lessons and units. For example, consider the data in Figure 7.5. A teacher may ask students to use a table such as this for an activity in which groups are looking at changes in life expectancy throughout America's history. She might assign one group the statistics found in the 1990 census reporting the period of 1989–1991. Here it is important for the teacher to add focusing questions that enable the students to use higher order thinking

FIGURE 7.4
Pie Chart Showing Percentages of Time Spent by a Sixth Grader During a 48-Hour Weekend Period

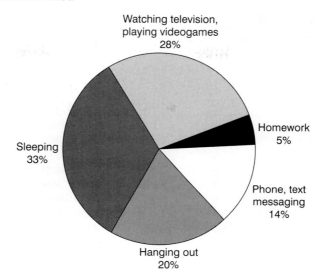

skills. The students may then suggest some hypotheses and generalizations that are based on their study of the data.

1. In which state was life expectancy longest for males? Females?
2. In which state was life expectancy shortest for males? Females?
3. How did the life expectancy of males and females in our state compare with states having the highest and lowest figures? With the national averages for men and women?
4. How do you account for the differences in life expectancies between males and females?
5. How do you account for the differences in life expectancies between the states that have the highest and the lowest figures?
6. Did you find any surprises? Why were you surprised?
7. Based on the information in the table, what can we conclude about the life expectancy of men and women in the late 1980s, early 1990s?

Computer programs such as spreadsheets are essential tools for students to use in analyzing and interpreting data. Students can manipulate the data to show how it can be represented in different forms. As a follow-up activity the teacher might ask the students to research and compare the life expectancy statistics reported in the 1990 census to those of today. Also, the fact that there is no racial distinction in the table of 1989–1991 should be noted and discussed. Students will be interested to find that the Center for Disease Control—Health Statistics reported in 2005 that

FIGURE 7.5
Life Expectancy, by Sex, 1989–91

Where Life Is Longest

The chart shows life expectancy at birth for each state and the District of Columbia, based on a study of death rates from 1989–1991. By that method, the national average was 71.8 years for men and 78.8 for women.

State	Male	Female	State	Male	Female
Alabama	69.6	77.6	Montana	73.1	79.5
Alaska	71.6	78.6	Nebraska	73.6	80.2
Arizona	72.6	79.6	Nevada	71.0	77.8
Arkansas	70.5	78.1	New Hampshire	73.5	80.0
California	72.5	79.2	New Jersey	72.2	78.5
Colorado	73.8	80.0	New Mexico	72.2	79.3
Connecticut	73.6	80.0	New York	70.9	78.3
Delaware	71.6	77.7	North Carolina	70.6	78.3
District of Columbia	62.0	74.2	North Dakota	74.4	81.0
Florida	72.1	79.6	Ohio	72.0	78.5
Georgia	69.7	77.5	Oklahoma	71.6	78.5
Hawaii	75.4	81.3	Oregon	73.2	79.7
Idaho	73.9	80.0	Pennsylvania	71.9	78.7
Illinois	71.3	78.3	Rhode Island	73.0	79.8
Indiana	72.0	78.6	South Carolina	69.6	77.3
Iowa	73.9	80.5	South Dakota	73.2	80.8
Kansas	73.4	80.0	Tennessee	70.4	78.2
Kentucky	70.7	78.0	Texas	71.4	78.9
Louisiana	69.1	77.0	Utah	75.0	80.4
Maine	73.0	79.6	Vermont	73.3	79.7
Maryland	71.3	78.1	Virginia	71.8	78.6
Massachusetts	73.3	79.8	Washington	73.8	79.7
Michigan	71.7	78.2	West Virginia	70.5	77.9
Minnesota	74.5	80.9	Wisconsin	73.6	80.0
Mississippi	68.9	77.1	Wyoming	73.2	79.3
Missouri	71.5	78.8			

Note. From Table H, page 10, U.S. decennial life tables for 1989–1991, Vol. 1, no. 3, some trends and comparisons of United States life table data: 1900–91. National Center for Health Statistics, Hyattsville, Maryland, 1991.

life expectancy has gone up and the gender gap has narrowed (CDC, 2005). This report corrects the omission of statistics for African Americans and includes a comparative racial and gender study that finds that life expectancy for white males is 75.4 years, black males is 69.2 years, white females is 80.5 years, and black females is 76.1 years. A teacher would be remiss not to ask students to speculate about why there exists a life expectancy difference among genders and races.

Analyzing Arguments

Whether presented in written or oral form, arguments often suffer from bias, distortion, and faulty logic. The ability to detect these elements in argumentation is critical to effective citizenship. Developing these skills requires continuous practice and application in the context of the research and analysis of subject matter. It also involves wide exposure to bias and distortion in all its forms, including that in the mass media, arguments of respected figures and demagogues alike, and even textbooks.

Detecting Bias and Distortion. It is far more effective for students to encounter bias and distortion in their daily life, rather than in an abstracted or edited form that typically appears in student texts. This suggests that a social studies classroom should be a forum for a wide array of materials from a diverse assortment of individuals and groups. Students should be encouraged to share cases of bias and distortion that they have encountered in materials. If the assortment of such materials collected is rich in examples, it may evoke controversy and even possible criticism, unless the purpose for its presence is clearly established. The teacher needs to make clear at the outset and reiterate periodically that *in no way does the presence of material illustrating bias and distortion imply either endorsement of its content or authors and sponsors.* It is necessary to establish some ground rules, consistent with school policies, concerning the types of materials that must be excluded and under what circumstances (e.g., pornographic material, racial hate literature in an emotionally charged multiracial class). This is a very slippery slope for teachers. Use great caution when selecting and displaying examples. This also pertains to guest speakers you might have address your students. Ideally, you will have heard the speaker so you will know exactly what is to be said. If this is not the case, at the very least you must establish ground rules about what can and cannot be said and shown. Should the speaker step over the line you must tactfully bring the presentation to a close.

Logical Reasoning. Arguments that are free from bias and distortion nonetheless may be flawed in their reasoning. Helping students detect errors in reasoning requires some work with logic. This in turn demands translating assertions and arguments into some form where they can be analyzed. One such form is a syllogism. **Syllogisms** are statements arranged in the following order:

All men and women are mortal.

Catherine is a woman.

Therefore, Catherine is mortal.

Casting Arguments in the Form of Syllogisms. Although most assertions and arguments do not appear neatly in a syllogistic form, they often can be recast with minor revisions and reorganization. Consider this hypothetical conversation between Harry and Sarah, 11th graders who have just read the proposed changes in upper-class lunchtime operations:

Harry: What are those sly seniors up to? They've just advocated the upper class be allowed to leave campus for lunch.

Sarah: Yeah? So what's the problem with that?

Harry: You know the seniors can never be trusted.

Sarah: You mean if they're pushing upper-class lunchtime privilege, there must be something wrong with it?

Harry: You got it.

Sarah: I see your point.

Organized as a syllogism, the argument mutually advanced by Sarah and Harry appears as follows:

If seniors support an action, something must be wrong with it.

They support the upper-class leaving campus for lunch.

Therefore, something must be wrong with the new lunch plan that they advocate.

In this case the *major premise,* the first statement in the syllogism, was inferred but never actually stated in the conversation—a frequent occurrence in discussions. When confronted with the inferred premise, Harry and Sarah likely would disavow it, since the seniors support many things with which they would find nothing wrong. If one were to accept the unstated major premise of the argument, it *would* logically follow that there must be something wrong with the upper class being allowed to leave campus at lunchtime. Thus, this example also illustrates how a logically *valid* argument can result from a premise that is *false.*

Testing the Validity of Syllogisms. One way that students can be helped to determine whether an argument is valid (i.e., the conclusion follows from the major premise) or invalid is through the use of circle diagrams. The one shown in Figure 7.6 diagrams the first syllogism that we presented. It demonstrates that the circle representing "Catherine" *must* be placed within the largest circle representing "Mortal People," since she has been placed within the circle "Men and Women."

The circle diagram shown in Figure 7.7 similarly illustrates how the circles can be used to uncover *invalid* arguments. For example:

All mechanical things are made by people and computers.

Airplanes are made by people and computers.

Airplanes, therefore, are mechanical things.

Since "Airplanes" may be placed *anywhere* within the circle "Things Made by People and Computers," it need not follow that they are one of the "Mechanical Things."

Programs to Develop Logical Reasoning Skills. Providing students with appropriate experiences involving logical reasoning extends beyond analyzing deductive arguments. The acquisition of such skills is a complex process that occurs slowly

FIGURE 7.6
Circle Diagram Showing Argument Is Logically Valid

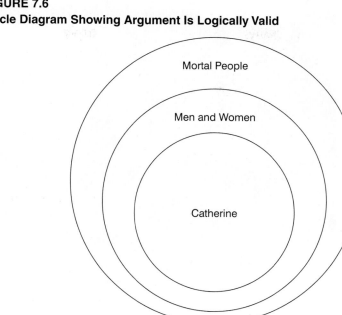

FIGURE 7.7
Circle Diagram Showing Argument Is Logically Invalid

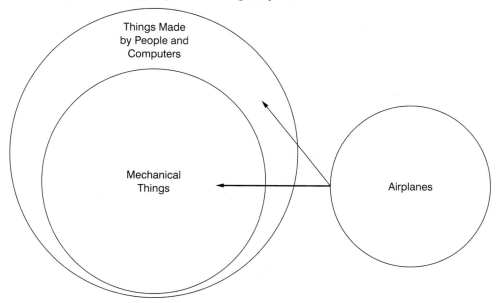

Preparing and conducting debates aids students in developing and applying reasoning skills.

over time. Further, stage theorists argue that these skills are related at least in part to the developmental level of the students (Cole & Cole, 1989; Santrock, 2008).

Social studies teachers must be skilled in differentiated instruction. Good comprehensive programs offer a wide range of instructional strategies and activities to teach skills to youngsters across all ages and developmental abilities. One such tried and true program, *Philosophy for Children,* has been developed by the Institute for the Advancement of Philosophy for Children (*Philosophy for Children,* 1987). The program includes materials for students in elementary, middle, and secondary grades. Some of the skills that the program attempts to develop include the following:

- Classifying and categorizing
- Defining terms
- Drawing inferences from premises
- Finding underlying assumptions
- Formulating causal explanations
- Searching for informal fallacies
- Predicting consequences
- Working with contradiction
- Identifying and using criteria

Howard Gardner's (2007) most recent work, *Five Minds for the Future,* emphasizes the need for citizens living at a time of great change and information overload to be able to develop ways of thinking that lead to timely decisions regarding both expected and unanticipated events. The comprehension skills noted above would certainly be foundational for Gardner's five minds. Consider the five minds and the need for each if one is to become a well-informed and proactive citizen of the 21st century:

- Disciplinary—Mastery of major schools of thought (including science, mathematics, history) and of at least one professional craft.
- Synthesizing—Ability to integrate ideas from different disciplines or spheres into a coherent whole and to communicate that integration to others.
- Creating—Capacity to uncover and clarify new problems, questions, and phenomena.
- Respectful—Awareness of and appreciation for differences among human beings.
- Ethical—Fulfillment of one's responsibilities as a worker and as a citizen (Gardner, pp. 1–6).

Processing Information from Pictures

Pictures represent a form of data that must be processed in order to extract meaning from them. Some of the most interesting teaching materials in the social studies are pictures or pictorial print materials. Visual materials can enrich and enliven instruction. Research data also suggest that imagery facilitates learning, especially with regard to visual learners (Gardner, 1993; Sommer, 1978; Wittrock & Goldberg, 1975; Santrock, 2008).

Types of Pictures. Teachers use many different types of pictures in teaching. Five types common to social studies instruction are noted here:

- Informational pictures
- Tell-a-story pictures
- Open-ended pictures
- Expressive pictures
- Political cartoons and propaganda posters

Many pictures, such as one showing mountains or the Washington Monument, appear to be self-explanatory and *informational*. Some help students see relationships or *tell a story*. Others are more *open ended,* permitting different viewers to read many varied interpretations of what is being communicated. These types of pictures can serve as springboards for discussion of issues.

Still other photos are *expressive*; they portray human emotions or arouse them in the viewer. Shots of starving people, war-ravaged areas, and little children are examples of expressive pictures. An additional type of picture, often containing a caption, makes a social or political statement and is typically characterized as a political cartoon.

Whether still or moving, photos can offer powerful examples of situations that exist in the world that students are unlikely to experience themselves. Often films depicting another time and/or culture, high interest for media-savvy teens, are the closest thing to an actual experience that students can have. Feature films and documentaries must be carefully prescreened to be sure that school policy is not violated. Films can be edited for appropriate use and wrapped into fact-finding and discussion sessions; in that way they can provide a meaningful cultural learning experience for your classroom. The beauty of the experience is that you are able to encourage a guided discussion and help students develop critical viewing skills that enable them to see other cultures as unique and not simply different (Vanden, 2007).

This would be an excellent opportunity to encourage you to flex your curriculum integration skills and consider using works of art in your social studies curriculum. Artists and their work enable you to read a culture, better understand the historical moment in which that piece was created, and understand the values the work represents (Stevens & Fogel, 2007). For example, during a repression when criticism of a government is unacceptable, it is often a country's artists who demonstrate their civil disobedience through subtleties that are painted, composed, built, etc., into the arts. It is your job to be aware of signals that the art is sending and thus better understand the historical significance of the art (Smith, 2007). World-class art museums as well as state art museums have websites with photos of collection items posted online that may be downloaded and used. Multiple intelligences theory tells us that we are all artists. Art may be the hook that reaches that nontraditional learner as well as offering you a chance to explore other means of teaching your social studies curriculum (Moore, 2007).

Using Political Cartoons in Instruction. Political cartoons and propaganda posters are visual forms that can be especially effective for dramatizing an issue in social studies instruction. However, they are often difficult for students to process (Steinbrink & Bliss, 1988), because they frequently embed complex concepts, require considerable prior knowledge, and employ visual metaphors.

Heitzman (1988, 2002) has provided a comprehensive annotated list of sources of political cartoons for use in the classroom as well as advice for teaching about elections with political cartoons. The cartoon by Auth shown in Figure 7.8, for example, encapsulates the rich irony that accompanies the cruel and endless tragedy of religious warfare in Lebanon. Sadly, it is as current today as it was in the early 1970s when it was drawn. The following questions could be used to process this and (with slight revisions) similar political cartoons or propaganda posters:

1. What do you see in the picture?
2. What does each of the figures and items in the picture stand for?
3. What is the issue that is represented in the picture?
4. What do you think the artist thought of each of the figures in the picture?
5. What would be an appropriate caption for the cartoon/poster?

FIGURE 7.8
Political Cartoon

Note. Cartoon from BEHIND THE LINES by Tony Auth. Copyright © 1975, 1976, 1977 by Tony Auth. Copyright © 1971, 1972, 1973, 1974, 1975 by *The Philadelphia Inquirer.* Reprinted by permission of Houghton Mifflin Company. All rights reserved.

Chronology Skills

Much of what we typically do both in our daily lives and in social studies classes involves *chronology*, some understanding of how people, places, items, and events are oriented in time. As adults, we are comfortable with related time concepts such as "a long time ago," "recently," "in the past," and "infinity." From a very young child's perspective, a basic concept of time involves understanding which items came first, which came last, and what typically happens as the result of the passage of units we call hours, days, weeks, months, or years.

For middle and secondary school students, chronology competencies evolve to include an understanding of the interrelationship of events and individuals over a temporal period. They also include a sense of what is meant by a unit such as a century. Eventually, it includes an understanding of the abstractness and arbitrariness of all units of time, whether they are measured in nanoseconds (billionths of a second), eons, or some new standard.

Comparative Conceptions of Time

In each society, the larger culture and various subcultures shape the ways in which individuals both conceive of time and respond to its passage. Thus, a Bostonian may come to characterize the pace of life in rural South Carolina as "slow" and that of Manhattan as "fast." On an international scale, this generalization means that diverse nations often view the past, present, and future in different terms.

On a planetary scale, different views of time are also possible. Hawking (1988), in *A Brief History of Time,* points out that contemporary physicists' perspectives on time in space are quite different from those people on Earth use to guide their daily lives:

> Consider a pair of twins. Suppose that one twin goes to live on the top of a mountain while the other stays at sea level. The first twin would age faster than the second. Thus, if they meet again, one would be older than the other. In this case, the difference in ages would be very small, but it would be much larger if one of the twins went for a long trip in a spaceship at nearly the speed of light. When he returned, he would be much younger than the one who stayed on Earth. This is known as the twins paradox, but it is a paradox only if one has the idea of absolute time at the back of one's mind. In the theory of relativity there is no unique absolute time, but instead each individual has his own personal measure of time that depends on where he is and how he is moving. (p. 33)

Recording Events on Time Lines

Activities that require students to arrange and view people, places, objects, and events as occurring in sequence—such as time lines—help to establish the perspective of chronology. Time lines provide a simple system for listing, ordering, and comparing events over some period. They function as a summary statement of a series of events. Also, they can represent a schema of how an individual has organized data into a meaningful chronological pattern.

Time lines may be horizontal or vertical. Also, any unit of time may be used, ranging from a day to centuries. Similarly, any context or theme may be the basis for a time line, for instance: "What I did today in the order I did it" or "The chronology of constitutional amendments."

Time lines function cognitively in several ways. Completed ones provide students with a summary of information concerning a series of occurrences over time. When students themselves construct time lines, they must first compare events and then structure them in a meaningful pattern.

To illustrate the differences in the two applications, consider the simple time line shown in Figure 7.9 that summarizes for a reader some major events over two decades. Processing the figure requires only that the reader *note* the order of events. Parallel time lines are effective ways for students to examine what is happening at the same time in different countries or on different world

FIGURE 7.9
Simple Time Line

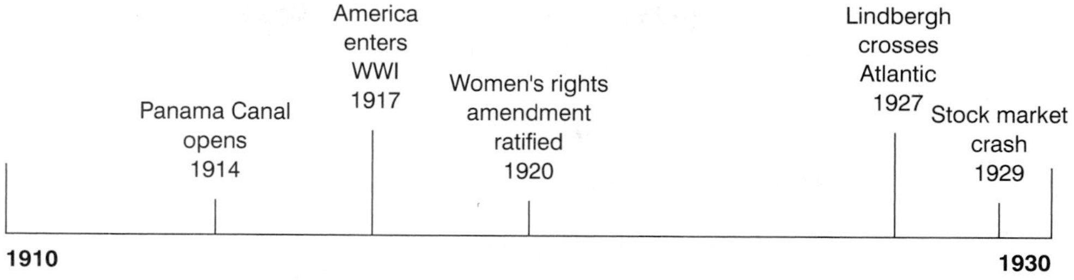

stages. Figure 7.9 could take on added significance if a parallel time line was included.

Alternately, consider a task that calls for you to *create* a time line. For example, begin by placing in the correct order of occurrence the following events: President Nixon's visit to China, the end of the Vietnam War, the first flight of the Wright brothers, the beginning of the Civil War, the assassination of President Kennedy, the invention of xerography, and the premiere of *Gone with the Wind*.

Compare your sequence with the following, arranged in ascending chronological order:

- The beginning of the Civil War
- The first flight of the Wright brothers
- The premiere of *Gone with the Wind*
- The invention of xerography
- The assassination of President Kennedy
- President Nixon's visit to China
- The end of the Vietnam War

Often time lines can be used to illustrate *causal relationships*, as well as temporal sequences. Genealogies are examples of such applications. To view a time line that addresses the changes in education over time, go to **www.ncsu.edu/chass/extension/ci** and click on "education time line." Educational eras are placed in an historic context. Here the parallel time line notations show simultaneous change on international, national, and local levels. Commercial time lines are readily available. Excellent examples may be found at Tom Snyder's site. Go to **www.teachtsp.com** for his Timeliners.

Spatial Skills

In an increasingly interdependent nation and world, citizens have greater need than ever before for skills that can better orient them in space. Competent citizens must be able to locate themselves and others spatially in order to travel, exchange ideas, and access artifacts. Spatial skills most often appear in social studies in the discipline of geography, but they are distributed throughout all areas of the curriculum. Identifying political boundaries, the locations of cities, landmarks, and land masses and determining the relationship of one object in space to another are all part of spatial understanding.

The Impact of Spatial Perspectives

Citizens also need to become more aware of how our spatial perspectives and vocabularies influence many of our social, political, and economic perspectives. Whether we view something as far away, densely populated, or growing, for example, may affect whether we decide to visit a region, seek a job there, or change our residence. Even the language we use in describing an area can skew our perspective. Collins (n.d.) has noted, for example, "Terms we select to describe other nations—and the present state of their social, economic, political development—influence students' perception of those nations."

As an illustration, for years Africa was characterized by teachers and texts as "the dark continent," creating a host of negative associations. Further, unlike most other regions of the world, the continent, rather than the nations within it, was studied as a whole, creating the misperception that there was a high degree of uniformity among all Africans. Some even thought Africa, the continent, was a country!

Using and Creating Maps in Instruction

The most common ways that individuals use to orient themselves spatially are through the application of existing maps and the creation of new ones. To a lesser extent, individuals reference globes. Maps and globes represent some region on the Earth. They do so, however, with varying degrees of distortion.

Map and Globe Distortions. Students should be sensitized to the relevant distortion and measurement issues associated with different projections. In representing regions on the Earth, maps and globes do so with varying degrees of distortion. Since the creation of the first maps, nations have often deliberately distorted the maps they used for political purposes. They have done this, among other ways, by extending or reshaping boundaries and rerouting rivers, as suits their interpretation of historical claims. Apart from those deliberate distortions, all projections of areas on the Earth's surface are functionally distorted in some ways because of the problem of translating a curved surface to a flat one.

In 1988 the National Geographic Society adopted the **Robinson projection** (Figure 7.10) as one that produced the least distortion for most nonspecialized map

FIGURE 7.10
A Robinson Projection

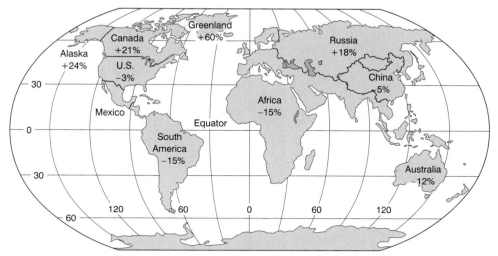

FIGURE 7.11
A Van der Grinten Projection

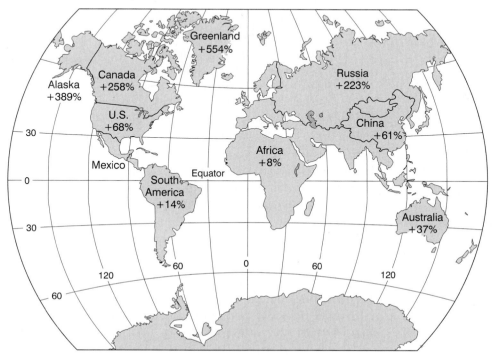

applications. It is compared with the traditional **Van der Grinten projection**, shown in Figure 7.11, that the Society had used since 1922 for most of its world maps.

Note the differences in the sizes and shapes of Greenland and the United States shown in each of the projections. Because of its location on the Earth, given seven different projections, the shape and size of Greenland will be different in each of them. Even in the Robinson projection shown in Figure 7.10, Greenland is still 60% larger than it should be. In the Van der Grinten projection, it is 554% larger.

Integrating Maps and Globes into All Social Studies Instruction

Jarolimek and Parker (1993) have suggested that maps can furnish eight basic types of information:

1. *Land and water forms:* Continents, oceans, bays, peninsulas, islands, straits

2. *Relief features:* Plains, mountains, rivers, deserts, plateaus, swamps, valleys

3. *Direction and distance:* Cardinal directions, distance in miles or kilometers and relative distance, scale

4. *Social data:* Population density, size of communities, location of major cities, relationship of social data to other factors

5. *Economic information:* Industrial and agricultural production, soil fertility, trade factors, location of industries

6. *Political information:* Political divisions, boundaries, capitals, territorial possessions, types of government, political parties

7. *Scientific information:* Locations of discoveries, ocean currents, location of mineral and ore deposits, geological formations, air movements

8. *Human factors:* Cities, canals, railroads, highways, coaxial and fiber-optic cables, telephone lines, bridges, dams, nuclear power plants. (p. 174)

Ideally, maps and globes should be an integral part of all social studies instruction. As they examine issues for which spatial perspectives would be instructive, students should be introduced to the wide range of maps and globes that exist. Teachers should also combine the development of spatial skills with others.

An example of a lesson that integrates spatial, research, and analysis skills is provided in Appendix C, Resource Figure 7.1. The issue that the lesson centers upon is: What special problems do landlocked nations face?

Students should also learn about the diverse types of questions that maps and globes can help answer. One of the most natural and functional ways to integrate maps and globes continuously into daily social studies instruction is to use them to answer important questions with spatial implications that the teacher or students generate while studying a subject.

Teachers should also help students recognize that, although one type of map or globe may suffice to answer a particular question, it may not be suitable for another. Apart from the traditional spatial questions of "How do I get from here to there?" or "Where is this place located?" maps and globes can help answer questions such as "What are the most promising areas in the United States to open businesses that cater to senior citizens?" or "Where in the world are most of the followers of the major religions?"

Dr. Lori Holcomb, a North Carolina State University professor and noted expert in teaching using technology integration, shares her views on our "Not so flat, but maybe it is?" world in the following Addressing the Issues commentary.

Identifying and Using Reference Sources in Developing Skills

Acquiring social, research and analysis, chronological, and spatial skills requires students to use a variety of reference sources. Virtually anything, including an individual, may serve as a reference for a particular question or problem.

Electronic reference sources, such as electronic card catalogs and databases, are widely used in many schools. Encyclopedias and collections of assorted reference works once housed only on library shelves are available on a single CD-ROM or on the Web. With so much information readily accessible through the Internet, it is even more important for students to have highly developed sophisticated citizenship skills. In a later chapter we will consider electronic reference sources in more detail.

Even though we are in the 21st century, teachers cannot be sure that all of their students have access to even the most basic of hard copy reference materials. In addition, the technology superhighway has not found its way to all schools and homes in our nation, so teachers cannot assume that all of their students have computers and Internet access. In areas of poverty and need the local library still fills the need for reference materials. Library skills are important and teachers must still teach the most basic of reference skills as well as how to find what is needed. Where computer-based references are used, technology skills are also required. A sampling of useful websites is noted in Appendix C, Resource Figure 7.2.

The notion that many sources can and should be considered as appropriate reference possibilities is an important one for students to learn. Similarly, they should understand that the basic criterion for judging the value of a reference work is "How useful and authoritative is it for solving a problem or answering a question?"

Sample Reference Works for Social Studies

Are your classroom reference cupboards bare and your technology resources slim? Is there only occasionally money for library or classroom purchases? Have you have been asked to suggest some "must have" materials? Here are some of the "low tech" print reference works that both teachers and students have found to be useful:

- *Album of American History.* This multivolume history of the United States is composed of pictures arranged chronologically.
- *Dictionary of American Biography.* This is a multivolume source of information on nonliving Americans who have made some significant contribution to American life. Included are politicians, artists, musicians, writers, scientists, educators, and many other types.
- *Dictionary of American History.* This multivolume work is arranged alphabetically and includes articles on a variety of historical topics, some famous and some not so well known.
- *Goode's World Atlas.* This is an authoritative and comprehensive atlas of the world.
- *The Illustrated History of the World and Its People.* In 30 volumes, a wealth of information is presented on the geography, people, history, arts, culture, and literature of individual countries of the world. There is also information on such topics as foods, religions, dress, holidays, festivals, customs, and educational systems of the countries.
- *Statesman's Yearbook.* A succinct thumbnail sketch of each country is provided in one volume.
- *The Story of America: A National Geographic Picture Atlas.* An extensive collection of visual, spatial, and narrative data on each of the states.
- *The Timetables of History.* In a chronologically organized single volume, a wide variety of important dates are included, covering seven major categories of American life. (online)
- *Worldmark Encyclopedia of the Nations.* This multivolume guide to nations is arranged alphabetically by the name of the country and provides basic information on each country's social, political, historical, economic, and geographical features.

Activities for Introducing Reference Materials

One way to introduce reference materials in a meaningful context is to create interesting, puzzling, or intriguing questions for students that require them to use such sources. The difficulty of the questions may be varied for different age and ability groups by providing more or fewer, obvious or subtle clues. The actual reference resources to be used in answering the questions may be made available within the classroom. As alternatives, students may be given a list of helpful reference materials or be allowed to use the school library to identify resources on their own.

Dr. Lori Holcomb,
North Carolina State University

Up until the 15th century, it was believed that the world was flat. In fact, many believed that the world was a flat disc that floated in the ocean. This "truth" was debunked when Columbus and his crew sailed west to find the East. However, the fear of sailing off the edge of the earth into oblivion almost caused Columbus's crew to mutiny and abandon the quest. The discoveries of the new world eventually lead to the belief that the world is in fact spherical.

Yet, despite all of the astronomical, mathematical, and geographical evidence that supports the world is in fact round, some are now reintroducing the argument that the world is flat. In the widely popular book by Thomas Friedman (2005), the notion of a flat world was introduced and argued. Living in a flat world means that people worldwide are equally able to collaborate, communicate, and compete. Advances in technology are connecting the world in ways never before possible. Boundaries and barriers for teaching and learning are quickly changing and disappearing due to the inclusion of technology.

So what does this all mean for teaching social studies in middle and secondary schools? It means that teachers and students have both the access and the opportunity to utilize technologies that will allow for learning to occur beyond the four walls of the classroom. It also means that the skills and tools that students will need to be competitive in a flat world are changing. Students will need to be able to locate information more readily and from a wider array of sources. Further, students will need to possess a knowledge base that goes beyond the classroom and the United States. Students will need to have a greater understanding for the world and how to be part of the global market. From an educational standpoint, in a flat world all aspects of the world are connected. A flat world also supports and fosters collaboration, self-directed learning, and problem-based learning. The following sections will highlight how a flat world ties in with a social studies curricula and framework.

Perhaps one of the greatest assets that technology offers is the access to an unlimited and wide array of information. In a flat world, documents, records, and collections are now readily available through national and international archives. On the United States' National Archive site (**http://www.archives.gov/**), students have access to a multitude of information and tools, including viewing the Charters of Freedom (Declaration of Independence, Constitution of the United States, and the Bill of Rights); tracing and researching family lineages; as well as reading the official text of public and private laws. Teaching with primary documents encourages and supports a varied learning environment for teachers and students. Primary documents also provide students with the opportunity to explore, research, analyze, and discuss key events in history. Students can work either independently or collaboratively. They can research topics such as the development of the industrialization of the United States using an array or primary documents. For example, they can trace the development of inventions critical to the industrial revolution as they view Thomas Edison's patent for the electric lamp or Alexander Graham Bell's patent for the telephone. Students could also use Edison's and Graham's patents as springboards for developing their own patents. Numerous educational possibilities exist. However, primary documents are not limited to the United States. International archives allow students to view and explore primary documents pertaining to wars, such as the Treaty of

Versailles. Historical artifacts are now readily available for students to use as they study and learn pivotal times in world history. Students across the world now have equal access to important historical archives.

The emergence of new technologies, such as Google Earth, have redefined teaching and learning. Google Earth (**http://earth.google.com/**) contains highly informative, multimedia-enhanced data about various places around the planet, overlaid on Google Earth imagery. Google Earth allows you to visit the far reaches of the world without leaving the classroom. Users can explore the magnificent pyramids of Egypt, view the Eiffel Tower, or travel along the Amazon River. Rather than reading and viewing two-dimensional text books, Google Earth allows students to view three-dimensional images. Through partnerships with other organizations, users can not only see high-resolution satellite imagery, but also read detailed information from various sources. As an educational tool, Google Earth can be utilized to address global concerns. For example, students can visit the Jane Goodall Institute to explore the Gombe National Park in Tanzania and track the chimpanzees. This activity not only allows students to learn more about chimpanzees and their behaviors, but also provides them with the opportunity to study different habitats. Further, over time, students can also document the impact of deforestation on the chimpanzee population. This in turn can serve as the foundation for discussions on global citizenship. Another option is to use the Google Earth overlay created by the United Nations Environmental Program. This overlay includes successive time-stamped images illustrating 100 areas of extreme environmental degradation around the world. Students can observe the before and after images of the deforestation of the Amazon and discuss the impact on the environment. Through this partnership, students can research and discuss the impact human growth and development has had on the world.

Subsequently, students could then strategize how to reverse the damaging effects of deforestation. Google Earth not only provides students with detailed information, but also serves as a venue for problem-based learning.

Similar to the notion of Google Earth, students can now visit and tour museums and art galleries around the world while still seated in the classroom. This allows students to study, critique, and connect art to various time periods and cultural influences. The Hermitage in St. Petersburg, Russia, offers a virtual tour of the museum allowing users to view its magnificent collections. This virtual tour provides insight into the tsars of Russia while also documenting the development of world culture and art from the Stone Age to the 20th century. Students are able to view firsthand how art reflected social and political eras across centuries. The Louvre Museum in France also offers virtual tours of its exhibits and paintings, where users can explore thematic trails designed to investigate a particular theme, movement, or period in depth. For example, there is a thematic trail for Alexander the Great. From this trail, students can learn about him via the collections of the Greek, Etruscan, and Roman antiquities departments. Throughout the thematic tour, each piece of art is carefully described including the relevance and importance that piece has toward understanding Peter the Great over the course of his life span. Virtual tours such as these afford students access to artifacts and important pieces of art that otherwise would not be available to them.

As we continue into the 21st century, it is becoming more and more evident that the world in which we live is flat. Advancements in technology have flattened the world, allowing for educational boundaries to disappear. In this flattened world, teachers and students now have access to a wealth of resources and information that are being utilized to transform education. Social studies education is poised to benefit greatly from a flattened world.

FIGURE 7.12
Problem Sheet

Problem Sheet

Directions: You are to discover the identity of Country X, a real country, described below. Use any reference sources that you wish. The ones that have been identified for you may be especially helpful. After you have discovered which country it is, list all of the references you consulted. Then tell whether each of the references helped you learn the identity of the country and in which way.

Data on Country X:

Country X

Country X differs from many other nations in several ways. It covers an area of 600,000 square miles with approximately 2,000,000 people. It is one huge plateau with the eastern half consisting mainly of plains with some mountains, while the western half is largely mountainous with some plains. Hundreds of lakes exist throughout the country, especially in the mountains, and in the hilly and mountainous regions, there are forests.

   In climate, Country X suffers from cold winds that sweep across the treeless plains and from great temperature extremes. For example, the temperature has risen to 105°F in the summer and to −50°F in the winter. Though there are many fish, the people have not really cultivated a taste for them, and exist chiefly on their livestock products and game.

Identity of Country X:
Reference sources used to determine identity:
Which were useful and in which way:

One type of activity that can be used to introduce reference materials in the context of solving interesting problems is a Problem Sheet. Consider the activity in Figure 7.12.

The Problem Sheet could contain some additional information that would make the solution easier. For example, the following additional pieces of data could be inserted into the paragraphs of the original description to give students more clues. These would make it easier to limit the list of countries that could match the description.

- There are about 2 people per sq. km. in the country. (2.8 million people, 1.5 million sq. km)
- One-third of the country is a desert, but only a small part of it is sandy. There is sufficient vegetation in the desert to support the feeding of camels and horses. Arable land is 1%.
- The lack of abundant raw materials and suitable transportation systems restricts industrial growth.
- The major occupation of the country is herding/agriculture (42%), though some small-scale industries have been started.

- The people of the country are largely nomadic, customarily dress in long flowing robes called *dels*, and live in canvas huts called *yurts*. This lifestyle is being eroded.
- There are no major ports or harbors because the country is landlocked and sandwiched between Russia and China. (Save this question until all are unable to find the answer. It is a giveaway.)

The country, by the way, is Mongolia. Any similar set of data that presents a puzzle or problem—whether it deals with a country, a city, an event, or an individual—can satisfy the same objective. The aim is to have students discover the functional value of reference sources through an interesting and challenging activity.

SUMMARY

In this information age it is not critical that students be reservoirs of facts and figures. Reference material is as close as a computer and can be accessed with the click of a mouse. What is important is for students to be able to discriminate among sources of credible information. Teachers must help students to understand how to use research and analysis skills and then interpret and compare the data that they have found. Chronology skills such as time lines give facts a frame of reference or context in which to be interpreted. Maps and globes provide the ultimate context by which to understand the relative and absolute location of geographic terms. When interpreting what a map is trying to tell us, it is important to use critical-thinking skills to note any subjective information that is being presented.

The development of the skills and competencies noted in this chapter are critical for students to become knowledgeable citizens of the world. This chapter has helped you to understand the importance of the skills that are needed to access and interpret the information needed by all citizens, especially those upon whom the nation's future depends.

ACTIVITIES

1. Locate five political cartoons. In your group, discuss how each might be used as a springboard for discussion in a secondary and/or middle school class.
2. Select a topic and create a Problem Sheet for a seventh-grade class. Use a real country, city, or person as the subject. Also, create a list of clues similar to those in the text that could be used to help students identify the subject. Try out the Problem Sheet with the members of the group and discuss age-specific possible modifications.
3. Locate instances of bias or distortion in reporting an event as they appear in several different newspapers or magazines. Explain how such materials might be analyzed in a middle-grade social studies class.

4. Develop a collection of different types of maps (either originals or copies) that could be used with middle grades and secondary students. To locate them, consult newspapers *(USA Today)* and periodicals, as well as reference works. For each map, list the types of questions that the map answers.

5. Examine a collection of different maps and identify the map symbols they employ. From them, construct a poster appropriate for grades 5 through 8 that includes an assortment of map symbols. Next to each symbol, place the name of the object that the symbol represents.

6. Develop a collection of different types of tables, charts, and graphs that deal with issues suitable for discussion with students in grades 9 through 12. To locate the materials, consult newspapers and periodicals, as well as library reference works and the Internet. For each table, chart, and graph, list the types of questions that it could answer. Also, indicate how each item might be used as a springboard for discussion with students.

7. Develop an activity for engaging students in grades 5 through 8 in mapping some spatial area such as their neighborhood. Field-test the activity with a group of five students for whom it is appropriate. Indicate the school and grade level of the students, provide copies of their maps, and describe and evaluate the results.

WEB RESOURCES

TechLINK

Teachers' Guide to Teaching with Political Cartoons: **www.education-world.com/a_curr/curr210.shtml**

America Memory's Learning Page: **http://memory.loc.gov/ammem/ndlpedu/index.html**

Newspapers in Education: **http://nieonline.com/**

High Beam Encyclopedia: **www.encyclopedia.com/**

Ibiblio: **www.ibiblio.org**

Mapping: **www.nationalatlas.gov, www.usgs.gov**

Conflict resolution: **www.teach-nology.com, www.peacegames.org, www.bam.gov/sub_yourself_conflict.html, www.kidsdhealth.org/teen/question/emotions/deal_with_anger.html**

Philosophy for Children: **www.cehs.montclair.edu/academic/iapc**

News for Students: **www.pbs.org/newshour/extra**

World Events from the United Nations: **www.un.org.News,**

Amnesty International: **www.amnsety.org**

UNICEF: **www.unicef.org/index.html**

U.S. Geological Survey: **www.interactive2.usgs.gov/learningweb/fun/map.asp**

Chapter 8

Social Concern in a Globally and Culturally Diverse World

Social Concern and Citizenship Education

The Morally Mature Citizen

The Dimensions of Concern

The Nature of Beliefs, Attitudes, and Values

Instructional Strategies for Examining Beliefs, Attitudes, and Values

Self-Concept Activities

Social Issues as a Curricular Focus

Curricular Framework for Analyzing Social Issues in the Classroom

Global Education in an Interconnected World

Peace Education

Multicultural Education

Issues in Multicultural Education

Designing Strategies for Multicultural Education

Guidelines for Selecting Appropriate Curriculum Materials for
Multicultural Education

Gender Issues in Multicultural Education

Current Affairs

Strategies for Analyzing Current Affairs

Teacher Positions on Controversial Issues

Summary

Activities

Web Resources

Mr. Williams wanted to go beyond the typical immigration unit he usually taught in his 11th-grade U.S. history class. This year, instead of starting with Ellis Island and the Age of Immigration, he asked his students to start with their personal immigration accounts.

Each student was asked to interview family members and conduct outside research to trace their own personal family immigration story. For some students in Mr. Williams's class, this meant learning about life as an indentured servant during the colonial era. For other students, it meant interviewing their parents about recently leaving their homeland and coming to America.

The students presented their findings as poetry, drama, digital video movies, songs, and collages. Mr. Williams then asked the students to identify themes

throughout the variety of personal immigration stories. From these themes, he and the students engaged in a lively discussion about immigration policy and legislation throughout U.S. history. Following the discussion, students were asked to establish personal priorities based on ethical decisions related to immigration.

Engle (1977) wrote, "A good citizen has many facts at his command, but more he has arrived at some tenable conclusions about public and social affairs. He has achieved a store of sound and socially responsible beliefs and convictions. His beliefs and convictions are sound and responsible because he has had the opportunity to test them against facts and values" (p. 2).

We characterize individuals of the type that Engle described as *concerned citizens*. The citizens are cognizant of and responsive in an informed manner to the larger social world around them. Their concern extends beyond local and personal issues to those at the regional, national, and international levels that affect the destinies of all humankind.

Concerned citizens also establish personal priorities and make ethical decisions with respect to issues of concern (Benninga, 1991). Appeals to citizens to advance our national interests often invoke themes that emphasize *patriotism* (i.e., support for your country) and *nationalism* (i.e., placing interests of your country above others). In contrast, advocates for a global perspective challenge us to consider "the greatest good for the greatest number" or the concerns of *all* nations, including our own.

One positive aspect of patriotism and nationalism is the creation of a sense of community, of belonging to a larger enterprise and sharing in a collective tradition. We identify with our nation's victories and defeats, pride, and shame in such events as the Olympic Games, explorations in space, and concern for the environment. Patriotism and nationalism can also be cohesive forces that bind citizens together. These forces can encourage people to work cooperatively, contributing to the next generation's welfare.

Extreme patriotism and nationalism, however, can lead to the oppression of dissident minorities and hatred and distrust of other nations. These forces can create barriers to greater understanding across cultures and reduce the opportunities for people to work together to achieve common goals. They can also create an exaggerated sense of superiority, as occurred in Nazi Germany. Additionally, in an era where an increasing number of nations possess both nuclear weapons and unstable political leadership, excessive patriotism and nationalism can threaten the very existence of the world.

Social Concern and Citizenship Education

We argued in earlier chapters that the three dimensions of reflection, competence, and concern characterize the effective citizen. Reflection and competence alone, without concern, are incomplete. To many Americans, it is obvious that among our citizens some people are highly reflective and competent—witness embezzlers, slumlords, drug lords, and tax evaders—but who lack a basic grounding in social concern. In carrying out our citizenship roles, the dimension of concern provides a focus for the exercise of reflection and competence.

It also heightens awareness that we are members of a pluralistic democratic society in an increasingly interdependent world where sensitivity for the welfare of others and our planet arguably should become the norm. It further reflects the assumption that, if our nation is to prosper and survive, the knowledge and skills we possess must be guided by our feelings and concern for others and the common social good, as well as our personal needs and aspirations.

The Morally Mature Citizen

During the past decades, educators, parents, and civic groups have expressed alarm over the lack of social concern evidenced by many youngsters in our society.

In this chapter, we examine illustrative areas in which teachers may contribute to the development of concerned citizens. Additionally, we consider some of the basic issues that arise from related classroom activities. As we shall see, analysis of matters of social concern may involve one or more of the instructional strategies we examined in earlier chapters.

The Dimensions of Concern

In a pluralistic society, citizens should be able to view issues from others' perspectives and to identify and resolve value conflicts. To make and act on social choices and commitments, concerned citizens also need well-grounded systems of beliefs, attitudes, and values. Additionally, since an important aspect of citizenship is deciding what are the right and the wrong things to do in a situation, individuals need to develop a sound ethical framework.

Each of us holds to some set of interrelated beliefs, attitudes, and values. We each have thousands of different beliefs, some important and some trivial, some objectively verifiable, and some not. Often people who share similar beliefs, attitudes, and values join together and become allies in common causes or interests. On the basis of shared beliefs, attitudes, and values, they join groups such as political parties, religious denominations, and community organizations. People also become friends for similar reasons.

By the same token, different beliefs, attitudes, and values can sharply divide us. Throughout history, such violent behavior as wars, inquisitions, riots, and genocides have resulted from the inability of nations, groups, and individuals to tolerate differences in others. The failure to understand or respect the differences in the beliefs, attitudes, and values of others can breed suspicion, fear, and hatred. It can lead to tension and engender hatred among groups; reduce social, economic, and political intercourse; and hasten the outbreak of hostilities and atrocities.

The Nature of Beliefs, Attitudes, and Values

A **belief** may be defined as any assertion an individual makes that he or she regards as true (Rokeach, 1968). A belief may not actually be true or a fact, but a person must think, feel, or act as if his or her assertions are factually correct in order for them to be beliefs. Throughout our lives, our belief systems typically undergo many changes as evidence gives us reason to cast aside old beliefs and acquire new ones. Examples of beliefs that some individuals hold are

The series of events known as the Holocaust never occurred.

Sports utility vehicles are dangerous to the environment.

Attitudes are closely related to beliefs. They are clusters of related beliefs that express our likes and dislikes, general feelings, and opinions about some individual, group, object, or event (Rokeach, 1968). We can have attitudes toward all sorts of groups or things—Latinos, people of Jewish faith, peace, the race car industry, the environment, beers, or even nonexistent entities, such as elves and centaurs. Beliefs and attitudes are derived from many sources, including relatives and friends, the mass media, peers, and different experiences (Triandis, 1971).

Values are the standards or criteria we use in making judgments about whether something is positive or negative, good or bad, pleasing or displeasing (Shaver & Strong, 1976). The standard we have, for example, for determining whether an individual's conduct is good or bad derives in part from our value of *honesty*.

It is important for students to understand that social studies textbooks and curricula are not value free. Textbook and curricula authors often claim to present unbiased facts. Authors make decisions about what should be included and omitted and what to present as favorable or unfavorable. Each textbook and each curriculum is value laden, meaning that it presents the author's point of view. We will discuss later in this chapter specific strategies that will help students uncover their own set of values and beliefs to identify how values and beliefs influence textbooks and curricula.

Instructional Strategies for Examining Beliefs, Attitudes, and Values

Teaching strategies often combine objectives relating to beliefs, attitudes, values, and ethical issues. Teaching materials and texts similarly often lump them together under headings such as "values education." Since beliefs, attitudes, and values are interrelated, a teaching strategy that focuses on one invariably has some impact on the others.

A starting point for instruction in the area of beliefs and attitudes is identifying where individuals stand on issues. The most fundamental beliefs and attitudes that students wrestle with are those related to self, referred to as *self-concepts*. Each of us forms our self-concept largely by our perception of how other individuals react toward us. The teacher who tells the student, "You do an excellent job on writing assignments," contributes to the child's self-concept of both writer and student.

Self-Concept Activities

It is important to integrate self-concept activities into the social studies classroom. **Self-concept activities** are tasks that encourage students to examine their personal views and attitudes. Activities, however, should safeguard the rights of students and their parents to privacy. Teachers should also recognize the limitations of their professional training in dealing with students who have histories of serious emotional problems. For some students, self-analysis can be traumatic and requires special professional supervision and counseling.

Given these caveats, let us consider different methods to help students examine their own self-concepts and how they influence their beliefs and attitudes.

Letter Disclosure. To help your students self-assess and represent themselves to you, they can write a "Dear Teacher" letter. This is a common practice used by teachers at the beginning of the school year to get to know their students, but can become much more helpful for the children as a self-analysis activity and for the teacher as a diagnostic tool. Students may write the letter telling about themselves in the voice of a parent, pet, friend, and so on. Telling about one's self in the voice of another frees writers to look more closely at themselves and disclose more information. It is also a mechanism for students to express thoughts and ideas that they are not comfortable sharing in class and a way for the teacher to provide them written feedback on their thoughts. An added bonus is that it provides the teacher with an excellent sample of the student's writing ability.

Attitude Inventories. A starting point for instruction in the area of beliefs and attitudes is identifying where individuals stand on an issue. An attitude inventory can be a composite of beliefs from many sources organized as an individual position. Additionally, it may include statements quoted from various sources or ones the teacher has created. Students also may be able to organize their own surveys and collect and analyze the results.

Consider the following statements of economic beliefs. Identify the ones with which you agree and explain your rationale:

- NAFTA is essential for fair trade among North American countries.
- The Internet has driven many small independent businesses into bankruptcy.

- Taxes should be levied to support universal health care.
- If peace were reached in the Middle East, gas prices would be more stable in this country.
- Most people on welfare could be self-supporting if they really wanted to be.

One of the ways in which beliefs and attitudes may be examined, compared, and discussed is through simple surveys or inventories, such as the one you just took. Through the process of examining the positions of others, it often is easier for students to become aware of and clarify their own beliefs and attitudes.

Student Debates. Student debates are another way to help students clarify their positions on complex social issues. Evans (1993) describes in Figure 8.1 how he uses debates with middle school students dealing with issues such as "John Brown: Criminal or Hero?"

BOX 8.1	Addressing the Issues: Teaching Character Education—Whose Job Is It?

Lev Vygotsky (1986) was tapped by the communist government to come up with a theory of education that was compatible with Marxism. His theory of cognitive socialization described children helping one another to learn, both as mentors to one another and in cooperative group activities. Teachers were teacher–mentors who helped their students to move from test proficiency levels to higher levels of achievement by providing scaffolding to climb from one level to another. In addition to academic considerations, teachers were expected to instruct children in the morals and expectations of society.

What is your job today regarding character education? Some parents feel that it is their responsibility to teach their values to their children. On the surface, this is a welcome change from the morally rudderless children who come through our doors having spent little quality time with positive, upstanding role models. This issue cuts across economic and social classes. Children of affluence and those of modest circumstances often experience an absence of parental supervision and guidance in their lives. The schools are expected to pick up the slack, with teachers as the first line of defense.

What can you do to teach character education? First, teachers must practice what they preach. If they expect respect, they must give it. If they want students to cooperate and exercise responsibility, teachers must do the same. To set up an environment to practice humane education, teachers must establish a well-organized, tightly run classroom. Procedures for operation should be established and posted. Consequences for failure to comply should be clearly understood and fairly enforced. Without an environment that enables teachers to teach and students to learn, positive behavior that teaches and demonstrates good character cannot be encouraged and developed. Teaching good character traits, one a month, does little to ensure practice unless the environment for practicing kindness, consideration, respect, cooperation, and other positive characteristics exists.

FIGURE 8.1

Classroom Debates as a Strategy to Analyze Complex Social Issues

---

Using Classroom Debates as a Learning Tool

Student debates are effective ways to foster cooperation, critical thinking, and enthusiasm for learning among middle school students. Teachers can use debates in almost any discipline, include students of all reading levels, and, when properly orchestrated, help students comprehend important and complex issues.

Political debates during election years can help students assess candidates and issues, whether at the presidential, congressional, or local levels. Student debates, however, are equally useful at any time and in any classroom. The curriculum itself should be a good source of topics—competing theories or historical disputes, for example—or current social and political controversies, such as abortion, women's rights, unemployment, foreign affairs, AIDS, education, and taxes.

I usually schedule debates at the end of a unit of study. As students investigate their debate topics and then listen to the debates of others, they add knowledge to the foundation of classroom lessons. Holding debates at the end of a study unit also provides me with an alternative form of evaluation, in lieu of a test, to help assess how well students have learned the material. I choose three interrelated topics relevant to the study unit just completed. For example, following a study of events leading to the Civil War, debate topics might be: "John Brown: Criminal or Hero?" "States Rights: Should States Be Allowed to Secede?" and "The Kansas-Nebraska Bill: Pro or Con?"

To stage a debate, I begin by dividing the class into three groups. I select members of these groups systematically to distribute evenly students of varying abilities. I then divide each group into two teams, one of which will argue for their chosen topic and the other against it. Each group then randomly selects a debate topic from among the preselected subjects. This random selection enables them to explore perspectives that may differ from their own.

Prior to the debate, students should spend at least one week investigating their particular issue and rehearsing opening statements and presentations. During this preparation phase, I provide research assistance appropriate to the aptitude of each class. For example, in some classes, it is enough to furnish students with magazines, newspapers, and other information. In other classes, I must highlight this material and explain how the students could use it effectively in a debate.

As homework assignments, I ask students to bring in any relevant information they can find about their topics. I also remind them to prepare for the unexpected by learning as much as possible about their opponent's topic.

After students have coordinated and gathered their information, they make posters and signs to illustrate their position and begin rehearsing their presentations. One or two days before the debate, I schedule a short rehearsal.

Note. From *Handbook on Teaching Social Issues,* (Bulletin 93), by R. Evans and D. Saxe (Eds.), 1996, Washington, DC: National Council for the Social Studies. Copyright 1996 by National Council for the Social Studies. Reprinted by permission.

In our complex, rapidly paced society, students are confronted with ethical issues that require background and in-depth understanding of a variety of viewpoints.

Social Issues as a Curricular Focus

The term *social issue* is used loosely in the social studies. Its meaning ranges from any topic that has social implications, to social problems, to any item of controversy (Olner, 1976). Social issues invariably touch on beliefs, attitudes, values, and ethical dilemmas. Issues may change over time, as old ones no longer affect large numbers of people and as new social phenomena arise. Advocates of an issue-centered curriculum argue that "in our rapidly changing world, the cutting edge of education must be at the emergence of new knowledge rather than at the persistence of old and frequently obsolete knowledge" (Evans, 1993).

An issue-centered curriculum calls upon students to master a set of core knowledge, skills, and dispositions (Evans & Saxe, 1996). Students are prompted to go beyond the basic rote memorization of facts and are called upon to critically interpret data, take a stance on a controversial issue, and clearly articulate their opinion. Hahn (1996) reports that students in an issues-centered classroom are more interested in the political arena, develop a greater sense of political efficacy and confidence, and become more interested in the issues that they have studied. Additionally, more students participate in class discussions and express more reflective thinking and in-depth understanding.

Curricular Framework for Analyzing Social Issues in the Classroom

As we considered in earlier chapters, several social studies educators have provided distinctive frameworks for identifying and shaping social issues for investigation within the social studies curriculum. The core of these frameworks rests with identifying a controversial question to guide the curriculum. Figure 8.2 highlights how traditional social studies units can be transformed into issue-based units with a framing question.

Fortunately, the advent of the Internet provides large quantities of primary sources and data for students and teachers. The following sites are examples of resources available to assist in issues-centered classrooms:

Documenting the American South: **http://docsouth.unc.edu**

American Memory: **http://memory.loc.gov/**

Perseus Digital Library: **http://www.perseus.tufts.edu/**

Virginia Center for Digital History: **http://jefferson.village.virginia.edu/vcdh/**

U.S. National Archives, Records, and Administration: **http://www.archives.gov/**

For concerned citizens to explore social issues unfettered requires a climate of freedom secured by their government. The First Amendment in the Bill of Rights

FIGURE 8.2
Transforming a Unit Topic into a Unit Issue

TRADITIONAL UNIT	ISSUE-BASED UNIT
The Women's Movement ——⟶	Has the Women's Movement of the last three decades helped or hurt American society?
Exploration in the New World ——⟶	Are the New World explorers to be praised or condemned for their efforts?
The First Amendment and Free Speech ⟶	When, if ever, should free speech be limited?
Immigration ——⟶	Immigration: Who should get in and why?
Global Pollution ——⟶	What should the U.S. do about global pollution?
The Legislative Branch ——⟶	Does Congress have too much power?
The Cradles of Civilization ——⟶	What makes a culture a "Civilization"?

Note. From "Table 1: Transforming a Unit Topic into a Unit Issue," by R. Evans & D. Saxe (Eds.), from *Handbook on Teaching Social Issues,* Bulletin 93, 1996, p. 91. © 1996 National Council for the Social Studies. Reprinted by permission.

is a concise and powerful guarantee of some of the most vital aspects of our daily lives, including freedom of speech:

> Congress shall make no law respecting an establishment of religion or prohibiting the free exercise thereof; or abridging the freedom of speech, or of the press; or the right of the people peaceably to assemble, and to petition the government for a redress of grievances.

The rights and reciprocal responsibilities that flow from our constitutional guarantees of freedom of speech have considerable significance for the social studies curriculum in middle and secondary schools. They provide a framework within which teachers can nurture development of the dimension of concern through an open examination of beliefs, attitudes, values, ethical dilemmas, and social issues.

In social studies classes, as students engage in open and candid discussions, teachers periodically will need to carefully structure classroom discussion. In Figure 8.3, Passe and Evans (1996) suggest a variety of discussion format styles.

Global Education in an Interconnected World

Global concern involves both an understanding of the nature and interdependence of other nations and an interest in their welfare. It also means a willingness to identify and make important decisions that may provide long-term benefits for the world, in general, at the expense of short-term national interests. Global education, in turn, refers to the process of engendering global concern in our citizens.

Some social studies educators have urged that the entire social studies curriculum adopt a global focus. Several projects have developed special materials for addressing salient global issues. One example is the *Choices for the 21st Century Education Project*. The Choices Project at the Watson Institute for International Studies at Brown University (**www.choices.edu/index.cfm**) has produced a series of inexpensive units for secondary students that address America's global policies. Sample units, which are updated periodically, are

- U.S. Immigration Policy in an Unsettled World (2006)
- Global Environmental Problems: Implications for U.S. Policy (2006)
- Responding to Terrorism: The Challenge for Democracy (2006)
- Conflict in Iraq: Searching for Solutions (2007)

In Chapter 10, we also consider some illustrations of how electronic networks that link schools and students around the nation and the world are being used to spur global education. These involve the transmission from computer to computer of information that includes print, video, and audio data. *World Classroom* (**www.mcn.org/ed/cu/liv/units/creative.html**) is an example of a program that attempts to engage students in developing a world community using telecommunications.

FIGURE 8.3

Format Styles

Socratic. Students sit in a horseshoe pattern (if feasible), with the teacher at the opening of the horseshoe or moving about inside. The teacher directs questions about a thought-provoking selection of text (not a textbook) to individual students, asking them to explain the meaning of a particular passage, define the issue posed, take a stand on the author's viewpoint, react to the opinion of another student, or provide evidence to support a contention, and so on (Adler, 1984).

Council. Students sit in one large circle. A talking stick is passed from student to student. Each person has the opportunity to speak, only when he or she has the stick. The guidelines are to talk honestly, be brief (one minute), and speak from the heart.

Quaker. Students sit in a large circle. Individual students may stand and move into the center of the circle—one person at a time—when moved to speak. Individuals may speak until they have completed all they want to say. Other than the individual speaking, students sit in silence throughout the activity; no questions or comments are allowed. Objects related to the topic may be used as props for student commentary; for example, on gender issues a Barbie doll or a baseball could be used.

Fishbowl. Students work in small groups discussing an issue or problem and send a representative from their group to sit inside the fishbowl—an inner circle of concentric circles. Student representatives inside the fishbowl discuss the issue or problem and attempt to reach a consensus. Students outside the fishbowl may communicate with their representatives by passing notes (Grambs & Carr, 1991).

Panel Discussion. A small group of students, seated in front of the class, hold a discussion on a topic, issue, or problem. Discussion is led by a moderator, usually the teacher. What will emerge is an informal conversation that is not as formally structured as a debate.

Debate. Two teams of students debate a resolution, pro versus con, in front of a class audience. The teams are given time to prepare arguments and counter-arguments. An opening statement from a member of the pro team is followed by a rebuttal statement from the con team, and then each member of the team is allowed a statement in turn, followed by rebuttal from the opposition. Following open debate and questions from the floor, team members may be asked to drop or reverse their roles.

Role Playing Debate. This is debate enhanced with specific biographical or situational roles. A debate on a zoning ruling, for example, might include an industrialist, a labor leader, and an unemployed worker.

Role Playing for Social Values. A small group of students prepares for and acts out a skit portraying a difficult, value-laden issue. Following the first enactment, the class discusses alternative choices, and members of the class are asked to act out their choices and the consequences they think will follow (Shaftel & Shaftel, 1967).

Mock Trial. Students assume the roles of judge (or a panel of judges), lawyers, witnesses, bailiff, jury, and so on. After being given role descriptions, students conduct a mock trial and jury deliberation.

Simulation. This is an activity in which students re-create an environment simulating some social situation of the past or present. This activity involves individual and group decision making.

Variations on Format Styles

There are many other variations on these formats, including the town meeting, congressional debate, presidential cabinet discussion, and personal decision making. Teachers should keep in mind the following aspects of conducting large-group discussion activities, especially when conducting one of the more complex ones:

- Set a context for the activity, providing sufficient background for the students so that they know the key facts and are clear about the key issue and its importance.

- Make sure the central question or resolution is simple, direct, and clear. The positions to be assumed by participants (pro, con, various roles, etc.) must also be clearly specified.

- Clarify procedures for students in advance and set behavior guidelines.

- Allow students time to prepare for the activity by studying their roles, ask questions and so on. If only a select number of students is involved in an activity, appoint "understudies" for key roles in case of absence.

- Write brief role descriptions for students, building in argument and evidence. A preferred option, when feasible, is to have students research their roles or positions.

- Ask students to think like the people in the roles they will play, and to argue from that viewpoint.

- Serve as moderator for the activity. After the class has gained experience with the exercise, appoint a student as moderator.

- After the activity, have a debriefing and connect the issue studied and the method to future lessons: What have we learned about this topic? What do we believe now? Why? What have we learned about participating in this type of discussion activity?

Note. From "Variations on Format Styles," by R. Evans & D. Saxe (Eds.), from *Handbook on Teaching Social Issues,* Bulletin 93, 1996, pp. 85–86. © 1996 National Council for the Social Studies. Reprinted by permission.

Peace Education

A number of organizations have promoted the theme of world peace as a focus for global education. These include *The Center for Teaching Peace* (**www.waging peace.org**), *The International Center for Cooperation and Conflict Resolution* (**www.tc.columbia.edu/centers/icccr**), and *The United States Institute for Peace* (**www.usip.org**).

The concerns of these organizations include teaching students about the ways that wars, violent acts, and general conflicts are initiated and how they can be avoided and controlled. These organizations also seek to acquaint students with the threat of potential nuclear destruction and the effects of warfare. They also promote alternative strategies for maintaining peace and stability throughout the world.

Some organizations also produce curriculum materials that promote peace education. Online resources for peace education are shown in Figure 8.4.

FIGURE 8.4
Online Resources for Peace Education

Teaching respect and tolerance for those who are diverse has become a primary educational focus. Peace education moved well beyond the utopian dreams of its 19th-century founders to realize very practical applications for this century.

Atrium Society: Peace education resources, newsletter, bookstore. Site feature: Bullying. ***www.atriumsoc.org***

Bucks County Peace Centers: Library of peace education/conflict-resolution materials, annotated list of peace education programs, plus a checklist for stereotyping awareness. ***www.ericdigests.org/1998-3/peace.html***

Center for the Study and Prevention of Violence: Blueprints for prevention, database, facts, and statistics. ***www.colorado.edu/cspv***

PeaceJam: Introduction to the lives of the heroes of peace. ***www.peacejam.org***

United States Institute for Peace: Articles on global peace issues, directory of funded projects, links to other peace organizations, publication reviews. ***www.usip.org***

World Wise Schools: Integrates global education into daily activities, including lesson plans for grades 6–9 and 10–12. Global cafe is excellent. ***www.peacecorps.gov/wws***

Multicultural Education

Each day's wave of current events reinforces our awareness that our globally interdependent world is a mélange of people of different colors, religions, languages, and customs. Our own nation is a microcosm of this diversity. In some classrooms throughout our country, it is not unusual to find 20 different languages spoken. Gaining insights into our wealth of diversity with its social, political, and economic implications is the essence of *multicultural education*.

Multicultural education has special significance for our nation because we have a rich mix of racial and ethnic groups. Also, multicultural education intersects with the major themes in our history and our abiding national commitment to equity in the treatment of citizens.

In the past half-century, the move for equity for all racial and ethnic groups in our society received a dramatic impetus from the civil rights struggles of the 1950s and 1960s and the attendant legislation and judicial rulings that they spawned. The wave of moral indignation and political restructuring generated by the succession of historic, often tragic, events that came to be known as "the civil rights movement" forced the nation to attack the roots of racism.

The movement began as a series of concrete, dramatic steps by a few brave individuals on behalf of fundamental justice for African Americans. By the 1980s, it had blossomed into an international outcry on behalf of people and groups everywhere who suffered oppression or injustice at the hands of those in power. In the United States, this movement included an introspective analysis of the treatment of ethnic groups that had suffered dramatically, consistently, and extensively from racism, such as Native Americans, Hispanic Americans, Latino Americans, and Asian Americans, as well as African Americans (see Box 8.2).

The outcry also forced an examination of our treatment of ethnic and religious minorities in general. By the close of the century, American ideals were globalized into a passion for social justice for all human beings and an increasing sensitivity for the rights of minorities across the world. Apartheid in South Africa and the treatment of Palestinians in the Middle East, for example, became and continue to be hotly debated political issues in our nation and around the world. The amorphous mass of displaced Americans, the homeless, and the homeless of the world, with neither home nor country, are part of the American political agenda. Currently our nation is grappling with issues of sexual orientation/identity and the influx of individuals of Hispanic origin.

Banks (1984) has contended that, in its role of supporting cultural pluralism and promoting multicultural education, the school should "help students to break out of their cultural enclaves and to broaden their cultural perspectives. Students need to learn that there are cultural and ethnic alternatives within our society that they can freely embrace" (p. 9). He observed further: "The major goal of multicultural education is to change the total educational environment so

BOX 8.2	Addressing the Issues: Enslaved People and Americans of Asian Heritage

Dorothy Redford, the curator of Summerset Plantation, a State Historic Site in the Coastal Plain of North Carolina, is a descendant of the enslaved people who first worked the fields of this rice plantation. She welcomes visitors to this unique State Historic Site, the only site developed with a focus on the enslaved people. While the "big house" is open to visitors, it is the outbuildings and the reconstructed quarters of the enslaved workers that are the focus of the historic site. Teachers who visit for a "day in the life of . . ." draw jobs out of a hat and must perform that job, and only that job, for the duration of the activity. You may be making brooms, hollowing out a drinking gourd, dipping candles, or cooking Hoppin' John. To really experience a day in the life of an enslaved person, you must realize that there was no choice of job offered. You did what you were told to do. Ms. Redford makes a deliberate point of calling the workers on the plantation "enslaved people." This drives home the point that they were forced to become slaves. Often, one word can be a powerful reminder of how horrible a situation actually was. The use of the term *enslaved* heightens our awareness of the brutality visited on a people robbed of their freedom.

Another dark time in our history involved the Americans of Asian heritage who were interned in camps in America during World War II. They, too, were done an injustice when they were taken from their homes and businesses and locked away in camps. It was feared that because they looked like the enemy and shared a common Asian heritage they might sympathize with the Japanese cause and spy for the enemy. The fact that many of the Americans of Asian heritage were second-generation American citizens did not seem to matter.

Do we unintentionally reinforce prejudice in the terms we use to refer to Americans whose cultural heritage is other than European? For example, Hispanic Americans, Asian Americans, and so on. When we posed this question to our preservice teachers, they admitted that they had never really thought about it, but wondered if it was an issue of individual comfort level. We should be called that which makes us most comfortable. If Dorothy Redford is correct and our awareness is heightened by the power of the word, should we use Americans of Hispanic heritage, Asian heritage, Native American heritage, African heritage, and European heritage? The rationale is that these terms might be more inclusive and recognize that we are Americans first, but still proud of our individual heritages. What do you think?

that it promotes a respect for the wide range of cultural groups and enables all cultural groups to experience equal educational opportunity" (p. 23).

What multicultural education advocates have proposed requires an ongoing commitment on the part of all teachers and schools, as well as key actors—such as parents—in the social environment beyond the school. Many skills associated with multicultural education are developed slowly over time. Some, such as perspective taking, are acquired only when students reach the appropriate developmental stage. And all are affected by family attitudes, the training individuals receive in the home, and the experiences they have outside of the school.

Issues in Multicultural Education

Is there such a thing as "an American culture"? To some extent, we all share in an amorphous cultural framework that makes us "American" (Spindler & Spindler, 1990). In addition, we have potential points of cultural reference that, should we care to use them, allow us to distinguish ourselves from the larger cultural American framework. We may choose to identify with one or more subcultures that are distinguished by distinctive ways of acting, thinking, and feeling (Kleg, 1993).

Cultural groups that are identified by ethnicity—**ethnic groups,** for example— view themselves as belonging together and gaining identification by virtue of their ancestry, real or imagined, and common customs, traditions, or experiences, such as language, history, religion, or nationality. Individuals often use the terms *cultural* or *ethnic* interchangeably in referring to themselves and others. Because many of the different groups in our nation prize those distinguishing characteristics that give rise to their individuality, we regard our nation as being *culturally pluralistic* or *multicultural.*

Our distinctive differences often divide us, as well as enrich us. The hatred and violence that spewed forth from Eastern Europe in the aftermath of Yugoslavia's disintegration is a chilling reminder, as are the ongoing conflicts in the Middle East. Racism, prejudice, and hostility still stalk the world, including our own nation: "Today racial and ethnic prejudices, discrimination, scapegoating, and other forms of aggression continue to characterize the human experience" (Kleg, 1993, p. 1).

The key issue in multicultural education for many is: How can we celebrate the richness and uniqueness of our diversity and the multiple perspectives that differing groups offer, while at the same time stressing the common bonds that unite and strengthen our nation politically, economically, and socially? The impassioned debate that continues over this issue touches many areas (Banks, 1991; Bullard, 1992; Martel, 1992; Ogbu, 1992; Ravitch, 1992). The fallout has implications for how textbooks, instructional materials, and curriculum in schools will be shaped in the future.

Addressing the issue of perspectives is crucial to multicultural understanding and, in fact, an informed analysis of all social data. For example, in his seminal text, *Red, White, and Black: The Peoples of Early America,* Nash (1982) argued that:

> [T]o cure the historical amnesia that has blotted out so much of our past we must reexamine American history as the interactions of many peoples from a wide range of cultural backgrounds over a period of many centuries. . . . Africans were not merely enslaved. Indians were not merely driven from the land. . . .
>
> To break through the notions of Indians and Africans being kneaded like dough according to the whims of invading European societies, we must abandon the notion of "civilized" and "primitive" people. . . .
>
> Africans, Indians, and Europeans all had developed societies that functioned successfully in their respective environments. None thought of themselves as inferior people. (pp. 2–3)

Similar to Nash, Benitez (1994) has advocated that teachers employ an "alternative perspectives approach" in teaching history. "With this approach," she wrote,

[T]he teacher presents historical events from alternative, i.e., non-male, non–Judeo-Christian, or non-Northwestern European, perspectives . . . . The following are examples using this approach:

- **Pre-colonial.** Discuss the concept of discovery with the students. Who was actually discovering whom? Point out that Asians immigrated via Alaska and that more than 500 native cultures thrived before the Europeans landed in North America.
- **Colonial.** Point out that the Spanish colonized more than one-third of the present United States, including Florida, Louisiana, Texas, New Mexico, Arizona, and California, and that some Spanish settlements preceded British settlements by almost a century. . . .
- **Seventeenth century through today.** Review the history of European settlements in North America from the perspective of the mainland American Indian. Ask students to write about or discuss how they would feel as an American Indian at several different historical junctures and vis-à-vis different groups of Europeans, taking into account the changing perceptions American Indians had of the white newcomers. Then ask students to write an essay entitled "The Invasion from the East" from the perspective of an American Indian. (p. 143)

Merryfield and Remy (1995) have emphasized the importance of involving students in firsthand experiences with people from different cultures as a way to gain insights into their perspectives. Samples of the strategies the authors advocate include:

Students practice active listening by interviewing people from another culture.

Example: Students interview a Vietnamese immigrant about his perspectives on refugees and political asylum.

Students work cooperatively with people from another culture toward common goals.

Example: Students work with employees from a local Honda plant to develop a video on "cross-cultural understanding and economic cooperation."

Students are immersed in another culture.

Example: Students raise money and plan a study tour to visit rain forests in Costa Rica. (p. 20)

An excellent source for understanding challenges faced by adolescents of diverse heritages is *Adolescent Portraits, Identity, Relationships and Challenges* (Garrod, Smulyan, Powers, & Kilkenny, 1992). Essays in this book address a wide range of themes, including ethnicity.

Designing Strategies for Multicultural Education

Banks (1993) has suggested that in social studies classes multicultural education might be advanced by including five different perspectives that represent different sources of information (Figure 8.5). Each perspective offers students a different insight from which to construct a more informed grasp of an historical event. Chapter 4 includes an illustration of how these five perspectives could be incorporated into a unit dealing with the Westward Movement. Lara Backus, a former classroom teacher, designed the lesson summaries in Box 8.3 as examples of teaching social studies with a social justice lens.

Apart from including multiple perspectives, some experiences that effective multicultural education programs might offer students include:

1. Learning how and where to obtain objective, accurate information about diverse cultural groups
2. Identifying and examining positive accounts of diverse cultural groups or individuals
3. Learning tolerance for diversity through experimentation in the school and classroom with alternate customs and practices
4. Encountering, where possible, firsthand positive experiences with diverse cultural groups enabling foundation building for cultural appreciation
5. Developing empathic behavior (trying to put yourself in the shoes of a person from a different cultural group) through role playing and simulations
6. Practicing using "perspective glasses"; that is, looking at an event, historical period, or issue through the perspective of another cultural group or gender

FIGURE 8.5
A Multiperspective Approach to Multicultural Education

Perspective	*Source of Information*
Personal/Cultural	Students' personal and cultural experiences
Popular	Mass media, pop culture, and films
Mainstream Academic	Research from mainstream scholars
Transformative Academic	Research that challenges mainstream findings or methodologies
School	Information in school texts and related media

Note. Adapted from "The Canon Debate, Knowledge Construction, and Multicultural Education," by J. Banks, 1993, *Educational Researcher*, 22, pp. 4–14.

BOX 8.3   Addressing the Issues: Social Justice Activities

Lara Backus,
UNC Doctoral Student

History Quiz Activity

Divide the students into four groups. Give each group a piece of chart paper face down. When you say "go," the students are to turn over the paper and list all of the historical figures that match the label on their paper. The group that lists the most will win a prize. Do not let the students look at their categories in advance or talk while completing the activity. Two groups are asked to list famous women, and the other two groups are asked to list famous men. Give them 5 minutes to list as many historical people as possible.

Discussion: When the game is over, have them count how many famous people they listed and then post them. The students will realize that the game was not fair and that the group that had famous women was at a disadvantage. Give all the students a prize for participating. Discuss why it was easier for the group who had men versus women. Discuss what famous women they were most familiar with and why.

Class Quilt Activity

Create a class quilt. Give each student a square of paper and have them divide it into fourths anyway they want to. Each section of the square represents a different aspect of their personal heritage.

In the first section the students create a symbol or draw where they are from. In the second section they draw or symbolize how they identify themselves racially/ethnically. In the third section the students draw or symbolize an aspect of their racial/ethnic heritage that they are proud of. In the final section they give the heritage of their names. Upon completion, use tape to attach the squares together.

Follow-up: After they have created the quilt have the students share what aspect of the activity was easy and what was difficult. Give the students the opportunity to explain why they thought it was more difficult than other aspects and what would have made it easier.

There are several opportunities to link these issues to schools, classrooms, and students. A discussion of schools could include the value of integrated schools versus majority schools; a discussion of classrooms could include whether the displays match the race/ethnicity of the students and what is the racial mix. There is also a tendency in schools to make race only a black and white issue. There are typically many other races and ethnicities present in a classroom. This is often found when teachers discuss Martin Luther King and school desegregation. Black and white kids could not go to school together, then they could. However, students of mixed race, Asian, or Hispanic are often overlooked in these conversations.

---

7. Improving the self-esteem of all students
8. Identifying and analyzing cultural stereotypes
9. Identifying concrete cases of discrimination and prejudice, including those taken from students' experiences

These nine types of experiences aim to heighten students' awareness of the diversity among us while respecting their own cultural anchors.

Guidelines for Selecting Appropriate Curriculum Materials for Multicultural Education

As they observe and participate in the evolving debates concerning the most appropriate forms of multicultural education, teachers should consider several general propositions. To aid in the selection of multicultural curriculum materials, a number of detailed guidelines exist. As an example, Etlin (1988) provided a basic five-point checklist for teachers to consider in assessing the appropriateness of multicultural materials:

1. Does the text or other items [instructional material] give proportionate coverage to our country's different ethnic groups?
2. Does it present them in the variety of roles and situations that all our country's people deal with, rather than limit them to one or two stereotypical contexts?
3. Does it present stories and historical incidents from the point of view of the people concerned, whatever their ethnic group, rather than that of the traditional single-culture U.S. society?
4. Does it use language that recognizes the dignity of the groups involved, not using demeaning slang terms? Does it avoid using dialect unless it's presented respectfully and serves a necessary purpose?
5. If it's fiction or a reader, does the story line avoid distributing power and competence on the basis of ethnic group stereotypes? (p. 11)

The National Council for the Social Studies (NCSS) has also published a more extensive set of guidelines for multicultural education, *Curriculum Guidelines for Multicultural Education* (1992). The document provides 23 categories of guidelines for evaluating a school's program, along with a rating form. The NCSS guidelines also develop a rationale for multicultural education.

Gender Issues in Multicultural Education

Multicultural education embraces the analysis of gender issues (King, 1990). As a reflection of the broader social ferment concerning equity for all groups within our society, discrimination on the basis of gender has come under increasing attack. **Sex-role stereotyping** is one aspect of gender issues. It refers to the practice of attributing roles, behaviors, and aspirations to individuals or groups solely on the basis of gender.

Discrimination based on gender may surface in any number of ways in school contexts. It may occur, for example, through teachers' patterns of activity assignments, group placements, the content of compliments and criticisms, and types of behavior tolerated. Examples range from the treatment of females in textbooks and curriculum materials (e.g., women are absent from historical periods or have stereotyped roles); to differential treatment of males and females in the classroom (e.g., girls are asked to bake the cookies for the party and the boys to set up the tables; number of times one gender is called on in class to answer; wait time allowed and reinforcing comments made); to erroneous assumptions about attitudes and cognitive abilities (e.g., girls are assumed to be more emotional than boys); to institutional practices that appear to favor one gender over another (e.g., males are favored over females for administrative positions).

Where sex-role stereotyping occurs in instructional materials, textbooks, and the mass media, probably one of the most effective ways for teachers to combat it is to challenge it directly. Teachers can first sensitize students to the presence of sex-role stereotyping through a newspaper activity similar to the one in Figure 8.6 and then analytically examine factual data and counterexamples. This approach can have the residual effect of alerting students to stereotypes of all varieties, including those that are racial, ethnic, or political (see Box 8.4). Another strategy is to provide students with curriculum materials and trade books that reflect the perspectives, contributions, and achievements of women (Zarnowski, 1988).

FIGURE 8.6
Activity to Sensitize Students to Sex-Role Stereotyping

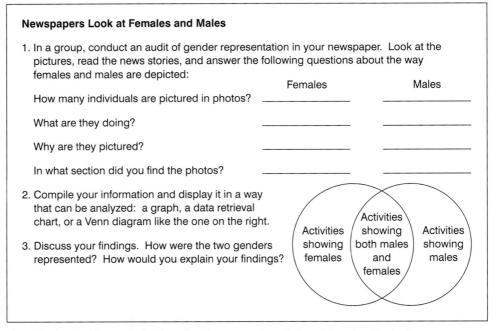

Note. Reprinted with permission from the Newspaper Association of America Foundation.

Because bad news sells better than good news, we are regularly shown horrific scenes of death and destruction on the evening news. Because they are so commonplace, even the most careful TV-watching, sharp-eyed, censoring parents often do not consider the impact that these scenes have on their children. From the footage of a father and son caught in the crossfire of troops in the Middle East to groups of people sold into modern-day slavery in Africa and small children working in sweatshops in India, children are overwhelmed with examples of our inhumanity to one another. Children feel deeply about injustice and cannot understand why a simple solution like stopping the gunfire, arresting the slave traders, or freeing the children from their looms cannot be used to solve the problem. They are unable to understand the history of the problems and the deeply felt views and attitudes of the peoples involved. Teachers must use care in judging how to evenly address national and international problems. Information gathering about the countries and people involved in conflict helps students to achieve a beginning-level, superficial understanding of elements involved in the problem. A deep and thoughtful discussion about the issue may be more than the students are developmentally able to understand.

Often, a problem closer to home is a little easier to comprehend. If students have a strong sense of place and community, they will immediately feel a connection to a local issue. If they do not, investing time in the local community will help them to build it. Most local problems will not address explosive war and peace issues, but are serious enough to have long-term consequences for the groups who need help.

Service projects that address issues of social action teach students that their generation can make a difference for someone else. Often, the issues speak to gender and ethnic inequality. Students may bring the issue to the class in the form of an "I don't understand why" statement. Homelessness, poor housing, industrial pollution, low wages for an honest day of hard work are all things that children believe have simple solutions. Giving them a chance to get involved and be part of the solution empowers them to know that they can make a difference in someone's life. Toy collection, refurbishing shelters, food drives, making posters that bring the problem to the community's attention, coats for kids, book donations, and community cleanups and plantings are all things in which any age group may participate and provide a good way to involve their parents. Some teachers and students become involved in worldwide issues, such as trick or treating for UNICEF or sponsoring a child in a foreign country. We cannot expect students to be proactive for peace and justice unless we enable them, even at a young age, to act and realize that they can make a difference.

Women's Perspectives in History. Gender issues extend beyond identifying stereotypes to include the subject of women's perspectives on events and issues. Noddings (1991/1992) noted: "If women's culture were taken more seriously in educational planning, social studies and history might have a very different emphasis. Instead of moving from war to war, ruler to ruler, one political campaign to the next, we would give far more attention to social issues" (p. 68). She has called for more attention in the social studies curriculum to issues and practices that she considers central to women's experiences (e.g., intergenerational responsibility and nonviolent conflict resolution). This supports the findings of developmental theorist Carol Gilligan and colleagues (1982, 1988, 1990). Her research showed that females more frequently made authoritative decisions that valued and preserved relationships, whereas males were more prone to authoritarian actions that strictly followed the rules.

As a special effort to redress the relative absence of women and their contributions and perspectives in written history, the field of women's history has developed. Underscoring the neglect of women in the history of our nation in 1987, the Congress, in declaring March *Women's History Month,* noted:

> [whereas] American women of every race, class, and ethnic background [helped found the Nation] in countless recorded and unrecorded ways [as servants, slaves, nurses, nuns, homemakers, industrial workers, teachers, reformers, soldiers, and pioneers; and] . . . served as early leaders in the forefront of every major progressive social change movement, not only to [secure] their own rights of [suffrage and equal] opportunity, but also in the abolitionist movement, the emancipation movement, the industrial labor union movement, and the [modern] civil rights movement; and . . . despite these contributions, the role of American women in history has been consistently overlooked and undervalued in the [body] of American history.

Although this appears to represent a step forward for the recognition of women's roles in history, one wonders why women's and other groups' contributions cannot simply be noted in the context of the history being studied throughout the year.

The National Women's History Project, **www.nwhp.org**, and the Upper Midwest Women's History Center, **www.hamline.edu/grad/whc-html/whc.html,** are examples of attempts to expand the focus of traditional history. These two organizations provide a woman's perspective on historical events as well as information concerning the vital roles that women have played in history. Both projects have produced an array of curriculum materials for K–12 social studies classes. These include biographies, videos, poster units, photos, and reference books. Materials deal with women in the United States and other nations.

Women in the World Curriculum Resources, **www.womenintheworld.com/wiwhc.html,** in contrast, uses dramatized accounts from world history to provide a female voice (see the sample activity in Figure 8.7). Using data from different periods in women's history, the project has created a series of teaching units that recount historical events through the eyes of fictitious young women.

One result of students' increased awareness of global and multicultural issues often is a developing sense of **social consciousness**. Social consciousness is an awareness that in society, citizens have both a right and a responsibility to identify and redress some social needs, in short, to help build a better world.

Social consciousness may be directed toward situations that can be easily changed and to actions that will have minimal impact on society. It can also be focused on problems that require complex changes and whose alterations will have far-reaching consequences. Ultimately, social consciousness also breeds

FIGURE 8.7
Sample Activity: Including a Female Voice in Studying World History

Women's Rights
Ancient Egypt and the United States

I. Read this definition:

Rights: A right is a privilege which a person is owed. It is guaranteed by law.

Examples: right to vote; right to a free education.

II. Hold a class discussion about the meaning of a *right.* What are some rights we have in the United States? Do students have any rights? Do children have any rights? Can rights be taken away? Do you think rights have to sometimes be fought for? Do the rights people have differ according to the society in which they live? Can you give an example of this?

III. Compared to women in other ancient civilizations, Egyptian women had many rights. The following *Rights of Women in Ancient Egypt and United States* form lists some of the rights women had in ancient Egypt. Use this form to compare their rights to women's rights today by asking the opinion of your mother or of any adult woman. Read her the rights of women in ancient Egypt listed on the form and ask if she also has these rights. Write her answer, "yes," "no," or "don't know" in the space provided.

IV. Then ask her: What other rights do you think women in the United States have? What other rights do you think women would like to have that they do not have now? Which of the rights listed do you think women had in the United States in the nineteenth century?

V. In class, poll the students to discover everyone's answers. Write the results on the chalkboard. *Discuss:* Were women's rights in ancient Egypt similar to those women have today? What additional rights do women have today? What changes have there been in women's rights in the United States since the nineteenth century? How do you think these changes came about?

More Research:

1. Using the rights listed on the *Rights of Women in Ancient Egypt and United States* form, find out if women in nineteenth-century America had these rights. Find out how women achieved the rights they did not have in the past.

2. Find out if women in classical, ancient Greece had the rights listed on the form.

3. Find out the meaning of these terms: *equal rights, civil rights, birthright, human rights, women's rights, copyright.* Have these rights always existed for everyone? Which groups have had to struggle for these rights?

(continued)

FIGURE 8.7
continued

Rights of Ancient Egyptian Women	Rights of Women in the United States
I. *In Egypt women had a right to:*	*Do American women have the same rights?*
	Answer no, yes, or don't know.
• keep anything they inherited from their parents when they married.	_____
• share equally with their husband any wealth both partners acquired within their marriage.	_____
• conduct business on their own.	_____
• own and sell property.	_____
• be a witness in a court case.	_____
• represent themselves in court.	_____
• make a will giving their wealth to whomever they wish.	_____
• adopt children.	_____
• go out in public and be in mixed company with men.	_____
• keep their own name after their marriage.	_____
• be supported by their ex-husband after a divorce.	_____
• work at jobs other than being a "housewife."	_____
• seek any employment they are qualified for.	_____

II. What other rights do women in America have? _____

_____

III. What other rights do you think women would like to have but do not now?

_____

_____

IV. Which of the rights listed do you think women had in the United States in the nineteenth century? _____

_____

Note. From "The Bird of Destiny," one unit in *Spindle Stories* series, by Lyn Reese, 1991, www.WomenInWorldHistory.com. Reprinted with permission.

social responsibility. Citizens of any age exhibit consciousness of social issues when they decide something in their society requires redress.

In a democracy, each citizen is relatively free to identify the social issues he or she wishes to address. In developing concerned citizens, teachers have the responsibility to encourage youngsters to identify areas of social need and the corresponding strategies for change. This requires giving students "the opportunity to contribute to the lives of others and to the improvement of the world around them" (Berman, 1990, p. 78).

The general message that a student should derive from activities that encourage social consciousness is that, for a society to prosper and improve, citizens must in some way give, as well as receive. Through citizenship, we receive a number of privileges as our birthright. At the same time, we also inherit the reciprocal responsibility to make some continuing contribution to our society.

Current Affairs

Engaging students in significant current affairs discussions invariably involves some aspects of global education, multicultural education, or social consciousness. By guiding students through an analysis and interpretation of the "news," as reported by the media, teachers can use current events as vehicles to address significant curricular objectives.

Our students live in a society in which we are inundated with current affairs information through the popular media, especially television. No matter where one lives in the United States or the world, it is possible to access televised news throughout the day by cable, satellite, or antenna reception. The various print media similarly afford us multiple opportunities to learn about current affairs.

Strategies for Analyzing Current Affairs

It's Friday. Time for current events!

Too often it happens that a certain day—usually the first or last of the week—is set aside in classrooms for "current events." When this practice occurs, students gain the impression that contemporary affairs are not an ongoing, vital part of everyday life.

Contemporary affairs at the local, national, and international levels should be incorporated naturally into the social studies curriculum throughout the year. Teachers should read a local paper regularly to identify significant events and issues. When current affairs have special significance, for the local community, the nation, or the world, they should also be allowed to take precedence over the regularly scheduled subject matter.

Incorporating emerging current developments into the existing curriculum can demonstrate the vitality of the social studies and how the past, present, and future are linked. Merryfield and Remy (1995) illustrated how one teacher, Connie White, at Linden McKinley High School in Columbus, Ohio, reflectively and flexibly fused emerging events with the existing curriculum. White was concluding a discussion of the Crusades just as the Gulf War erupted.

> Although she had planned to teach a unit on African civilizations next, she decided to continue with the Arabs and focus on their achievements and their connections to the world today. She began with a discussion in which her students began to make connections with their previous work on Arab civilizations and the current conflict in the Persian Gulf. The students then worked in cooperative groups to develop timelines of historical antecedents and the role of the area in global conflicts. They used their information from the timelines to make transparencies of the changing borders in the Middle East so that as a class they could examine how power had changed hands over hundreds of years and the role of conflict in the region. (pp. 37–38)

To provide different viewpoints and stimulate discussion, Ms. White invited guest speakers. She also had students simulate a peace conference after they determined which countries should be included. Later, as a culminating activity, students shared their views concerning global conflicts with their counterparts in Geneva, Switzerland. This was done via the Internet (discussed in Chapter 10).

Bulletin Boards, Activities, and Current Events. Students, especially in the middle grades, should be encouraged on an ongoing basis to bring to class or place on a special **living bulletin board** (i.e., one that grows as the class feeds it) pictures and articles that represent events that especially interest or puzzle them. Similarly, as each new unit or lesson is introduced, a teacher may encourage the class to identify materials or share information from the news that relates to the subject matter under study. An easy way to make your own "country specific" bulletin board is to project a transparency of that country onto a large piece of paper that has been taped to the wall. Outline the country on the paper, label it, and have the students bring in news articles that are country specific to tape to the paper. Any spare class time can be used to read about what's going on "inside" the country (see Box 8.5).

A teacher may also periodically stimulate an analysis of contemporary affairs by action-oriented activities. An example is a simulated newscast where the class is divided into "news desks." These might be the local, state, national, and international "desks."

Students can be assigned to one of the four desks and asked to prepare the evening's report of events at these levels. After brainstorming what the news is at their desk, each of the groups can select a newscaster to report the news. After the "newscast," the results can be discussed by the whole class for inaccuracies, interrelationships, and omissions—much like they might analyze real newscasts. Be sure to videotape the activity.

In a less complex world, teachers taught current events on one particular day. The speed of communication now enables us to know and discuss current events that have happened only minutes before. Teachable moments arise from unexpected happenings. How will you handle them?

Current events often evoke great emotion, and in the retelling of what has been seen or heard, facts can become muddled. First, the class needs to fact-find. What do we know to be true? How has it been verified? The Internet is an excellent source for up-to-the-minute information, provided that you can access CNN or major newspaper websites. Second, the K-W-L approach (What do we know? What do we want to know? What have we learned?) helps to organize our facts, determine what information is still needed, and evaluate what we have learned. Third, under the K part of the approach, you can fact-find from the perspective of a newspaper reporter and answer the 5 W questions: who, what, when, where, and why? Finally, information can be posted and amended as the event plays out.

Using current events as a teaching tool is a very important part of any curriculum. Students become aware of other places, problems, opinions, and cultures and should be helped to understand something other than the Americentric perspective that we are so used to using as our frame of reference.

An effective way to familiarize students with regions of the world is to post outlines of these regions on the classroom wall. These world segments can be made very easily by using a transparency of an outline of a region, projecting it up onto a large piece of paper that is taped to a wall or blackboard, and tracing the outline onto the paper. Students can then cut out the region (leaving a border on the outline to note adjoining countries), label the region, and post it on the wall. As the events occur in a group's region, they can post the news story, pictures, or K-W-L minichart right on top of the region. Having the information posted enables students to reread the story and study the issue in their spare time. Those not in that region's group can still help their friends by alerting them to current stories that they might want to cut out and add.

Current events work may be as local as your classroom or as global as halfway around the world. Both are important and each can influence the other. Students need to see their connection to others, a connection that makes us all citizens of the world.

Using Newspapers and Print Materials. Some of the major sources of print materials for learning about contemporary affairs are newspapers and periodicals. Many of the printed materials that are available at the "adult" level actually are written at a very low reading level, and they contain a number of instructive visual and chart materials (e.g., *USA Today*). However, their intelligent use requires some understanding of how newspapers select, construct, often bias and distort, and feature stories (Kirman, 1992). We will consider these and other issues related to printed materials in more detail in Chapter 9.

Many newspapers and periodicals feature local or "colorful" news at the expense of national and international affairs. Among the major exceptions are *The New York Times* and the *Washington Post*. These are sold throughout the United States in most major metropolitan areas and are excellent sources of information for social studies teachers and secondary students. Many newspapers, both foreign and domestic, are available online. Students will find the slant of the news in the foreign papers interesting. Global issues receive much more coverage than information about the United States. Useful websites for following the news include: **www.africanews.org, www.times.spb.ru, www.bbcnews.org,** and **www .nytimesnewspaper.com.**

Student Versions of Newspapers and Periodicals. Some publishers have also produced versions of weekly newspapers and periodicals for students that have an instructor's guide for the teacher. These publications are especially adapted for students in the middle and secondary grades and include materials that attempt to be both objective and interesting. Nonetheless, they have some of the same limitations as other printed materials.

Two examples of student newspapers are *Junior Scholastic* and *WorldWise*. Examples of periodicals are *COBBLESTONE* and *CALLIOPE*. These publications include teacher's manuals that suggest activities and discussion topics.

Teacher Positions on Controversial Issues

Invariably, at some point in the discussion of controversial issues, students wish to know what the teacher thinks. For a teacher to suggest that he or she had *no* opinion would be silly or dishonest. It also is likely to puzzle students. If it is important for them to form a position on the issue, why hasn't the teacher done so?

Teachers have several options when such a question arises. They may state their positions at that point or suggest that they have a tentative position but would like to hear all of the students' arguments before making a final decision. Alternately, they may indicate that they have a position but would rather not state it until the discussion is finished and students have made their own decisions. When teachers really have no opinion because of the nature of the issue, they should share this fact and the reasons.

It is important for students to understand that in a controversy the positions of those in authority, including that of the teacher, are not necessarily the best or the correct ones. Moreover, in many controversies, authority figures (and often "authorities" on the subject of the controversy) take competing positions. The most prudent course for all citizens is to seek out all points of view, to consider the facts, to come to a tentative conclusion, and to keep an open mind to new arguments.

SUMMARY

Teaching facts and concepts is much more straightforward than helping students to examine beliefs and attitudes, address moral dilemmas, and argue social issues. Framing these issues within our global society makes teaching today a complex task. It is important for students to examine their own beliefs and attitudes so that they may understand what is true and what is misconception.

Although we warn students not to believe everything that they read, see, and hear, sometimes they must be schooled in the subtle, and not so subtle, discrimination that occurs in everyday life. It is a teacher's obligation to make sure that the material has been carefully screened for pictures, facts, and omissions that represent discrimination. Ethnic and gender diversity are often slighted, and a real effort must be made to be sure that materials are inclusive and used as a matter of course. Equally important is the material that we use to teach global awareness. It is important that we value and respect other cultures. It is easy to fall into the trap of teaching a foreign culture as "different," a word some may take to mean "odd" or "weird." A much better approach is to examine a culture as unique and point out that, while things may be done differently in this culture, we have many things in common. Newspaper and the Internet are excellent sources of up-to-date information. Media, in general, is one way to update our textbooks. Always preview any Internet sites you are going to use and provide the URLs so surfing is kept to a minimum.

The next chapter helps you tackle the subject of literacy in the social studies classroom. You can have the best plans, supplemental material, and assignments in the world, but if you cannot make the reading–social studies connection, your students will struggle. What is the reading–social studies connection, you ask? Read on!

ACTIVITIES

1. In your community, identify five significant social issues that you believe a concerned citizen should examine or become involved in. Also, develop a rationale for why you think these issues are especially important. Discuss your conclusions.
2. Develop an attitude inventory related to the topic you have selected that is appropriate for children in grades 5 through 12. Then identify a class to field-test the inventory. Discuss the results and any changes you would make based on your experiences.
3. Develop a list of five ethical or moral dilemmas that students should explore as a part of the social studies curriculum. Support each of your dilemmas with a rationale and suggested teaching strategies.
4. Locate a cartoon, letter to the editor, or article from the local newspaper that you feel reflects racial, ethnic, or gender bias. Identify what you view as the bias and explain why. Discuss how you could use this piece of media with students to teach a lesson on bias.
5. Select a social studies textbook. Review the textbook and inventory the photographs throughout the text. Evaluate the textbook's representation of diverse populations. Discuss how you can teach your students to be critical consumers of textbooks.

WEB RESOURCES

National Women's History Project: **www.nwhp.org/**

National Association for Multicultural Education: **www.nameorg.org/**

Harvard University's Civil Right's Project: **www.civilrightsproject.harvard.edu/**

Multicultural Pavilion: **www.edchange.org/multicultural/**

Online Modules for Global Educators: **www.coe.ohio-state.edu/mmerryfield/globalresources/default.htm**

American Model United Nations: **www.amun.org/**

Teaching About Human Rights, Tolerance, and Refugees: **www.unrefugees.org/educationalresources.cfm**

Character Education Partnership: **www.character.org/**

Part

Analyzing and Improving Social Studies Teaching and Learning

CHAPTER 9   Comprehending, Communicating, and
               Remembering Subject Matter

CHAPTER 10   Using Technology to Enhance Social Studies
               Instruction

CHAPTER 11   Adapting Social Studies Instruction to
               Individual Needs

CHAPTER 12   Evaluating and Assessing Student Learning

Chapter 9

Comprehending, Communicating, and Remembering Subject Matter

Comprehending Social Studies Subject Matter

   Building on Existing Knowledge in Reading

   Strategies for Improving Reading Comprehension

   Specific Strategies

Reading and Social Studies Text Materials

   Using Adolescent Literature in Social Studies Instruction

   Reading Newspapers and Periodicals

   Visual Literacy

Communicating Social Studies Subject Matter

   Listening and Speaking

   Integrating Writing into the Social Studies Curriculum

   Technology Tools in Writing

Remembering Social Studies Subject Matter

   Imagery and Memory

   Structured Mnemonic Techniques

   Notetaking Techniques

English as a Second Language (ESL)

Summary

Activities

Web Resources

The students in Ms. Smith and Ms. Pickel's classroom were engaged in an in-depth discussion about personal liberties. The discussion was focused on a recent court ruling that dealt with freedom of speech. The students shared differing opinions and cited court rulings and the Bill of Rights to support their statements. They had used their textbook, the school library, and the Internet to research their arguments. They found the U.S. Supreme Court's multimedia website, Oyez (www.oyez.org), to be most helpful in learning about related court rulings. The students' desks were arranged in a circle and they took turns stating their opinion and questioning one another.

These students were engaged in a Paideia seminar. A Paideia seminar is an instructional method based on didactic instruction, coaching of academic skills, and a seminar discussion. The Paideia seminar is one method of enhancing literacy skills through the social studies; it involves readings, writing, and speaking. Literacy skills are among the most important skills that assist students in their development of becoming a reflective and competent citizen.

249

Unfortunately, student reading problems pose an especially serious obstacle to learning in the area of social studies, since much of the subject matter appears in written form. Further, reliance on nonprint materials, even when they do exist, often limits students' opportunities for reflective analysis and precludes use of primary source data. Reading competencies are also required in everyday citizenship roles, from being an informed consumer to comprehending the ballot in a voting booth.

As we have considered in earlier chapters, social studies instruction directed toward developing the reflective, competent, and concerned citizen incorporates many elements of planning. It includes strategies for organizing and presenting subject matter in ways that achieve the teacher's goals and objectives. Such instruction also aids students in comprehending, communicating, and remembering the social studies subject matter they encounter.

Comprehending Social Studies Subject Matter

Contemporary perspectives on reading underscore that readers are not passive receivers of information from printed materials. Rather, they interact with text and construct meaning from it. The result may or not be the same meaning that the author intended.

Comprehension, as reading educators use the term, is a complex act representing a number of different cognitive processes. These include recognizing words and relating them to previously learned information and making inferences. What readers actually comprehend from a passage of text "depends upon their knowledge, motives, beliefs, and personal experiences" (Camperell & Knight, 1991, p. 569).

It should also be noted that the subject matter of social studies often deals with places and cultural practices that students may never have encountered. Additionally, the field draws heavily on abstract concepts (e.g., democracy, detente, alienation). Social studies also embraces subject matter that includes many specialized concepts and complex visual and tabular data (e.g., filibuster, political cartoons, GNP tables).

The three essential components of reading comprehension in the social studies are building on prior knowledge, strategies for engagement, and metacognition.

Building on Existing Knowledge in Reading

Prior knowledge can be defined as a combination of the learner's preexisting attitudes, experiences, and knowledge (Kujawa & Huske, 1995). Regardless of their ages or abilities, students' existing knowledge (i.e., prior knowledge) is a critical variable in reading comprehension: "All readers, both novices and experts, use their existing knowledge and a range of cues from the text and the situational context in which the reading occurs to build, or construct, a model of meaning from the text" (Dole, Duffy, Roehler, & Pearson, 1991, p. 241). Often this knowledge base is incomplete, or students fail to relate it to the information in the text.

The existing knowledge also may be inaccurate or at variance with texts, in which case students are likely to ignore or reject the new information. Teachers who connect new content to students' prior knowledge will assist students' comprehension by helping the students link the content to their culture and experience (Beyer, 1991). It is essential for teachers to be aware of students' prior knowledge and to use specific strategies to maximize that knowledge.

Strategies for Improving Reading Comprehension

Beyond their existing knowledge, students bring to the reading process various strategies that they use with varying degrees of effectiveness to construct meaning from text.

Dole et al. (1991) have summarized five powerful strategies, supported by cognitively based research, that students can use to improve their comprehension of any texts, including social studies materials:

- Determining importance
- Summarizing information
- Drawing inferences
- Generating questions
- Monitoring comprehension

Determining importance involves assessing which items the author considers to be important. This may include understanding how a text is structured as well as how to look for clues as to what is important.

The strategy of *summarizing information* relates to selecting what is significant, synthesizing data, and then representing passages of text, either orally or in writing.

Drawing inferences involves integrating prior knowledge with the information given in text to draw conclusions (e.g., inferring the character is browsing the Internet after reading "she spent the afternoon surfing the Internet").

The strategy of *generating questions* in this context refers to students generating their own questions about text.

Monitoring comprehension consists of students being aware of how much they understand about text and how to remedy omissions or confusion, or metacognition. **Metacognition,** or thinking about thinking, is the awareness of one's own learning. The basic steps for metacognition are connecting prior knowledge to new knowledge, using effective comprehension strategies, and monitoring or reflecting on the thinking process.

Specific Strategies

Helping students comprehend social studies subject matter typically involves aiding them in reading textbooks, newspapers, periodicals, reference works, and adolescent literature. Approaches that incorporate well-grounded instructional strategies in reading and social studies can advance teachers' goals for both areas. Seven techniques that meet these criteria are the K-W-L technique, discussion webs, graffiti, reading guides, concept (or semantic) maps, graphic organizers, and data-retrieval charts.

The K-W-L Technique. The **K-W-L technique** (Carr & Ogle, 1987; Ogle, 1986) is a basic way to (1) initiate study of a unit by motivating students and activating their prior knowledge, and (2) assess what they have learned after the unit is concluded. The K-W-L technique can be used as a whole-class activity, group activity, or individual activity.

Consider a unit of study on the Bill of Rights. At the outset of the unit, a sheet similar to the one shown in Figure 9.1 is given to each student or group (Young & Marek-Schroer, 1992). After brainstorming, a cumulative list of *known* items is compiled. The process then is repeated for the items students *want to know* about the Bill of Rights. At that point, the teacher may also include additional questions that the text analysis will address.

In the next step, students consult the list of items in the W column. They also confirm or refute the accuracy of the items in the K column. As a final step, the students list in the L column what they have *learned* from their readings. Alternately, the teacher may use some of the different forms of assessment discussed in Chapter 12 to determine what students have learned.

FIGURE 9.1
Illustration of the K-W-L Technique

	K-W-L Chart	
	Bill of Rights	
K (What we *know* about the Bill of Rights)	W (What we *want* to know)	L (What we *learned*)

Discussion Webs. A **discussion web** (Duthie, 1986) may be used to help students organize arguments or evidence from text. It is suitable for issues or questions that are not resolved or for which there are balanced pro and con arguments.

An example of a web is given in Figure 9.2. As shown, a web begins with a teacher question related to materials that students have read: Should the United States have dropped the atomic bomb on Japan? The format that follows is flexible, but students, individually or in small groups, need to locate information that supports both sets of answers; for example, under the "No" column, a student writes "Thousands of innocent civilians were killed or maimed in some way."

After completing the web, students discuss the findings and then take an individual position on the issue (e.g., "Yes. Without the bomb, it would have taken an invasion of Japan to end the war. This would have caused a lot of casualties on both sides").

Graffiti. **Graffiti** is an effective strategy to help students brainstorm what they know about a topic. It is also an effective way for the teacher to assess prior knowledge or to assess student comprehension. The teacher begins a graffiti exercise by preparing sheets of newsprint with a different question or subtopic. Students are divided into small groups and instructed to respond to the prompt on the newsprint in a short time period (e.g., 2 minutes). Each student in the group has a marker and contributes to the "graffiti" on the paper. After the time is up, the newsprint is passed along to the next group. Students must then respond to the prompt posed on their new piece of paper, but they cannot repeat something that is already written on the piece of paper.

FIGURE 9.2
A Discussion Web

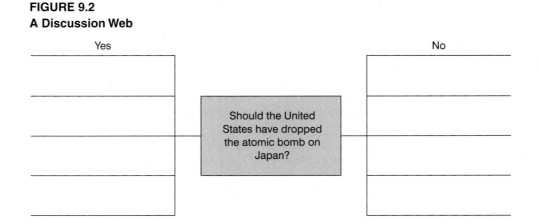

An example of graffiti in a class studying the American Revolution and colonial America may include prompts such as:

- List the events leading to the Revolutionary War.
- Who were the colonial leaders and what were their contributions?
- What was life like for a colonial American? How did this differ by geographic region?
- How was life different for colonists in America than their previous life in Europe?

Reading Guides. **Reading guides** help students organize the information from their reading. They are effective tools to assist students with scaffolding and metacognition. They help students comprehend the information and can be used to monitor learning.

Reading guides should begin by asking students to take stock of the reading material. If it is a textbook, review the table of contents to learn how the text is organized. What structures are in place to guide student reading (e.g., chapter summaries, subtopics)?

Once students have reviewed the reading selection as a whole, there should be specific questions to guide student reading. Questions should focus on main ideas and help readers make connections throughout the text. Students should also be required to paraphrase or summarize text selections or the entire reading.

Concept Maps. Concept (or semantic) mapping is a flexible technique that has several different applications in social studies instruction, including aiding students' comprehension (see also Chapters 4 and 6). The technique encourages students to organize categories of concepts and identify relationships among them.

Many variations of the concept mapping technique exist (e.g., Novak & Gowin, 1984). Basically it begins with the teacher or students identifying a series of major concepts in a narrative (e.g., a chapter), including one that is the central concept. These concepts then are organized and linked through a diagram that illustrates logical connections.

The organization of the concepts typically is hierarchical, but some applications omit this condition. In some way, however, the central or overarching concept should be identified, either by assigning it the largest circle or placing it at the top or the center of the page. In one variation, the teacher creates a partial map. This shows some of the concepts and linkages to demonstrate relationships and model the technique, and then students are asked to complete the map.

Figure 9.3 illustrates the application of this approach with a concept map made by a sixth-grade student characterized as a "low achiever" (Novak & Gowin, 1984, p. 41). The map represents the student's organization of information after reading a textbook chapter. The teacher supplied the concepts of *feudalism, kings, guilds,* and *church* shown in the figure, and the student then completed the map.

FIGURE 9.3
**A Concept Map for History Prepared by a Previously Low-Achieving
Student in Sixth Grade**

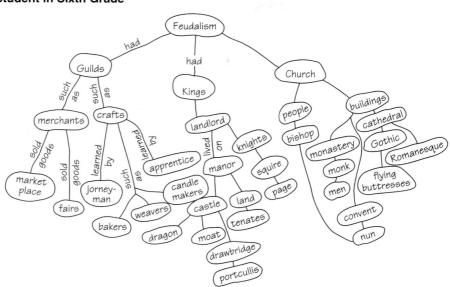

Note. From *Learning How to Learn* (p. 41), by J. D. Novak and D. Bob Gowin, 1984, Cambridge, UK: Cambridge University Press. Reprinted with the permission of Cambridge University Press.

In a different type of application, Ms. Devereaux, a ninth-grade teacher, began the study of the federal budget by listing the target term *federal budget expenditures* on the board in the center circle. Then she asked students to brainstorm some of the specific items that are included in the federal budget. Their responses, which include items such as student loans, interest on savings bonds, and social security, were recorded on the board. Ms. Devereaux also added some of her own items to the list. After the brainstorming and listing, she and the class also constructed some simple categories of the federal budget under which their responses were grouped:

Entitlements

Defense spending

Interest on the national debt

Other programs

Then she asked the class to construct individual maps that later were used to organize the information. One student's partially completed map is shown in Figure 9.4. Students were also instructed to include new items as they were encountered in readings and discussions.

FIGURE 9.4
Partially Completed Concept Map

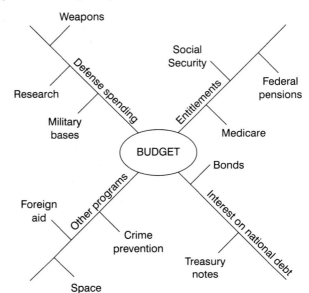

Graphic Organizers. Similar to concept maps, **graphic organizers** are representations of the relationships among major themes in a reading passage. They can be used by students before reading material as a way to discern how the teacher or author has structured information. Alternately, they can be used at the end of a reading session to serve as a summary.

Typically, graphic organizers appear as hierarchical diagrams or verbal overviews that show relationships. For example, in an American history class, a teacher might begin a discussion of the New Deal programs by first overviewing the ways in which the actions of the Roosevelt administration constituted a departure from the past administrations. Similarly, an American government class could be given a chart outlining the structure of the executive branch before examining each of the major units. Computer programs such as Inspiration (**www.inspiration.com**) are creative and easy ways to integrate graphic organizers in the classroom.

Bean, Sorter, Singer, and Frazee (1986) provide a clear example of a diagram used in a world history class that serves as an organizer (shown in Figure 9.5). Whereas the text for the class discussed several specific revolutions, such as the French Revolution, the authors used the organizer to show students the general properties of all revolutions.

Data-Retrieval Charts. As considered in Chapter 6, **data-retrieval charts** allow teachers and students to organize data from written text in a way that

FIGURE 9.5
Graphic Organizer for a World History Class

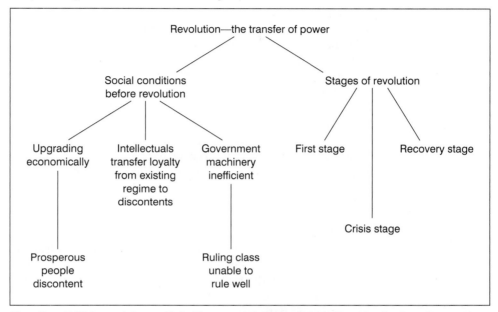

FIGURE 9.6
Sample Data-Retrieval Chart

	Natural Resources	Standard of Living	Major Social Problems	Major Exports
Countries				
Costa Rica				
Mexico				
Argentina				
Guatemala				

highlights important relationships. The format they employ offers comparisons and analyses that are not included in typical text discussions. The data-retrieval chart shown in Figure 9.6 illustrates how a teacher can offer students a skeleton that aids them in organizing information in their social studies textbook chapter.

Reading and Social Studies Text Materials

An extensive body of research has documented the limitations of existing social studies text materials from a variety of perspectives (e.g., Armbruster & Gudbrandsen, 1986; Beck & McKeown, 1988, 1991; Garcia, 1993; Siler, 1986–1987). From a cognitive perspective, for example, one major criticism of social studies textbooks—especially history texts—is that they lack depth, compartmentalize information, and fail to aid students in linking passages and discovering cause–effect relationships. Another charge is that they discourage hypothesis development and problem solving.

What characteristics specifically would make social studies texts seem "**considerate**" or "friendly" to a reader? Singer (1986) summarized the features of such texts in five categories: text organization, explication of ideas, conceptual density, metadiscourse, and instructional devices (see also Armbruster, 1984; McCabe, 1993):

1. *Text organization* refers to statements of purpose and rationale, organization of material, suggestions concerning how to learn from the text, and the like, provided for the reader. Included are a uniform writing style throughout the text and consistent use and placement of questions and rhetorical devices. Other such aids would be time lines and cause–effect and comparison charts.
2. *Explication of ideas* refers to straightforward statements of facts and ideas. Included is the definition of new terms as they are introduced, the provision of necessary background information, and the relating of new knowledge to prior knowledge. Also included is the explication of some organizing point of view or theory for the text, if one exists.
3. *Conceptual density* refers to the number of new concepts, ideas, and vocabulary items included in the text. The greater the number of these and the fewer the explanations through the introduction of main ideas and examples, the more complex is the learning task for the student.
4. *Metadiscourse* has been likened to a conversation between the author and the reader about the text. The discussion may cover any topic and typically uses the first-person form of narration.
5. *Instructional devices* refer to text features that help the user better comprehend its meaning. Among these features are tables of contents, headings, cues, annotations in the margins, inserted questions, and indices.

Researchers (Armbruster & Anderson, 1984; Armbruster, Anderson, & Meyer, 1991) have identified strategies for helping students identify and use the organizing structures in their texts. These are known as **frames,** ways of visually conceptualizing significant content of texts.

Frames represent important ideas and relationships in text. They may take many forms: data charts, tables, diagrams, and concept maps. Since authors of

FIGURE 9.7
Frame for the Westward Movement

The Westward Movement		
	Pioneers	*Native Americans*
What were their goals?		
What were their plans?		
What actions did they take?		
What was the outcome of their actions?		

texts seldom provide frames, teachers and students have to create them. Once they are constructed, evidence suggests that they facilitate learning from social studies texts (Armbruster et al., 1991), as well as other subjects.

Consider the following application of frames to a social studies text describing the westward movement, as shown in Figure 9.7. The teacher has identified four major categories of information that structure the text's narrative concerning the pioneers and Native Americans: *goals, plans, actions,* and *outcomes.*

Using Adolescent Literature in Social Studies Instruction

Pick up a social studies textbook for any grade and read a sample chapter. Did it hold your interest?

Apart from their structural limitations, which we have already discussed, some of the most biting criticisms of social studies textbooks are that they are dull, lifeless, disjointed, and lack a point of view. They have also been criticized for omitting the pageantry, myths, stories, issues, and anecdotes that are part of the vitality of social studies. Further, their critics charge that they provide only a single, allegedly objective, account of events; they also lack an "acknowledgment that there even exists more than one lens through which to examine social and political events and phenomena" (Beck & McKeown, 1991, p. 488).

Adolescent literature is an antidote to some of the major problems that textbooks have. A wealth of books designed for middle and secondary grades exist. They offer the promise of exciting and colorful in-depth alternative portrayals of issues, ethical dilemmas, social models, events, persons, and places by outstanding authors and illustrators. Historical fiction is well documented as a tool to incite students' interest and make learning meaningful. It helps students to understand that history is about individual lives and not just a list of dates and themes. Historical fiction also helps tell the stories that have been omitted from the textbook.

Adolescent literature can enrich and enliven social studies.

Too often, textbooks tell history as the traditional canon and omit the stories of immigrants, women, and people of color. Historical fiction provides students a window into the lives of individuals of different racial, ethnic, and gender backgrounds. Lindquist (2007) touts the advantages of using historical fiction in her classrooms and has created a list of criteria for selecting historical fiction:

The historical fiction you choose should:

- present a well-told story that doesn't conflict with historical records,
- portray characters realistically,
- present authentic settings,
- artfully fold in historical facts,
- provide accurate information through illustrations, and
- avoid stereotypes and myths. (Criteria section).

To highlight books she has used with her students, Lindquist (2007) presents the list on the next page, and suggested instructional strategies.

Semantic maps, discussed earlier, can be used to structure the analysis of adolescent literature. Norton (1993) provided a detailed illustration of how a middle-grade class used maps in their study of World War II in conjunction with reading Lois Lowry's *Number the Stars*. This is an account set in Denmark of how the Resistance aided Jews. The teacher placed the title of the book in the center of the map, with four spokes extending from it: conflict, themes, setting, and characterization. After students working in groups completed the book, they filled in details as shown in Figure 9.8.

Title and Author	Brief Summary	Teaching Strategy
With Every Drop of Blood: A Novel of the Civil War by James Lincoln Collier and Christopher Collier	In this first-rate novel, two young men are caught up in the Civil War: Johnny is on a bold mission to supply Rebel troops, while Cush, a Yankee, is a runaway slave. They form an unlikely alliance during the final days of the war.	I feel that getting kids to look at things from more than one point of view is important. One way to do this for this novel is to have kids write journal entries from each boy's point of view. Kids fashion journals out of half sheets of paper. This seems to stimulate creativity, because staring at a whole sheet of blank paper can be intimidating!
Under the Blood-Red Sun by Graham Salisbury	As Japanese-Americans living in Hawaii, Tomi and his family face prejudice and hatred after the attack on Pearl Harbor. Father is taken to an internment camp and Grandfather disappears. Tomi discovers how people respond to crisis.	My students spend a period constructing a survey to see what members of the community know about Japanese-American internment. They pool their information; do simple statistics with mean, mode, and median; and create charts.
The Captive by Joyce Hansen	This novel chronicles the life of a young Ashanti boy from his captivity in West Africa to his life as a slave in Salem, Massachusetts, and then to freedom with African-American ship captain Paul Cuffe.	I have students create symbols for the major events in the main character's life. I give them enough exposure to the time period so that their symbols are culturally accurate as well as intellectually on target. Then I have students organize the symbols into a pictorial time line.
The Glory Field by Walter Dean Myers	This novel is about the experiences of five generations of an African-American family on Curry Island, South Carolina. The book encompasses the Lewis family's joys and challenges, beginning with the first slave boat that landed on the island.	It's fun for students to compose a five-generation newspaper. I divide the class into five groups, assign each group a generation, and cut a piece of notebook paper lengthwise for each student. Each student writes an article on his or her strip representing experiences and points of view of the generation. Kids use black felt-tip pens to write their final drafts, I tape the articles together, and we photocopy the newspaper.

FIGURE 9.8
A Semantic Map Showing Conflict, Themes, Setting, and Characterization

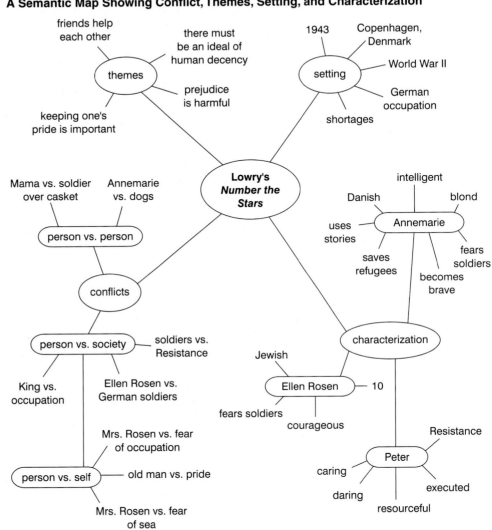

Note. Semantic map from Donna E. Norton, "Webbing and Historical Fiction." *The Reading Teacher, 46*(5), pp. 432–436. Reprinted with permission of the International Reading Association. All rights reserved.

To help middle- and secondary-grades social studies teachers locate outstanding books, the National Council for the Social Studies (NCSS) has published *An Annotated Bibliography of Historical Fiction for the Social Studies, Grades 5 through 12* (Silverblank, 1992). Also, each year in the April/May edition of *Social Education*, the NCSS publishes a list of notable trade books in the field of social studies published during the past year, some of which are appropriate for the middle grades. The list includes works written for grades K through 8 that emphasize human relations and different cultural groups. The list is available online each year at **www.socialstudies.org/resources/notable/**.

Biographies. Biographies designed for youngsters are especially useful in social studies. Zarnowski (1990) provided a detailed set of strategies for using biographies in social studies instruction in her book, *Learning about Biographies*. One of the techniques she recommended is drawing relationships between the events in the life of the subject and those in history.

Picture Books. Picture books are a surprising treasure for the middle and secondary social studies classroom. Unfortunately, many teachers believe picture books are just for the elementary classroom. But, once a middle or secondary teacher uses a picture book for grades 6–12 students, they are typically pleasantly surprised at student reaction.

Picture books are an effective tool to "hook" students at the beginning of a unit. For example, the book *You Forgot Your Skirt, Amelia Bloomer* is a fun picture book that can be used to introduce a lesson on women's suffrage. The book tells the story of Amelia Bloomer and her resistance to wearing traditional women's skirts. She went against social norms and wore "bloomers." Amelia Bloomer later became friends with Elizabeth Cady Stanton and Susan B. Anthony and helped advocate for women's rights.

Picture books are a creative resource to personalize history during a unit. Take, for example, *Amelia and Eleanor Go for a Ride*. This book tells the true story of Amelia Earhart and Eleanor Roosevelt quietly leaving a formal White House dinner one night to take an airplane ride over Washington, D.C. Readers find great delight in connecting these two independent women and their little-known excursion. Reading this picture book during a unit on the Great Depression is a creative way to personalize Eleanor Roosevelt and bring her persona to life out of the textbook.

Picture books are a valuable source to help tell the stories that are omitted from traditional textbooks. *Baseball Saved Us* is a picture book that tells the story of a young Japanese American boy who was sent to live in an American internment camp in Idaho. The little boy's will to live and survive is driven by his dreams of a baseball career. He plays baseball on a daily basis and dreams of life at home. His story personalizes the internment camps in the United States during World War II. His story is one that is often left out of textbooks. Asking students to compare this account to the account in their textbook is a useful activity at the end of the World War II unit.

Reading Newspapers and Periodicals

Newspapers and *periodicals* have many of the same problems as textbooks. On the one hand, they offer students a wealth of data on contemporary affairs and help bridge the gap between the real world and that of the school curriculum (see instructional applications of current events in Chapter 8). To properly interpret and process the information these media contain, however, most students—even good readers—need assistance.

Although they share many elements in common with textbooks, newspapers and periodicals present some special reading challenges. Effectively reading newspapers and periodicals includes being able to:

1. *Separate headlines from the substance of an article.* This involves being aware that a headline is often an interpretation of what the article is about made by someone other than the author.
2. *Identify and correctly use common colloquialisms, metaphors, acronyms, and cryptic expressions.* This includes an awareness of how frequently such expressions are used.
3. *Compare different accounts of the same event.* This involves searching for cause–effect relationships and separating what appears to be fact from opinion.
4. *Identify the big idea in a story.* This involves separating the important points from the peripheral or colorful but nonessential ones.
5. *Recognize how information is categorized and organized.* This includes identifying the structure of newspapers and periodicals and recognizing the nature of the contents within each section.

Many local newspapers host a program, Newspapers in Education (NIE), that provides weekly and daily resources for teachers and students related to current events and the newspaper. Check with your local newspaper or visit **www.nie.online.com** to learn more about their NIE program. Newspapers are useful in integrating social studies (see Box 9.1).

Visual Literacy

Research data suggest that learning through imagery, such as pictures, is often easier than through other forms. Pictorial data enliven lessons and spark interest in social studies activities. There are a variety of still pictures and visual materials available for teaching social studies, including paintings, photos, slides, drawings, dioramas, and transparencies. Old magazines and newspapers, as well as commercially prepared materials, are treasure troves of visual materials that can be used as springboards for social studies lessons. For students to comprehend visual data with social data effectively, however, they need to understand how to *read* pictures.

BOX 9.1	Addressing the Issues: Why Integrating Social Studies and Language Arts is So Important for Social Studies Teachers and Their Students

It is hard to argue with the importance of reading and writing in today's society. Even with shortcuts and fail-safe measures, we have to keep our i's dotted and t's crossed (with spelling and grammar checks); we all must know and practice good literacy skills. As an added incentive, we are tested, or rather our students are tested, to see if we have taught them properly so that they can make the grade. Literacy skills can get rusty if you do not read or write outside the classroom. Today, teachers are faced with students who are more watchers than readers. The skills these children bring to the classroom show their lack of literary practice—thus the rush to increase the amount of time spent reading and writing. This usually comes at the expense of another subject, such as social studies. Good teachers realize that they can teach reading and writing skills through the social studies. As an added bonus, they can emphasize character education, another specific area that teachers are pressured to include in their curriculum.

Newspapers provide excellent sources for combining language arts, social studies, and character education. Students can look for specific individuals in the news whose timely actions exemplify a particular character trait, like courage, responsibility, or integrity, and write about how each of them demonstrated the trait. The writer could then reference herself and relate a way that she has shown that quality.

Shorting social studies education weakens the foundation that helps us all to develop our sense of place. We need to know the roots of our common heritage, as well as appreciate the special cultures that many of our people have brought to our country. Pride is a powerful incentive that enables us to persevere and try our best in all our subject areas in school. The ball is in the court of elementary social studies. Because elementary teachers teach it all, they can model how to teach social studies in every subject area. Theirs can be a true integrated curriculum. Middle school teachers, too, feel the pressure to increase language arts instructional time. As a result of robbing social studies time in the elementary and middle school, high school teachers now bemoan the lack of preparation that students bring to high school civics, world history, and American history classes. By emphasizing social studies as an important subject and using it when appropriate as subject matter for the other disciplines, we can help our students to become learned historians with good citizenship qualities while they are practicing their skills in reading, writing, speaking, and listening.

Techniques for Reading Still Pictures. Reading visual material effectively requires some of the same techniques that print reading does. It involves more than merely perceiving what is visually present. In reading visual materials, viewers try to answer a series of basic questions. These include points such as:

- Identifying which data the picture presents (What is presented?)
- Distinguishing whether the information represents fact or fiction (Is this an actual or recreated version of reality?)
- Relating the data to other information (What bearing does this have on what is known already?)
- Summarizing the data (What would be an appropriate title or caption for the item?)

Projection devices, such as an overhead projector or LCD panel, are helpful tools in displaying an image for the entire class to see. It is effective to lead students through photo analysis by asking students to complete tasks such as:

- If you were in the background of this image, what would you hear? Describe the conversation and background noises.
- Imagine you are one of the people in this image. Describe what you see, hear, feel, smell, and touch.

In Chapter 7, other considerations for processing pictures and constructing meaning from them were discussed. These encompass an examination of the varieties of pictures that appear in the social studies, including political cartoons.

Communicating Social Studies Subject Matter

In addition to becoming more effective readers, students need to communicate effectively in their citizenship roles. Communication involves *listening, speaking,* and *writing.* In the home, the marketplace, at work or play, in addition to reading, all of us must listen, speak, and write effectively to achieve some of our most fundamental goals and live in harmony with others.

Reading, listening, speaking, and writing are interrelated. "Each informs and supports the other" (Strickland, 1990, p. 20). Instructional approaches that attempt to integrate all these elements into meaningful activities for students are often characterized as **whole-language approaches.** By integrating these four dimensions throughout the social studies curriculum, teachers can better prepare students for their roles as citizens.

Listening and Speaking

Much of students' cognitive development depends on opportunities to engage in social discourse. This includes interactions within and presentations to groups, where feedback is available. As they engage in dialogue with others, students clarify and advance their own thinking, as well as influence and persuade others. Part of the social studies curriculum should assist students in becoming effective in communicating their ideas through listening and speaking to other individuals and interacting in small and large groups.

Some students, as they enter school, appear to be skillful listeners; they already have learned to wait quietly until another finishes speaking. Becoming a good listener, just as with becoming a good speaker, requires practice. The basic characteristic of good listeners seems to be that they allow senders to complete their messages without interruption and they interpret correctly the senders' main points. Both conditions are necessary for effective listening.

In the classroom, helping students become good listeners includes teaching them to take turns in talking and to wait for acknowledgment before speaking. It also requires that the teacher delay calling on impulsive speakers. Posting a simple set of rules to encourage listening and speaking in structured teacher-led discussions can be a helpful reminder to students.

Some techniques that help foster effective listening and speaking are

- Requiring that all students periodically restate or review what another said earlier
- Providing criteria for self-analysis of speaking abilities
- Having students "interview" one another, record the interview, and play the interview as a podcast
- Creating games or role-playing enactments to provide practice in letting everyone speak and listen
- Periodically asking students to take notes when others give reports or short presentations
- Having students listen to public speakers or media figures and then asking them to paraphrase what they just heard
- Encouraging students to practice giving their reports at home using a tape recorder

A self-evaluation form that students may use to monitor their own discussion habits in groups is shown in Figure 9.9.

FIGURE 9.9
Pupil Self-Evaluation Form for Discussions

What Do I Do in Discussions?

	Sometimes	Always	Never
1. Do I do most of the talking?	_____	_____	_____
2. Do I usually talk only a little?	_____	_____	_____
3. Can I follow the suggestions of others?	_____	_____	_____
4. Do I get angry when others do not agree with me?	_____	_____	_____
5. Do I interrupt others?	_____	_____	_____
6. Do I take turns talking?	_____	_____	_____
7. Do I stay on the subject?	_____	_____	_____
8. Am I a good listener?	_____	_____	_____

Integrating Writing into the Social Studies Curriculum

Like reading, speaking, and listening, writing is an integral part of effective citizenship (Bragaw & Hartoonian, 1988; "*Civitas*," 1991). Stotsky (1990) has written:

> [W]riting has been as much a part of the history of democratic self government as reading, and is essential to public speaking. In the course of American history, as local self government developed, so too did the kind and amount of writing that people needed to do as citizens . . . .
>
> Writing is also a vital support for the most direct way that citizens can express themselves and participate in civic or political life: as public speakers. Finally, writing for academic purposes can stimulate the moral reasoning and the independent reading and thinking that lie at the heart of both academic study and responsible public discourse. (p. 72)

Stotsky suggested some of the basic ways that students can use writing in their citizenship roles:

- To personalize civic relationships and/or express civic identity (e.g., thank-you letter to a civic official)
- To provide information or services (e.g., community newsletter)
- To evaluate public services (letter of request to a public service)
- To advocate a position on a public issue (letter to the editor)

In addition to these types of civic writing, teachers could integrate the following types of writing into social studies activities:

Recording in journals

Writing poems

Creating Web pages

Constructing data-retrieval charts

Preparing information for databases in computer programs

Creating captions for cartoons

Taking notes

Writing book reviews

Writing reports

Developing scripts for movies

Constructing advertisements and brochures

Writing newsletters

Some roles or audiences that students might assume for their writing activities are outlined in Figure 9.10.

FIGURE 9.10
Audiences for Social Studies Writing

ad agencies	characters in novels	movie stars
administrators	doctors	pen pals
artists	historical figures	politicians
athletes	hospital patients	salespersons
cartoonists	journalists	scientists
Chamber of Commerce	lawyers	teachers
community figures	older or younger students	television stations

Note. From *Content Reading Including Study Systems: Reading, Writing and Studying Across the Curriculum* (p. 121), by C. M. Santa, L. Havens, M. Nelson, M. Danner, L. Scalf, and J. Scalf, 1988. Reprinted with permission of the publisher.

The RAFT Technique. An example of a basic technique to make students more effective writers in the context of the social studies curriculum is *RAFT*, developed by Vandervanter (cited in Santa et al., 1988). The technique helps students improve their essays by teaching them to consider four major dimensions in their writing:

- Role they are assuming, such as a woman in colonial times or the inventor of the polio vaccine
- Audience to whom they are writing, such as an employer or a patient
- Format for the written communication, such as a diary or an advertisement
- Topic (plus an action verb), such as urging an industry to stop polluting a stream or clarifying a misunderstanding with a friend

Technology Tools in Writing

Among the tools that teachers can use to assist students in improving their writing are various types of word-processing computer programs. These encourage students to experiment with language, sentence and paragraph structure, and the sequencing of ideas and to construct multiple drafts. Such programs also allow students to prepare banners and newsletters. Many word processors have editing features that allow students to track their revisions and allow a peer or teacher to make comments within the document.

Beyond the traditional word processor, students today are using multimedia to represent what they are learning in the social studies classroom. Students may design Web pages, digital video movies, or PowerPoint presentations to synthesize information on a particular unit. There are a variety of software programs and pieces of hardware that facilitate multimedia learning in the social studies classroom.

MidLink Magazine (**www.ncsu.edu/midlink/**) is one example of middle school students' using the Web to share projects for their social studies classroom. Through this site, students from across the world are able to contribute their projects and share them with a world audience. A recent project completed by middle school students is called "Coming to America." Students researched the experiences of Asian and European immigrants at the turn of the 19th century and wrote historical fiction that explores the economic, political, and social aspects of the time period.

Digital historical narratives are an example of students using multimedia software to foster reading and writing skills. Digital historical narratives are short digital movies (1 to 3 minutes) that students create using tools such as iMovie, MovieMaker, or PrimaryAccess. Students select historical images and write a narration to accompany the images. Then, they record their voice as the narration. Sample digital historical narratives are available through Documenting the American South's Classroom website: **http://docsouth.unc.edu/classroom/narratives/classroom.html.**

Comic Life is another piece of software that students can learn to facilitate reading and writing skills. Using the Comic Life software, students can create a number of products such as comics, story boards, brochures, or photo albums. With relative ease, students can develop creative reports, biographies, time lines, or conceptual maps. Or more information about Comic Life, visit **www.macinstruct .com/node/69**.

The act of producing the narrative provides a strong active learning experience, in which the learner must research the topic, actively construct meaning from the primary documents available, craft a written story that conveys that understanding to others, and finally, create a movie that uses the documents to accompany the narration in a visually compelling manner.

Remembering Social Studies Subject Matter

An adjunct to helping students comprehend subject matter as they read text materials is aiding them in *remembering* such information (see Box 9.2; Mastropieri & Scruggs, 1991; Torney-Purta, 1991). To the extent that teachers and text authors

---

BOX 9.2   Addressing the Issues: Making Study Skills a Part of Your Program

In the 1970s, a study skills technique called SQ3R was all the rage. It is still applicable to today's instruction and is a simple way to teach your children how to use a book chapter's layout as a way to reinforce the reading. SQ3R stands for Survey, Question, Read, Recite, Review. First, ask your students to examine the title and headings of the chapter. Second, have them turn the title and the headings into questions and try to imagine what each part is all about. Third, students read the chapter. Fourth, have them go back to the title and the headings and recite what that part was about. Finally, they review the chapter, look at the questions at the end, and try to answer them. As an update, we suggest reading through the questions before actually reading the text. Reading for a purpose (to answer the questions) results in greater comprehension.

systematically organize data for more efficient remembering, they assist students in creating schemata and referencing, activating, and applying prior knowledge.

The subject of memory traditionally has suffered from association with the rote learning of nonfunctional information. In reality, students frequently are required in social studies classes to remember a great number of names, places, events, dates, and general descriptive information to clarify and link new knowledge in meaningful ways. This need includes remembering names, places, events, dates, patterns, and general descriptive information.

Imagery and Memory

Creating an image related to an element of subject matter often can assist us in remembering of information (Bower, 1972; Richardson, 1980; Wittrock, 1986). In an extensive review of 23 studies, Levie and Lentz (1982) concluded that drawings and pictures have a powerful effect on learning from printed instructional materials. In all but one study, students learned more from materials that included related illustrations or pictures than from materials without illustrations. Research also indicates that spatial information may be learned more effectively from maps than from verbal descriptions.

Wittrock's (1986) model of generative learning predicts that both memory and comprehension are facilitated when students relate new information to be learned to their prior knowledge and generate a representation of the relationship. Students who wished to remember the various battles of the Civil War, for example, might visually imagine Bull Run as a bull, Gettysburg as a Getty gasoline station, and so on.

Structured Mnemonic Techniques

Several specific memory strategies, or **mnemonic techniques,** exist for social studies applications, some dating back to the early Romans and Greeks (Bellezza, 1981; Wittrock, 1986). Mnemonics involve either imagery or verbal devices or some combination of the two. Two mnemonic strategies that have applications to social studies instruction are the first-letter technique and the keyword technique.

First-Letter Technique. The **first-letter technique** involves taking the first letter of each word to be remembered and composing a word or sentence from the letters. For example, to remember the list of American presidents in correct chronological order, one may remember a rhyme such as "Watch *a* *j*olly *m*an *m*ake . . ." (Washington, Adams, Jefferson, Madison, Monroe).

Another application of the first-letter technique is to create an acronym composed of the first letters of the items you wish to remember. For example, suppose you wish to remember the names of the Great Lakes: Huron, Ontario, Michigan, Erie, and Superior. Remembering the simple acronym *HOMES*, which is composed of the first letters of the names, will help you recall the five lakes.

The Keyword Technique. Another mnemonic device, the **keyword technique**, was initially used for learning foreign language vocabulary (Atkinson, 1975). It since has been applied to a variety of types of information, including social studies data, and has several variations (see Mastropieri & Scruggs, 1991). This technique involves first identifying a word to be related to the one to be remembered and then generating an interactive image between the two words (Levin & Pressley, 1985).

Based on their extensive review of the related research, Pressley, Levin, and Delaney (1982) concluded: "The evidence is overwhelming that use of the keyword method, as applied to recall of vocabulary definitions, greatly facilitates performance" (pp. 70–71). Their conclusion was based on the analysis of studies in which both concrete and abstract words were the learning tasks, and the subjects were of varying ages.

Mastropieri and Scruggs (1991) suggested that the application of the keyword technique consists of three steps:

1. Create a keyword by casting the terms to be learned into a term that sounds similar and that can be represented visually in some concrete way. (Example: Apples to represent Annapolis, the capital of Maryland.)
2. Relate the keyword to the information to be learned in a picture, image, or sentence. (Example: Visualize apples getting married.)
3. Verbally review the relationships by first recalling the keyword, noting the relationship in the visual image, and then stating the correct response. (Example: Recall the word *apples*, note what the apples were doing in the image, and assert that Annapolis is the capital of Maryland.)

Notetaking Techniques

Effective notetaking techniques can also facilitate both comprehension and remembering of subject matter in social studies texts and lectures (see Slater, Graves, & Piche, 1985). One effective notetaking technique uses a **split-page approach**, as illustrated by Spires and Stone (1989) in Figure 9.11.

Students are directed to divide the page into two columns. The left column, which takes up one-third of the page, is for listing key concepts and ideas. The right column is for related supporting information.

Spires and Stone (1989) found that the notetaking strategy was particularly effective when students learned to ask themselves the following questions before, during, and after a lecture:

Planning (before taking notes):

How interested am I in this topic?

If my interest is low, how do I plan to increase interest?

Do I feel motivated to pay attention?

What is my purpose for listening to this lecture?

FIGURE 9.11
Split-Page Method of Notetaking

Lecture Topic: "Social Control"	
Definition of social control	Ways of conditioning or limiting actions of individuals to motivate them to conform to social norms.
Two types of social control	(1) internalized (2) externalized
Internal control	Individuals accept norms of group or society as part of own personality (e.g., refrain from stealing not because afraid of arrest but because believe stealing is wrong).
	Most effective means of socially controlling deviant behavior.
External control	Set of social sanctions (informal or formal) found in every society.
Informal sanctions	Applied through actions of people we associate with every day (i.e., the *primary* group).
	May range from gesture of disapproval to rejection by primary group.
Formal sanctions	Applied by agents given that function by society (e.g., law enforcement).

Note. Figure from Hiller A. Spires and P. Diane Stone (1989), "The Directed Notetaking Activity: A Self-Questioning Approach." *Journal of Reading, 33*(1), October, pp. 36–39. Reprinted with permission of the International Reading Association. All rights reserved.

Monitoring (while taking notes):

Am I maintaining a satisfactory level of concentration?

Am I taking advantage of the fact that thought is faster than speech?

Am I separating main concepts from supporting details?

What am I doing when comprehension fails?

What strategies am I using for comprehension failure?

Evaluating (after taking notes):

Did I achieve my purpose?

Was I able to maintain satisfactory levels of concentration and motivation?

Did I deal with comprehension failures adequately?

Overall, do I feel that I processed the lecture at a satisfactory level? (p. 37)

English as a Second Language (ESL)

Nearly 10% of the public school population has limited proficiency in English (Kindler, 2002). The implications of the growing number of students in our classrooms who are ESL learners are severe. Many of these students leave their regular classroom for English lessons, but they spend the majority of their school day in a regular classroom. Given that 42% of public school teachers have an ESL student in their class, it is more important than ever for social studies teachers to understand how they can effectively meet the needs of this population of students.

The role of culture and community are vital to making school a positive experience for ESL students. To begin, teachers should make every child feel welcome in the classroom. This may take the form of simply learning to correctly spell and pronounce the ESL learner's name or inviting the ESL student to share aspects of his or her culture with the class. The teacher and the class community should seek to learn about the ESL student's native culture. Barriers to learning may easily be removed once there is an understanding about the ESL student's prior experiences and schooling. At the same time, the teacher should share aspects of local culture. Something as routine as a fire drill alarm can be quite unsettling to a new ESL student.

Teachers should encourage students to use their native language to help them learn social studies. Teachers should not try to teach ESL students alone. Teachers should partner with ESL specialists in the school or community to identify the best strategies to help each student learn. Teachers should also allow students to help one another. Partnering a new ESL student with a more veteran ESL student is one way to help both students learn. It is also important to make parents of these students feel welcome in the school. This may mean sending a letter home to parents in their native language or holding parent conferences during times that parents are available to come to school or in a local community center.

Specific instructional methods such as using graphic organizers and implementing cooperative learning are effective in helping ESL students master the social studies content, while also increasing their language proficiency. Technology tools also are useful strategies to assist the ESL learner. Bilingual software or translating devices found on websites such as **www.altavista.com** allow the student to read and listen to content in both the native language and in English. The chart on the next page further highlights methods of differentiating instruction for bilingual learners.

NCSS published a special bulletin, *Passport to Learning: Teaching Social Studies to ESL Students* (2003), that focuses on this topic. Included in this bulletin are specific instructional strategies and lessons for the different social sciences, such as:

- Use cooperative learning strategies to help students build their schema and ask questions in a smaller group.

What Strategies or Activities Can Help Bilingual Learners Understand Class Lectures?	What Can Help Bilingual Learners to Participate More Effectively in Class Discussions?	What Strategies or Activities Can Help English Language Learners To Read Grade-Level Texts?	What Strategies or Activities Can Help Bilingual Learners Develop Their Writing Proficiency in English?
Provide an outline with blanks student can fill in during lecture	Allow more wait time	Use pre-reading, during-reading, and after-reading activities	Discuss and share before writing
Pause for asking neighbor question	Use Think, Pair, Share	Make connections and build on prior knowledge	Practice outlines, graphic organizers
Provide pre-lecture notes, agenda	Play readers' theatre	Provide time lines	Allow peer editing
Build/connect with background knowledge	Don't correct mistakes, model/repeat answer using correct language, but focus on meaning not form	Teach how to summarize/paraphrase/ take notes	Practice every day
Tape lectures	Use thumbs up/down	Use lower level on same subject	Practice writing in first language
Summarize at beginning	Wait until most students have their hands up to call upon someone	Read aloud	Use warm-ups/ quick writes
Let students teach small topics	Create an accepting class community	Break into small sections	Write letters/ e-mails
Use an outline or graphic organizer	Explore ideas in writing before discussion	Use reading conferences	Use group writing/ shared writing
Have class routines	Have provocative questions that everyone can relate to	Make cartoon strips	Have pen pals/ E-pals
Use games/ dramas	Have students hold up cards of opinions	Use pre-reading strategies: key points, word mapping, context for understanding text, vocabulary, concept	Focus on authentic writing— prompts and audience
			Use cartooning

- Use the "V.I.P.S." in speaking to students. V stands for voice: quality and pitch; I stands for intonation: proper enunciation; P stands for pausing: for comprehension and response; and S stands for speed: giving time to process the language.
- Assess student knowledge of social studies content based on language proficiency and comprehension.
- Incorporate students' cultural experiences into classroom instruction.

The lesson described in Figure 9.12 is one example of teaching social studies content that addresses issues of English language learners.

FIGURE 9.12
Whom Should We Allow In?

Intermediate Fluency

One of the thorniest dilemmas facing our nation concerns immigration to the United States. This exercise allows students to consider whether some people should be given preference over others as immigrants to the United States. Acting as a facilitator, the teacher must be prepared for spirited student discussion and to work through some potentially prejudiced viewpoints. Because of the inherently controversial nature of the topic, the classroom teacher should use his or her professional judgments as to whether the activity is a suitable one for his or her class. Despites these caveats, this exercise underscores the difficulties of choice that confront us, especially when those choices concern our fellow human beings.

Materials

Student resource sheet (Whom Should We Allow In?")

Strategy

1. Place students in groups of three or four. Explain that they are a panel of U.S. immigration officials who will be reviewing the backgrounds and credentials of ten people trying to gain entry into the United States. Because immigration is restricted to certain quotas per year, only four of the applicants can be allowed in.

2. Distribute "Whom Should We Allow In?"to each student, allowing ELL students to have access to their bilingual dictionaries. Direct students to silently read through the cases first and, individually, rank them from most desirable (1) to least desirable (10) as U.S. citizens. After everyone has ranked the applicants as individuals, each group is to discuss its rankings, consider which characteristics should be most sought in immigrants, and decide which four applicants will be allowed entry into the U.S.

   [Alternate Strategy: You may also want to first present the scenarios with visuals and gestures and then group students to rank them.]

3. Ask each group to write its list of four (in rank order) on the board.

4. As a class, discuss the rankings and the discussions that led to their final decisions. Ask: Whom did you pick first—why?

5. Bring closure to the lesson by leading a discussion using the following questions:
   a. What is the most important thing to help you decide who can come to the United States?
   b. Should political immigrants be given priority over those who immigrate for economic reasons? [Explain, if necessary: a political immigrant is someone who comes to live in the U.S. because his or her political beliefs are not the same as the government's political beliefs in his or her country. An economic immigrant comes to live in the U.S. to find better job prospects.]
   c. Would your rankings be different if you could place certain conditions on the applicants (e.g., ineligibility for public assistance or learning English)?
   d. What might happen if the United States decided to stop all immigration into the country?
   e. Do you think the United States will ever need to stop immigration entirely? Why or why not?

(continued)

FIGURE 9.12
Continued

Ricardo Flores:

1. 34-year-old farmer from small town in Mexico where there is guerrilla violence
2. has a family (wife, mother, and four children) who will come with him
3. skilled agricultural worker who is willing to accept any work available; wife and mother also willing and able to work
4. speaks only Spanish.

Chandra Patel:

1. 42-year-old physician from India
2. he and his family (wife and three children) want a new start in the U.S.
3. Dr. Patel is internationally well-known as a cardiologist
4. will move to Atlanta where his uncle and two cousins live.

Michael Collins:

1. 29-year-old computer programmer from Ireland
2. has a high level of education and experience in computer science
3. has no family or friends in the U.S.
4. is HIV-positive.

Francine Bouvier:

1. 21-year-old fashion model from France
2. well-known in the U.S.; has been on the cover of several magazines
3. wants to become an American citizen eventually
4. speaks little English but is starting a language course soon.

Lydia Martínez:

1. 65-year-old retired school teacher from Cuba
2. is sick and cannot get necessary medicines and treatment in her native country
3. has two children in Miami who are willing to give her a home
4. speaks only Spanish.

Li Chang:

1. 25-year-old factory worker from China
2. has one child with his wife but would like to have more (the "one-child policy" in China makes it difficult for them to have another child)
3. would like to settle in San Francisco where there is a large Asian community.

Sonya Petrov:

1. 14-year-old gymnast from Russia
2. would like to move with her parents to the U.S. to increase Sonya's career prospects; they have hopes of her joining the American Olympic team
3. all three are fluent in English.

François Pamphile:

1. 50-year-old taxi driver from Haiti
2. single, no family
3. cannot make a living in Port-au-Prince because of his country's political and economic problems
4. speaks French, Creole, and some English.

Hans Deutch:

1. 34-year-old German with a petty criminal record
2. has been studying English for the past year
3. is willing to work at any job available although he has training as a diesel mechanic.

Note. Figure from "Whom Shall We Allow In" by B. C. Cruz, J. W. Nutta, J. O'Brien, C. M. Feyten, and J. M. Govoni, 2003, *Passport to Learning: Teaching Social Studies to ESL Students*. Bulletin No. 101. Copyright 2003 by National Council for the Social Studies. Reprinted by permission.

SUMMARY

Students have a lot to remember these days. As one teacher points out, "Social studies doesn't ever decrease the materials we have to learn. We keep adding more material with each passing year!" This chapter has introduced you to different ways of helping students sort social studies information and categorize it to make it easier to understand and remember. It has also looked at the importance of the format of the text and how to aid students who are trying to keep all the facts and concepts straight. Newspapers and trade books are important additions to the curriculum and can offer a personalized encounter with events and people that may receive only a mention in the textbook. Integrating social studies into all areas of the curriculum ensures that students learn and appreciate the stories of themselves and others. Adding the personal touch to your social studies program through the use of dramatic narrative makes your classroom an exciting place for you and your students. Another tool for teaching and learning that heightens interest and provides timely instruction opportunities is technology. This chapter has also taken into account the growing population of ESL students in our schools and suggested methods to assist in their development of social studies content and skills. In the next chapter we will look at many ways to incorporate technology into the social studies curriculum.

ACTIVITIES

1. Select a social studies textbook. Create (a) a graphic organizer for any chapter within the text, (b) a data-retrieval chart for another chapter, and (c) a frame for another chapter. Compare your results and discuss how they could scaffold students' learning.
2. Select one of the technology applications mentioned in this chapter (Inspiration, Comic Life, iMovie, MovieMaker, Web authoring). Explore the technology and discuss how you could use it to teach a specific unit of study.
3. Identify five metaphors in newspapers or periodicals. Then explain how you would try to explain them to a middle school student using the guidelines in the chapter.
4. Identify and read four trade books for students that address significant social issues. List the author, title, publisher, and copyright date for each, along with a brief summary of the book and the issue it raises. To identify some appropriate works, consult NCSS's list of notable trade books.
5. Interview a teacher who has worked with an ESL student. Ask the teacher what strategies were most effective to help the student learn social studies content. Inquire as to what strategies were more effective to learn about the student's prior experiences and cultural background.

WEB RESOURCES

TechLINK

MultiMedia Mania: **www.ncsu.edu/mmania/**
ReadingQuest.org: **www.readingquest.org**
HowToStudy.org: **www.howtostudy.org/resources/howh/index.htm**
National Paideia Center: **www.paideia.org/**
Scholastic: **http://teacher.scholastic.com/**
Dave's ESL Café: **www.eslcafe.com/**

Chapter 10

Using Technology to Enhance Social Studies Instruction

Integrating Technology into Today's Classrooms

Internet Applications for Social Studies Instruction

Media Literacy

Web-Based Resources for Teachers and Students

Telecollaboration

Software Applications for the Social Studies Classroom

Simulation Software

Database and Spreadsheet Software

Multimedia Editing Software

Mapping Software

Personal Digital Assistants in the Social Studies Classroom

Technology Challenges

Internet Safety

Copyright

Digital Divide

Emerging Technologies: Challenges of the Future

Summary

Activities

Web Resources

Imagine we have planned a visit to Ms. Hooper's ninth-grade geography classroom. The classroom is charged with energy and abuzz with activity. At first blush, however, to the untutored eye the class appears chaotic and lacking focus and structure.

Ms. Hooper spots us at the door and waves us into the room. She is hovering over a computer station, brainstorming with a small group of students, who she explains later are working together to learn more about the social and biological effects of stream pollution.

The students, still in the preliminary stages of their research, first surveyed some basic reference materials such as the online version of Encyclopaedia Britannica. *Now, the students are deep into the recesses of the Internet, searching for data and information to help them better understand the issues surrounding stream pollution. Ms. Hooper is reminding the students of the Internet search strategies she had demonstrated a few weeks ago. The strategies will help the students narrow their searches and find the most helpful information.*

Once the students have gathered preliminary information, they will develop a series of questions that they hope to be able to answer. One group of students is using the Internet to download topography maps. They will then use ArcView to access GIS (geographic information systems) data.

Nearby, two students are using digital video editing software to edit the interviews they conducted with scientists and county commissioners. They plan to splice the video clips together with news clippings they have found from news sources around the world related to stream pollution.

Down the hall in the library, a team of students is searching through texts for information that may be helpful. These students are reading not just the traditional books available on their school library's bookshelves, but also through books available online through digital libraries.

In a quiet corner, a student with a cellular phone is explaining the class's project to a state environmental official, who gives the student some contacts and telephone numbers. The official also volunteers to e-mail several sets of relevant charts and an important article describing the social costs of pollution.

At another spot in the back of the room, two other students are engaged in a synchronous online dialogue with students in Costa Rica who are researching a similar topic. The students are typing in real time to one another to learn about how stream pollution impacts communities across the world.

Through the window, we can see a team of students making their way down to the stream that borders the school property. These students have been using personal digital assistants (PDAs) to gather, record, and analyze data related to the stream's pollution over time.

Ms. Hooper uses a similar PDA to record the students' activities throughout class. She finds using a PDA to track student work to be an effective classroom management tool, especially when her students are engaged in such diverse activities as they have been today.

Integrating Technology into Today's Classrooms

All the technologies employed in the school we have just described are, in fact, available and in use in social studies classrooms. Ms. Hooper provides for her students a technology-rich environment that is highly functional in relation to her curricular goals. Her students freely and comfortably use technology tools to access authentic data and to learn more about real-world problems. In a sense, technology breaks through the traditional four walls of the classroom and empowers students to engage in powerful learning experiences.

In social studies classrooms, it has been proven that computers can help students to quickly access in structured ways great amounts of information to aid in hypothesis development and problem solving, simulate important social issues, and better organize and synthesize new information. Above all, computers can challenge and excite students.

Computers are becoming more and more a part of everyday instruction in classrooms across the nation. For example, in 1994, only 35% of public elementary and secondary schools, and 3% of all instructional rooms, had access to the Internet. Today, this figure has increased to 99% of public schools and 93% of instructional rooms (National Center for Education Statistics, 2005). As mentioned in Chapter 1, the International Society for Technology in Education (ISTE) has developed a series of National Educational Technology Standards (NETS) for both teachers and students. These standards were created under the philosophy that technology has the potential to establish new learning environments in classrooms. Figure 10.1 demonstrates how new learning environments can evolve through incorporating new technology strategies into the classroom.

FIGURE 10.1
Establishing New Learning Environments

Incorporating New Strategies	
Traditional Learning ⟶ Environments	**New Learning Environments**
Teacher-centered instruction	Student-centered learning
Single sense stimulation	Multisensory stimulation
Single path progression	Multipath progression
Single media	Multimedia
Isolated work	Collaborative work
Information delivery	Information exchange
Passive learning	Active/exploratory/inquiry-based learning
Factual, knowledge-based learning	Critical thinking and informed decision making
Reactive response	Proactive/planned action
Isolated, artificial context	Authentic, real-world context

Learning to use new technologies for classroom instruction can be exciting and overwhelming. However, it is important to stop and consider two questions before using technology applications in the classroom (Harris, 1998):

1. Will technology allow me to do something with my students that I could not do before technology?
2. Will technology allow me to do something with my students better than I'm doing it now?

Internet Applications for Social Studies Instruction

The Internet was created in 1969 by the Pentagon to help researchers and the military expedite the sharing of information around the world. Increasingly, however, it is being used by teachers and students to access and share information and break down the barriers between schools and real-world learning (Martorella, 1997; Pawloski, 1994). The Internet also serves to reduce the isolation that many classroom teachers feel and increases the potential for collaborative activities (Kearsley, 1996).

The Internet has prompted a revolution in *what* we teach and *how* we teach. In 1993, there were approximately 130 websites; today there are hundreds of millions (Leiner et al., 2000). Teachers and students are no longer limited by the resources within a school to learn about a topic. Rather, they now have access to millions of resources such as e-texts, movie clips, art, data, primary sources, and maps.

Media Literacy

With the number of online documents growing exponentially, it is essential for students to develop media literacy skills. Media literacy skills assist students in identifying and sorting through websites to find the most appropriate ones to use. Literacy was once limited to text-based or oral instruction. As means of communication have evolved with technology, literacy has evolved to include hypertext documents, multimedia projects, and online communication.

Media literacy is a set of skills that students will use for a lifetime as citizens in our global society. Skills such as effectively using search engines are one example of media literacy skills. Students must be able not only to locate appropriate information but also to critically read, analyze, evaluate, and make inferences.

There are two primary categories of search engines—mechanical search engines and human-operated directories. Mechanical search engines use web robots to cull through websites looking for pertinent documents. Examples of mechanical search engines are Alta Vista (**www.altavista.com**) and Google (**www .google.com**). Human-operated directories locate online resources by using virtual libraries and categories of resources. Yahoo (**www.yahoo.com**) is an example of a human-operated directory.

There are a number of online guides and tutorials available for teachers and students that provide more information about media literacy skills and provide updated information on searching the Web. Examples of these resources are

UCBerkeley Search Strategies: **www.lib.berkeley.edu/TeachingLib/Guides/ Internet/Strategies.html**

Education World, "Surfing for the Best Search Engine Techniques": **www .educationworld.com/a_tech/tech078.shtml**

Web-Based Resources for Teachers and Students

Web-based resources for teachers and students can be categorized into different genres. Figure 10.2 lists the different categories of online resources and gives a definition and an example of each.

WebQuests are one of the more common uses of Web-based resources in the social studies classroom. WebQuests may be considered both teacher and student resources because they have both a teacher and student page. The teacher page offers suggestions to the teacher on how to implement the WebQuest. The student page guides students through specific resources in search of information on a particular topic. WebQuests encourage students to use inquiry methods to learn more about specific topics. Box 10.1 provides more information on WebQuests.

Telecollaboration

Telecollaboration is another example of how teachers and students can use the Internet in the social studies classroom. **Telecollaboration** is the collaborative learning process that occurs when individuals connect via the Internet. Telecollaboration holds out the promise of cross-cultural insights and sharing of information from regional, national, and international sites. It also affords students in social studies classes the opportunities to obtain timely and reality-based data for research projects. In addition, it allows students to obtain multiple perspectives, including global ones, on an issue. According to Harris (1998), telecollaborative classrooms turn traditional classrooms into global classrooms. Such classrooms expose students to "differing opinions, perspectives, beliefs, experiences, and thinking processes; allow students to compare, contrast, and/or combine similar information collected in dissimilar locations; and provide a platform where students can communicate with a real audience using text and imagery" (p. 55).

Harris (1998) has defined three categories of telecollaborative activities: *interpersonal exchanges*: students and teachers connect via the Internet with geographically disparate individuals; *information collection and analysis*: students gather

FIGURE 10.2
Genres of Web-Based Resources

Category of Web-Based Resources for Teachers	Definition	Example
Professional Tools	Online tools that assist teachers in managing class activities (e.g., lesson plan generators)	Kathy Schrock's Teacher Tools: *http://school.discovery.com/ teachingtools/teaching tools.html*
Professional Resources	Online resources that provide helpful information to assist in class instruction (e.g., lesson plans)	America Memory Learning Page: *http://memory.loc.gov/ammem/ ndlpedu/index.html*
Content Resources	Online resources that enhance teacher content knowledge on a particular subject	Documenting the American South: *http://docsouth.unc.edu*
Professional Development	Online opportunities for teachers to engage in professional development	Tapped In: *http://ti2.sri.com/tappedin/*

Category of Web-Based Resources for Students	Definition	Example
Primary Sources	Online primary sources that allow students to do the work of a historian	National Archives Digital Classroom: *www.archives.gov/ digital_classroom/*
Reference Materials	Online reference resources (e.g., encyclopedias or dictionaries)	Library Spot: *www.libraryspot.com/*
Teacher/School Generated Resources	Websites that enhance communication between school and home by providing students and/or parents with information (e.g., homework suggestions or letters home to parents)	Education World's Cool Schools: *www.education-world.com/ cool_school/*
Student Generated Websites	Student projects that have been posted online	MidLink: *www.ncsu.edu/midlink/*

BOX 10.1 Addressing the Issues: Teaching with WebQuests

Meghan McGlinn
Doctoral student, School of Education
The University of North Carolina at Chapel Hill

WebQuests are Web-based, group-inquiry projects that have potential for enlivening the social studies classroom. These projects enable students to develop in-depth understanding and to think critically and creatively in analyzing and synthesizing information on a topic. Designed by Bernie Dodge and Tom March in 1995, a WebQuest is an "inquiry-oriented activity in which some or all of the information that learners interact with comes from resources on the Internet . . ." (Dodge, 1998). The WebQuest provides background information, specifies the task or product that students will complete, the process for students to follow in completing their work, and the Web sites students are to use in their research. The process usually consists of students in small groups identifying individual research assignments then regrouping to share their information and to design a product in common which they will present to the rest of the class.

Any teacher of U.S. History knows that the Gilded Age is one of the most difficult units to teach. While the Gilded Age covers a relatively short period of time (around 1880–1914), it includes the development of important themes in American History, among them industrialization, urbanization, immigration, and the Progressive Movement. Each of these themes is rich in content and includes a variety of concepts key to understanding subsequent events in American history. The textbook I used devoted several chapters to this unit and its many themes. Unfortunately, time dictated that devoting weeks of study to this time period would not allow for anything but a cursory study of more contemporary American history as the semester progressed. I faced a dilemma: How could I help my students understand the important themes of the Gilded Age in the most efficient manner?

For help, I turned to a WebQuest titled "The Gilded Age" which I retrieved from a group of examples listed on Bernie Dodge's WQ page. This WQ had everything I was looking for—an interesting product, the major themes of the Gilded Age incorporated collaborative roles for students to take, and a page of resources for students to examine. I still had my students keep up with their textbook readings and we sometimes spent half of the class time discussing and clarifying the reading. I scheduled the remaining time for group work developing the "Gilded Age Documentary" PowerPoint presentations that would be the WQ's final product. After several weeks, the students came together to give their presentations and take notes on their classmates' work. The WQ became a major part of the assessment of the unit along with a traditional objective test.

To prepare for work on the WQ I described my expectations for work in the lab and provided a copy of the opening Web page to explain the purpose of a WQ. I also previewed the student roles of "Historian," "PowerPoint Engineer," "Producer," and "Media Specialist" before we went to the lab by explaining the job descriptions and expectations. I asked students to rank their first choices among the list of roles and I assigned groups by honoring their requests as much as possible.

I altered the original WQ somewhat by adding a "goal log" requirement for the "Producer" to keep a running log of student goals and performance each day. When the students first came together they discussed what remained in the project to be accomplished and what specifically each person would be working on that day. At the end of the work period, the students would come back together to record what actually had been completed. This provided a nice way to facilitate the group work as well as a method to assess their use of class time (a portion of the rubric). I also allowed my students to create individual templates for their PowerPoint presentations rather than create one large "documentary" with

(continued)

BOX 10.1   Continued

individual slides formatted similarly. I used the rubric provided by the WQ as a starting point and made additions that reflected my goals for student mastery of the subject.

Every year when my students studied W.W.I., I introduced a project in which they divided into groups and created a newspaper realistic to the time period (roughly between 1910–1920). My objective for the project was for students to put themselves in the time and examine issues domestic and foreign, cultural and economic, that might have appeared in a newspaper of the day. Obviously the project also meant students had to work at synthesizing information, writing, editing, group skills, and creativity in order to create a layout that looked like a newspaper. Students chose the name of the paper and the city of publication. I required a number of specific article topics but the students also chose a variety of items to incorporate into their design. On the whole, this project was very successful; students seem to enjoy working in a group and engaging in development of the newspaper. It is always hard for them at first to pick the date and title, but once they do, they decide fairly quickly which article topics to include and which items to develop.

My main concern with the project became collecting resources for student use and creating a space for their access. I was increasingly aware of tremendous amounts of online texts, photographs, audio files, and drawings from W.W.I. collected in digital libraries and on Web pages and wanted to incorporate these into my teaching. I liked the way my project was organized, the roles it included, and the final product, so I decided to create a WQ based my original project idea. The final product or purpose of my WQ "W.W.I.: A War to End War" remained to create a W.W.I. newspaper but I added specific group roles and expectations for newspaper editor, researcher/writer, and artist. The resource page provided links to all of the electronic sources that I felt were the most interesting and rich in content, and I also included a rubric with assessment information. By using a WQ format, my students could easily access not only the directions for the assignment but also resources useful for their investigations and writing away from my classroom.

WQ definitely provides a break from traditional, teacher-centered instruction in my classroom. Not only does it encourage students to take more control of their learning but also it provides an outlet for creativity and individual strengths. Students who felt more comfortable about using technology often helped their classmates learn techniques for navigating a Web page or creating a PowerPoint presentation. At the same time students who enjoyed researching history had the opportunity to do so. Most importantly the products provided the opportunity to showcase talents (artistry, creativity, humor, and technical ability) that under other circumstances may not have been made apparent in social studies class. Overall the WQ provided a highly motivating activity for my students and a chance to engage in the work of real historians as they developed a more meaningful understanding of the past.

Resources

Caswell, T., & DeLorenzo, J. (1998). *The gilded age WebQuest: Documenting industrialization in America.* Retrieved April 22, 2003, from Oswego City School District, New York, website: **www.oswego .org/staff/tcaswell/wq/gildedage/student.htm**

Dodge, B. (1998). The WebQuest Page. Retrieved on October 20, 2003, from San Diego State University, website: **http://webquest.sdsu.edu/**

McGlinn, M., & McGlinn, J. (2003). *The great war to end war.* Retrieved October 20, 2003, from UNC-Asheville, website: **www.unca.edu/~mcglinn/ WWIwebquest.htm** authentic data and create projects to share and analyze with others; and *problem solving*: collaborative activities engage students in critical thinking and problem-based learning. Examples of each of these categories may be explored through Harris's Virtual Architecture website (**http://virtual-architecture.wm.edu/**).

The Global School House (**www.gsn.org/**) is another excellent resource for identifying telecollaborative projects. For example, *Life on the Streets* is a project developed by high school students in San Diego. The students were all homeless at one time and tell the story of homelessness through the eyes of students. This powerful project invites students from around the globe to share their stories of homelessness in their community.

Methods of Telecollaboration. Through the Internet, students and teachers can engage in collaborative learning experiences using e-mail, discussion boards, Web logs, real-time chat, and videoconferencing.

E-mail is the familiar form of telecollaboration. We use it daily to correspond with friends, family, and colleagues. This asynchronous text-based tool is also an effective technology tool that can be used to expand the classroom. Through projects such as ePals (**www.epals.com/**), teachers can design lessons that link students with other students across the world. The students can then communicate with one another via e-mail to discuss various issues. Teachers are able to register for projects or submit projects. The "War-Affected Children" project is one example of how ePals can be used to provide a forum for students to discuss the impact of war on students through the work of Graça Machel, the wife of Nelson Mandela.

E-mail can also help students hone their communication skills. Since e-mail protocols promote focused writing (i.e., identifying audience and the purpose of the message), revising and editing are important before sending. Because the message will be sent out over a public forum to an unseen audience, students also tend to be motivated to produce an exemplary communication.

Discussion boards and Web logs are two other examples of telecollaboration tools. Discussion boards are Web-based forums that thread online posts. Typically, they are often text based. Most often, posts are organized, or threaded, by the subject. To view a sample discussion board, visit the NCSS Web page (**www.ncss.org/**) and select "discussion board" from the menu.

Web logs are online personal journals that students and teachers can create and contribute to over time. They can be used as student portfolios or as a class portal where teachers post homework or class notes. Web logs can also be used to facilitate collaborative writing or peer review of writing. Web logs can support multimedia such as recorded sound or video clips. For more information on Web logs and to view Web logs, visit Weblogs in Education (**www.weblogg-ed.com/**) or Blogger.com (**http://new.blogger.com/**).

Real-time chat and videoconferencing are two synchronous telecollabora-tives that support simultaneous communication. Planning synchronous activities may take a bit more coordination, because teachers must consider factors such as the time zone of the partner school and the equipment that is being used. Software such as Skype or Microsoft NetMeeting can be downloaded for free to facilitate real-time chat discussions. These discussions may link students with other students or they may link students with scholars and experts in the field.

Videoconferencing allows students to see and hear each other in real time. Software programs such as Skype, SightSpeed, or Microsoft NetMeeting support videoconferencing and are user friendly. The Global School House has a special portal dedicated to videoconferencing. Visit the portal to learn more about equipment needed and upcoming projects for you and your students (**www.globalschoolhouse. org/cu/aglance.html**).

Software Applications for the Social Studies Classroom

In addition to the plethora of Internet-based resources for social studies teaching and learning, there are numerous software applications for the classroom. Teachers should examine software as critically as they do traditional print materials and media. This requires that they become conversant with the capabilities and limitations of existing software through the use of objective evaluation criteria.

Evaluation of instructional software should occur at two levels. One addresses general technical and instructional issues such as whether the software functions flawlessly or gives clear directions. Numerous guidelines have been developed for teachers to conduct objective evaluations at this level (e.g., Roberts, Carter, Friel, & Miller, 1988). A second level of evaluation focuses on the way in which subject matter is represented in the software (for instance, whether it is factually correct and addresses significant objectives). For more information on software evaluation, visit **www.clrn.org/home/**.

Simulation Software

Simulation software engages students in authentic activities that typically require critical-thinking skills. Software simulations have the capacity to stimulate lively discussions, whether used as an individual, small-group, or whole-class activity with a large monitor. As with noncomputer simulations, teachers need to carefully structure an activity and engage students in reflection and generalization. An example of a simulation software collection is Tom Snyder's *Decisions Decisions* series. Each of the software programs presents students with a dilemma that they must work to resolve in small groups. Each student is assigned a role and given information pertinent to that role. The issues to be addressed range from the campaign trail to feudalism to the Revolutionary War.

Database and Spreadsheet Software

Students can use database and spreadsheet software to access or input data which can then be manipulated and analyzed. Microsoft Excel is an example of spreadsheet software. Databases and spreadsheets are an effective tool for engaging students in critical-thinking skills.

For example, suppose a class research project involves collecting data concerning the nature, scope, and seriousness of the problem of homelessness in America. The teacher has divided the class into 10 groups, each responsible for five states. After some discussion, the teacher and the groups identify the basic questions they would like to have answered from their research:

- Who are the homeless (e.g., gender, number of children)?
- How extensive is the problem of homelessness (e.g., number)?
- Where is the problem of the homeless the greatest in the United States (e.g., states with the highest percentage)?
- How much are local and state governments doing to solve the problem of the homeless (e.g., state expenditures, types of shelters provided)?

One group lists on a large sheet of paper the categories of data that it recommends the class collect and enter into the database according to the procedures specified in the software manual. Other groups make further recommendations. The teacher points out some changes in the categories that are required by the protocols of the database (e.g., not using commas in recording numerical data). The class as a whole then finally adopts a common list of categories. As a next step, students proceed to do research and mathematical calculations to identify the required information, then enter the data under each category. Once this is accomplished, students can use the database to answer their questions.

Spreadsheet software engages students in social mathematics (Hannah, 1985– 1986). It enables them to make numerical tabulations quickly, make predictions from extrapolations, and show the impact of one variable on another (e.g., effects of increases in cigarette taxes on the federal budget). Within spreadsheets, numerical data are entered in columns and rows, and results may be represented as tabular data or in the forms of graphs and charts. Once data are entered in a spreadsheet, it can "crunch" the numbers to quickly answer questions. Although most spreadsheets appear foreboding and complex to use, some, such as Excel, are suitable for student use.

Multimedia Editing Software

Definitions abound, but essentially, the term **interactive multimedia** refers to some combination of video, sound, graphics, and images orchestrated by a computer. "Interactive multimedia—the marriage of text, audio, and visual data within a single information delivery system—represents a potentially powerful tool for teachers and students throughout the curriculum" (White, 1990, p. 68). *Interactivity* refers to the fact that the user controls his or her path through a program.

Interactive multimedia technologies show promise of aiding social studies teachers in motivating students and translating abstract ideas into more concrete examples (Martorella, 1997). The effective and full use of these electronic aids, however, will depend on how skilled social studies teachers become in their applications. As Simon (1990) has underscored, "It is increasingly clear that as powerful new technologies and software proliferate, teachers will need to learn more about these new tools on a continuous basis" (p. 8).

Emerging multimedia systems can incorporate sounds and images from digital video, CD-ROMs, still images, scanned pictures, or documents. For example, a student report on immigration might include text-edited clips of oral history interviews with immigrants describing their arrival in the United States. The student might weave music and news reports throughout the oral histories to help describe the political and social background during the era when the interviewees immigrated to the United States.

Software such as Apple's iMovie has made digital video editing extremely user friendly. Students are also motivated to create and edit digital videos. One example of student-created videos is having students re-create historical events based on what they have learned in class. For example, imagine after studying a unit on Ancient Greece, students could write and produce a video as if they were visiting Athens during ancient times. For more examples of how teachers are using iMovie and other multimedia in the social studies classroom, visit **www.apple.com/education/**.

It is important to remember that it is not the medium itself that necessarily makes it effective as an instructional vehicle, although visual media often transmit information more effectively than others. Rather, it is the teacher's understanding of how one form of data can serve an important instructional purpose and advance students' thinking. Often, for example, it is more effective for instructional purposes that a teacher repurpose the media (use media in a way different from what its author intended). Consider a short film that shows people from a culture quite different from our own engaged in some typical activity. Initially the film might be shown with the sound turned off. At the conclusion of the viewing, students might be asked a basic question: "What did you see?"

The class's response could be recorded on a sheet of paper and then covered with another sheet of paper. As a next step, the class could be subdivided into three groups. The first group would be asked to observe how time was used by the participants in the film. A second group would be asked to focus on the people and what each person did. The third group would be responsible for observing which things the people used and how.

The same film clip then would be shown a second time. After this viewing, each of the groups would be asked to summarize its members' individual observations and to report its findings to the class. Again, the observations would be recorded on a sheet of paper and then covered. At this point, the teacher could elect to stop or to repeat the reviewing of the film, each time recording the latest rounds of observation of each group.

Typically, each new viewing will reveal additional observations that were missed in earlier sessions. The simple observational framework of time, people, and things corresponds to that used by anthropologists in ethnographic field-work. In a social studies class, the framework provides an interesting vehicle for systematically processing visual data.

Mapping Software

Geographic information systems (GIS) software allows students to represent and manipulate data through the "layering" of maps. GIS integrates electronic data-base with spatial data to create visual displays. We are surrounded by GIS applications daily, from the maps generated in MapQuest to the tracking of mail and packages. GIS is a valuable tool for the social studies classroom that enables students to collect and create their own data, analyze demographic data, visualize historic events, and explore change over time (Alibrandi & Palmer-Moloney, 2001). The National Geographic MapMachine is one example of a social studies online resource that is powered by GIS. MapMachine has predetermined categories such as political, culture, or climate that students can overlay on a world map. Visit **http://plasma.nationalgeographic.com/mapmachine/** to try the MapMachine for yourself.

Google Earth is another powerful technology tool that allows students to learn in a way impossible before the Internet. Google Earth (**http://earth.google .com/**) is a free, Web-based project that uses satellite imagery, maps, terrain, and buildings to create digital maps. Students can create local maps and explore faraway places through the power of technology. One classroom teacher reports that the students in his World Geography class regularly use Google Earth to plan trips to faraway places and then "fly" to their destination.

Personal Digital Assistants in the Social Studies Classroom

Personal digital assistants (PDAs) are becoming more prevalent in schools today. Most PDAs are the size of a small stack of index cards and can be purchased for as little as $100. Teachers and students are using PDAs, or handhelds, to create or edit word-processed documents, send e-mail, search the Web, or record audio or video. Peripherals for handhelds, such as collapsible keyboards, global positioning systems, digital cameras, phones, audio recorders, and MP3 players further enhance the capabilities of this tool.

As described in the opening scenario of the chapter, teachers are using PDAs to assist in classroom management tasks such as monitoring student behavior, recording student participation, or grading student assignments. When teachers are provided with classroom sets of handhelds, issues related to digital divide (discussed on p. 295) are greatly lessened by providing a device for each student.

Students are using handhelds to manage their assignments and to have ubiquitous access to technology. Many textbook companies now have online versions of their texts that students can download onto their PDA. This means that students are able to access their assignments any time, any place. Student use of PDAs is also leading to a more collaborative learning environment because it is so simple for students to share writing assignments and to collaborate on group projects. For more information on PDAs in the classroom, visit **www.palmone.com/us/ education/** or **http://www.concord.org/work/themes/handhelds.html**.

Technology Challenges

Coupled with the innovative resources that can be used in the social studies classroom are technology challenges that every teacher must address. The challenges include issues related to Internet safety, copyright, and the digital divide.

Liz Moore/Merrill

Increasingly, schools are using advanced video and computer technologies to enhance instruction.

Internet Safety

Teachers and parents should be well educated about safety issues before allowing students to use the Internet. The two most common risks for students who use the Internet are access to inappropriate materials and communication with cyberpredators. A **cyberpredator** is someone who inappropriately communicates with a student through the Internet. Sadly these communications sometimes lead to face-to-face meetings which may be dangerous for the student. To help prevent inappropriate communication and to limit student access to such materials on the Web, every school should have an acceptable use policy (AUP). An AUP is an agreement between parents, students, and the school concerning access of information on the Internet and publication of student photos and student work on the Internet. For more information on Internet safety and to view sample AUPs, visit **www.coedu.usf.edu/internetsafety/**.

Copyright

Copyright is another area of technology integration that can be troublesome for teachers. Students often do not realize the inappropriateness of copying and pasting documents, photos, and multimedia files within their work. It is essential for teachers to address copyright issues with students. To begin, teachers should help students understand the importance of citing all work that they reference or quote. It is just as important to give authors and developers credit for work they have generated on the Internet as authors who have published books or articles.

Once students gain an understanding of this concept, it is important to introduce them to the basics of citing original works. For more information on copyright issues in the classroom, visit **www.ncsu.edu/midlink/citing.html**.

Digital Divide

Despite the seemingly wide infiltration of technology into our schools and society, there is still a large digital divide between those who have access to computers and those who do not. Over 40% of the computer users today are from the United States and Canada ("Global Internet Trends," 2001). Yet, in the United States, there is great disparity between those who have computers in schools and those who do not. There is also a disparity between those who have computers at home and those who do not. Approximately one-third of the U.S. population uses the Internet at home; however, only 16.1 percent of Hispanics and 18.9 percent of African Americans use the Internet at home (U.S. Department of Commerce, 2000; NTIA, 2000).

The digital divide is about more than just access. Issues of connectivity and culturally relevant technology must be embraced to ensure that everyone not only has access to technology, but also has skills to use the technology, and that the means and materials are culturally relevant. The impact of this disparity is severe and must be addressed by teachers. It is important to know your students and to be aware of their access to technology. Beyond this, however, is a greater awareness about resource allocation within and across school systems. As social studies teachers, we must consider the educational and cultural impacts the divide has on our society. For more information on the digital divide, visit **www.digitaldivide network.org/**.

Emerging Technologies: Challenges of the Future

What technological developments that can enrich the teaching of social studies loom on the horizon? Martorella (1997) foresaw a scenario for technologies in which the excitement would not be the bells and whistles, but the constructivist learning principles that were enabled through effective integration of technology.

We have entered the era where the lines between elements of technology and learning are becoming blurred. Integrated sound and still-motion images of all types, all regulated by computers with increasing capabilities, have become the norm. Telecollaborative technology applications continue to become more sophisticated and less expensive.

Both the memory and storage capacity of computers continue to grow, even as the computer itself shrinks in size. Gordon Moore, the founder of Intel Corporation, speculated that computer chip density doubles every 24 months (Moore, 1965). This means that memory sizes, processor power, and so on, all follow the same rate of growth. For example, today's Palm m100 has the same amount of memory as the computer that guided Apollo II to the moon in 1969. The exponential changes in technologies will continue to grow and impact social studies teaching and learning.

Gradually, too, more and more technological advances will be easier for teachers to apply and incorporate into their instruction. The telephone will become the standard of technological "user friendliness" that newer computer-based tools emulate. Telephone companies, now empowered to challenge cable companies, will flood our homes with a smorgasbord of video data, from popular films to educational programs. All of these data will be easily stored in the new generation of computers.

Advancing cellular and radio technologies will extend current capabilities of cell phones so that soon we will be able to complete transactions over our cell phones much as we now do using an Internet-based computer. Satellite technologies and distance-learning techniques will be refined and extended to all schools to further extend their access to information and reduce isolation.

The Internet will be faster and more easily accessible by all citizens; thereby, our reach will extend beyond our borders to other nations of the world. This will make education truly global. Besides communicating over the Internet, students and teachers will also be able to tap into an expanding repertoire of comprehensive databases.

Even our concept of a book will undergo changes. Electronic books that fit in the palm of your hand, have clear resolution, and provide complete texts will inch their way into the schools. The new electronic tools will allow students to do key word searches, experiment with the text, or even create large type size to compensate for poor vision.

The challenge for us as teachers of social studies is both exciting and demanding. We must determine which roles technology and the rich informal educational system beyond the school can play most appropriately in the development of reflective, competent, and concerned citizens.

SUMMARY

Once the sleeping giant of technology has been awakened, social studies instruction will never be the same again (Martorella, 1997). This chapter has examined the challenges and opportunities afforded teachers because of the technology explosion. Students can travel the world in a matter of seconds, access documents long out of print, research up-to-the-minute facts for reports, and connect to their peers in other schools, states, and countries. Technology integration has changed the landscape of curriculum design and delivery. In an article in *Theory and Research in Social Education,* Postman (2000) ponders things new and old. Are all new things always progress and all old things always obsolete? How would you answer these questions? Technology has allowed us to adapt social studies instruction to the individual needs of our students. There are many other ways to accomplish this, and in Chapter 11 we will examine differentiated instruction in the social studies.

ACTIVITIES

1. Conduct a technology inventory in a local middle or secondary school. Visit the school and make a list of specific technologies you observe being used by teachers and students. If possible, interview teachers and students to learn more about their use of technology in the social studies. Discuss those things that surprise or impress you.
2. Using the categories of online resources identified in Figure 10.2, locate additional Web-based resources for teachers and students. Discuss how they could be used by teachers and/or students.
3. Design a multimedia presentation that is an exemplar of the new learning environments discussed in Figure 10.1.

4. Identify new and emerging technologies that were not mentioned in this chapter. Participate in a demonstration of the technology and describe how it can be used to enhance social studies instruction.
5. Visit one or more of the online resources mentioned in the chapter. Develop a lesson plan that illustrates how you could implement the resource into social studies teaching and learning.

WEB RESOURCES

New York Digital Library: **http://digital.nypl.org/**
Perseus Digital Library: **www.perseus.tufts.edu/**
Center for Electronic Texts in the Humanities: **www.ceth.rutgers.edu/**
The Census Bureau: **www.census.gov/**
Center for History and New Media: **http://chnm.gmu.edu/**

Adapting Social Studies Instruction to Individual Needs

Matching Social Studies Instruction to Students' Developing Capabilities

Symbolic, Enactive, and Iconic Social Studies Activities

Social Discourse in the Classroom

Social Studies for the Middle Years

Exemplary Middle-Grades Schools

Exemplary Middle Grades' Social Studies Programs and Teachers

High School Social Studies

Individualized Instruction and Individual Differences

Individual Differences Among Students

Individual Styles of Thinking and Learning

Thinking and Learning Styles

Matching Thinking Styles to Instruction

Matching Learning Styles to Instruction

Organizing the Classroom for Individualized Instruction

Computers

Multilevel Reading Materials

Learning Contracts

Using Jackdaws®, Artifact Kits, and Teacher-Made Materials for Individualizing Instruction

Instructional Resources for Individualizing Instruction

Equity for Those with Disabilities

Individuals with Disabilities Education Improvement Act of 2004 (IDEA 2004)

Mainstreaming

Strategies for Mainstreaming Students for Social Studies Instruction

Equity for the Gifted

Societal Perspectives on the Gifted

Identifying the Gifted

Approaches to Gifted Education

Gifted Students in Social Studies Classes

Summary

Activities

Web Resources

Marty, Lena, Jason, and Hakeem attend a magnet high school with 2,800 other students. They come from neighborhoods all over the city. Their GPAs are similar so they may share some of their classes. Because the school has magnet status, there will be a plethora of courses to take that address the unique learning characteristics that each student brings.

In a democracy, a public educational system must be sensitive to this uniqueness and attempt to provide all students with equal opportunities for reaching their full potential. Ideally, this means teachers should capitalize on students' special strengths and enable the students to use those strengths to help themselves address their limitations.

In a pluralistic society, students often arrive at the school door more different than alike. Their differences may include languages, religious beliefs, intellectual abilities, physical and psychological challenges, traditions, and customs. Regardless of their race, religion, ethnicity, intellectual capabilities, gender, and other characteristics, all students deserve an equal chance to learn and succeed.

Teachers can achieve equitable treatment of students by suspending their initial judgment on what they can expect of each student with respect to classroom performance, learning, behavior, and aspirations. When a teacher's preconceived expectations are that a particular individual will be industrious, bright, well behaved, and will bring rich experiences and high learning ideals to the classroom, these views are likely to affect positively the teacher's behavior toward the student. By contrast, if the teacher associates negative labels with students, whatever those descriptors may be, the teacher's behavior toward the students may be negative (Good & Brophy, 1991; Erb, 2005).

Matching Social Studies Instruction to Students' Developing Capabilities

Treating students as individual learners requires providing them with social studies materials and activities that are appropriate to their levels of development. Psychologists and educators frequently use the term **development** to refer to four basic types of changes—physical, social/emotional, moral, and cognitive—that individuals continue to undergo (Santrock, 2008).

Examples of marked physical developmental changes over time include variations in height and weight, the size of various parts of the body, and general motor ability (Van Hoose, Strahan, L'Esperence, 2001). Illustrations of differences in social development often are more subtle. As a youngster grows to understand which patterns of behavior in social situations are considered acceptable or valued by others and which are not, social development progresses. This process requires learning to function effectively in social settings within both peer and adult cultures. It means learning what is considered to be appropriate with respect to dress, language, customs, courtesies, and many other social protocols. Teachers and parents notice that there is a great deal of peer group membership shifting. Someone will belong to one group today and be in another group tomorrow. This is all part of trying to find the identity that fits the individual, and the group is the testing ground. Students shift their look and behavior, their social and moral values to match those of the group. While groups may set their own identities, Vygotsky (1986) emphasized that it is the teacher whose responsibility it is to transmit the social and moral values of the culture to her students.

In recent years, especially with the advent of NCLB legislation, educators increasingly have focused on the process of cognitive development. As students advance in years, they typically interpret and respond to intellectual tasks in qualitatively different ways. Their processes of reasoning and problem solving and their understanding of the physical and social world undergo significant changes. Among other things, youngsters alter their views concerning space, time, quantity, morality, and cause–effect relationships.

Bruner (1973), whose theories draw heavily on the work of Piaget, has suggested a threefold schema to explain how cognitive development occurs. His research indicates that we learn through one of three basic modes: the **symbolic mode** (words), the **enactive mode** (doing), the **iconic mode** (imagery).

Symbolic, Enactive, and Iconic Social Studies Activities

During each of these stages, Bruner argued, learning occurs predominantly through either interpreting symbols, such as spoken or written words, or doing something, or viewing images. As an example, students might read an account of the event (symbolic mode) and then view a film dramatization of the Tea Party (iconic mode). Alternately, they might learn more about the Boston Tea Party by role-playing the event (enactive mode). Teachers can facilitate students' learning by presenting them with activities that capitalize on their current dominant mode of thinking/learning. The diversity in learning approach and style, as well as achievement level, that all students bring to the classroom necessitates differentiated instruction (Tomlinson, 1999).

Developmental growth, Bruner argued, involves mastering each of the increasingly more difficult modes of representation, enactive to iconic to symbolic. It also includes development of the ability to translate each form into the other (Bruner, 1973). For instance, translation might occur through a discussion of what had been observed and learned from a picture, such as occurs when a student is shown a painting of the Battle at Lexington Green and is asked to write a paragraph describing the event. It is important to offer alternate approaches to learning. Your class may have students with levels of reading from poor to excellent with many students reading somewhere in between. Assigning a chapter to be read and questions to be answered as your sole approach to teaching social studies is not viable for today's learners.

Social Discourse in the Classroom

Regardless of the mode through which students acquire information, it is essential that they have opportunities to communicate their findings and raise questions. In addition, they must be able to ask the big questions that pertain to the topic of study. As you know, social discourse involves students in sharing experiences, taking roles, discussing, disputing, and listening in small- and large-group activities.

As students increasingly interact with others, they begin to internalize the existence and significance of alternative points of view. Social discourse in social studies instruction, whether in small groups or class discussions, can also be instrumental in refining and improving students' thinking. (Remember Vygotsky's intermental and intramental.) When students engage in whole-class discussion, guided by teachers, they interact in a verbal give-and-take and defend and explain their ideas. This enables them to not only share their thoughts, but test them. In short, students' conversations in groups, when they have purpose and guidelines, stimulate both social and cognitive growth. Achieving a balance in your classes that gives everyone a chance to participate and be heard without being judged is critical.

Whole-class discussions, if properly framed and monitored, enable the class to develop a camaraderie that is vital to building respect and appreciation for ones' classmates. For example, modeling a process desired for an upcoming assignment, and doing that modeling with the whole class, enables the teacher to accomplish several goals. Everyone, especially those who are visual and auditory learners, is much better able to understand exactly what is required for the assignment. During the process, the teacher may reference one student's comment and note its similarity to another's remark. Because lower level students are more likely to take part in a discussion where reading and writing skills are not required, it is possible for the teacher to note the similarity of low and high level students' comments, thus subtly showing the class that there is much that all levels of students have in common (Beal, 1996).

Social Studies for the Middle Years

As students move from childhood to early adolescence, the needs and capabilities of middle-grade students (typically those in grades 6 through 8) often appear to change from moment to moment. One social studies educator, Brown (1982), has observed:

> In terms of the total life-span, the transition from pre-adolescence to early adolescence is a metamorphic development of monumental proportions, having extraordinary consequences for the individual and widespread implications for social studies educators. Dramatic changes occur at this time in the areas of physical, mental,

emotional, and social growth and development. Not only is the overall transition into adolescence highly significant, but the customary uneven rates of change in these areas, either independently or through interaction, often result in complex patterns of development which necessitate important considerations for teaching and learning. (p. 30)

Students in the middle grades are making the transition between Piaget's stages of concrete operations and formal operations. Their thinking is becoming increasingly abstract and complex. They are developing reflective thinking skills, a surer grasp of time, and a wider range of analytical skills.

Brown (1982) offered an example of a social studies activity involving reflective and hypothetical–deductive thinking that a student at the stage of formal operations is able to complete but that one at the stage of concrete operations could not: "If the United States dollar rose in value to be worth five Canadian dollars . . . how would life (in both countries) be affected?" (p. 39).

Students in the middle years are also undergoing shifts in their moral and social orientation. Chapin and Messick (1989) have noted, for example: "Socially, middle-grade children are entering the age of reciprocity in friendship and human relations. They are able to see that their actions have social consequences. When they are in a group, they are eager to seek fairness. They relish opportunities to make rules, establish consequences for breaking them, and carry out enforcement of the rules" (p. 94).

Exemplary Middle-Grades Schools

In recognition of the developmental characteristics and needs of early adolescents, middle schools were developed in the 1960s. Over the years, they have replaced the traditional junior high school. The effective middle school differs from the old junior high, which was often seen as a miniature high school, in more respects than grade organization (Allen, Splittgerber, & Manning, 1993; George & Alexander, 2002). Creating an effective middle school involves a transformation in the way that teachers, administrators, support professionals, and staff work with students and one another and allocate instructional time (Allen & Stevens, 1994; "Social Studies in the Middle School," 1991; Stevenson, 1992; Erb, 2005). The four hallmarks of an excellent middle school include block scheduling, team organization (two-teacher teams preferred), advisor/advisee, and exploratory subject offerings.

Among their recommendations, George and Alexander (2002) have suggested that middle schools include the following features:

- *Guidance.* Each child should have an adult who is responsible for providing advice on academic, social, and personal matters. The advisor is the champion of that child and serves as the child's bridge between the school and home. Advisor/advisee groups are small and should meet daily so that the advisor can help the child deal with issues in a timely fashion. Small groups ensure that the advisor and the advisees can engage in meaningful discussion.

- *Transition/Articulation.* There should be a smooth articulation between elementary and high school, and all learning experiences should be carefully coordinated. A detailed plan must be put into place at the elementary, middle, and high school levels to ensure that smooth transitions occur for students as they move up to new challenges, expectations, and operating procedures.
- *Block Time Schedule/Interdisciplinary Teams.* There should be blocks of instructional time in the daily schedule, and students should be taught by interdisciplinary teams of teachers who implement curriculum integration.
- *Appropriate Teaching Strategies.* A variety of effective teaching strategies that provide differentiated instruction should be employed.
- *Exploratory.* There should be a variety of elective courses or activities, including intramural athletics, for students.
- *Appropriate Core Curriculum/Learning Experiences.* A core of learning experiences and skills should be required of all students.

An earlier foundation-building task force report, *Turning Points* (Carnegie Corporation, 1989), made recommendations similar to those of George and Alexander. It also called for students and teachers to be teamed and stay together through the middle grades. *Great Transitions* (Carnegie Corporation, 1994) and *Turning Points 2000, Education of Adolescents in the 21st Century* (Jackson, Davis, & Tirozzi, 2001) have followed up to examine the progress that has been made since 1989. Both documents are important studies, and each suggests that there is much more work to be done to realize the goals of the first *Turning Points* in 1989.

Exemplary Middle Grades' Social Studies Programs and Teachers

What type of social studies teacher is needed for the emerging middle school? Buckner (1994) identified two lists of characteristics that he contended excellent middle-level teachers have. One dealt with *personal characteristics* and the other with *professional characteristics*.

Personal characteristics: "look like they feel good about themselves, demonstrate warmth and kindness, are optimistic, are enthusiastic, are flexible, are easy to talk with, are humorous, are friendly, are respectful toward students" (Buckner, 1994, p. 18).

Professional characteristics: "are easy to understand, are fair when grading, are available when students need to speak with them, provide extra help for those students who need it when beginning unfamiliar material, are well organized for class, use a variety of activities and materials in class, ask easy, average, and difficult questions, really know the subjects they teach, are careful to compliment students for doing a good job, are careful to correct students who do not pay attention, let students have some say in homework assignments, [and] do not use the textbook each and every day of class" (Buckner, 1994, p. 18).

Examine the two lists of characteristics, and identify in each list the characteristics that *you* regard as the most important. Compare your analyses with the following responses of 394 middle-school students who completed the survey.

The 394 middle-level students in the study ranked the following as the top *personal* characteristics: are willing to listen, are respectful toward students, accept students, demonstrate warmth and kindness, are easy to talk with, and are friendly (Buckner, 1994, p. 18). With regard to the top *professional* characteristics, students identified the following: really know the subjects they teach, are easy to understand, are fair when grading, and provide extra help for those students who need it (Buckner, 1994, p. 18).

High School Social Studies

Social studies in the high school is more complex by virtue of the many different social science courses available to students. Both middle and high school courses have their own particular sets of standards they must address; however, the stakes are often thought to be higher in high school because of the end-of-course and advanced placement (AP) tests. Those who believe that middle schoolers and their parents are not stressing about future college entrance scores are incorrect. Middle school teachers can recount any number of stories about "helicopter" parents. These individuals hover and swoop in to handle any issue, especially grade related, that pertains to their child. Their constant action is just one sign that the push to get the high grades needed for college admission starts well before high school.

High school teachers will tell you that the social studies knowledge base and the skills built in middle school are critical for success in high school social science courses. Middle and high school teachers must work together to emphasize the need to give the social sciences the same instructional time as math, science, and language arts courses. Mandates to diminish instructional time for social studies in favor of the NCLB tested subjects will erode the middle school social studies foundation and leave high school teachers playing catch-up when these students come to their classes.

In addition to the issue of middle school social studies preparation and its influence on high school educators and the curricula is the sharp focus that is being put on graduation rates at the secondary level. National statistics that show increasing numbers of secondary students failing to complete their high school education have alerted states' lawmakers who are mindful that national economic prosperity is directly related to a highly skilled, taxpaying, law-abiding workforce. The high school dropout rate is a multilayered problem that speaks to the knowledge and preparation of the lawmakers and voters themselves, administrators, teachers and students, as well as funding priorities of state and national governments. Your study of students' development characteristics, teaching and learning approaches, as well as the in-depth knowledge you bring in your content area should indicate to you that addressing the dropout rate is a complex matter. Educational shortcomings are not solved by blaming just one group or going back to a 1950s approach to education, "drill and kill followed by spit-back testing." Joining your local, state, and national teacher organizations (NEA, ACT) and national interest groups (NMSA, NCSS) and becoming proactive and involved in all levels of education policy making will ensure that there is a knowledgeable voice in the conversation, yours.

Your authors believe that the personal and professional characteristics noted for exemplary middle school teachers are equally applicable to secondary teachers. We also believe that teachers would say that the personal characteristics— willing to listen, being respectful, accepting, etc.—are ones they would also like to see in their students and students' parents.

Individualized Instruction and Individual Differences

The rise of middle schools and related curricula is but one manifestation of how educators attempt to individualize instruction for developing students. In its simplest form, **individualized instruction** makes provisions for some set of differences among learners. Since there are many differences among students, it would be impossible for a single teacher to consider all of them for any given learning task. Typically, teachers select some set of differences that they regard as especially significant to their students' success and provide for those differences in the instructional program. They then consider the resources available and begin to develop strategies and materials for instruction.

Individual Differences Among Students

Some differences are relatively easy to address and involve only modest adjustments in classroom practices. An illustration is moving a student who has reduced visual acuity or hearing difficulties to the front center row. Others may require major reorganization of the classroom or even of an educational system.

For example, it is widely accepted that all students enter kindergarten or the first grade at approximately the same chronological age. However, they are not all the same developmental age and therefore the time when students are really ready to enter formal education differs. Recognizing this would require fundamental changes in both legal statutes and school admission policies. Nationally, the Head Start Preschool program has given youngsters from more modest circumstances early schooling to get them ready with the skills and experiences needed for kindergarten. Some states have developed programs seeking to address developmental differences. For example, North Carolina has implemented the More at Four program.

Some differences among students that have been used in the past as a basis for individualizing instruction include the following:

Prior knowledge	Reading abilities
Attention spans	Developmental capabilities
Achievements	Learning and thinking styles
Vision problems	Motivational levels
Hearing problems	Cultural experiences
Interests	Physical settings preferred for learning
Interpersonal skills	Amounts of time needed to complete a task

When teachers select some set of these or other differences to address with special instruction, they engage in a form of individualized instruction.

Individual Styles of Thinking and Learning

A critical element for teachers to consider in individualizing social studies instruction is the dominant pattern or *style* students use to acquire new information. To address a student's preferred learning style you must provide alternative teaching approaches and learning environments. Teachers sensitive to students' styles try to find the best match between the learning task and the styles of individual students. This includes the match between the teacher's teaching style and the learner's learning style.

Thinking and Learning Styles

The term **thinking** (or **cognitive**) **style** refers to the pattern we typically follow in solving problems, engaging in thinking, and generally processing information. Individuals may vary their thinking style from one task to another, but one style usually is dominant and stable over a period of years (Witkin, Moore, Goodenough, & Cox, 1977). Researchers report that thinking styles develop early in life and influence not only the ways we learn but also our career choices (Witkin et al., 1977).

Learning styles are similar to thinking styles in that they also represent patterns that we typically follow in learning. **Learning styles** are the set of preferences we express about the conditions for learning something. Certain learning style differences appear to be biological, whereas others are developed through experience (Dunn, Beaudry, & Klavas, 1989).

Matching Thinking Styles to Instruction

Witkin and his associates have identified two basic thinking styles that may be applied to classroom instruction, **field independent** and **field dependent** (Witkin et al., 1977). Still applicable today, these styles enable the teacher to know better how to tailor instruction. Some of the characteristics of each type are summarized below:

Field-Independent Individuals

- Can deal effectively with unstructured problems
- Are task oriented
- Are relatively unconcerned with social interaction
- Can deal effectively with abstract thinking
- Are intrinsically motivated

Field-Dependent Individuals

- Are relatively effective in remembering information that has social content
- Prefer group activities
- Prefer highly structured tasks and activities
- Are extrinsically motivated

Teachers who wish to adapt their social studies instruction to account for differences in thinking styles among students could offer alternative choices such as structured (dependent) versus unstructured (independent) assignments (Guild & Garger, 1985). Similarly, teachers could offer guidelines for activities that provide open-ended (independent) versus specific and detailed (dependent) instructions.

They could also ensure that alternatives in instructional strategies are available such as discovery (independent) versus expository (dependent) approaches. Further, they could offer students choices between working alone (independent) or in groups (dependent) on tasks.

Matching Learning Styles to Instruction

In contrast to our thinking style, our learning style may vary over time and from task to task. It may also include a host of visual, auditory, or kinesthetic factors that influence how we learn. To illustrate, applying Bruner's theory of the three modes of learning discussed earlier in this chapter, we may prefer to learn something by *observing* two- or three-dimensional items (iconic mode). Alternately, our preference may be to rely on the *spoken* or *written word* (symbolic mode). A further preference might be for *hands-on* activities that emphasize learning by doing (enactive mode).

Learning styles may also be influenced by conditions such as the temperature or ambience within a classroom, seating arrangements, our mood and motivations, our physical state, the sounds around us, and the time of day that is optimal for learning (Dunn et al., 1989). Our learning style may even include the hemisphere of our brain that appears to be the dominant one in processing information (McCarthy, 1990; Sousa, 2001).

When adapting instruction teachers must consider first those conditions that they can actually control. Those mentioned above are not always all within your control. Select and correct those which you can. Next, of critical importance is your assessment of your students' individual learning styles. Once you have made this assessment and you are able to select the most prominent styles used by your students, you can then tailor your instruction to include those styles. There are any number of survey tools to use to assess learning styles and instructional preferences. (See WEB RESOURCES at the end of the chapter.)

The 4MAT System. Other approaches focus on providing alternative instructional strategies that are responsive to students' dominant preferences. The **4MAT system,** for example, assumes there are four major learning styles, all equally valuable (McCarthy, 1990):

- *Style One.* Learners are primarily interested in personal meaning.
- *Style Two.* Learners are primarily interested in understanding facts.
- *Style Three.* Learners are primarily interested in how things work.
- *Style Four.* Learners are primarily interested in self-discovery.

McCarthy contended that students need to learn through all four styles, not just their preferred one. She also stated that they should engage in activities that draw on both hemispheres of the brain.

Multiple Intelligences. More widely recognized than the 4MAT is the theory of **multiple intelligences (MI).** Developed by Howard Gardner in 1983, the theory postulates that individuals learn through at least eight comprehensive modes or intelligences:

- *Bodily-Kinesthetic Intelligence.* Ability to use our bodies to indicate ideas and emotions
- *Interpersonal Intelligence.* Capacity to distinguish emotions, feelings, and motives of others
- *Intrapersonal Intelligence.* Ability to introspect and act flexibly on self-insights
- *Linguistic Intelligence.* Ability to communicate effectively either orally or in writing
- *Logical-Mathematical Intelligence.* Capacity to reason clearly to facilitate mathematical operations
- *Musical Intelligence.* Ability to distinguish, manipulate, and communicate musical elements
- *Spatial Intelligence.* Capacity to distinguish and manipulate spatial and visual elements (Gardner, 1983, 1991, 1993, 2000)

Gardner (1991) has written: "We all are able to know the world through language, logical mathematical analysis, spatial representation, musical thinking, the use of the body to solve problems or make things, an understanding of other individuals, and an understanding of ourselves" (p. 12). Where individuals differ, he maintains, is in the relative strengths of each type of intelligence and in the ways we use them to accomplish various tasks. Standardized tests are prepared for those whose strengths are in linguistic and logical mathematical intelligences. Often students do not test well because their dominate mode of operation is other than those two. Teachers must be mindful of presenting lessons, assignments, and assesment measures, using differentiated instruction so that the multiple learning styles are addressed.

Developing special instructional strategies for identifying learning styles, such as in the 4MAT system or the multiple intelligences approach, requires study and practice. Mentors are an excellent resource and online information is plentiful. Ask your mentor for help in preparing lessons that match teaching and learning styles for your classes.

A number of learning style inventories have been developed. They may employ paper-and-pencil measures that ask students to indicate their preferred conditions for engaging in learning activities. There are any number of multiple intelligences tests that can be found through an Internet search. These tests can be

Howard Gardner's theory of multiple intelligences offers a framework for individualizing social studies instruction.

downloaded and taken with pencil and paper or taken online and scored at the site. Students enjoy taking these surveys and are often surprised by what they learn about themselves. Studies undertaken since 2000 at North Carolina State University have found that when adolescents are taught about development theories (Piaget, Erikson, Kohlberg, Gilligan, Vygotsky, Gardner, Charity James, Garbarino) and understand what is happening to them socially, cognitively, emotionally, and morally, they are empowered to make significant improvements in their academic and social life. Beal's studies pose the question of why we do not teach development theories to youngsters who are undergoing changes significant to their lives (Beal, 2003).

Organizing the Classroom for Individualized Instruction

Among the tools that social studies teachers in the middle and secondary grades have found especially useful for differentiating instruction are *computers, multilevel reading materials,* and *learning contracts.* Each of these tools enable teachers to tailor instruction and offer students an opportunity to learn through a medium or environment that is responsive to individual needs or strengths.

Computers

Computers have the capacity to enliven and enrich social studies instruction through brilliant color representations and graphics, as well as timely website information. Computers offer the teacher options that enable differentiation of lesson, assignment, and assessment. Appropriate software can accommodate a range of attention spans, motivational levels, and learning paces of students. Students can work individually or in small groups, at their own speed, and on their own level. They can use the computer to practice skills or extend their understanding of a topic. If students are absent and have access to a computer they can keep up with assignments and material covered in class. Many teachers have their own websites that contain daily assignments, messages, and instructions, among other things (Risinger, 2006).

Multilevel Reading Materials

The individual differences in the levels at which students read in the middle and secondary grades are often vast. This phenomenon is an especially serious obstacle to learning in the area of the social studies where much of the subject matter in schools typically is available in written form.

Previously, we have considered how providing students with varied reading materials and strategies for comprehension affords them opportunities for success, even though their individual reading abilities may vary considerably. By using an interesting and varied mix of reading materials students can seek their own levels of proficiency and challenge, progressing as their comprehension and self-confidence grows. Where multilevel supplemental reading materials are used, the basal textbook can serve as a *basic* reference work, consulted as needed. "Remaindered" book sales often have volumes with beautifully photographed locales. Yard sales can also be a good source of *National Geographic* magazines, travel books, and young adult literature that is social studies specific. Using your wits and a little money can provide a wealth of cheap, multileveled resource materials. When using supplemental material that is clearly on an elementary level, but needed by students of limited reading skills, consider introducing such material into the classroom as a resource that students may use when they research and prepare work that they might also want to share with younger family members, when they tutor in the lower grades, or help ESL students become proficient in English. If a child with no English skills is placed in your classroom, remember books on tape and begin with simple stories that allow the student to follow along with the words as she/he hears them spoken. Because this suggestion is obviously a very elementary approach that uses elementary level materials, you will have to work with your class on ways that the new ESL student can be made to feel good about the materials being used and the progress being made.

Learning Contracts

Learning contracts are a simple way to provide students with individualized learning tasks, while clarifying the objectives of an activity. They also help students learn to establish reasonable deadlines and work schedules. Further, contracts can help teachers with managerial tasks, such as keeping track of which students are working on different projects and what their deadlines are.

There is no set format for a learning contract. Typically, the contract spells out (1) what a student agrees to do, (2) which resources will be used and in what ways, (3) how to determine when each phase of the activity has been completed, and (4) when the activities will be completed. The contract is actually an outgrowth of the teacher's rubric, that is, what the teacher has decided needs to be done, what approaches will be used, and what the desired outcomes should be. An example of a basic learning contract for the middle grades is given in Figure 11.1.

FIGURE 11.1
A Learning Contract for an Eighth-Grade Class

Contract for the "Powers of the President" Assignment

I, _____, am contracting to complete the activities listed below for the "Powers of the President" assignment.

1. Complete all of the activities in the artifact kit.
2. Pick one activity from the Activity Sheet and follow all of the steps.
3. Select one of the software programs in the computer corner and answer the questions on the sheet in the corner.
4. Read two of the books on the reading list.
5. Have a conference with the teacher to discuss what I have learned.

Student's Signature: _____ Date: _____

Teacher's Signature: _____ Date: _____

Using Jackdaws®, Artifact Kits, and Teacher-Made Materials for Individualizing Instruction

Individualizing instruction may require materials that are designed by the teacher for use with a particular class. One example is the use of an artifact kit (Dowd, 1990; Rasinski, 1983). Loosely defined, **artifact kits** are collections of various kinds of resource materials built around a single theme, with the focus being an individual, a document, an event, an issue, or a place (see Box 11.1). Some examples of topics are:

Henry V   Japanese American Internment
The Magna Carta   The French Revolution
Reconstruction   The Struggle for Suffrage
Abraham Lincoln

Both teachers and students can contribute items to an artifact kit. You might begin to build your artifact kits by collecting items and placing them in individually categorized file folders, that is until file folders are no longer big enough to hold your collections. Typically, each kit is housed in an attractive and sturdy container or box that holds all of the relevant materials. These may include some combination of artifacts and three-dimensional objects such as clothes, utensils, models, and coins; copies of primary source materials such as historical documents,

BOX 11.1	Addressing the Issues: Connecting Across Your State with a Regional Jackdaw

The Travelin' Trunk was a project that connected an elementary class of students in the mountains of North Carolina with their counterparts on the coast. Two teachers who had met at a statewide social studies conference formulated a plan to help their fourth graders learn about their own region and at the same time get an intimate look at their neighbors across the state. In the fall, both teachers had their students brainstorm characteristics of their specific region. What really represented the mountains or the coast? How did the people make a living? What cultural activities and crafts were specific to their area? Students in both locations spent the first semester researching and writing about their region and collecting artifacts to include in a trunk that represented their region's life and lifestyle. Parents and community neighbors got involved, made suggestions, and donated items for the trunk. During the semester-long process the students and teachers in each region exchanged letters, got to know one another, and kept each other informed about their progress.

In the spring, the students from the mountains hand-delivered their trunk to their counterparts on the coast. The coastal class took their guests on a tour of the area. This way, when their mountain friends opened the coastal trunk back home in their classroom, they would better understand the things packed inside. Many of the students from the mountains had never been to the beach, eaten freshly caught boiled shrimp, or tried to throw out a fishing net.

Both the students and the teachers felt this was one of the best projects that they participated in all year. Not only did they examine their own area and learn to appreciate its culture and the need to preserve it, but they also got an in-depth look at another region of their state. Each group of students developed a strong sense of place and an appreciation for their neighbors. Activities accommodated individual student learning needs and contained instructions for both concrete and abstract projects. Students enjoyed seeing and using the copies of original source documents because it helped them realize that the use of original source documents may be subjective, depending on the user's interpretation. By meeting and exchanging trunks each group better understood the other's "take" on life.

advertisements, maps, legal documents, birth certificates, and letters; books, magazines, articles, charts, and pictures; and teacher-produced items such as dioramas and drawings (Dowd, 1990).

As an illustration, Dowd (1990) noted that an artifact kit created by The Institute of Texan Cultures in San Antonio with the theme "Early Texan Frontier Life" was housed in an old pioneer trunk and contained a washboard, a quilt, a bonnet and dress, a coffee pot, and lye soap. Another artifact kit, "The Cape Lookout Lighthouse Keeper's Trunk," packed with everything needed to care for and service a lighthouse, is sent around North Carolina to classes studying the Cape Lookout lighthouse. Some excellent commercial artifact kits, "Jackdaws," are also available from Jackdaw Publications, but they are limited in the types of materials they contain. (Even though teachers usually refer to all artifact kits as "Jackdaws," the term when used to describe such kits is a registered trademark of Golden Owl Publishing Co. of Amawalk, New York.)

Artifact kits should be designed to be self-instructional and for the use of a single student or a small group of two to three students. They should accommodate individual student needs and allow them to freely explore all of the materials in the kit. Beyond the opportunity for self-exploration, teachers should include structured cues and tasks to help students focus on key points and issues. To simplify analyses, different colored sheets should be used for different types of information. It should be noted that kits may also be used simply as a resource material. They do not have to include suggested activities or instructions for small group use.

In addition to the collection of materials, artifact kits should contain the following:

- One or two sheets that list all of the items in the kit (affix one inside the top of the box) (Figure 11.2)
- Any special instructions on how the materials are to be examined
- A set of questions designed to stimulate students' thinking as they examine the materials
- Commentary sheets that provide appropriate background or context for the materials included
- A set of activities to be done in conjunction with an examination of the materials
- A list of references and readings for students
- Special instructions for how to divide tasks if a small group is to use the kit

Note that the teacher should have all of the above sheets on file so that lost sheets may be quickly replaced.

Instructional Resources for Individualizing Instruction

Effective individualized instruction requires a variety of resources within a classroom. These include technology tools such as the following:

Technology Tools

Listening hook-up with multiple sets of headphones

Computer, printer, CD-ROM drive, and modem for Internet connection or wireless connection

Record player (may be needed for older resources)

Tape player

Videotape machine

Videodisc player

CD player

Overhead projector

FIGURE 11.2
Artifact Kit Contents

1. Outline of Cherokee dates and events. Taken from J. Ed. Sharpe's book *The Cherokees Past and Present*.

2. Map of the boundaries of Cherokee country. Taken from *The Cherokees Past and Present*.

3. Broadsheet on Cherokee origin and history.

4. Broadsheet on Cherokee government.

5. Symbol of the seven clans of the Cherokee. Taken from *The Cherokee Past and Present*.

6. Broadsheet of the Cherokee religion.

7. Cherokee poem "The Corn Maiden." Taken from Mary Newman Fitzgerald's book *The Cherokee and His Smokey Mountain Legends*.

8. Carved wooden figure of the Eagle Dancer. Taken from Rodney Leftwich's book *Arts and Crafts of the Cherokee*.

9. Broadsheet of the Cherokee language.

10. Cherokee alphabet. Taken from Samuel Carter III's book *Cherokee Sunset: A Nation Betrayed*.

11. Cherokee glossary. Taken from *The Cherokees Past and Present*.

12. Clipping from the Cherokee newspaper, the *Cherokee Phoenix*. Taken from *Cherokee Sunset: A Nation Betrayed*.

13. Broadsheet on Cherokee dwellings.

14. Arts and crafts of the Cherokee. Taken from *The Cherokee Past and Present*.

15. Cherokee crafts.

16. Arrowheads.

17. Cherokee Memorial to U.S. Congress, December 29, 1835. Taken from the *American Heritage Book of Indians*.

18. Various photographs dealing with the "Trail of Tears."

19. Map of the "Trail of Tears." Taken from *Cherokee Sunset*.

20. Map of the Cherokee Reservation in Oklahoma. Taken from *Cherokee Sunset*.

21. Photo of John Ross.

22. The story of Tsali, a Cherokee hero. Taken from *The Cherokee and His Smokey Mountain Legends*.

23. Broadsheet on the contributions of the Indians. Taken from *The Cherokee and His Smokey Mountain Legends*.

Note. From *The Cherokee Indians,* by J. Allen, 1991. Unpublished manuscript.

Students also need a collection of multimedia and print materials similar to the list that follows.

Multimedia and Print Materials

Collections of photographs and pictures

Globe and maps

Models

Dioramas

Tapes, records, compact discs, computer software, and video cassettes

Study prints

Simulation games

Artifacts and artifact kits

Compasses

Posters

Magazines and newspapers

Historical fiction works

Nonfiction and biographical informational books

Textbooks

Reproductions of historical documents

Timelines

Teacher-made materials

Reference works

Cartoons

Charts, graphs, and tables

Travel folders

Catalogs

Almanacs and Yellow Pages

Atlases

Equity for Those with Disabilities

Of all the categories of students vying for individualized instruction in our schools, citizens with disabilities have received the most attention in the past decades. The basic issue is how to provide instruction appropriate to their special needs.

In recent years, there has been considerable progress in addressing the needs of students with disabilities. Once the level of awareness toward those with disabilities was raised, many organizations and businesses voluntarily changed policies and procedures that created hardships. The passage of federal, state, and local laws has also expanded access to public facilities through requirements for provisions such as ramps at sidewalks and Braille instructions in elevators.

Individuals with Disabilities Education Improvement Act of 2004 (IDEA 2004)

Schools, like other institutions in our society, have been affected by governmental statutes and regulations concerning those with disabilities. The most significant of these was the Individuals with Disabilities Education Act, usually referred to as IDEA. Its predecessor, PL 94-142, passed in 1975 (and renamed in 1990, and most recently reauthorized in 2004), stated, in effect, that if any school system in the United States wished to receive special federal funding, it had to make provisions by 1980 for "free, appropriate, public education" for all students.

The most recent authorization of IDEA (PL 105-17), affected all students with disabilities, regardless of their impairments. Such disabilities include the following:

Speech impairment

Other health impairments, including attention deficit hyperactivity disorder (ADHD) and Tourette syndrome

Hearing impairment

Learning disability

Visual impairment

Orthopedic impairment

Intellectual disabilities

Emotional/behavioral disorder

Autism

Physical impairment

Traumatic brain injury

In practice, however, the vast majority of mainstreamed students with disabilities are classified in just five categories: learning disabilities, emotional/behavioral disorders, speech impairments, intellectual impairments, and other health impairments. The largest category of students served in the five noted is the category of "other health impairments" because it includes those with ADHD.

One of the lingering controversies surrounding students with special needs concerns the labeling or classifying of these students. The issues center on the validity of the process, particularly where there is considerable weight given to scores on IQ tests. Critics of current practices contend that, given the normal variance in such tests and their dependence on culturally bound references, it seems likely that many students have been improperly labeled.

The category of "learning disability" is particularly susceptible to misapplication; the actual criteria used to classify students as learning disabled often are difficult to distinguish from those that teachers informally use to describe a student as a "slow learner" or "not working up to potential." Many teachers who struggle with entire classes of students with low motivational levels, poor self-concepts, and a variety of educational, social, and economic deficits would argue that labels are less meaningful than specific strategies that attempt to match instructional programs with the needs and abilities of individual students. Figure 11.3 shows ways for communicating with people with disabilities.

As a result of controversy about the diagnosis of learning disabilities, the 2006 regulations for implementing IDEA 2004 have adopted the concept of "response-to-intervention" as a component of learning disabilities identification. States may now use student response to "research-supported instruction provided at increasingly more intense levels" to determine whether a student's academic difficulties are due to insufficient or inappropriate instruction. Many school districts now employ a three-tiered model, only the last and most intense of which actually includes special education. This change will make it increasingly incumbent on general education teachers, especially in language arts and mathematics, to implement instruction that is supported by research and to document that it is being implemented with sufficient intensity to determine whether the target student identified is responding positively.

Fortunately, many procedures for documenting student response of academic or behavior interventions have been demonstrated to help classroom teachers make data-based instructional decisions that support all students, not just those with disabilities. Probably the most widely used is curriculum-based measurement (CBM). CBM incorporates frequent, brief probes (1–5 minutes) taken from the curriculum being taught. Ideally, students chart their own performance on a weekly basis, and they and their teachers use the charts to set goals and guide instruction (Fuchs & Fuchs, 1986). Several CBM manuals and tools, including those for computer graphing to monitor reading and math skills, can be downloaded from **www.interventioncentral.org**.

A Least Restrictive Educational Environment. One significant provision of IDEA for social studies teachers is that students with disabilities have the right to be educated in the general education program with their nondisabled peers to the maximum extent possible and in the "least restrictive" educational environment. What this last provision means in practice has been the subject of considerable debate and varying interpretations. Many different implementations of the provision exist in schools across the nation.

Individualized Education Plans. In addition to the provisions already mentioned, IDEA contains a section requiring the development of an individualized education

FIGURE 11.3

Ten Commandments for Communicating with People with Disabilities

1. Speak directly rather than through a companion or sign language interpreter who may be present.

2. Offer to shake hands when introduced. People with limited hand use or an artificial limb can usually shake hands and offering the left hand is an acceptable greeting.

3. Always identify yourself and others who may be with you when meeting someone with a visual disability. When conversing in a group, remember to identify the person to whom you are speaking. When dining with a friend who has a visual disability, ask if you can describe what is on his or her plate.

4. If you offer assistance, wait until the offer is accepted. Then listen or ask for instructions.

5. Treat adults as adults. Address people with disabilities by their first names only when extending that same familiarity to all others. Never patronize people in wheelchairs by patting them on the head or shoulder.

6. Do not lean against or hang on someone's wheelchair. Bear in mind that people with disabilities treat their chairs as extensions of their bodies. And so do people with guide dogs and help dogs. Never distract a work animal from the job without the owner's permission.

7. Listen attentively when talking with people who have difficulty speaking and wait for them to finish. If necessary, ask short questions that require short answers, or a nod of the head. Never pretend to understand; instead repeat what you have understood and allow the person to respond.

8. Place yourself at eye level when speaking with someone in a wheelchair or on crutches.

9. Tap a person who has a hearing disability on the shoulder or wave your hand to get his or her attention. Look directly at the person and speak clearly, slowly, and expressively to establish if the person can read your lips. If so, try to face the light source and keep hands, cigarettes and food away from your mouth when speaking. If a person is wearing a hearing aid, don't assume that they have the ability to discriminate your speaking voice. Never shout to a person. Just speak in a normal tone of voice.

10. Relax. Don't be embarrassed if you happen to use common expressions such as "See you later" or "Did you hear about this?" that seems to relate to a person's disability.

Note. Reprinted with permission of Irene M. Ward and Associates, copyright 1993.

plan (IEP) for each student determined to have a disability and requiring special education and related services. An IEP is a written plan with specific details concerning a student's present level of educational performance, the educational program to be provided for the student, and the criteria that will be used to measure progress toward the objectives. The student's parents and the student, where appropriate, are to be involved in the development of an IEP. If the student is or may be participating in the general education environment, the IEP team must also include at least one general education teacher. Federal law does not determine the form of the IEP, states or school districts do. However, the form must include the basic components indicated above.

Many states and local school districts have developed sample formats for use by local school districts in developing an IEP. Figure 11.4 is an example of one such format.

Mainstreaming

School practices associated with the provision for a least restrictive educational environment are often referred to as *mainstreaming* those with disabilities. This means bringing them into the mainstream of public education by placing them in regular classrooms for at least part of their school day. In fact most students with disabilities spend the largest part of each day in general education. An assumption of IDEA is that students with disabilities will advance socially, psychologically, and educationally when they are not isolated from other students. Further, the assumption is that they will be better prepared for the realities of the world if they learn to function in normal environments. The law also assumes that the experiences of nondisabled students participating with students with disabilities should help break down stereotypes and negative attitudes.

In many schools, some students with disabilities have always been mainstreamed. Students in wheelchairs and those with poor eyesight, hearing problems, and assorted psychological disorders, for example, have been assimilated into many classrooms long before legislation required it. Among other things, what IDEA and earlier legislation attempted was to increase both the scope and number of all types of students with disabilities who would be mainstreamed. It also sought to establish the legal right of all students to such education, whether the schools wished to provide it or not.

The basic social intent of PL 94-142 was to bring all individuals with disabilities, as much as is possible, fully into the mainstream of society, including its schools. The "least restrictive environment" provision of PL 94-142, and now IDEA 2004, does not require that all students with disabilities be placed in regular classrooms or that all aspects of their education occur there. It does, however, place on school districts the burden of proof to show that some part of these students' education cannot take place in a regular classroom setting.

FIGURE 11.4
Sample Format for Developing an IEP

Individualized Education Program/Service Delivery Plan
(To be completed after Part 1 of the IEP is developed)

Student: _____

School: _____

ID#: _____ Grade: _____

Check Purpose
[ ] Initial Entry   [ ] Change in Placement
[ ] Annual Review   [ ] Change in Identification
[ ] Reevaluation   [ ] Other: _____

I.   AREA OF IDENTIFICATION (ELIGIBILITY) (mark only primary condition)*

[ ] Academically Gifted
[ ] Autistic
[ ] Behaviorally-Emotionally Handicapped
[ ] Deaf-Blind
[ ] Hearing Impaired
[ ] Mentally Handicapped
   [ ] EMH   [ ] S/PMH   [ ] TMH
Other Needs: _____

[ ] Multihandicapped
[ ] Orthopedically Impaired
[ ] Other Health Impaired
[ ] Specific Learning Disabled
[ ] Speech-Language Impaired
[ ] Traumatic Brain Injured
[ ] Visually Impaired

II. RELATED SERVICES
[ ] None
[ ] Audiology
[ ] Counseling Services
[ ] Occupational Therapy
[ ] Physical Therapy
[ ] Speech-Language
[ ] Transportation
[ ] Other _____

*Child meets the eligibility criteria of the State Board of Education and is in need of special education.

III. LEAST RESTRICTIVE ENVIRONMENT (PLACEMENT)
A.   AMOUNT OF TIME IN EXCEPTIONAL EDUCATION:

Type of Service	Sessions per Wk./Mo./Yr.	Min. Per Session	Hours Per Wk.
Consultation	_____	_____	_____
Direct Special Education	_____	_____	_____
Related Services	_____	_____	_____
_____	_____	_____	_____
_____	_____	_____	_____
Total	_____	_____	_____

B.   CONTINUUM OF SERVICES: Check the services considered by the committee, and circle the decision reached. Give reason(s) for options rejected and the decision reached. A continuum of services must be considered.
[ ] Regular - Less than 21% of day (up to 1 hour 15 min.)
[ ] Resource - 21% - 60% of day (1 hr. 15 min. to 3 hrs. 30 min.)
[ ] Separate - 61% or more of day (excess of 3 hrs. 30 min.)
[ ] Public Separate School - 100%

[ ] Private Separate School - 100%
[ ] Public Residential - 100%
[ ] Private Residential - 100%
[ ] Home/Hospital - 100%

PRESCHOOL
[ ] Regular* - Up to 6 hours per week
[ ] Resource* - 6 to 18 hours per week
[ ] Separate* - more than 18 hours per week
[ ] Public Separate School - 100%
   *Applicable only in a classroom setting

[ ] Private Separate School - 100%
[ ] Public Residential - 100%
[ ] Private Residential - 100%
[ ] Home/Hospital - 100%
[ ] Home/Family - minimum 1 hour per week

AGENCY: Check where the student is receiving special services.
[ ] 1. LEA/School in Attendance Area   [ ] 3. Another LEA
[ ] 2. LEA/School Not in Attendance Area   [ ] 4. Other _____

Reason(s) for options rejected _____
_____
_____

Reason(s) for decision reached _____
_____
_____

C.   REGULAR PROGRAM PARTICIPATION: Circle the regular class(es) in which the student is enrolled and list the letter(s) for any modification(s) in the blank provided.

____ Reading	____ Library	____ History	____ For. Lang.	____ Vocational
____ English	____ Music/Art	____ Science	____ Physical Educ.	____ Recess
____ Spelling	____ Economics	____ Health	____ Chapter 1	____ Homeroom
____ Math	____ Social Studies	____ Writing	____ Remediation	____ Other
____ Language Arts	____ Lunch	____ Assemblies		

Appropriate classroom modification(s), if any:
a. Grading
b. Peer Tutoring
c. Oral Test
d. Abbreviated Assign-
   ments

e. Alternative Materials
f. Extended Test Time (Tchr. Test)
g. Large Print Books
h. Audio Tapes
i. Tape Recorder

j. Interpreter
k. Auditory Trainer
l. Assistive Devices
m. Computer/Typewriter/
   Word Processor

n. Other _____
_____
_____
_____

Note. From Wake County Public School System, Raleigh, NC. Copyright © 1993. Reprinted with permission.

Strategies for Mainstreaming Students for Social Studies Instruction

Glazzard (1980) has developed a list of 44 specific suggestions for what teachers can do to adapt classrooms for mainstreamed students. Her suggestions cover six categories of disabilities.

There are also a number of instructional strategies that can facilitate mainstreaming of special students for subject-matter instruction (see Curtis, 1991; Ochoa & Shuster, 1981). Some of the most successful approaches have involved the cooperative learning techniques we have discussed previously.

Examples of how the physical environment of the classroom might be adapted to accommodate various disabilities include removing barriers to facilitate easy movement and seating students with special needs near the front of the classroom and by the doors. Other ways to assist students involve tape-recording and providing outlines, notes, and study guides of lessons and attaching Braille labels on materials (Barnes, 1978). Additional strategies include allowing students to answer test questions orally and allowing those who have orthopedic impairments to be dismissed a few minutes early for their next classes. If you establish an environment that accepts and supports all learners and builds on each student's strengths, you will lay a strong foundation for mainstreaming success.

Susan Osborne, former Director of Graduate Studies for the Department of Curriculum and Instruction in the College of Education at North Carolina State University, is a professor of special education specializing in learning disabilities and attention problems. Colleagues and students seek her out for advice on teaching and learning strategies that help meet needs of children who are learning disabled. In Box 11.2, she provides suggestions for helping students recall important information. These approaches will help the students with special needs who are mainstreamed into your classroom as well as other learners who find memory joggers helpful.

Sanford (1980) offered a number of strategies and guidelines that are specific to social studies instruction in a mainstreamed classroom. To aid students with visual problems in geography instruction, for example, he advocated the use of tools such as Braille atlases, relief maps and globes, dissected maps of continents and countries, and landform models featuring three-dimensional tactile maps.

Osborne emphasizes the importance of using teaching techniques and approaches that address a range of students' needs and abilities. She points out that establishing, repeating frequently, and actually directly teaching classroom rules is important to a student's understanding of how to function in a classroom. For example, what does being prepared for class actually mean? She notes that giving lots of positive feedback for appropriate behavior, both social and academic, establishing and posting a schedule and reviewing it orally, making expectations clear, making sure directions are not beyond the reading level of the students in the class, and using mnemonics to teach factual information are all important

BOX 11.2   Addressing the Issues: Including Students with Special Needs

Susan Osborne
Associate Professor of Graduate Special Education, North Carolina State University

Students with learning problems including Specific Learning Disabilities, Emotional/Behavioral Disorders, Attention Deficit Disorders, and other high incidence disabilities generally participate with their nondisabled peers in social studies classes. Many students with these disabilities have particular difficulties with organizing information to be learned and with activating mental strategies to connect new information to information that is already familiar.

Teachers often express concern about how to include these students and help them learn and retain information required by today's high stakes testing. Fortunately, there has been considerable research in recent years in improving learning in content area instruction for students who struggle academically. Much work has been done, for example, by Margo Mastropieri and Tom Scruggs to enable middle grades students with disabilities activate strategies that will help them remember important information. One strategy that uses visual imagery is the key word approach. This is a three-step process in which students (1) recode by associating an unfamiliar word with a familiar one that sounds similar; (2) relate the actual word to the familiar one through visual imagery; and (3) retrieve the new term by recalling the mental picture. Mastropieri and Scruggs (1998) recall a middle school student with mild intellectual disabilities who had learned state capitals using key words the previous year. This student challenged

a research assistant to quiz her on state capitals. The research assistant asked the student the capital of Florida. The student replied correctly and explained that she remembered the association between Florida (flowers) and Tallahassee (television) because she had made a mental picture of a television with flowers on it to help her remember. Of course there are many other strategies we can use to help our students remember information. Some of these are acronyms like the widely used COPS strategy designed by Schumaker, Nolan, and Deshler (1985) to prompt students to proofread their final drafts for:

Capitalization (first words and proper nouns)

Overall Appearance (legibility, margins, indention of paragraphs)

Punctuation (end punctuation, commas)

Spelling

The best thing about such strategies is that they tend to boost performance for all students, not just those with difficulties in memory or in actually performing the skills that they have mastered.

Resources

Intervention Central: **www.interventioncentral.org**

Mastropieri, M. A., & Scruggs, T. E. (1998). Enhancing school success with mnemonic strategies. *Intervention in School & Clinic, 33,* 201–299.

Schumaker, J. B., Nolan, S. M., & Deshler, D. D. (1985). *Learning strategies curriculum: The error monitoring strategy.* Lawrence, KS: University of Kansas Center for Research on Learning.

procedures to ensure a student's success in the classroom. As Osborne points out, this kind of structuring for a classroom helps all students succeed, not just those with disabilities.

Bender (1985) has advocated extensive use of visual materials, such as various graphic organizers, with special students in social studies classes. He observed that many students with disabilities learn better when subject matter is presented through some visual representation. Keep in mind that even when seated in the front, some students cannot copy from the front board or screen. They are unable to make that board to paper written translation. Provide them with a copy of the material so they may be able to participate and study.

For administering social studies tests to mainstreamed students with mild disabilities, Wood, Miederhoff, and Ulschmid (1989) have made a number of suggestions, including the following:

1. Give examples of how students are to respond.
2. Provide directions both orally and in writing.
3. Offer alternative ways to test the same item (e.g., orally or written).
4. To reduce errors, let students circle correct answers rather than use answer sheets.
5. Use only one type of question (e.g., multiple choice) per sheet.
6. If a modified test is required for a mainstreamed student, design it to look like the regular one.

In some cases, materials for students with certain disabilities are available through your school media center and special agencies. For example, students with visual and hearing disabilities are served by several agencies that loan special social studies materials. Many community agencies offer the use of these materials, or they may be secured from the following organizations:

American Foundation for the Blind
15 West 16th Street
New York, NY 10011
www.afb.org/default.asp
AFB education section: **www.afb.org/info_documents.asp?collectionid=8**

American Printing House for the Blind
1839 Frankfurt Avenue
Louisville, KY 40206
www.aph.org/index.html

Captioned Films for the Deaf
Special Office for Materials Distribution
Indiana University Audiovisual Center
Bloomington, IN 47401
www.cfv.org/

Equity for the Gifted

Another category of special students in our schools is the **gifted**. In 1978 when the Congress passed the Gifted and Talented Children's Act, members asserted boldly, "The nation's greatest resource for solving national problems in areas of national concern is its gifted and talented children." The gifted are arguably critical to the future of our nation and the world. They enrich and enlighten us through their contributions to literature and the visual and performing arts. They produce our scientific breakthroughs and new technologies. Our societal problem solvers, national leaders, great artists, and top scientists come from their ranks.

In these and other ways, gifted and talented individuals are an important national resource. Whether we nurture and wisely use this resource depends in great measure on what special provisions our educational systems offer.

Societal Perspectives on the Gifted

American society historically has existed in a state of tension concerning the gifted student (Laycock, 1979; Delisle, 1991). One school of thought maintains that the gifted are an elite who are well qualified to look out for themselves without any special help. This perspective reasons that schools filled with average students and those with special problems should focus their limited resources on the majority, not the gifted minority.

At the same time, our society promotes the notion of excellence and the ideal that individuals should strive to achieve all that their abilities allow. Schools are alternately chided and prodded when they ignore this societal goal. We exhort our schools to help produce exceptional individuals who will keep our nation in the forefront of the world in areas such as technology, industrial productivity, space, the arts, peacekeeping, human rights, and standards of living. When we seem to lag or fall behind, as in the 1950s in the space race with the former Soviet Union, and in the 1960s when the economic engine of Japan was in high gear, we initiate national crash programs and offer special incentives to stimulate the education of talented individuals.

Identifying the Gifted

Who are the gifted? Definitions vary considerably, but most gifted individuals possess some combination of the following characteristics (Marland, 1972):

Leadership abilities	Special academic aptitudes
Creativity	General intellectual abilities
Artistic abilities	Psychomotor abilities

Most states and local school districts have created operational meanings for those characteristics that they use to define gifted students. For example, a school may consider a score of 130 or above on an individual IQ test as an indicator of general intellectual ability. Such procedures, however, have come under attack on the grounds that they are too limiting and favor students reared in the mainstream culture (Baldwin, 1978; Frasier, 1989). The critics favor alternative procedures and instruments to identify giftedness in students whose backgrounds are dissimilar to the majority of students (Sisk, 1987).

Approaches to Gifted Education

Schools that provide for the special needs of the gifted usually employ some variation of three organizational approaches to their programs (Maker, 1982; Sisk, 1987). One approach is to group students in one or more subjects by *ability*. For example, students judged to be gifted in social studies might be placed together, either by grades or across several grades (multiage grouping). A variation of this approach is to place all students designated as gifted together for all subjects.

A second approach is to keep students within a regular classroom setting, but to provide *enriched* learning experiences in one or more subjects. Enrichment may be provided within the regular classroom setting or through so called "pull-out" programs, where gifted students are taken from their classrooms to special programs one or more times a week.

The third basic approach emphasizes *accelerating* students' progress in mastering subject matter. Either through special in-class activities or other types of special programs, students advance as rapidly as they are capable through the study of a subject. When the subject matter has been mastered, a student advances to the next level of material. They may also focus in more depth on the same topic. This may be through "postholing" (digging down) to achieve greater depth of knowledge of the subject or consideration of more complex, reflective issues regarding the topic (Tomlinson, 1999). Schools that offer accelerated learning through AP (advanced placement) courses enable students to take end-of-course tests. High scores may be used as credit for some college courses.

Providing for gifted students is a serious matter for parents, teachers, and schools. School systems that do not provide agreed-upon measures and programs for their gifted students may be taken to court to force compliance.

Gifted Students in Social Studies Classes

Sisk (1987) has observed that the "social studies, more than other subjects, offers gifted students a chance to deal with real problems in the world, problems that have their roots in the past, direct application to the present, and implications for the future" (p. 171). Several different sets of characteristics that seem to distinguish general giftedness in social studies have been identified (Jewett, 1960; Plowman, 1980; Sisk, 1987; Torrance & Sisk, 1998).

Consider a sixth-grade class composed of students who have demonstrated exceptional *cognitive abilities* in the area of social studies. Signs of exceptional cognitive abilities in the area of social studies might include the following:

With respect to *verbal ability*, the student exhibits signs of:

1. A high level of language development
2. A vast store of information
3. Advanced comprehension through use of abstract thinking
4. Facility in speaking and in expressing complex ideas

5. Asking many and often original questions
6. Unusual curiosity and originality in questions
7. Ability to engage in sustained, meaningful, give-and-take discussions
8. An exceptional memory
9. Large vocabulary
10. Varied interests

With respect to *written work*, the student exhibits signs of:

1. An unusual capacity for processing information
2. A special knack for seeing unusual or less obvious relationships among data
3. A pattern of consistently generating original ideas and solutions
4. Unusual examples of cause-and-effect relationships, logical predictions, and frequent use of abstractions
5. An unusual ability to accurately synthesize large bodies of information
6. The capacity to use with ease a number of different reference materials in solving problems and testing hypotheses
7. Advanced reading ability
8. Unusual ability to understand alternative points of view or to place oneself in another's shoes
9. A large storehouse of information
10. Creativity

It is not coincidental that students with either or both abilities are usually very well read.

Among the ways in which special social studies programs for the gifted have been provided to address the special cognitive abilities described above are the following:

- *Using Alternative Materials at Advanced Reading Levels.* Example: Using 11th-grade and above leveled materials on American history to supplement or replace normal 8th-grade American history text and program.
- *Using Exclusively Discovery Approaches and Simulations and Role-Playing Techniques.* Example: Substituting the usual narrative expository study of a topic with a series of discovery lessons and simulation and role-playing activities that are open ended and require consideration of alternatives and problem solving.
- *Using a Special, Alternative Curriculum.* Example: Substituting a year's course of study in geography, economics, or anthropology for the standard basal text in the 12th grade.
- *Employing Mentors Specializing or Working in Areas Related to the Social Studies Curriculum.* Example: Under the guidance of a mentor specialist, having a student conduct a project to obtain data regarding the ethics of seal hunting (Figure 11.5).
- *Emphasizing Problem-Solving Assignments and Activities.* Example: Reorganize the sixth-grade curriculum around a series of units that involve problem-solving tasks.

FIGURE 11.5
Plan for a Mentorship Activity

		Finalized Plan for a Community-Based "Mentor-Directed Enrichment Project"	
		Mentor's Name ___Jeannie G.___ Pupil's Name ___Grania M.___ Project Topic ___Sealing: Right or Wrong?___ Project Meeting Time ___Friday Afternoons 1:00-3:00 or longer___	
		Week # Learning Activities (Including Resources)	**Related Learning Outcomes**
Phase I Planning proposal		1. (a) Mentor writes up proposed project in his or her area of expertise (b) University instructor and enrichment teacher use proposal to match mentor to an interested pupil	(a) Preparing for first meeting with pupil
Phase II Agreeing on finalized project plan		2. (a) Introduce proposal and topic (b) Find out what Grania knows about seals and sealing, and what her attitudes are (can change project plan if necessary) (c) Prepare questionnaire for next week's interview, and role-play an interview using tape recorder	(a) Increasing intrinsic motivation (b) Planning an enrichment project (c) Posing answerable questions (d) Interviewing skills (e) Practicing courtesy
Phase III Carrying out the project plan		3. (a) Visit Vancouver Aquarium to observe seals (b) Interview (tape record) seal trainer discussing what seals are like (c) Take slides of seals; sketch them	(a) Observation skills (b) Interviewing skills and confidence (c) Background knowledge about seals (d) Artistic skills
		4. (a) At school, Grania decides which sketches, slides, and information are to be used in her presentation (b) Read materials on seals and compare to observations made at aquarium	(a) Decision-making and organization skills (b) Comparing and contrasting
		5. (a) Assess project thus far (review) (b) Prepare and rehearse questions for next week's interview with Gordon Rogers (a "pro-sealer" from Newfoundland) and the following week's interview with someone from the Greenpeace organization (anti-sealing)	(a) Grania has greater voice in preparing questions (b) Brainstorming imaginative questions
		6. (a) Interview Gordon Rogers (b) Obtain leads to other pro-sealing sources	(a) Gain a "pro-sealer's" point of view firsthand (b) Refine interviewing skills
		7. (a) Interview spokesperson from the Greenpeace organization (b) Obtain leads to other anti-sealing resources (c) Obtain materials to be used in presentation (including visuals)	(a) Gain an anti-sealing point of view firsthand (b) Refine interviewing skills
Phase IV Completing and presenting the project		8. (a) Organize the material to be used in the class presentation (b) Mount Grania's sketches (c) Mold clay seals; paint them (d) Prepare posters to display pro and con information	(a) Decision-making and organization skills (b) Lettering posters (neatness)
		9. (a) Role-play the class presentation (mentor demonstrates; pupil practices) (b) Objectively present both pro and con information to allow class members to decide for themselves if sealing is right or wrong	(a) Speaking skills and self-confidence (b) Objective reporting of controversial information
		10. (a) Pupil gives class presentation and answers questions about what she liked best about her project, and so forth.	(a) Public speaking skills (b) Thinking "on one's feet" while answering questions

Note. From "Mentor-Assisted Enrichment Projects for the Gifted and Talented," by William A. Gray. In the November issue of *Educational Leadership, 40,* p. 19 © 1982 Association for Supervision and Curriculum Development. Used with permission. Learn more about ASCD at www.ascd.org.

- *Focusing on Research as Conducted by Social Scientists*. Example: Organizing several units around the use and analysis of primary and secondary source materials. For example: Enable students to ask big questions and address issues that are of interest to them.
- *Studying Problems and Cutting-Edge Issues*. Example: Focusing the entire seventh-grade curriculum that deals with world cultures on the problem of world hunger, how different countries have been affected by it, what the projections for the future indicate, and what are some scenarios of how the world of the future could be different if a solution to the problem could be found.
- *Use of Student Projects*. Example: As an alternative to studying about communities in the basal text, students design, carry out, and evaluate with teacher assistance a series of projects to better understand their local community.

SUMMARY

One advantage of having students from different parts of a region, country, or the world is the diversity that it brings to your classroom. Differing heritages, abilities, languages, and interests require that a teacher use differentiated instruction. In the 1970s, individualizing meant you prepared a different approach and lesson for every student that you taught. Today, we recognize that, while teachers are very good, they cannot nor do they wish to individualize a whole classroom of children. Teachers today seek to know the learning styles of each student that they teach, and they vary the assignments and their own teaching styles to best meet the needs of their students. They assess progress in a number of different ways. Years of rote learning and paper-and-pencil tests have given way to new approaches to teaching and learning that better meet the needs of students and teachers. NCLB and the emphasis on standardized testing of discrete facts sends us back to the old style of teaching that does not support and encourage abstract thinking and learning.

Children with special needs bring a new challenge to the classroom teacher. Laws require that specific measures must be taken to ensure that children with special needs have an equitable opportunity to realize their potential. Often school districts provide aides that accompany a child with special needs. These aides help facilitate the child's learning in the regular classroom. They also help the classroom teacher understand how to provide for that child's learning in the context of the regular classroom. It is important that when we discuss diversity in our classrooms that we realize that it is not just the color of one's skin that contributes to a diverse classroom. There are many forms of diversity—cultural, ethnic, gender, and ability, to mention a few.

This chapter has discussed ways to meet the different needs of your students in the context of a social studies classroom. Chapter 12 will examine more completely how to evaluate and assess your students' progress.

ACTIVITIES

1. Visit a classroom in either a middle or a secondary school that includes a diverse group of learners. Identify all of the ways that the classroom is diverse and that the teaching and learning approaches the teacher uses respond to the diversity. Discuss your findings.

2. Select a local school district in your area and determine how it identifies gifted students in the elementary, middle, and secondary schools. Determine which of the three approaches to gifted education discussed in the chapter the district employs. Discuss your findings.

3. Contact Harvard Project Zero Development Group, Longfellow Hall, Appian Way, Cambridge, MA 02138 (**http://pzweb.harvard.edu/**), for a list of schools that are implementing multiple intelligences (MI) theories. Contact one of the schools to learn about results.

4. Select any middle or secondary school social studies basal textbook. Pick a topic or a sample of subject matter that is part of the text narrative (symbolic mode). Develop a sample activity to illustrate how the same material could be taught to a youngster through the iconic mode. Repeat the process for the enactive mode.

5. Construct an artifact kit dealing with any social studies topic. Follow the directions and suggestions within the chapter.

WEB RESOURCES

National Association for Gifted Children: **www.nagc.org/**

Council for Exceptional Children: **www.cec.sped.org/**

ERIC Clearinghouse on Disabilities and Gifted Education: **www.ericec.org/**

Library of Congress: **www.loc.gov**

Learning Styles Network: **www.learningstyles.net/**

Learning Styles Profile for Secondary and Middle: **www.youngzones.org/learning_styles.html**

Evaluating and Assessing Student Learning

The Dimensions of Evaluation

Grades, Assessments, and Standards

The Use and Misuse of Tests

Norm-Referenced Tests

Criterion-Referenced Tests

The National Assessment of Educational Progress

National Standards and National Testing

Performance Assessments

Social Studies Performance Assessments and Portfolios

Teacher-Made Paper-and-Pencil Tests

Posttests and Pretests

Constructing Essay Test Items

Constructing Objective Test Items

Test Software

Evaluating Reflection, Competence, and Concern

Assessing Reflection

Assessing Competence

Assessing Concern

A Framework for Evaluating the Outcomes of Social Studies Instruction

Matching Evaluation and Instructional Goals and Objectives

Summary

Activities

Web Resources

Mr. Holman was excited about his first year as a social studies teacher. He had many ideas about the creative strategies he intended to use with his high school social studies students. He couldn't wait to meet his new colleagues so that he could share ideas with them and learn from their years of teaching experience.

He was baffled, however, on the first day of teacher workdays to meet his new colleagues. It seemed all they talked about was the state end-of-course exam. He was surprised by their focus on the state standards and state exam that the students would have to take. The emphasis among his new colleagues seemed to be on how to ensure that a high percentage of the students passed the test. Mr. Holman realized at this time that he must not only implement the creative teaching strategies that he intended to use in his classroom but also understand the different dimensions of evaluation.

Increasingly, teachers and schools are being asked to provide specific indicators of student learning and comparisons with their classmates' achievements in social studies. Tests, grades, assessment, and evaluation have become integral parts of the process of schooling. Teachers are expected to provide reasonable and clear answers to basic parent questions such as, "What did my youngster—not the class—learn in social studies this year?"

The Dimensions of Evaluation

Evaluation can be seen as a way of making a decision about the value of something based on some systematically organized data. Literally, the term means "to determine or judge the value or worth of something or someone." Parents and other societal groups look to educators for evaluations of how successful our schools have been in achieving their objectives. Students, more basically, wish to know simply, "How am I doing?" Evaluation has many objective and subjective dimensions; it involves much more than "giving tests" and labeling students. The National Council for the Social Studies developed a position statement on the testing and evaluation in the social studies. In this statement, NCSS states: "To gauge effectively the efforts of students and teachers in social studies programs, evaluators must augment traditional tests with performance evaluations, portfolios of student papers and projects, and essays focused on higher-level thinking" (1991, p. 285).

The American Education Research Association (AERA) has also developed a position statement on testing and evaluation in the schools. This position statement contains a list of conditions that are essential for implementation of high-stakes testing. The list includes:

- Protection against high-stakes decisions based on a single test
- Adequate resources and opportunity to learn
- Validation for each separate intended use
- Full disclosure of likely negative consequences of high-stakes testing programs
- Alignment between the test and the curriculum
- Validity of passing scores and achievement levels
- Opportunities for meaningful remediation for examinees who fail high-stakes tests
- Appropriate attention to language differences among examinees
- Appropriate attention to students with disabilities
- Careful adherence to explicit rules for determining which students are to be tested
- Sufficient reliability for each intended use
- Ongoing evaluation of intended and unintended effects of high-stakes testing

We first will consider some of the nuances, issues, and mechanics associated with different dimensions of evaluation. Then we will move beyond them to examine how a teacher develops an evaluation framework. This is what guides teacher decisions about what is important in the curriculum and how best to assess what students have learned.

Grades, Assessments, and Standards

Grades are one of the shorthand ways of communicating the results of an evaluation. "Hank got an A in social studies" means that the teacher evaluated his performance and decided it was exceptional. In the absence of a grade, a sentence, symbol, or other means could have served the same purpose. Grades, however, are often used because they are easy to record, communicate to others, and compare.

Perhaps most significantly, grades can be reduced to quantifiable terms. This means that separate evaluations from different subjects, each totally unrelated, may be merged and used to form a new, single evaluation; for example, "Reba was a 3.35 student."

In contrast to grades, **assessments** are those systematic ways we use to collect our data. They encompass measures such as simple charts for keeping track of the number of times a student asks questions in a social studies class and comprehensive collections of student work. Assessments may also include paper-and-pencil measures, such as tests that are used to measure how much subject matter a student has learned.

Standards are related to both assessment and evaluation. They are the criteria teachers use for making judgments. Standards determine what every student should know, how carefully something should be assessed, and what is satisfactory performance or an acceptable level of learning. Teachers' standards determine whether they are regarded as "easy" or "tough."

The ultimate purpose of grades, assessments, standards, and evaluation should be to validate and improve teaching and learning. Teachers should use assessment data to enhance student learning. Consequently, assessment should be an ongoing part of social studies instruction rather than a culminating activity.

The Use and Misuse of Tests

Testing has assumed a large role in our society over the past 60 years. Tests and testing will probably dog students throughout at least the early part of their lives and occupational careers. It is safe to say that students who enter a public school in the United States will take countless tests of all types before they graduate. College and the world of work will likely present yet another battery of tests for the student to take.

Although tests can aid the teacher in some aspects of evaluation, they are often inappropriate measures of what a student has learned. Tests, especially paper-and-pencil tests, sometimes are used on occasions where other tools would be more efficient or suitable. It seems obvious, for example, that it would be inappropriate to use a paper-and-pencil test dealing with art to discover whether students were exceptional artists. Rather, we likely would have a qualified artist or panel judge their artwork. So it is with many aspects of achievement in the social studies. If we wish to evaluate how well students can use data to solve a problem or to determine how effectively they apply techniques of research, for example, student productions or projects probably are more appropriate than a test.

Critics of existing testing practices also point to their potential negative consequences (e.g., Darling-Hammond & Lieberman, 1992; Mitchell, 1992). One particularly penetrating criticism of many tests is that they are biased with respect to ethnicity, social class, and gender. In addition, Darling-Hammond and Lieberman (1992) also have charged:

> Because of the way in which the tests are constructed, they place test-takers in a passive, reactive role, rather than a role that engages their capacities to structure tasks, produce ideas, and solve problems . . . . Teaching has been geared to the tests, reducing students' opportunities for higher-order learning . . . . Many studies have found that because of test-oriented teaching, American students' classroom activities consist of listening, reading textbook sections, responding briefly to questions, and taking short-answer and multiple-choice quizzes. They rarely plan or initiate anything, create their own products, read or write something substantial, or engage in analytical discussions or in projects requiring research, invention, or problem solving. (p. B1)

Norm-Referenced Tests

Two basic types of social studies tests that students typically are required to take throughout their school careers and beyond are norm-referenced and criterion-referenced tests. **Norm-referenced tests** allow teachers to compare their students with the norms or results obtained from the performance of a sample group of other students on the same test (Williams & Moore, 1980). They provide answers to a question such as, "How does the performance of this 10th-grade class compare with that of other 10th graders?"

Standardized Social Studies Tests. So-called **standardized tests** are those that have standardized sets of instructions for administering the tests to ensure uniform test-taking procedures, such as California Achievement Tests. They have been administered to a given population and contain scores and percentiles. Usually, the items on a standardized test have been refined over time. For example, three types of questions have been eliminated through field tests and trials: (1) those that are poorly worded or ambiguous; (2) those that most students answer correctly; and (3) those that most students answer incorrectly.

Major sources of information on all of the standardized tests currently available, including those in the area of social studies, are the *Mental Measurement Yearbooks* and *Tests in Print*. They are available in most college libraries and contain information such as a description of a test, where it can be purchased, and one or more critiques of its strengths and weaknesses. Some examples of standardized tests for the social studies are *California Achievement Tests, Iowa Tests of Basic Skills*, and *Sequential Tests of Educational Progress*.

Teachers should realize that the subject matter sampled in standardized tests *may not correspond to what is being studied in any individual classroom*. This may occur since the specific subject matter and curriculum for a given grade level may vary from district to district. As a consequence, standardized tests often exclude social studies information and skills that are considered to be important to teachers. Further, as Darling-Hammond and Lieberman (1992) have cautioned, "They are inappropriate tools for many of the purposes that they are expected to serve, including tracking students, determining promotions, and allocating rewards and sanctions to students, teachers, and schools" (p. B1).

In sum, as they use and interpret the results of standardized tests, teachers should consider carefully whether what the tests measure matches the objectives of the classroom social studies program. Unless a clear match exists, the standardized test is useful only as a general diagnostic measure of what students know.

Criterion-Referenced Tests

In comparison to norm-referenced tests, **criterion-referenced tests** allow teachers to compare the performance of their students against some standard of what they should know (Popham, 1988). To develop large-scale criterion-referenced tests, school districts contract with test publishers to develop suitable materials for the school's curriculum. These tests provide answers to questions such as, "How does the performance of our students compare with the criterion of what we expected them to know or demonstrate?" An example of a criterion would be: Given an unlabeled globe of the world, a student will be able to correctly identify 80% of the world's major waterways.

The National Assessment of Educational Progress

In 1969, after 6 years of gestation, a consortium of states embarked on a national project known as the Nation's Report Card or the **National Assessment of Educational Progress (NAEP)**, which is still in existence. The NAEP was an attempt by states to begin collecting evaluation data across the various participating states. It attempts to measure student growth in various areas of the school curriculum, including areas of the social studies.

Samples of students from across the United States have been included in the ongoing NAEP project. Findings have been reported for age groups 9, 13, and 17. Tests are repeated on a cyclical basis, and results are published and made available to the general public, as well as participating school districts. Report cards for specific areas such as U.S. history, civics, and geography are included within the data sets. All report cards and more information are available online at **http://nces.ed.gov/nationsreportcard/**.

National Standards and National Testing

In recent years, some groups both separate from and within NAEP have also called for the establishment of **national standards** for subjects within the curriculum. For example, the 1994 Goals 2000: Educate America Act called for the development of voluntary national standards by the year 2000. These standards would establish what all students in the United States should know and when they should know it.

To date, all the major professional organizations have worked on standards related to the social studies curriculum. Their efforts are represented in the History Standards Project, addressing the area of history; the Geography Standards Project, dealing with geography; the National Council on Economic Education Standards, focusing on the discipline of economics; National Standards for Civics and Government, covering civics and government; and the NCSS Curriculum Standards for the Social Studies, addressing the social studies as a whole.

For more information on each of these sets of standards, visit the following websites:

Center for Civic Education: **www.civiced.org/**

National Council on Economic Education: **www.ncee.net/**

National Center for History in the Schools: **www.sscnet.ucla.edu/nchs/**

National Council for Geographic Education: **www.ncge.org/**

National Council for the Social Studies: **www.ncss.org/**

As noted in Chapter 2 (refer to Figure 2.5), NCSS developed a set of standards to guide social studies teachers. The NCSS standards consist of 10 thematic strands that are to be included at every grade level. Attached to each strand is a set of specific performance expectations that should be used to guide assessment. For example, Figure 12.1 illustrates the relationship of Standard 9, Global Connections, to performance expectations across the grades.

FIGURE 12.1
Specific Performance Expectations for Standard 9, Global Connections

Social studies programs should include experiences that provide for the study of *global connections and interdependence,* so that the learner can:

Early Grades	Middle Grades	High School
a. Explore ways that language, art, music, belief systems, and other cultural elements may facilitate global understanding or lead to misunderstanding;	a. Describe instances in which language, art, music, belief systems, and other cultural elements can facilitate global understanding or cause misunderstanding;	a. Explain how languages, art, music, belief systems, and other cultural elements can facilitate global understanding or cause misunderstanding;

FIGURE 12.1
continued

Early Grades	Middle Grades	High School
b. Give examples of conflict, cooperation, and interdependence among individuals, groups, and nations;	b. Analyze examples of conflict, cooperation, and interdependence among groups, societies, and nations;	b. Explain conditions and motivations that contribute to conflict, cooperation, and interdependence among groups, societies, and nations;
c. Examine the effects of changing technologies on the global community;	c. Describe and analyze the effects of changing technologies on the global community;	c. Analyze and evaluate the effects of changing technologies on the global community;
d. Explore causes, consequences, and possible solutions to persistent, contemporary, and emerging global issues, such as pollution and endangered species;	d. Explore the causes, consequences, and possible solutions to persistent, contemporary, and emerging global issues, such as health, security, resource allocation, economic development, and environmental quality;	d. Analyze the causes, consequences, and possible solutions to persistent, contemporary, and emerging global issues, such as health, security, resource allocation, economic development, and environmental quality;
e. Examine the relationships and tensions between personal wants and needs and various global concerns, such as use of imported oil, land use, and environmental protection;	e. Describe and explain the relationships and tensions between national sovereignty and global interests, in such matters as territory, natural resources, trade, use of technology, and welfare of people;	e. Analyze the relationships and tensions between national sovereignty and global interests, in such matters as territory, economic development, nuclear and other weapons, use of natural resources, and human rights concerns;
f. Investigate concerns, issues, standards, and conflicts related to universal human rights, such as the treatment of children, religious groups, and effects of war.	f. Demonstrate understanding of concerns, standards, issues, and conflicts related to universal human rights;	f. Analyze or formulate policy statements demonstrating an understanding of concerns, standards, issues, and conflicts related to universal human rights;
	g. Identify and describe the roles of international and multinational organizations.	g. Describe and evaluate the role of international and multinational organizations in the global arena;
		h. Illustrate how individual behaviors and decisions connect with global systems.

Note. From *Curriculum Standards for the Social Studies* (p. 44), by National Council for the Social Studies, 1994, Washington, DC: Author. © National Council for the Social Studies. Reprinted by permission.

The NCSS also encouraged educators to combine its standards with those proposed by other projects. Following this suggestion, educators could construct "customized" curricula to meet local needs.

Performance Assessments

As we have seen, proposals for national standards and testing frequently also embrace the use of **performance** (or authentic) **assessments** as part of an overall program of evaluation. These assessments are a way of measuring student learning that requires the active construction of responses in the context of performing real (sometimes called "authentic") tasks (Perrone, 1991). Among other features, performance assessment approaches typically tap multiple sources of information to determine what students have learned in every phase of the social studies program.

Although performance assessments may employ paper-and-pencil tests, these have a limited role in the total evaluation process. Tests that assess only knowledge of social studies subject matter cannot provide thorough and comprehensive measures of social studies learning. They typically pass over knowledge of processes and skills.

Among those types of learning that paper-and-pencil tests of knowledge typically ignore in the social studies are the ability to:

- Identify, clarify, and solve an open-ended problem
- Use spatial tools such as maps, globes, and compasses to locate objects
- Identify cause–effect relationships among social data
- Develop, execute, and critique an oral presentation to argue on behalf of a position or valued principle
- Generate and test hypotheses and generalizations
- Apply and relate concepts
- Take and defend an ethical position
- Organize a body of related information into a graph, chart, or table
- Conduct an interview to gather social data
- Write a report summarizing important similarities and differences among issues, events, and individuals
- Evaluate the evidence presented in competing arguments

Social Studies Performance Assessments and Portfolios

To redress the limitations of paper-and-pencil tests, teachers frequently employ portfolios of performance (or authentic) assessments (see Armstrong, 1994). A **portfolio** consists of samples of a student's work accumulated in a folder over a period of time. Additionally, it may include observations and comments regarding a student's

FIGURE 12.2
Standardized Testing Versus Authentic Assessment

Standardized Testing	Authentic Assessment
• Creates a mythical standard or norm which requires that a certain percentage of children fail.	• Establishes an environment where every child has the opportunity to succeed.
• Pressures teachers to narrow their curriculum to only what is tested on an exam.	• Allows teachers to develop meaningful curricula and assess within the context of that program.
• Emphasizes one-shot exams that assess knowledge residing in a single mind at a single moment in time.	• Assesses on an *ongoing* basis in a way that provides a more accurate picture of a student's achievement.
• Focuses too much importance on single sets of data (i.e., test scores) in making educational decisions.	• Provides *multiple* sources of evaluation that give a more accurate view of a student's progress.
• Treats all students in a uniform way.	• Treats each student as a unique human being.
• Discriminates against some students because of cultural background and learning style.	• Provides a *culture-fair* assessment of a student's performance; gives everyone an equal chance to succeed.
• Regards testing and instruction as separate activities.	• Regards assessment and teaching as two sides of the same coin.
• Produces scoring materials that students often never see again.	• Results in products that have *value* to students and others.
• Focuses on "the right answer."	• Deals with *processes* as much as final products.

Note. From *Multiple Intelligences in the Classroom* (p. 116), by Thomas Armstrong. Alexandria, VA: Association for Supervision and Curriculum Development. © 1994 ASCD. Used with permission. Learn more about ASCD at www.ascd.org.

activities by parents and teachers. Some key differences between standardized testing and authentic assessment are displayed in Figure 12.2.

Portfolios are intended to provide a holistic view of a student's capabilities in social studies. Optimally, the student and the teacher should review portfolios periodically throughout the year to chart progress. As technology becomes ubiquitous in today's classrooms, more and more students are creating digital portfolios. Digital portfolios allow more creativity to link content throughout the product and when they are Web-based the viewing audience is expanded. Student productions for a portfolio might include the following types of items:

- Written essays, papers, projects, and exercises
- Skits, debates, oral reports, panels, and role playing

- Cooperative learning group outcomes
- Skill demonstrations (e.g., using reference materials and interviewing techniques)
- Creations of products (e.g., dioramas, oral history collections, exhibits, videotapes, audiotapes, artifacts, photographs, bulletin boards, posters, card sorts, and timelines)
- Rating forms, checklists, and observation forms
- Diaries, journals, and logs
- Experiments
- Teacher anecdotal records
- Teacher interviews

Teacher-Made Paper-and-Pencil Tests

Some of the most frequently used evaluation devices in the middle and secondary grades are **teacher-made paper-and-pencil tests.** These often include features and items that resemble those found in norm-referenced and criterion-referenced tests. They differ from commercially prepared tests largely in the uses to which they are put and in the procedures used to develop them.

Posttests and Pretests

As one dimension of evaluation, teachers typically give tests *after* students have studied a subject. These are often referred to as **posttests.** Tests can also be used as diagnostic measures to determine what students know *before* they begin study of a topic. Used in this fashion, such measures are called **pretests.**

Pretests can provide direction for the shape of a unit by identifying students' interests and gaps or misconceptions in their knowledge. Comparison of scores with those on the posttest also can indicate how much students actually have achieved as a result of instruction. The K-W-L technique, described in Chapter 9, is an illustration of how this can be done.

A number of specialized books, materials, and guidelines exist to help teachers construct their own tests (e.g., Airasian, 1991; Popham, 1988; TenBrink, 1994). Once a teacher has determined that student achievement can best be measured through a teacher-made test, several basic choices exist. These generally consist of identifying or creating *essay* and *objective test* items.

Constructing Essay Test Items

Essay questions are an especially effective way to measure students' ability to organize, analyze, apply, synthesize, and evaluate in their own words information they have learned. Essay questions require students to use abstract thinking and provide students with the freedom to think broadly and to express themselves in different ways. Student essays, however, often are difficult to assess with objectivity. Further, of necessity, they can cover only a narrow range of objectives in a short period of time. They also are time consuming to score and allow students to digress.

In some cases, essay questions also penalize students who have in reality learned a great deal but have trouble expressing themselves in standard English. Translating concrete objects and ideas into abstractions represented by essay answers is a cognitive task that is related both to development and to language facility. Those for whom English is a second language, for example, often have more difficulty in stating something in their own words than in demonstrating learning by selecting, identifying, applying, or demonstrating among alternatives.

General Guidelines. Following are two basic guidelines for constructing well-designed essay questions.

1. Use clear, specific, and simple language.
   a. Yes: Describe three major ways in which the economic systems of the United States and China differ.
   b. No: Elaborate briefly on the distinctions between the economic systems of the United States and China.
2. Limit the scope of the question and the expected answer as much as possible.
   a. Yes: Identify two significant presidential characteristics that Kennedy and Theodore Roosevelt shared.
   b. No: How was Kennedy like Theodore Roosevelt?

Before teachers present essay questions to students, they should construct a model answer for each question. The model should list the major points, items, or type of discussion the teacher will accept as correct, partially correct, or satisfactory (TenBrink, 1994). It also should indicate the relative weights that will be assigned to each element in the answer.

For example, note the short-answer essay question given in Figure 12.3 (Scott Foresman, 1983). Let us assume the question is worth a total of seven points and that there are seven elements in a correct answer, each worth one point. The teacher will accept the following three elements as correct for the middle area: Both were important men, both wanted to govern wisely, and both led political parties.

Under *Jefferson's Views*, the teacher will consider as correct any two of the following three items: As little government as possible is best; common people should have power; and farming should be a major industry. For *Hamilton's Views*, the teacher will accept any two of these: Strong federal government is best; wealthy should have power; and strong businesses are necessary.

An alternate approach to scoring an essay question is to use a **rubric**. Using this technique, the teacher reads the essay and scores it using a rubric such as the sample rubric on page 346. Students are assessed on different components of the essay and given a final grade.

FIGURE 12.3
Assessment Item: Short-Answer Essay

Diagramming Two Different Views

Thomas Jefferson and Alexander Hamilton were both very important men during the beginning of the United States. Both men wanted the country to be governed wisely, but each had views that were very different.

While Hamilton felt that the federal government should be strong, Jefferson believed that as little government as possible would be best for the people. Hamilton felt that the wealthy should run this government. Jefferson believed that common people should have the power.

Jefferson wanted farming to be the country's main industry. Hamilton felt that strong businesses that provided many jobs were necessary. Both men led political parties that supported their own beliefs. Jefferson and his followers became known as Republicans. Hamilton and his followers became known as Federalists.

Complete this Venn diagram. In the middle area, summarize three things that Jefferson and Hamilton shared in common. Then summarize each man's differing views below his name.

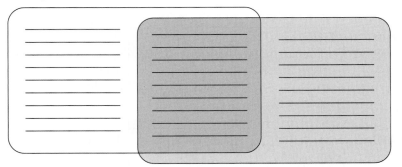

Note. Excerpt p. 39 from *America Past and Present Workbook: Teacher's Edition,* by Schreiber, Stepien, Patrick, Remy, Gay and Hoffman. Copyright © 1983 by Scott Foresman and Company. Reprinted by permission of Pearson Education, Inc.

Constructing Objective Test Items

The term *objective* in the context of testing refers to the way in which responses to a question will be graded, not to the nature of the question itself. Deciding to include one item instead of another on a test to represent learning is a *subjective* judgment of the teacher.

Objective test items are relatively easy to grade quickly and are not susceptible to teacher bias in scoring. They also permit many objectives to be addressed in a short period of time and do not penalize students who lack verbal skills. On the other hand, objective items encourage guessing and are often more difficult and time consuming to construct than essay questions. They also afford students no opportunity to demonstrate divergent thinking.

Sample Rubric for Assessing a Student Essay

Points	1 Weak	2 Basic	3 Proficient	4 Strong	Total
Brief summary of novel	Summary does not reflect comprehension	Gives an overview, but no evidence of understanding	Presents the information	Well-developed, concise summary	
Critique of novel	Does not present a critique	Presents surface-level critiques without evidence	Presents critiques with evidence	Presents critiques and supports with evidence and suggestions	
Comparison of historical account with other sources	Little or no evidence of source comparison	Initial comparison of sources	Detailed comparison of sources	Highly creative and thorough comparison of multiple sources	
Grammar and Spelling	Frequent grammar and/or spelling errors; no evidence of proofreading	Three or more grammar and/or spelling errors	Two or fewer grammar and/or spelling errors	Well-written with no grammar and/or spelling errors	
Timeliness	Handed in three or more days late	Handed in two days late	Handed in one day late	Handed in on time	
Total					
Comments					

Types of Objective Test Items.   Types of objective test items most appropriate for use in the social studies are *multiple-choice, alternative response,* and *matching* questions. There are many variations of each form possible, as well. Several of the texts cited in the references section provide comprehensive instructions on constructing each of these types.

A fourth form of objective test item, *completion* or *fill in the blank,* also exists and is used by some social studies teachers. Typically, however, its use in social studies is fraught with problems. Clear and unambiguous items are difficult to construct. Also, students can often respond with many reasonable completion items, besides the correct one.

Consider, for example, this poorly constructed completion question: "_____ _____ was the author of the _____ of _____." The correct answer expected is the set of four words, "Thomas," "Jefferson," "Declaration," and "Independence." In reality, however, myriad plausible alternative sets of answers are equally correct (e.g., "John," "Steinbeck," "Grapes," and "Wrath").

An example of each of the three types of objective items recommended—multiple-choice, alternative response, and matching questions—follows, accompanied by some guidelines on the writing of the item.

Multiple-Choice Questions. The largest of the 50 states in terms of population is which of the following?

a. Wyoming

b. Delaware

c. West Virginia

d. Rhode Island

Some basic guidelines for writing multiple-choice questions include the following:

- The stem (the first part) should state the question or issue.
- All choices should be plausible, related, and, ideally, approximately the same length.
- Use four options and avoid use of the options "All of the above" and "None of the above," which often confuse students.
- Preferably the stem should be stated in a positive form, avoiding the use of terms such as *not* and *never*.
- Organize the stem around one idea only.

Alternative Response Questions. All of the following statements deal with the newspaper article you have been given. If the statement is true according to the article, circle the *T* next to it. If it is false, circle the *F*.

T   F   The country has been experiencing economic problems.

T   F   Agriculture is a major part of the economy.

Some basic guidelines for writing alternative response questions include the following:

- Each statement should include a *single* point or issue.
- Avoid statements designed to "trick" or mislead students if they do not read carefully.
- Avoid terms such as *always, never, all, generally, occasionally*, and *every*, which signal the correct answer.

Matching Questions. Look at the two sets of items that follow. The set on the left lists cities, and the one on the right gives states. In front of the set of cities is a blank space. Write in each space the letter of the state that belongs with the city.

___ Denver	a.	North Carolina
___ Philadelphia	b.	California
___ Camden	c.	South Carolina
___ Raleigh	d.	Pennsylvania
___ Tampa	e.	Colorado
___ Los Angeles	f.	Rhode Island
___ Providence	g.	Wyoming
	h.	New Jersey
	i.	Virginia
	j.	Florida

Some basic guidelines for writing matching items questions include the following:

- The items in each column should be related.
- The directions should state clearly what the student is to do and any special limitations on the use of choices (e.g., whether items can be used more than once).
- Generally, there should be more choices than can be matched.
- The order of the items in each set of choices should be either alphabetical or random.
- The number of items in the shorter column should be less than 10 to avoid students wasting time by searching through long lists.

Test Software

Publishers of basal textbook programs now include computer software with banks of test items that are correlated with the subject matter of the text. This type of software allows easy modifications of tests and sharing of items with other teachers. A number of commercially developed software programs also make it possible for teachers to create an entire test. Examples are *Test Generator, Test Quest,* and *QuickTests.*

A number of Web pages now also provide teachers access to generate assessment tools online. *Kathy Schrock's Guide for Educators* (**http://school.discovery .com/schrockguide/**) is one example of a website that provides teachers the opportunity to quickly create customer-made assessment tools such as quizzes, puzzles, and activity sheets. This site also provides sample rubrics that can be used to assess student work, specifically multimedia student projects.

Evaluating Reflection, Competence, and Concern

Effective, meaningful evaluation is transacted for some significant purpose. We conduct evaluations to determine the relative effectiveness of significant components of our instructional program and to validate student achievement.

We have suggested throughout this text that in social studies our ultimate goal should be the development of reflective (head), competent (hand), and concerned (heart) citizens. Correspondingly, the evaluation system and the assessments we devise should tap each of these three dimensions of the effective citizen. Moreover, our objectives and our curricular programs should guide the character of our evaluation and assessment system, rather than the reverse.

In the preceding sections, we have considered some issues associated with evaluation and a repertoire of assessment strategies that can aid in the evaluation process. We now will examine some sample assessment items specifically related to measuring the dimensions of reflection, competence, and concern that we considered in earlier chapters. The items illustrated will include a mix of the following types of performance assessments:

test items	cooperative learning outcomes
research sheets	creation of products
teacher interviews	checklists
rating scales	

Results from each of these forms of assessment may be accumulated in individual student folders. These products, or illustrative samples of them, can be reviewed periodically to evaluate student progress.

Assessing Reflection

We have characterized reflective citizens as those who have knowledge of a body of facts, concepts, and generalizations. Reflective citizens are also capable of channeling that knowledge into action in the form of problem solving and decision making. The achievement of instructional objectives related to the development of these characteristics can be measured in a variety of ways.

Let us consider some different sample items, which are arranged by the type of assessment used. For each type, the dimension of reflection it attempts to assess is listed and an example is given.

Using an Essay Test Question to Assess Reflection

Dimension: Identification of critical attributes of a concept

Example: List the criterial attributes of the concept of revolution.

Using a Multiple-Choice Test Question to Assess Reflection

Dimension: Developing a generalization from facts

Example: Examine the graphs shown in Figure 12.4 and answer the questions that follow them.

Dimension: Forming a hypothesis

Example: Imagine a homeless man standing on a busy corner crying. Why do you think he is crying?
a. He can't find a place to sleep.
b. The people around him won't help him.
c. It is an act to generate a handout.
d. He has no inner strength.

Using a Research Sheet to Assess Reflection

Dimension: Identifying cause–effect relationships

FIGURE 12.4
Multiple-Choice Test Question

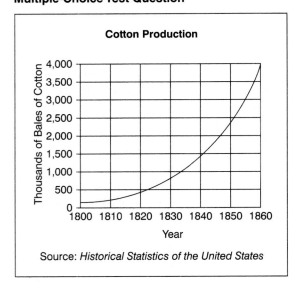

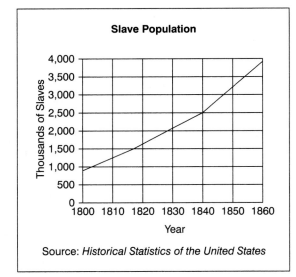

What might be concluded about the relationship between cotton production and slaves?
a. To produce more cotton, fewer slaves were needed.
b. To produce more cotton, more slaves were needed.
c. Cotton production was not related to slavery.
d. An increase in slaves caused a decrease in cotton production.

Note. From *The American Nation* by Prentice Hall © 1986 by Prentice Hall, Inc. Used by permission. From *The American Nation Teacher's Resource Guide* by Prentice Hall © 1986 by Prentice Hall, Inc. Used by permission.

Example: Read each statement carefully. Then, for each statement write the *cause* of the event.*

a. Thousands of Cubans fled their island and came to the United States.
   Cause:
b. In the 1960s some women's groups called for "equivalent pay."
   Cause:
c. In recent years many Hispanics have been elected to public office.
   Cause:
d. Migrant farm workers had little chance to get an education.
   Cause:

Dimension: Relating facts and generalizations

Example: Consider the following generalization: "The end of World War II caused major economic problems for the world." Identify five sets of facts that support this generalization. Record each set of facts using the Procedure Sheet that you were given for this report.

For your references, consult the books that have been set aside in the library. When you have completed the research sheet, place it in your social studies portfolio.

Assessing Competence

Competent citizens, as described earlier, have a repertoire of talents that include social, research and analysis, chronology, and spatial skills. Paper-and-pencil tests are often sufficient to measure such skills. As with many other skills in life, however, some citizen competencies can best be demonstrated through actual performance.

Checklists are inventories that show, from demonstrations with real tasks, which skills students have mastered. They may be completed by the teacher or the student and are especially useful for objectives that are either–or types (i.e., either the student achieved the objective or not).

Rating scales appear in many different forms (e.g., attitude inventories introduced in Chapter 8). Unlike checklists, they can be used to measure the *degree of progress* students have made. For example, a teacher may assess whether a student has demonstrated considerable or minimal growth in an area, rather than merely check "has made progress" or "has not made progress."

Let us examine some different sample assessment items that include checklists and rating scales. For each item, the dimension of competence it attempts to measure is listed, followed by an example.

Using the Creation of a Product to Assess Competence

Dimension: Demonstrating map-making skills

*This example from *The American Nation Teacher's Resource Guide*, p. D127, © 1986 by Prentice Hall, Inc. Used by permission.

Example: Create a map that shows someone who is traveling by car from our school how to get to the Crossroads Shopping Mall. In your map, include the features listed on the attached sheet. Also, consult your compass and use it in constructing the map. When you have completed the map, ask two people who can drive if they could locate the mall using your map. Based on their answers, make any final changes that are needed. Then place the map in your social studies portfolio.

Using a Checklist to Assess Competence

Dimension: Use of reference materials

Example: A checklist similar to the one in Figure 12.5 could be constructed to assess students' use of simple reference materials. When a student has demonstrated the skill satisfactorily, a check is made next to the student's name.

Using Rating Scales to Assess Competence

Dimension: Group skills

Example: Each student working within a group would be rated on each of the characteristics in Figure 12.6.

FIGURE 12.5
Sample Checklist for Reference Sources

Reference Sources Checklist	Mary	Bill	Tara	Fred	Jo
1. Uses picture captions and titles to organize information	—	—	—	—	—
2. Uses glossaries and dictionaries to identify word meaning	—	—	—	—	—
3. Uses dictionaries as aids to pronunciation	—	—	—	—	—
4. Uses a variety of reference works	—	—	—	—	—
5. Uses an atlas	—	—	—	—	—
6. Uses the telephone directory and the Yellow Pages as sources of information	—	—	—	—	—
7. Uses an index to locate information	—	—	—	—	—
8. Uses newspapers and magazines as sources of information	—	—	—	—	—
9. Writes letters to obtain information	—	—	—	—	—
10. Constructs computer databases	—	—	—	—	—

FIGURE 12.6
Group Participation Rating Sheet

Student's Name _____ Date _____

Group Members _____

Date Group Formed _____

Each of the characteristics of group participation will be rated as follows:

    5 = Consistently Exhibited
    4 = Frequently Exhibited
    3 = Occasionally Exhibited
    2 = Seldom Exhibited
    1 = Not Exhibited

Characteristics   *Rating*

  1. Accepts ideas of others   ____

  2. Initiates ideas   ____

  3. Gives opinions   ____

  4. Is task oriented   ____

  5. Helps others   ____

  6. Seeks information   ____

  7. Encourages others to contribute   ____

  8. Works well with all members   ____

  9. Raises provocative questions   ____

10. Listens to others   ____

11. Disagrees in a constructive fashion   ____

12. Makes an overall positive contribution to the group   ____

                                                      Total Rating   ____

Additional Comments:

Using the Creation of a Product and Teacher Interview to Assess Competence

Dimension: Constructing a timeline to organize major events

Example: Make a timeline that shows what you think are the major events that occurred between 1929 and 1942 in the United States. Then, be prepared to explain to the teacher in a conference why you felt these events should be included.

Using Cooperative Learning and the Creation of a Product to Assess Competence

Dimension: Establishing factual claims

Example: Students are assigned to a Jigsaw II cooperative learning group (see Chapter 5). Each expert is given a different sheet of factual claims that have been made concerning the Columbus voyages and their impact. Each expert is required to research the information on his or her sheet and determine what the best evidence suggests. Following the Jigsaw II procedures, each expert briefs the other members on the findings. Each group then creates a poster that lists "claims" and "facts."

Assessing Concern

We have characterized concerned citizens as those who are aware of and exercise fully and effectively their rights and responsibilities as members of our society. They are also aware of and responsive to the larger social world around them. In addition, they are willing to make commitments and act on social issues at the local, regional, national, and international levels. Concerned citizens also establish personal priorities and make ethical decisions with respect to significant values and issues of greatest concern to them.

In assessing students' progress toward developing dimensions of concern, teachers may find tools such as checklists, research sheets, anecdotal records, and rating scales especially helpful. These instruments can be equally valuable as pretests or posttests.

Let us consider some different sample items. For the item, the dimension of concern it attempts to measure is listed, followed by an example.

Using a Research Sheet to Assess Concern

Dimension: Perspective taking

Example: From our study and discussion of the colonial period, what can you say were the attitudes of these different groups toward their experiences? List as many things as you can for each group. Then try to put yourself in the shoes of the English, the Africans, and the Indians, and offer some reasons for *why* they might have felt this way (see Figure 12.7).

FIGURE 12.7
Sample Research Sheet

How the English Felt	Why They Felt This Way
_____	_____
_____	_____
How the Africans Felt	Why They Felt This Way
_____	_____
_____	_____
How the Native Americans Felt	Why They Felt This Way
_____	_____
_____	_____
_____	_____

Note. Based on _Getting Together with People_, (p. 37), by N. E. Wallen, 1974, Reading, MA: Addison-Wesley.

Using an Essay Test Question to Assess Concern

Dimension: Taking a stand on ethical dilemmas

Example: "Examine the problem scenario on page 211. Answer questions 2 and 3. Then suppose that you had taken the opposite position. What are some reasons you might give to support your stand?"

When everyone is finished, we will break into groups to discuss your answers.

Using a Checklist to Assess Concern

Dimension: Developing sensitivity to alternative points of view

Example: A checklist similar to the one in Figure 12.8 could be constructed by individuals working in a group. If a student has demonstrated the behavior, a check is made next to his or her name.

FIGURE 12.8
Checklist of Student Behaviors Related to Sensitivity for Alternate Points of View

	Tod	Abe	Jean	Rea
1. Is open to new ideas	___	___	___	___
2. Listens while others speak	___	___	___	___
3. Is willing to change his or her mind	___	___	___	___
4. Does not ridicule others' ideas	___	___	___	___
5. Does not engage in name calling	___	___	___	___
6. Does not reject those who disagree	___	___	___	___
7. Supports others' rights to speak	___	___	___	___
8. Is curious about ideas different from his or her own	___	___	___	___

A Framework for Evaluating the Outcomes of Social Studies Instruction

To this point, we have been examining assessment techniques associated with evaluation. Let us now consider a scenario in which a teacher, Ms. Schwartz, armed with these techniques, develops an evaluation plan from the ground up. Suppose at the beginning of the year, she is engaged in designing an evaluation framework for the first report card period.

After some reflection about her students, she decides the following assessment procedures will be appropriate and adequate as measures of their learning in social studies:

- Scores from teacher-made tests
- Anecdotal records of class interaction
- Checklists of group participation skills
- Ratings on individual projects
- Ratings on oral reports
- Scores from a standardized test
- Checklists of written assignments

The further decision she makes is related to the percentage of the total evaluation that should be assigned to each of the seven measures. Again, Ms. Schwartz made a subjective judgment. That is, she decided which indicators would be more important than others in determining student progress.

Ms. Schwartz decided that ratings of individual projects should receive the greatest weight. Her rationale was that a great deal of class time during the evaluation period would be spent on project activities. Correspondingly, she assigned the

FIGURE 12.9
A Sample Evaluation Framework

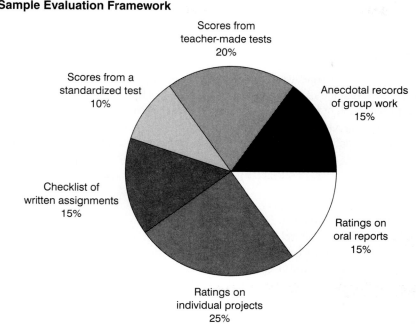

smallest percentage to a standardized test, since only one would be given, and it would cover only a small set of subject-matter objectives addressed by the course.

The sizes of the remaining five pieces were determined on a similar basis. (If Ms. Schwartz had deemed it appropriate, all of the pieces could have been of an equal size or of some other proportion.) Once she had made her decisions about the relative importance of the different components of the course, her evaluation framework, as shown in Figure 12.9, was established.

Matching Evaluation and Instructional Goals and Objectives

In making her evaluation decisions, Ms. Schwartz looked to the goals and specific instructional objectives she had established for the social studies program. The seven elements of her evaluation framework addressed all aspects of the program considered to be important for the time period considered. These elements also encompassed those areas in which the class would spend most of its time during the evaluation period.

In addition to an evaluation pie chart, an **evaluation grid** sometimes is useful for determining whether all the teacher's goals or objectives have been reflected in the evaluation framework and in which ways. It involves listing all of the instructional

FIGURE 12.10
Evaluation Grid

Important Goals	How Achievement of the Goals Will Be Assessed
Identify major ethnic groups within the United States and some of the traditions associated with each of them.	Ratings on an oral report Individual projects A teacher-made test
Learn research techniques associated with locating information from written materials.	Skill demonstrations Samples of individual student papers Anecdotal record

goals or objectives that the teacher considers to have been important in one column. In the next column are matched those ways in which student achievement of the goals or objectives are to be measured (e.g., through ratings on an oral report). A portion of a sample evaluation grid is shown in Figure 12.10.

SUMMARY

Chapter 12 has summarized the role that assessment plays in the social studies classroom. It has also provided you with suggestions and ideas for implementing appropriate assessment activities in your classroom. We hope that as you prepare for your first day of teaching, you will have the excitement and enthusiasm that Mr. Holman did in the opening scenario of this chapter. Keeping in mind that the essence of social studies instruction is the head, heart, and hand, we hope that you will nurture the enthusiasm and excitement that is a part of your first teaching experience.

ACTIVITIES

1. Select a unit from your state or local standard course of study. Outline the content, suggested activities, and resources. Design appropriate assessments for the unit, including authentic and standardized.
2. Interview five middle or secondary students. Ask them what role evaluation and assessment plays in their views of school and learning. Specifically, ask them about their experiences with standardized tests and authentic assessments (give them examples).
3. Examine a standardized test for social studies. Note its name, the publisher, the copyright date, and the grade level at which it is used. Also identify the different forms of questions that are included (e.g., multiple choice) and

the topics or subjects that it covers. Discuss your reactions and how you would best prepare students for the test.

4. Interview three social studies teachers about their views on evaluation and assessment. Specifically ask them how they feel national and state legislation impacts the social studies curriculum taught in their classroom.

5. Review one of the NAEP's report cards for U.S. History or Civic Education. What can we learn from these reports? What role do these results play in social studies teaching and learning in your future classroom?

WEB RESOURCES

ERIC Clearinghouse on Assessment: **http://ericae.net/**

The Nation's Report Card: **http://nces.ed.gov/nationsreportcard/**

Instructional Module Assessment: **www.edutopia.org/Assessment/GW_contact.html**

Kathy Schrock's Guide to Assessment: **http://school.discovery.com/schrockguide/assess.html**

RMC's Online Resources for Assessment: **www.rmcdenver.com/useguide/assessme/online.htm**

Appendix A

NCSS Standards and Performance Expectations

I. Culture

Social studies programs should include experiences that provide for the study of *culture* and *cultural diversity*, so that the learner can:

Middle Grades

a. compare similarities and differences in the ways groups, societies, and cultures meet human needs and concerns;

b. explain how information and experiences may be interpreted by people from diverse cultural perspectives and frames of reference;

c. explain and give examples of how language, literature, the arts, architecture, other artifacts, traditions, beliefs, values, and behaviors contribute to the development and transmission of culture;

d. explain why individuals and groups respond differently to their physical and social environments and/or changes to them on the basis of shared assumptions, values, and beliefs;

e. articulate the implications of cultural diversity, as well as cohesion, within and across groups.

High School

a. analyze and explain the ways groups, societies, and cultures address human needs and concerns;

b. predict how data and experiences may be interpreted by people from diverse cultural perspectives and frames of reference;

c. apply an understanding of culture as an integrated whole that explains the functions and interactions of language, literature, the arts, traditions, beliefs and values, and behavior patterns;

d. compare and analyze societal patterns for preserving and transmitting culture while adapting to environmental or social change;

e. demonstrate the value of cultural diversity, as well as cohesion, within and across groups;

f. interpret patterns of behavior reflecting values and attitudes that contribute or pose obstacles to cross-cultural understanding;

g. construct reasoned judgments about specific cultural responses to persistent human issues;

Note. From "Ten Themes from the Executive Summary" in *Expectations of Excellence: Curriculum Standards for Social Studies*, pp. x–xii, by National Council for the Social Studies, 1994, Washington, DC. © National Council for the Social Studies. Reprinted by permission.

I. Culture *(continued)*

Middle Grades

High School

h. explain and apply ideas, theories, and modes of inquiry drawn from anthropology and sociology in the examination of persistent issues and social problems.

II. Time, Continuity, & Change

Social studies programs should include experiences that provide for the study of *the ways human beings view themselves in and over time*, so that the learner can:

Middle Grades

a. demonstrate an understanding that different scholars may describe the same event or situation in different ways but must provide reasons or evidence for their views;

b. identify and use key concepts such as chronology, causality, change, conflict, and complexity to explain, analyze, and show connections among patterns of historical change and continuity;

c. identify and describe selected historical periods and patterns of change within and across cultures, such as the rise of civilizations, the development of transportation systems, the growth and breakdown of colonial systems, and others;

d. identify and use processes important to reconstructing and reinterpreting the past, such as using a variety of sources, providing, validating, and weighing evidence for claims, checking credibility of sources, and searching for causality;

e. develop critical sensitivities such as empathy and skepticism regarding attitudes, values, and behaviors of people in different historical contexts;

f. use knowledge of facts and concepts drawn from history, along with methods of historical inquiry, to inform decision making about and action taking on public issues.

High School

a. demonstrate that historical knowledge and the concept of time are socially influenced constructions that lead historians to be selective in the questions they seek to answer and the evidence they use;

b. apply key concepts such as time, chronology, causality, change, conflict, and complexity to explain, analyze, and show connections among patterns of historical change and continuity;

c. identify and describe significant historical periods and patterns of change within and across cultures, such as the development of ancient cultures and civilizations, the rise of nation-states, and social, economic, and political revolutions;

d. systematically employ processes of critical historical inquiry to reconstruct and reinterpret the past, such as using a variety of sources and checking their credibility, validating and weighing evidence for claims, and searching for causality;

e. investigate, interpret, and analyze multiple historical and contemporary viewpoints within and across cultures related to important events, recurring dilemmas, and persistent issues, while employing empathy, skepticism, and critical judgment;

f. apply ideas, theories, and modes of historical inquiry to analyze historical and contemporary developments, and to inform and evaluate actions concerning public policy issues.

III. People, Places, & Environments

Social studies programs should include experiences that provide for the study of *people, places, and environments*, so that the learner can:

Middle Grades

a. elaborate mental maps of locales, regions, and the world that demonstrate understanding of relative location, direction, size, and shape;

b. create, interpret, use, and distinguish various representations of the earth, such as maps, globes, and photographs;

c. use appropriate resources, data sources, and geographic tools such as aerial photographs, satellite images, geographic information systems (GIS), map projections, and cartography to generate, manipulate, and interpret information such as atlases, databases, grid systems, charts, graphs, and maps;

d. estimate distance, calculate scale, and distinguish other geographic relationships such as population density and spatial distribution patterns;

e. locate and describe varying landforms and geographic features, such as mountains, plateaus, islands, rain forests, deserts, and oceans, and explain their relationships within the ecosystem;

f. describe physical system changes such as seasons, climate and weather, and the water cycle and identify geographic patterns associated with them;

g. describe how people create places that reflect cultural values and ideals as they build neighborhoods, parks, shopping centers, and the like;

h. examine, interpret, and analyze physical and cultural patterns and their interactions, such as land use, settlement patterns, cultural transmission of customs and ideas, and ecosystem changes;

i. describe ways that historical events have been influenced by, and have influenced, physical and human geographic factors in local, regional, national, and global settings;

High school

a. refine mental maps of locales, regions, and the world that demonstrate understanding of relative location, direction, size, and shape;

b. create, interpret, use, and synthesize information from various representations of the earth, such as maps, globes, and photographs;

c. use appropriate resources, data sources, and geographic tools such as aerial photographs, satellite images, geographic information systems (GIS), map projections, and cartography to generate, manipulate, and interpret information such as atlases, databases, grid systems, charts, graphs, and maps;

d. calculate distance, scale, area, and density, and distinguish spatial distribution patterns;

e. describe, differentiate, and explain the relationships among various regional and global patterns of geographic phenomena such as landforms, soils, climate, vegetation, natural resources, and population;

f. use knowledge of physical system changes such as seasons, climate and weather, and the water cycle to explain geographic phenomena;

g. describe and compare how people create places that reflect culture, human needs, government policy, and current values and ideals as they design and build specialized buildings, neighborhoods, shopping centers, urban centers, industrial parks, and the like;

h. examine, interpret, and analyze physical and cultural patterns and their interactions, such as land use, settlement patterns, cultural transmission of customs and ideas, and ecosystem changes;

i. describe and assess ways that historical events have been influenced by, and have influenced, physical and human geographic factors in local, regional, national, and global settings;

III. People, Places, & Environments *(continued)*

Middle Grades

j. observe and speculate about social and economic effects of environmental changes and crises resulting from phenomena such as floods, storms, and drought;

k. propose, compare, and evaluate alternative uses of land and resources in communities, regions, nations, and the world.

High school

j. analyze and evaluate social and economic effects of environmental changes and crises resulting from phenomena such as floods, storms, and drought;

k. propose, compare, and evaluate alternative policies for the use of land and other resources in communities, regions, nations, and the world.

IV. Individual Development & Identity

Social studies programs should include experiences that provide for the study of *individual development and identity*, so that the learner can:

Middle Grades

a. relate personal changes to social, cultural, and historical contexts;

b. describe personal connections to place—as associated with community, nation, and world;

c. describe the ways family, gender, ethnicity, nationality, and institutional affiliations contribute to personal identity;

d. relate such factors as physical endowment and capabilities, learning, motivation, personality, perception, and behavior to individual development;

e. identify and describe ways regional, ethnic, and national cultures influence individuals' daily lives;

f. identify and describe the influence of perception, attitudes, values, and beliefs on personal identity;

g. identify and interpret examples of stereotyping, conformity, and altruism;

h. work independently and cooperatively to accomplish goals.

High school

a. articulate personal connections to time, place, and social/cultural systems;

b. identify, describe, and express appreciation for the influences of various historical and contemporary cultures on an individual's daily life;

c. describe the ways family, religion, gender, ethnicity, nationality, socioeconomic status, and other group and cultural influences contribute to the development of a sense of self;

d. apply concepts, methods, and theories about the study of human growth and development, such as physical endowment, learning, motivation, behavior, perception, and personality;

e. examine the interactions of ethnic, national, or cultural influences in specific situations or events;

f. analyze the role of perceptions, attitudes, values, and beliefs in the development of personal identity;

g. compare and evaluate the impact of stereotyping, conformity, acts of altruism, and other behaviors on individuals and groups;

h. work independently and cooperatively within groups and institutions to accomplish goals;

i. examine factors that contribute to and damage one's mental health and analyze issues related to mental health and behavioral disorders in contemporary society.

V. Individuals, Groups, & Institutions

Social studies programs should include experiences that provide for the study of *interactions among individuals, groups, and institutions*, so that the learner can:

Middle Grades

a. demonstrate an understanding of concepts such as role, status, and social class in describing the interactions of individuals and social groups;

b. analyze group and institutional influences on people, events, and elements of culture;

c. describe the various forms institutions take and the interactions of people with institutions;

d. identify and analyze examples of tensions between expressions of individuality and group or institutional efforts to promote social conformity;

e. identify and describe examples of tensions between belief systems and government policies and laws;

f. describe the role of institutions in furthering both continuity and change;

g. apply knowledge of how groups and institutions work to meet individual needs and promote the common good.

High school

a. apply concepts such as role, status, and social class in describing the connections and interactions of individuals, groups, and institutions in society;

b. analyze group and institutional influences on people, events, and elements of culture in both historical and contemporary settings;

c. describe the various forms institutions take, and explain how they develop and change over time;

d. identify and analyze examples of tensions between expressions of individuality and efforts used to promote social conformity by groups and institutions;

e. describe and examine belief systems basic to specific traditions and laws in contemporary and historical movements;

f. evaluate the role of institutions in furthering both continuity and change;

g. analyze the extent to which groups and institutions meet individual needs and promote the common good in contemporary and historical settings;

h. explain and apply ideas and modes of inquiry drawn from behavioral science and social theory in the examination of persistent issues and social problems.

VI. Power, Authority, & Governance

Social studies programs should include experiences that provide for the study of *how people create and change structures of power, authority, and governance*, so that the learner can:

Middle Grades

a. examine persistent issues involving the rights, roles, and status of the individual in relation to the general welfare;

b. describe the purpose of government and how its powers are acquired, used, and justified;

High school

a. examine persistent issues involving the rights, roles, and status of the individual in relation to the general welfare;

b. explain the purpose of government and analyze how its powers are acquired, used, and justified;

VI. Power, Authority, & Governance *(continued)*

Middle Grades

c. analyze and explain ideas and governmental mechanisms to meet needs and wants of citizens, regulate territory, manage conflict, and establish order and security;

d. describe the ways nations and organizations respond to forces of unity and diversity affecting order and security;

e. identify and describe the basic features of the political system in the United States, and identify representative leaders from various levels and branches of government;

f. explain conditions, actions, and motivations that contribute to conflict and cooperation within and among nations;

g. describe and analyze the role of technology in communications, transportation, information processing, weapons development, or other areas as it contributes to or helps resolve conflicts;

h. explain and apply concepts such as power, role, status, justice, and influence to the examination of persistent issues and social problems;

i. give examples and explain how governments attempt to achieve their stated ideals at home and abroad.

High school

c. analyze and explain ideas and mechanisms to meet needs and wants of citizens, regulate territory, manage conflict, establish order and security, and balance competing conceptions of a just society;

d. compare and analyze the ways nations and organizations respond to conflicts between forces of unity and forces of diversity;

e. compare different political systems (their ideologies, structure, institutions, processes, and political cultures) with that of the United States, and identify representative political leaders from selected historical and contemporary settings;

f. analyze and evaluate conditions, actions, and motivations that contribute to conflict and cooperation within and among nations;

g. evaluate the role of technology in communications, transportation, information processing, weapons development, or other areas as it contributes to or helps resolve conflicts;

h. explain and apply ideas, theories, and modes of inquiry drawn from political science to the examination of persistent issues and social problems;

i. evaluate the extent to which governments achieve their stated ideals and policies at home and abroad;

j. prepare a public policy paper and present and defend it before an appropriate forum in school or community.

VII. Production, Distribution, & Consumption

Social studies programs should include experiences that provide for the study of *how people organize for the production, distribution, and consumption of goods and services*, so that the learner can:

Middle Grades

a. give and explain examples of ways that economic systems structure choices about how goods and services are to be produced and distributed;

High school

a. explain how the scarcity of productive resources (human, capital, technological, and natural) requires the development of economic systems to make decisions about how goods and services are to be produced and distributed;

VII. Production, Distribution, & Consumption *(continued)*

Middle Grades	High school
b. describe the role that supply and demand, prices, incentives, and profits play in determining what is produced and distributed in a competitive market system;	b. analyze the role that supply and demand, prices, incentives, and profits play in determining what is produced and distributed in a competitive market system;
c. explain the difference between private and public goods and services;	c. consider the costs and benefits to society of allocating goods and services through private and public sectors;
d. describe a range of examples of the various institutions that make up economic systems such as households, business firms, banks, government agencies, labor unions, and corporations;	d. describe relationships among the various economic institutions that comprise economic systems such as households, business firms, banks, government agencies, labor unions, and corporations;
e. describe the role of specialization and exchange in the economic process;	e. analyze the role of specialization and exchange in economic processes;
f. explain and illustrate how values and beliefs influence different economic decisions;	f. compare how values and beliefs influence economic decisions in different societies;
g. differentiate among various forms of exchange and money;	g. compare basic economic systems according to how rules and procedures deal with demand, supply, prices, the role of government, banks, labor and labor unions, savings and investments, and capital;
h. compare basic economic systems according to who determines what is produced, distributed, and consumed;	h. apply economic concepts and reasoning when evaluating historical and contemporary social developments and issues;
i. use economic concepts to help explain historical and current developments and issues in local, national, or global contexts;	i. distinguish between the domestic and global economic systems, and explain how the two interact;
j. use economic reasoning to compare different proposals for dealing with a contemporary social issue such as unemployment, acid rain, or high-quality education.	j. apply knowledge of production, distribution, and consumption in the analysis of a public issue such as the allocation of health care or the consumption of energy, and devise an economic plan for accomplishing a socially desirable outcome related to that issue;
	k. distinguish between economics as a field of inquiry and the economy.

VIII. Science, Technology, & Society
Social studies programs should include experiences that provide for the study of *relationships among science, technology, and society*, so that the learner can:

Middle Grades	High school
a. examine and describe the influence of culture on scientific and technological choices and advancement, such as in transportation, medicine, and warfare;	a. identify and describe both current and historical examples of the interaction and interdependence of science, technology, and society in a variety of cultural settings;

VIII. Science, Technology, & Society *(continued)*

<table>
<tr><td>

Middle Grades

b. show through specific examples how science and technology have changed people's perceptions of the social and natural world, such as in their relationship to the land, animal life, family life, and economic needs, wants, and security;

c. describe examples in which values, beliefs, and attitudes have been influenced by new scientific and technological knowledge, such as the invention of the printing press, conceptions of the universe, applications of atomic energy, and genetic discoveries;

d. explain the need for laws and policies to govern scientific and technological applications, such as in the safety and well-being of workers and consumers and the regulation of utilities, radio, and television;

e. seek reasonable and ethical solutions to problems that arise when scientific advancements and social norms or values come into conflict.

</td><td>

High school

b. make judgments about how science and technology have transformed the physical world and human society and our understanding of time, space, place, and human-environment interactions;

c. analyze how science and technology influence the core values, beliefs, and attitudes of society, and how core values, beliefs, and attitudes of society shape scientific and technological change;

d. evaluate various policies that have been proposed as ways of dealing with social changes resulting from new technologies, such as genetically engineered plants and animals;

e. recognize and interpret varied perspectives about human societies and the physical world using scientific knowledge, ethical standards, and technologies from diverse world cultures;

f. formulate strategies and develop policies for influencing public discussions associated with technology-society issues, such as the greenhouse effect.

</td></tr>
</table>

IX. Global Connections

Social studies programs should include experiences that provide for the study of *global connections and interdependence*, so that the learner can:

<table>
<tr><td>

Middle Grades

a. describe instances in which language, art, music, belief systems, and other cultural elements can facilitate global understanding or cause misunderstanding;

b. analyze examples of conflict, cooperation, and interdependence among groups, societies, and nations;

c. describe and analyze the effects of changing technologies on the global community;

</td><td>

High school

a. explain how language, art, music, belief systems, and other cultural elements can facilitate global understanding or cause misunderstanding;

b. explain conditions and motivations that contribute to conflict, cooperation, and interdependence among groups, societies, and nations;

c. analyze and evaluate the effects of changing technologies on the global community;

</td></tr>
</table>

IX. Global Connections *(continued)*

Middle Grades

d. explore the causes, consequences, and possible solutions to persistent, contemporary, and emerging global issues, such as health, security, resource allocation, economic development, and environmental quality;

e. describe and explain the relationships and tensions between national sovereignty and global interests, in such matters as territory, natural resources, trade, use of technology, and welfare of people;

f. demonstrate understanding of concerns, standards, issues, and conflicts related to universal human rights;

g. identify and describe the roles of international and multinational organizations.

High school

d. analyze the causes, consequences, and possible solutions to persistent, contemporary, and emerging global issues, such as health, security, resource allocation, economic development, and environmental quality;

e. analyze the relationships and tensions between national sovereignty and global interests, in such matters as territory, economic development, nuclear and other weapons, use of natural resources, and human rights concerns;

f. analyze or formulate policy statements demonstrating an understanding of concerns, standards, issues, and conflicts related to universal human rights;

g. describe and evaluate the role of international and multinational organizations in the global arena;

h. illustrate how individual behaviors and decisions connect with global systems.

X. Civic Ideals & Practices

Social studies programs should include experiences that provide for the study of *the ideals, principles, and practices of citizenship in a democratic republic*, so that the learner can:

Middle Grades

a. examine the origins and continuing influence of key ideals of the democratic republican form of government, such as individual human dignity, liberty, justice, equality, and the rule of law;

b. identify and interpret sources and examples of the rights and responsibilities of citizens;

c. locate, access, analyze, organize, and apply information about selected public issues—recognizing and explaining multiple points of view;

d. practice forms of civic discussion and participation consistent with the ideals of citizens in a democratic republic;

High school

a. explain the origins and interpret the continuing influence of key ideals of the democratic republican form of government, such as individual human dignity, liberty, justice, equality, and the rule of law;

b. identify, analyze, interpret, and evaluate sources and examples of citizens' rights and responsibilities;

c. locate, access, analyze, organize, synthesize, evaluate, and apply information about selected public issues—identifying, describing, and evaluating multiple points of view;

d. practice forms of civic discussion and participation consistent with the ideals of citizens in a democratic republic;

IX. Civic Ideals & Practices *(continued)*

Middle Grades

e. explain and analyze various forms of citizen action that influence public policy decisions;

f. identify and explain the roles of formal and informal political actors in influencing and shaping public policy and decision making;

g. analyze the influence of diverse forms of public opinion on the development of public policy and decision making;

h. analyze the effectiveness of selected public policies and citizen behaviors in realizing the stated ideals of a democratic republican form of government;

i. explain the relationship between policy statements and action plans used to address issues of public concern;

j. examine strategies designed to strengthen the "common good," which consider a range of options for citizen action.

High school

e. analyze and evaluate the influence of various forms of citizen action on public policy;

f. analyze a variety of public policies and issues from the perspective of formal and informal political actors;

g. evaluate the effectiveness of public opinion in influencing and shaping public policy development and decision making;

h. evaluate the degree to which public policies and citizen behaviors reflect or foster the stated ideals of a democratic republican form of government;

i. construct a policy statement and an action plan to achieve one or more goals related to an issue of public concern;

j. participate in activities to strengthen the "common good," based upon careful evaluation of possible options for citizen action.

Appendix B

Sample of a Social Studies Textbook Evaluation Form

AMERICAN HISTORY

SOCIAL STUDIES
Grades 8, 11–12, and A.P. History

TEXTBOOK EVALUATION FORM

DIVISION OF INSTRUCTIONAL MATERIALS & TECHNOLOGY
DEPARTMENT OF CURRICULUM & INSTRUCTION
MEMPHIS CITY SCHOOLS—MEMPHIS, TENNESSEE
copyright 1990

LIST SECTION TOTALS BELOW
A. TEXTBOOK DEVELOPMENT _____
B. PUBLISHER _____
C. COST _____
D. PHYSICAL FEATURES _____
E. ORGANIZATION _____
F. INSTRUCTIONAL FEATURES _____
G. INSTRUCTIONAL CONTENT _____
H. TEACHER'S EDITION _____
I. ANCILLARY MATERIALS _____
   TOTALS—SECTIONS A–I _____

Complete one form for each textbook evaluated for each grade level or course.

Name of Textbook _____

Name of Publisher _____

Name of Series _____

Name of Committee _____ Evaluation Date _____

RESPOND TO ALL OF THE STATEMENTS LISTED BELOW BY USING THE FOLLOWING SCALE.

STRONGLY DISAGREE 0   1   2   3   4   5   6 STRONGLY AGREE

N - **Not Applicable**   AGREE
       No Information

A. **TEXTBOOK DEVELOPMENT**
   1. There is evidence that the development team of authors, advisors, and consultants includes a wide range of people (Grades 1–12 and university teachers). _____
   2. There is evidence that the text and ancillary materials were successfully field-tested. _____
   3. The field-test data were used to refine and improve the text and ancillary materials. _____
   4. The textbook reflects current thinking and knowledge (consider the publication date). _____
   5. The textbook can be used successfully for the next six years. _____

   Textbook Development Total _____

B. **PUBLISHER**
   1. The publisher will provide, at no cost, sufficient professional consultants to help implement the program. _____
   2. The publisher will provide, at no cost, continuous consultant services to meet school and classroom needs. _____
   3. The publisher will correlate its program to the MCS's social studies objectives within a reasonable time period. _____
   4. Reliable and quality service has been provided in the past by the publisher. _____
   5. The consultants provided at the hearing were knowledgeable and competent. _____

   Publisher Total _____

Note. From Division of Instructional Materials, Department of Curriculum and Instruction. Memphis City Schools, Memphis, TN. Used with permission.

C. COST
1. The cost of the textbook is comparable to the cost of other textbooks in the field. _____
2. The cost of ancillary materials is comparable to the cost of other ancillary materials in the field. _____

Cost Total _____

D. PHYSICAL FEATURES OF THE TEXTBOOK
1. The size and weight of the text are appropriate for the age of the student. _____
2. The type size and style are clear and appropriate for the age group. _____
3. The binding and cover are durable. _____
4. The paper quality is good. Nonglare paper is used. _____
5. The page layout is uncluttered and balanced. There is sufficient white space for easy reading. _____
6. Provisions for emphasis (heavy type, boxes, color, italics, etc.) are clear and appropriate. _____
7. The illustrations, tables, figures, graphs, charts, and maps are free from sexual and cultural bias. _____
8. The illustrations, tables, figures, graphs, charts, and maps are relevant and functional. _____
9. The cover is attractive, well designed, and appealing to students. _____

Physical Features of the Textbook Total _____

E. ORGANIZATION OF TEXTBOOK
1. The table of contents shows a logical development of the subject. _____
2. The glossaries/appendices are clear and comprehensive. _____
3. There is uniformity in lesson format within a single text. _____
4. The unit/chapter introductions are clear and comprehensive. _____
5. The unit/chapter summaries suitably reinforce the content. _____
6. There are sufficient, relevant, and well-placed unit/chapter tests. _____
7. There are sufficient, relevant, and well-placed practice exercises. _____
8. The references, bibliographies, and resources are sufficient. _____

Organization of Textbook Total _____

F. INSTRUCTIONAL FEATURES OF TEXTBOOK
1. The text is written in clear, simple, and logical terms. _____
2. Sentence structure and grammar are correct. _____
3. The style of writing improves comprehension. _____
4. The text provides sufficiently for individual differences. There are suggestions and alternative resources/activities for enrichment as well as for remediation. _____
5. The reading level is appropriate. _____
6. Key vocabulary is made clear in context or in the glossary. _____
7. End-of-lesson questions review key ideas and vocabulary. _____
8. Atlas and gazetteer sections reinforce the lesson. _____
9. Skills are introduced, taught, and maintained throughout the text. _____
10. The activities appeal to a wide range of student abilities and interests. _____

11. The students are sufficiently encouraged to develop skills beyond literal comprehension. _____

12. New concepts are identified in an easily distinguishable manner (boldface type, etc.). _____

13. There are opportunities for students to apply their skills to interesting, real-world situations. _____

14. There are sufficient activities for independent research and reports.

15. Content is presented in chronological order. _____

Instructional Features of Textbook Total _____

G. INSTRUCTIONAL CONTENT OF TEXTBOOK

1. The objectives listed in the proposed curriculum guide under Strand I can be successfully taught using this textbook. _____

2. The objectives listed in the proposed curriculum guide under Strand II can be successfully taught using this textbook. _____

3. The objectives listed in the proposed curriculum guide under Strand III can be successfully taught using this textbook. _____

4. The objectives listed in the proposed curriculum guide under Strand IV can be successfully taught using this textbook. _____

5. The objectives listed in the proposed curriculum guide under Strand V can be successfully taught using this textbook. _____

6. The objectives listed in the proposed curriculum guide under Strand VI can be successfully taught using this textbook. _____

7. The objectives listed in the proposed curriculum guide under Strand VII can be successfully taught using this textbook. _____

8. The objectives listed in the proposed curriculum guide under Strand VIII can be successfully taught using this textbook. _____

9. The objectives listed in the proposed curriculum guide under Strand IX can be successfully taught using this textbook. _____

10. The objectives listed in the proposed curriculum guide under Strand X can be successfully taught using this textbook.

11. The objectives listed in the proposed curriculum guide under Strand XI can be successfully taught using this textbook. _____

12. Map/Globe skills are an integral part of the lesson. _____

13. Map/Globe skills are reinforced in content-related activities. _____

14. Critical thinking skill development is provided at the lesson, chapter, and/or unit level. _____

15. Coverage of the content is adequate and balanced. _____

16. Sufficient examples of relationships between past and present are provided. _____

17. Covers important historical events and people. _____

18. Biographies of famous people are highlighted. _____

19. The content is actual and factual. _____

20. Historical events are clearly presented and supported by quotations and examples from firsthand accounts. _____

21. Includes all social studies disciplines (history, geography, government, etc.). _____

INSTRUCTIONAL CONTENT OF TEXTBOOK—CONTINUED

22. Emphasizes responsibilities of citizenship in a democratic society. _____
23. Controversial issues are treated factually and objectively. _____
24. The content is free of biases and prejudices. _____
25. The content is free of sexual and cultural stereotypes. _____
26. Contributions of the sexes and various cultural groups are reflected fairly. _____

Instructional Content of Textbook Total _____

H. TEACHER'S EDITION/RESOURCE PACKAGE

1. The teacher's edition is easy to use. _____
2. The teacher's edition is comprehensive, well organized, and contains sufficient information for even the inexperienced teacher. _____
3. Step-by-step plans are included on how to implement the student's text in the classroom. _____
4. Objectives are clearly stated. _____
5. Scope and sequence for each level is provided. _____
6. Sufficient, complementary assessment tools are included. _____
7. Supplementary components are referenced in the teaching plans at the appropriate place. _____
8. Teaching techniques are suggested that improve instructional effectiveness. _____
9. Includes provision for reteaching skills and concepts related to objectives. _____
10. Sufficient activities and optional strategies are provided for enrichment and remediation. _____
11. Answers to exercises and tests are provided on the facsimiles of the student pages. _____
12. Lists of key vocabulary are included for each unit. _____
13. Includes a variety of strategies for teaching skills and alternative strategies for reteaching. _____
14. The size of type is suitable. _____

Teacher's Edition Total _____

I. ANCILLARY MATERIALS

1. Duplicating/blackline masters are of high quality. _____
2. Printed and/or audiovisual materials being provided at no charge are of high quality and enhance instruction. _____
3. Quality printed and/or audiovisual materials are available at no charge to conduct independent inservice and to aid the individual teacher. _____
4. Transparencies that are being provided at no charge enhance instruction. _____
5. Software components are available to aid the individual teacher to enhance instruction, meet individual needs, and for remediation. _____

Testing and Management System

6. Tests are provided for assessment of facts, vocabulary, main ideas, and skills. _____
7. Sufficient, relevant, and well-placed unit/chapter tests are provided. _____
8. End-of-level tests (end-of-book) are provided. _____
9. Placement, diagnostic, and assessment tests provided are reliable and valid. _____

10. Reproduction rights to placement, diagnostic, and assessment tests are provided to the Memphis City Schools at no charge. _____

Workbooks

11. Workbooks are clear and well organized. _____
12. Practice relates to previously taught skills, vocabulary, and concepts. _____
13. Material extends understanding—not merely "busy work." _____
14. Include a variety of activities and response formats. _____
15. Workbooks are simple enough for independent work. _____
16. Workbooks are appealing to a wide range of students. _____
17. Sufficient amount of writing space is given. _____

Ancillary Materials Total ══════

We, the duly constituted members of the Textbook Adoption Committee, do hereby certify that the information contained in this document represents a consensus opinion that is supported by the undersigned.

1._____
(Name, School, Date)

2._____
(Name, School, Date)

3._____
(Name, School, Date)

Appendix C

Resource Examples Cited in Text

Excerpt from Lesson on Poverty from the "Episodes in Social Inquiry Series"

Lesson 1

DISCUSSION OF MOTIVATIONAL PICTURES AND REPORT ON QUESTIONNAIRE ABOUT POVERTY

OBJECTIVES

1. To stimulate interest in the subject of poverty.
2. To find out how much the class knows about poverty and what their attitudes toward the poor are.
3. To give concrete meaning to the word *poverty* and to show the diversity of its symptoms and effects.

SUGGESTED TEACHING PROCEDURE

At the start of this lesson, distribute the student texts and have students examine the six pictures in the text showing people in poverty.

(1) *Common elements in poverty.* After the pictures have been examined, ask the students what all the pictures have in common. Some will probably say, "They are all pictures of poor people," or "They are about poverty." But what makes them think these people are poor? What sorts of things do the poor have in common? This discussion should elicit some of the characteristics of poor people: powerlessness (e.g., children and the aged lack political and economic power), despair, hopelessness, apathy, low level of living as reflected in poor and crowded housing, inadequate diet, shabby clothes, and worn and broken furniture. It is not necessary to spend much time discussing the characteristics of poverty since these are dealt with in more detail later in the episode.

(2) *Diversity among the poor.* A more important question to ask is: How do these pictures *differ* from each other? Students will see that there is great diversity among the poor. The poor include the young and the old, people of all ethnic groups (whites, blacks, Indians, etc.), urban and rural dwellers, and people who are healthy as well as those who are disabled. One of the objectives of this lesson is to give concrete meaning to the word *poverty* and to show the diversity of its symptoms and effects.

(3) *Using pictures as data suggesting the nature of poverty.* Following the opening discussion of similarities and differences in the pictures, you may want to have the students respond to the questions asked about each picture. These questions are designed to encourage students to think about areas of poverty touched on later in the episode. Students should begin to see that poverty is more than just a shabby, run-down physical environment or unemployment or lack of money. They should be on the way to discovering that poverty is a condition that allows us to make predictions about a poor person's relationships with other people and his connection with the institutions of society. They should begin to see that income or property is a clue that tells us where we stand in relationship to other

(continued)

RESOURCE FIGURE 1.1
continued

people. Students should also start to see that although we often see poverty in psychological terms (frustration, despair, apathy), these states of mind are generated by conditions in the social order.*

You will notice that there are no answers given to the questions. The questions are to develop interest in the study of poverty and to encourage student thinking about areas to be covered later. As discussion leader, you should strive to elicit as many and as full responses as possible from the students. (You will have a similar role in many of the lessons that follow.) Permit students to challenge each other's statements. But be sure to leave enough time for the tally committee chairman to report on the questionnaire administered earlier.

* None of these things should be explicitly stated (at least by the instructor) at this time. They point to an enlarged conception of poverty and its meaning that should emerge throughout the study of this episode.

Note. From *Sociological Resources for the Social Studies, Instructor's Guide for the Incidence and Effects of Poverty in the United States* (pp. 16–17), 1969, Boston: Allyn & Bacon. Copyright © 1969 by Pearson Education. Reprinted by permission of the publisher.

RESOURCE FIGURE 3.1
Middle Grades Activity with Multidisciplinary Emphasis

Lesson Plan

Chunnel Vision

by Jody Smothers Marcello

This lesson plan is designed for use with the May 1994 *National Geographic* article "The Light at the End of the Chunnel," by Cathy Newman. The article focuses on the social and historical implications of connecting France and Great Britain via the English Channel Tunnel—or Chunnel. For the first time in their history, the British have a "land" link to the Continent. This lesson explores the importance of the Chunnel—a name coined from "channel" and "tunnel"—through geographic and historical perspectives.

Connection with the Curriculum
Geography, history, math, English, current events, social studies, art

Teaching Level: Grades 6–8; adaptable for higher and lower grades

Geographic Themes: Human/Environment Interaction, Movement, Region, Location, Place

Materials:
May 1994 *National Geographic*
Paper and pencil for creating sketch maps
Atlases or pull-down maps of the United Kingdom, France, and Europe
Set of encyclopedias
Art supplies (see alternative activity)

Introducing the Lesson
To launch the lesson, have students formulate mental maps of the English Channel region. Before the students read the article, ask them to sketch a map of the region based on their mental maps, and make a list of what they know about the Channel, including its size. Then distribute photocopies of the maps in this lesson. Have students compare their sketch maps with the photocopied maps. Acquaint the students with the Channel's true location and dimensions (approximately 350 miles long and 21 to 100 miles wide). How wide is the English Channel at the point of the Chunnel?

Now ask the students to read the *National Geographic* article. You may wish to read the article to younger students and review the illustrations with them.

Mapping the English Channel and Its Environs
On the inset map, ask students to identify and label the North Sea, Atlantic Ocean, English Channel, France, and Great Britain. (Great Britain is the portion of the United Kingdom that comprises England, Scotland, and Wales.) On the larger map, have them use an atlas as a reference to label the countries, the capitals, the cities, and towns marked with a dot, and the Seine and Thames Rivers.

Cities and towns shown on the map:
In Belgium: Antwerp, Brussels, Ostend.
In France: Amiens, Caen, Calais, Cherbourg, Coquelles, Dieppe, Le Havre, Paris, Rouen.
In the Netherlands: Hoek van Holland, Rotterdam.
In the United Kingdom: Dover, Folkestone, Harwich, London, Newhaven, Portland, Portsmouth, Reading, Southampton.

(continued)

Present an overview of the area, highlighting the significant regions and place-names on both sides of the Channel. As you present place-names, ask students to identify the names familiar to them from history, drama, literature, and music. In addition, ask the students to refer to an atlas to see which names from this region have been given to cars (e.g., Plymouth, Calais), cows (e.g., Jersey, Guernsey), and other objects in our culture. Discuss—or ask the students to research—the etymology of some of the place-names. Would a "Plymouth" or "Portsmouth" be found inland? Why or why not? What do the suffixes "-ton," "-ham," "-ford," "-chester," and "-shire" mean?

English Channel History

The English Channel has long played an integral part in England's, and subsequently Great Britain's, history. Discuss with the students why Great Britain has been called an "island fortress" and the English Channel a "moat."

Divide students into eight groups. Ask each group to research one of the events in the numbered list on the following page. (School encyclopedias will work well for this assignment.) Each group should prepare a report for the class that focuses on the questions listed on the next page. As part of each report, a map should be prepared and used as a visual aid when groups report orally to the class.

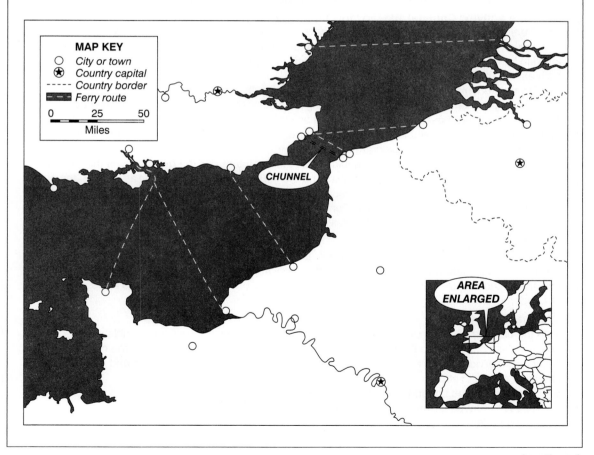

(continued)

Historic Events

1. First Invasion of England by the Celts: 500 B.C.
2. Roman Conquest of England: 55 B.C.–A.D. 80s
3. Germanic Invasions of England: mid-400s
4. Norman Conquest of England (Battle of Hastings): 1066
5. Hundred Years War: 1337–1453
6. Defeat of the Spanish Armada: 1588
7. D Day Invasion of Normandy: June 6, 1944
8. Completion of Chunnel: May 1994

Research Questions

- Who have been foes of the English?
- Did the Channel protect England? If so, how?
- What groups have been able to invade England?
- In what cases did the Channel aid an invasion, either of England or of France?
- How did this event change England and the course of English, European, or world events?

Alternate Activity: Chunnel Masterwork (Tapestry of Events)

The Bayeux Tapestry, illustrated and described in an August 1966 *National Geographic* article, depicts the story of William the Conqueror's Norman Conquest of England in 1066, the last time England was invaded by an enemy. The English Channel played a large role in this event, as it did in other events both earlier and later in England's history.

Divide students into eight groups. Assign each group the task of making a panel of a "tapestry" representing one of the significant events in English history listed above. The groups may use a rectangle or a square of canvas to embroider a scene, or they may sketch onto the canvas in pencil and use tubes of fabric paint for color. They can also use large construction or craft paper and paints or computer software drawing programs.

At the heart of each panel, they should depict the important role the geography of the English Channel played in the event. If possible, examine the 1966 *National Geographic* article with the class to see the tapestry. (A picture of a portion of the tapestry appears in the *World Book Encyclopedia* entries about England and the Norman Conquest.) Discuss how this tapestry is a record of both history and geography, "a picture story for an illiterate public," and yet a masterwork of artistry.

Chunnel Routing

Have students use road maps of Great Britain, London, France, Paris, Belgium, and Brussels and the map included with this lesson that shows ferry crossings and the Chunnel to generate their own maps showing the specific routes travelers could take on a trip from London to Paris or London to Brussels.

Chunnel Savings

With the building of the Chunnel, the trip from London to Paris by train will be possible in just three hours. Ask students to use the map, with their labels, to figure out how much time the new three-hour passenger service will save over a traditional train-and-ferry trip between London and Paris. They should use this schedule:

- The train leaves London at 8:33 A.M. and arrives in Dover at 10:16 A.M.
- The ferry leaves Dover at 10:45 A.M. and arrives in Calais at 12:20 P.M.
- The train leaves Calais at 12:40 P.M. and arrives in Paris at 2:32 P.M.

Chunnel Flow

The article "The Light at the End of the Chunnel" notes that only 30 percent of the round-trips through the Chunnel are expected to originate in France. Ask students to speculate on the factors that might create this uneven flow, with many more of the round-trips starting at Great Britain.

Chunnel Math

- The Chunnel passageway is 31 miles long. What is the average speed of a train that travels through the tunnel in the 35 minutes scheduled for the passage?
- About two years after it opens, the Chunnel is expected to carry eight million passengers a year. Given that total, how many riders will the trains carry each day?

$$\frac{8,000,000 \text{ riders}}{12 \text{ months}} = \frac{666,666 \text{ riders}}{1 \text{ month}}$$

$$\frac{666,666 \text{ riders}}{1 \text{ month}} \times \frac{1 \text{ month}}{30 \text{ days}} = \frac{22,222 \text{ riders}}{1 \text{ day}}$$

- Have students calculate the volume of traffic in a local area in or near the school. For example, how many students per day travel up and down your school's busiest hallway or stairwell? Ask students to study different intersections in town and count the number of cars that go by at several times during the day—as well as the number of passengers per car—and then estimate the number of people passing through the intersections each day. (Students may want to compare their results with those of students in neighboring communities that may be larger or smaller than theirs.) Compare the findings with the number of passengers they calculated to be traveling through the Chunnel each day.

Chunnel Power

The shuttle trains using the Chunnel will require 160 megawatts of electricity, equal to the peak load of a city of 250,000. Have students investigate the amount of power used by trains in the United States or by the Shinkasen, Japan's Bullet Train. Ask them to find out from their local power company the peak megawatt load of their community. (For example, 20 to 21 megawatts of power is the maximum electrical power load in the author's hometown of 8,500 people, in Alaska. This peak results from many homes being electrically heated; the peak occurs in midwinter, when heat demands are high. The maximum megawatt load may be different in other towns of similar population where a majority of homes are heated by gas, for example.)

Chunnel Plans

Define and discuss the concept of infrastructure. Then have students make a list of harbors, subway systems, airports, rail systems, major roads, tunnels, bridges, and ferry terminals—as well as utility facilities (for telephones, water, gas, electricity, steam, and wind or solar power)—in their local area or surrounding region. What is the importance of infrastructure?

What are some considerations for public works projects of the scope and nature of the Chunnel? Have teams of students devise a plan for the infrastructure that would support the Chunnel or a local proposed public works project. Then have the teams compare their plans and check to see whether each team has given consideration to all necessary factors.

(*continued*)

Chunnel Discussion Questions

- What factors need to be considered in building a bridge between two land masses? In digging a tunnel?
- Why did the Seikan Tunnel of Japan take 18 years to build, whereas the Chunnel took less than 7 years?
- How is the completion of the Chunnel likely to affect the ferry service lines between England and France? (See the map.)
- The English Channel is known as the world's busiest sea passage. Will the opening of the Chunnel affect this status? Why, or why not?
- Why is the Battle of Hastings (October 14, 1066) considered a battle that changed the course of history?
- How did the Battle of Hastings make England once more a part of Europe?
- How did the 1805 Battle of Trafalgar keep Great Britain safe from Napoleon, who had been planning an invasion of Great Britain since 1803?
- It has been said that the English Channel "helped shape the independent character of the British people." How might that be so?
- How has the building of the Chunnel changed the English and French landscapes, and how has it changed the human/environment interaction in the Channel region?
- Why did the French and English finally agree to the Chunnel? What specifically did former Prime Minister Thatcher and President Mitterrand see as the benefits of this project?
- How does the Chunnel serve as a symbol of the European Union?

Extension Activities

- Research the Channel Islands and have students make an illustrated map that characterizes the uniqueness of the islands, their political ties to Great Britain, and their location near France.
- Map other transportation links of the world, including canals (e.g., Suez Canal, Panama Canal, Main-Danube Canal) and other busy water passageways (e.g., Strait of Gilbraltar, Strait of Malacca, Strait of Hormuz, the Bosporus, Korea Strait). Have students research and discuss who controls these passageways, why they may be called choke points, and how they have played important roles in world events.
- It has taken expert swimmers an average of 12 hours to cross the English Channel. Have students make a timeline of the swimmers who have crossed the Channel and record the crossing time of each one.

References

Allen, Bryan, "Winged Victory of *Gossamer Albatross*," *National Geographic*, Nov. 1979, 640–651.

Guterl, F. V., and R. Ruthen, "Chunnel Vision: An Undersea Link Between Great Britain and France," *Scientific American*, Jan. 1991, 22–26.

National Geographic Atlas of the World, National Geographic Society, Washington, D.C., revised sixth edition, 1992.

National Geographic Picture Atlas of Our World, National Geographic Society, Washington, D.C., revised 1993.

Setton, Kenneth M. "900 Years Ago: the Norman Conquest," *National Geographic*, Aug. 1966, 206–251 [out of print].

Slave Resistance

A. Objectives

1. To understand why open rebellion was rarely undertaken.

2. To list different ways slaves resisted their condition.

3. To enact through the Readers' Theatre an example of the minor resistance which pervaded slaves' interactions with masters.

B. Lesson Background Materials

Slave resistance ranged from adopting a mask of humility, which gave an illusion of utter dependence, to open revolt, which culminated in the massacre of whites. Students tend to be interested in the sensational forms of resistance. While revolts did occur, they should not be overemphasized. There were hundreds of conspiracies to revolt, but only a few ever actually took place. Nat Turner's Rebellion in Virginia in 1831 is the most famous. Turner's revolt resulted in the murder of 55 white men, women, and children and the deaths of as many blacks in the aftermath. To white Southerners, almost more chilling than the number of deaths was Turner's intelligence and status as the trusted slave of a relatively kind master. If Turner could rebel, then any slave might rise up against any master.

Violent and open rebellions were much more common in Latin America than in North America. This difference was due to weaker military control, easier access to unsettled areas, a greater imbalance of blacks to whites and a greater imbalance of males to females. The existence of families among slaves in the United States was crucial in restraining violent revolts.

Slaves committed countless acts of individual rebellion in day to day living. They often worked slowly or pretended to be stupid when asked to learn a skill. They were careless about property—losing farm tools, damaging equipment and abusing farm animals. Arson was a particularly effective means of revenge; it required little effort and was difficult to detect. Feigning illness was commonplace, especially during harvest or other periods of heavy work. The most pervasive form of resistance was simply masking one's true nature by adopting a role. The role might be a child-like dependence on the master, a stubborn stupidity, or a mask of apathy. Frederick Douglass wrote that he had never heard a slave, while still a slave, say that he or she had a bad master. Masters took comfort in the outward subservience of slaves, but it was a very uneasy comfort bolstered by patrols and the lash.

Running away was another option. Typically, runaways were young males who ran off alone and hid in neighboring woods or swamps. Usually they would be caught or would return on their own after a few days alone without food. But some

(*continued*)

slaves managed to escape. There were colonies of runaway slaves in the isolated swamps or mountains of the South, especially in Florida, where they became allied with Seminoles and other tribes of Indians. Another means of permanent escape was the Underground Railroad, a series of safe houses and stations organized by abolitionists, where slaves could hide on their journey north to freedom. The most famous "conductor," Harriet Tubman, led 300 slaves out of the South on nineteen separate trips.

C. Lesson Activities

1. In an exploratory discussion consider why slaves, with a few notable exceptions, did not openly revolt against their condition.

    a. Remind students of the laws reviewed in DOCUMENT B, "The Alabama Slave Code of 1852," which made rebellion difficult.

    b. Explain that masters were brutal to slaves who were even suspected of plotting to rebel and that slaves wanted to protect their families and friends from reprisals. Because most slaves did not openly rebel does not mean they quietly accepted slavery; they resisted in many ways. These acts of resistance were often disguised and typically difficult to prove.

2. Have students read DOCUMENT E, which includes "James Henry Hammond's Instructions to His Overseer" and additional excerpts from the "Alabama Slave Code of 1852" (these readings are sufficiently clear that a simplified version is thought unnecessary). These rules and laws suggest ways slaves resisted their masters.

    a. Discuss with students what they would do as slaves to resist their condition. Some students may say they would kill their masters or run away. Slaves did those things, but not as frequently as one might suppose. Explain that slaves disguised their feelings from masters. In the presence of whites, slaves were always playing roles, acting in the ways they believed to be in their best interest. This gave them more private space for living, lulled masters, and gave slaves a measure of control over owners.

    b. Remind students of the patrols and the rules against slaves having weapons or gathering in groups. Also remind students of Bruce's slave inventory, which showed that many women and children were slaves. For the most part, slaves were too tightly controlled and too concerned with the relative well-being of their loved ones to risk open rebellion.

3. Shift the discussion to ways slaves could resist slavery without getting caught. Remind students of the "Tar Baby" story. See if students understand that stories, songs, and other forms of cultural expression were all ways to resist slavery. Often masters were oblivious to resistance of this sort.

Through careful questioning, students should come to recognize some of the more common forms of slave resistance. Questions might include:

    a.   Why would a master care if a slave or a slave's house was unclean?

    b.   What does neglect of tools mean?

    c.   Since all tools eventually wear out or break, could masters or overseers know if a tool was broken on purpose?

    d.   What difference does it make to the master if slaves drank alcohol?

    e.   Why was setting a fire punishable by death?

    f.   Why was breaking into a white person's house at night punishable by death?

Explain that slaves disguised their feelings from masters. In the presence of whites, slaves were always playing roles, acting in the ways they believed to be in their best interest. This gave them more private space for living, lulled masters, and gave slaves a measure of control over owners. Have students list forms of rebellion. These might include:

a.	Breaking tools	f.	Pretending stupidity
b.	Losing tools	g.	Lying
c.	Working slowly	h.	Stealing
d.	Running away	i.	Arson
e.	Feigning illness		

4.   Pass out DOCUMENT F, "Slavery and the Domestic Slave Trade in the United States." Explain that it is part of a letter written by Ethan Allen Andrews in 1835 and published in 1836 as part of a book about American slavery. The conversation is a distillation of many similar ones Andrews had heard throughout the South.

    a.   Divide the class into groups of three. Have students read the document silently.

    b.   Have volunteers choose parts for a performance for the class.

5.   As a concluding activity, students might write a brief paragraph on slave resistance from a slave's point of view.

D. Evaluating the Lesson

Have students imagine they are former slaves explaining to their grandchildren, long after the abolition of slavery, about the ways they resisted slavery. They should write a short paragraph about the way they behaved and why.

(*continued*)

STUDENT RESOURCE: DOCUMENT E

James Henry Hammond's Instructions to His Overseer*

(Primary Source)

The following is the order in which offences must be estimated and punished:

1st *Running away*
2nd *Getting drunk or having spirits*
3rd *Stealing hogs*
4th *Stealing*
5th *Leaving plantation without permission*
6th *Absence from house after horn blow at night*
7th *Unclean house or person*
8th *Neglect of tools*
9th *Neglect of work*

The highest punishment must not exceed one hundred lashes in one day and to that extent only in extreme cases. The whip lash must be one inch in width or a strap of one thickness of leather 1½ inches in width, and never severely administered. In general fifteen to twenty lashes will be sufficient flogging.

*Manual of Rules, [c. 1840–1850] James Henry Hammond Papers, Library of Congress

Alabama Slave Code of 1852

(Primary Source)

Additional excerpts:*

1. *Every slave who breaks into and enters a dwelling house in the night time, with the intention to steal or commit a felony, must, on conviction, suffer death.*

2. *Any slave who breaks into and enters a dwelling house in the day time, or any other building in the day or night time, must, on conviction, be punished by stripes, not exceeding one hundred, and by branding in the hand, one or both.*

3. *Every slave who robs, or commits an assault and battery with intent to rob any white person, or willfully maims. . . any white person, or attempts to poison, or to deprive any white person of life, by any means. . . must, on conviction, suffer death.*

4. *Every slave who willfully and maliciously sets fire to or burns any dwelling house, or out house appurtenant thereto, store house, banking house, ware house, or other edifice, public or private, corn crib, gin house, cotton house, stable, barn, cotton in the heap to the value of one hundred dollars, or in bale to any value, or any ship or steam boat, must, on conviction, suffer death.*

* From *The Code of Alabama*, prepared by John J. Ormand, Arthur P. Bagby, and George Goldthwaite. Montgomery: Brittain and DeWolf, 1852. (pp. 234–245, 390–393, 589–597)

Note. From *Slavery in the Nineteenth Century* (pp. 51–58), by J. Pearson and J. Robertson, 1991, by permission of the National Center for History in the Schools, www.nchs.ucla.edu. Reprinted with permission.

RESOURCE FIGURE 4.2
Sample Lesson Plan Format

Patterns of Prosperity

Creating and using thematic maps require students to gather information, to identify factors for analysis, and to form hypotheses about the geographic theme "regions"— areas defined by certain shared characteristics. This lesson shows students how to create one kind of thematic map and to compare the relative wealth of the various countries in South America. The activity was developed for use with middle-school students.

Objectives

- To understand the meaning of the geographic theme *regions* and the term *per capita income.*
- To research data from maps, almanacs, and other sources.
- To map numerical data for geographic regions.
- To analyze and compare patterns of data on quartile maps.

Background Discussion

Ask students to define the term *region* and to give examples of regions (polar region, the Middle East, Chinatown, an economic region). Encourage students to give some local examples. Tell students they will be comparing per capita income data of the countries of South America and studying regions that share common economic characteristics.

Materials

A wall map of South America or an atlas; a current almanac; an outline map of South America; *The Development Data Book,* World Bank Publications, Washington, D.C., 1984. (This book contains social and economic statistics for 125 countries.)

Schedule of Activities

Day 1
- Have students look at maps of South America and speculate about which might be the wealthiest and the poorest countries. They should write down their predictions, giving reasons for their choices.

- Discuss the term *per capita income,* making sure that students understand how the figures are determined.

- Assign students to look up the per capita income for each country in South America in an atlas or an almanac.

- Have students compare this data with their speculations to see how correct they were.

Day 2
- Explain how quartile mapping is done:
  — Rank the per capita income data of each country from highest to lowest.

(continued)

RESOURCE FIGURE 4.2

continued

> — Divide the ranked data into four equal parts (as nearly as possible). Each of these parts is called a quartile.
>
> — Define the range (highest to lowest figures) of each quartile.
>
> — Assign a color to each quartile—the darkest colors for the highest figures and lightest colors for the lowest figures.
>
> — Create a key that shows the per capita income range that each color represents.
>
> • Have students fill in the outline map using the four colors from the key.
>
> • Analyze the data on the map.
>
> — Did the map turn out as predicted? If not, why not?
>
> — Discuss the factors students think could be related to the per capita income of a country. List these on the board. (Possible answers might include population, resources, value of exports, arable land, labor, literacy, industries, GNP, political or governmental influences. This information is available in an atlas or an almanac.) Keep this list for the next day.
>
> *Day 3*
>
> • Divide the class into small teams. Tell each team that it will be making a second quartile map.
>
> • Review the factors listed on the board on Day 2. Discuss which factors could be represented by numerical data.
>
> • Ask each team to select one factor—literacy, for example—for which numerical data can be found in an atlas or an almanac. Have teams collect data on that factor for each country.
>
> • Have students speculate on which factors they think would be related most closely to per capita income. Discuss why they think so. Have each group map its set of data, using quartiles.
>
> • Have the teams compare their new quartile maps with the per capita income quartile map. How closely do they match? Which data matches most closely? What are some possible reasons for differences?
>
> • Summarize the lesson with the following questions:
>
> — What is per capita income, and what does it tell us about a country or region?
>
> — Why does per capita income vary in different countries or regions?
>
> **Related Activities**
>
> Have students collect data for other regions of the world or for regions within the United States and follow this same activity.

Note. From *Teaching Geography: A Model for Action* (pp. 53–55), 1988, Washington, DC: National Geographic Society.

RESOURCE FIGURE 4.3
Sample Lesson Plan Format

Unit Title: United States History (Early Beginning Through Reconstruction)
Lesson Title: Causes of the Civil War Lesson 2.3

1.   **Gaining Attention**

Show the following list of wars on a transparency:

French and Indian War 1754–1769
Revolutionary War 1775–1781
Civil War 1861–1865
World War I 1914–1918
World War II 1941–1945
Korean War 1950–1953
Vietnam War 1965–1975

2.   **Informing the Learner of the Objective**

Learners will be expected to know the causes of the Civil War and to show that those causes also can apply to at least one of the wars listed on the transparency.

3.   **Stimulating Recall of Prerequisite Learning**

Briefly review the causes of both the French and Indian War and the Revolutionary War as covered in Lessons 2.1 and 2.2.

4.   **Presenting the Stimulus Material**

(a) Summarize major events leading to the Civil War:
— rise of sectionalism,
— labor-intensive economy,
— lack of diversification.

(b) Identify significant individuals during the Civil War and their roles:
— Lincoln,
— Lee,
— Davis,
— Grant.

(c) Describe four general causes of war and explain which are most relevant to the Civil War:
— economic (to profit),
— political (to control),
— social (to influence),
— military (to protect).

5.   **Eliciting the Desired Behavior**

Ask the class to identify which of the four causes is most relevant to the major events leading up to the Civil War.

6.   **Providing Feedback**

Ask for student answers and indicate plausibility of the volunteered responses.

7.   **Assessing the Behavior**

Assign as homework a one-page essay assessing the relative importance of the four causes for one of the wars listed on the transparency.

Note. Effective Teaching Methods, 3/e, by G. D. Borich, 1996, Upper Saddle River, NJ: Merrill/Prentice Hall. Copyright 1996. Adapted by permission of Prentice Hall, Inc., Upper Saddle River, NJ.

The Trial of Napoleon Bonaparte

The purpose of this trial is to judge the actions of Napoleon Bonaparte. Was he a great leader and patriot, or was he a power-hungry dictator? The year is 1815, and his last 100 days as a general have ended on the fields of Waterloo. What are we to do with this man? Our task is to examine his life and produce a verdict on the charge of "crimes against humanity," a charge later used against the Nazis after World War II. Be careful, because the Congress of Vienna—which is sponsoring this trial—may not be completely innocent!

The Cast of Characters/Students

Courtroom Personnel:

 The Judge: _____

 The Lawyer(s) for the Quadruple Alliance: _____

 The Lawyer(s) for the Defense: _____

 The Court Clerk/Sheriff: _____

Witnesses for the Prosecution (representing the Quadruple Alliance):

 Prince Metternich of Austria: _____

 Czar Alexander I of Russia: _____

 Lord Castlereagh of Great Britain: _____

 The Duke of Wellington of Great Britain: _____

 A Prussian Nationalist Soldier: _____

 An anti-Napoleon French soldier who fought in Russia: _____

 A British merchant and trader: _____

 Others (see your teacher): _____

Witnesses for Napoleon:

 Napoleon: _____

 The Chief Justice of the French court: _____

 A French schoolteacher: _____

 A loyal French officer who fought at Austerlitz: _____

 A loyal French soldier: _____

 A French peasant: _____

 An Italian nationalist: _____

 Others (see your teacher): _____

Preparation and Expectations for the Participants

1. The chief responsibility of the judge and clerk/sheriff is to be familiar with courtroom procedures. They will be responsible for conducting the trial and making sure all participants are following proper legal procedure. These two members must complete, before the trial, a minimum two-page summary of their respective duties in a trial. A summary can be done by each person, but it is recommended that the summary be completed jointly: this summary should follow the suggested order of trial listed below. The judge and clerk/sheriff are expected to cover what their characters will say and how they will deal with lawyers and witnesses during the trial. You can talk to the teacher for references about these duties. This summary must be typed or neatly written; it will be distributed to the rest of the class before the trial to help facilitate the smooth operation of the activity.

2. The lawyers must understand how each witness (their own or the hostile witnesses) will contribute to their legal strategy. Each legal team must complete an introductory speech that outlines: the witnesses they will call in their favor; the weaknesses of the opposing side's case; and the major arguments of their own case. They will also write a closing statement that summarizes the arguments in favor of their case; explains the weaknesses of the other side's arguments and witnesses; and provides a recommendation on sentencing. Lawyers should write this conclusion before the trial by anticipating what will happen, but they should also leave room on the conclusion to add details that may emerge during the trial. Finally, the lawyers will write at least six questions for each of their own witnesses that highlight their witnesses' title and position, experience regarding Napoleon, and their consensus on the best questions. The lawyers will also need to create two or three questions for their cross-examination of hostile witnesses. These questions should put the witness on the defensive and reinforce the arguments of the cross-examining lawyers.

3. Each witness must prepare a 200- to 300-word summary of his or her character. The summary should include the character's upbringing, position, general political beliefs and opinions toward Napoleon. Those witnesses who are not specific historical characters may have to create much of their character, as long as it is within reasonable limits and nothing inaccurate about Napoleon is said. These nonspecific characters are important for what they represent about Napoleon, not who they are in particular (sorry!). The witness must also create 6 to 10 likely questions they would face from the lawyers. An appropriate answer for each question will be required. These will be shared with their lawyers. Ask your teacher for appropriate kinds of questions.

Suggested Order for the Trial of Napoleon Bonaparte

A. Opening the Trial

    1. The entry of the judge.

    2. The opening statement by the clerk/sheriff.

    3. The entry of the prisoner.

B. Taking Pleas

    1. The introduction of the lawyers.

    2. The reading of the charge against the accused.

    3. The plea of the prisoner.

(continued)

C. The Case for the Prosecution

1. The opening statement of the prosecution lawyers.

2. The examination of the prosecution witnesses, with cross-examination and rebuttal.

D. The Case for the Defense

1. The opening statement of the defense lawyers.

2. The examination of the defense witnesses, with cross-examination and rebuttal.

E. Summations by Counsel

1. Defense lawyers.

2. Prosecution lawyers.

F. The Verdict

1. The decision of the jury regarding guilt and sentencing.

G. Closing the Trial

1. The exit of Napoleon and the judge.

Notes to the Teacher

1. Like any mock trial, many things will have to be improvised. Each witness, for example, may have to create many elements of his or her character. Napoleon's witnesses, for example, can be fictional, as long as they summarize Napoleon's various achievements. As a teacher, you'll have to decide for yourself about selecting roles, costuming, timing, etc. This can be stressful, but it's also very creative and rewarding!

2. You will need many resource books for this project. Ask your librarian well ahead of time to pull all of the available books. A particularly good resource, and one that helped me create this mock trial, is Charlie and Cynthia Hou's *The Riel Rebellion: A Biographical Approach*. The teacher's guide, in particular, has some excellent ideas on the roles of the judge, the clerk/sheriff, and the lawyers. Another good legal resource is a Law 12 textbook, *All About Law* (3rd edition). Chapter 7 is especially helpful with trial procedure. Incidentally, even though this trial is supposedly set in nineteenth century Europe, the courtroom procedures I've employed are from modern Canadian criminal law.

3. Preparation is very important; it can be tedious but it makes a world of difference for the actual trial. You should read through the expectation and suggested order pages with the entire class and make sure everyone knows what to do. (A limited "dry run" is recommended to familiarize everyone with trial procedure.) This and the library research may take three to five one-hour classes. The trial and wrap-up should take two classes.

4. I recommend that a very responsible and outgoing student is selected as the judge. You should also have strong students acting as lawyers. They will have to be resourceful, thorough, and able to interact with others (especially when creating questions). Finally, avoid hassles—don't have a separate jury, because they tend not to do much. Let the whole class decide!

Note. Developed by Colin Welch, Fraser Valley Distance Education School, Chilliwack, B.C. Canada. Reprinted with permission.

RESOURCE FIGURE 7.1

Lesson That Integrates Spatial Skills Development and Application

---

Understanding the Dilemma of Landlocked Nations

Thirty of the world's independent nations are without access to the sea—they are landlocked. With some exceptions, landlocked nations are generally small, developing countries with numerous social and economic problems. This lesson plan explores the background essential to understanding the problems that landlocked nations face.

Objectives

- To define the geographic theme "location."
- To define the term "landlocked" and to identify the world's landlocked nations.
- To identify advantages and disadvantages of being landlocked in both a historical and a contemporary context.
- To research social and economic data about landlocked countries and to draw conclusions about the economic development of such countries.
- To identify the origin of problems that landlocked nations face.
- To investigate how certain countries came to be landlocked.
- To speculate on places that could become landlocked in the future.

For Discussion

- What is a landlocked nation?
- Many goods in international trade are shipped by sea for at least part of their journey. What does this mean to countries without coastlines? (Examples: Dependence on neighboring countries; delays in receiving goods; tariffs; and transportation costs.)
- Identify some countries that lost their coastlines in war.
- Using examples from current events, identify places that could become landlocked in the future.

Follow-Up Activities

- Divide the class into two groups. Assign one group to report on the historical and current advantages of being landlocked. Assign the second group to report on the disadvantages. Discuss the relative merits of each viewpoint.
- Ask the class to do research on landlocked countries, using almanacs, encyclopedias, textbooks, and other resources. Display information about each country on a chart. List generalizations that can be made about landlocked nations. Point out exceptions.
- Have each student select two countries—one that is landlocked and one that is not—and use a data book or an almanac to analyze statistics about them. Suggest that students pay special attention to indicators of social and economic development, such as life expectancy, adult literacy, population growth rate, and GNP per capita. Then have each student write an essay comparing the two countries.
- Have students select and read about a landlocked nation and then prepare an oral report about the country's problems. Have students include the importance of relative location on each country's problems.

Note. From Teaching Geography: A Model for Action (pp. 36–39), 1988, Washington, DC: National Geographic Society. Copyright 1988 by National Geographic Society. Reprinted with permission.

RESOURCE FIGURE 7.2
Some Internet Starting Points

State Information

A good starting point for information on specific states is the Library of Congress Web page on state and local government. Its URL is *http://lcweb.loc.gov/global/state/stategov.html*

There you will find links to various indexes of state information, as well as links to individual states. Some state sites are listed below.

- California Home Page *(www.ca.gov/)*
- Connecticut Government Information Page *(www.state.ct.us/)*
- Florida Government Information Locator Service *(www.dos.state.fl.us)*
- Georgia Home Page *(www.state.ga.us/)*
- Idaho Home Page *(www.state.id.us/)*
- Illinois Home Page *(www.state.il.us/)*
- Access Indiana Information Network *(www.ai.org/)*
- Info Louisiana *(www.state.la.us/)*
- Mississippi Home Page *(www.state.ms.us/)*
- New Jersey In Touch Home Page *(www.state.nj.us/)*
- Welcome to New York State *(www.state.ny.us/)*
- New Mexico Home Page *(www.state.nm.us/)*
- North Carolina Public Information *(www.state.nc.us/)*
- Oregon Online *(www.oregon.gov)*
- South Carolina Home Page *(www.myscgov.com)*
- Texas Government Information Page *(www.texas.gov/)*
- Virginia Home Page *(www.state.va.us/)*
- West Virginia: A Welcome Change *(www.state.wv.us/)*

Information on Specific Subject Areas

- For American History, try American Memory: Historical Collections for the National Digital Library *(www.memory.loc.gov/ammem/amhome.html)*
- For World History, try World Wide Web Virtual Library: History *(www.ku.edu/history/VL)*
- For World Geography/World Cultures, try Global Gateway World Culture and Resources *(http://international.loc.gov/intldl/intldlhome.html)*

General Educational Information

Education is among the fastest-growing areas of the Web. Below are some good starting points.

- Classroom Connect *(www.classroom.com).* Here you can find a newsletter for educators, plus regularly updated educational links, lesson plan pointers, and sample Web pages from schools.
- Global SchoolNet Foundation *(www.gsn.org).* This nonprofit organization provides links and activities to connect schools located around the world.
- Prentice Hall Home Page *(http://www.phschool.com).* See Prentice Hall's website for classroom resources, special online events, and a professional development center.

A myriad collection of text and multimedia exists for each day's news. Up-to-date news can be found at the following Internet addresses:

www.abcnews.com

www.cbsnews.com

www.cnn.com

www.foxnews.com

References

4 of 10 censorship attempts succeed. (1993, September 2). Raleigh, NC: *The News & Observer,* p. 9a.

Airasian, P. (1991). *Classroom assessment.* New York: McGraw-Hill.

The American nation teacher's resource guide. (1986). Upper Saddle River, NJ: Prentice Hall.

Alibrandi, A., Beal, C., Wilson, A., Thompson, A., Mackie, B., Sinclair, N., Owens, V., & Hagevik, R. (2001). Students reclaim their community's history: Conducting interdisciplinary research with technological applications. In M. Christenson, M. Johnston, & J. Norris (Eds.), *Teaching together: School/university collaboration to improve social studies education* (pp. 61–70). Silver Spring, MD: NCSS.

Alibrandi, M., & Palmer-Moloney, J. (2001). Making a place for technology in teacher education with Geographic Information Systems (GIS). *Contemporary Issues in Technology and Teacher Education* [Online serial], *1*:4. Available: **www.citejournal.org/vol1/iss4/currentissues/socialstudies/article1.htm**

Allen, H. A., Splittgerber, F. L., & Manning, M. L. (1993). *Teaching and learning in the middle level school.* Upper Saddle River, NJ: Merrill/Prentice Hall.

Allen, M. G., & Stevens, R. L. (1994). *Middle grades social studies.* Boston: Allyn & Bacon.

Armbruster, B. B. (1984). The problems of "inconsiderate" text. In G. G. Duffy, L. R. Roehler, & J. Mason (Eds.), *Comprehension instruction: Perspectives and suggestions.* New York: Longman.

Armbruster, B. B., & Anderson, T. H. (1984). Structures of explanations in history textbooks or so what if Governor Stanford missed the spike and hit the rail? *Journal of Curriculum Studies, 16,* 181–194.

Armbruster, B. B., & Gudbrandsen, B. (1986). Reading comprehension instruction in social studies programs. *Reading Research Quarterly, 21,* 36–48.

Armbruster, B. B., Anderson, T. H., & Meyer, J. L. (1991). Improving content area reading using instructional graphics. *Reading Research Quarterly, 26,* 393–416.

Armstrong, T. (1994). *Multiple intelligences in the classroom.* Alexandria, VA: Association for Supervision and Curriculum Development.

Arnold, J., & Beal, C. (1995). *Service with a smile* Raleigh, NC: North Carolina Middle School Association.

Aronson, E., Blaney, N., Stephan, C., Sikes, J., & Snapp, M. (1978). *The jigsaw classroom.* Beverly Hills, CA: Sage.

Atkinson, R. C. (1975). Mnemonics in second language learning. *American Psychologist, 30,* 821–828.

Atwood, V. (1982). A historical perspective of social studies. *Journal of Thought, 17,* 7–11.

Backler, A. L., Patrick, J. P., & Stoltman, J. P. (1992). Geography in U.S. history: A video project. *The Social Studies,* 58–63.

Baldi, S., Perie, M., Skidmore, D., Greenberg, E., & Hahn, C. (2001). *What democracy means to ninth-graders: U.S. results from the International IEA Civic Education Study* (NCES 2001-096). U.S. Department of Education, National Center for Education Statistics. Washington, DC: U.S. Government Printing Office.

Baldwin, A. Y. (1978). *Educational planning for the gifted: Overcoming cultural, geographical, and socioeconomic barriers.* Reston, VA: The Council for Exceptional Children.

Banks, J. (1984). *Teaching strategies for ethnic studies* (3rd ed.). Boston: Allyn & Bacon.

Banks, J. (1991). Multicultural literacy and curriculum reform. *Educational Horizons, 69,* 135–140.

Banks, J. (1993, June–July). The canon debate, knowledge construction, and multicultural education. *Educational Researcher, 22,* 4–14.

Barber, B. (1992). *An aristocracy for everyone: The politics of education and the future of America.* New York: Ballantine.

Barnes, E. (1978). *What do you do when your wheel-chair gets a flat tire? Questions and answers about disabilities.* New York: Scholastic Book Services.

Barr, R. D., Barth, J. L., & Shermis, S. S. (1977). Defining the social studies. *Bulletin, 51.* Washington, DC: National Council for the Social Studies.

Baum, W. K. (1977). *Oral history for the local historical society.* Nashville, TN: American Association for State and Local History.

Beal, C. (1996). *Case study on the use of reading/writing workshop to teach English language arts to at-risk adolescents.* Unpublished doctoral dissertation, North Carolina State University, Raleigh.

Beal, C. (2002). To Russia with technology. *Social Education, 66:4,* 166–172.

Beal, C. (2003, February). *Research report on Help Yourself, Yourself, a university and middle grades program seeking to help preservice and practicing teachers learn, understand and teach development theories to their students promoting student self-knowledge to improve academic and social responsibility taking.* The Eighth Annual Southeastern Association of Educational Studies Conference, Chapel Hill, NC.

Bean, T. W., Sorter, J., Singer, H. G., & Frazee, C. (1986). Teaching students how to make predictions about events in history with a graphic organizer plus options guide. *Journal of Reading, 29,* 739–745.

Beane, J. (1997). *Curriculum integration: Designing the core of democratic education.* Columbus, OH: Teachers College Press.

Beane, J. (2005). A reason to teach. Creating classrooms of dignity and hope. Portsmouth, NH: Heinemann.

Beane, J. A. (1990). *A middle school curriculum from rhetoric to reality.* Columbus, OH: National Middle School Association.

Beck, I. L., & McKeown, M. G. (1988). Toward meaningful accounts in history texts for young learners. *Educational Researcher, 17,* 31–39.

Bednarz, S., Acheson, G., & Bednarz, R. (2006). Maps and map learning in social studies. *Social Education, 70:7,* 398–404.

Bellezza, F. S. (1981). Mnemonic devices: Classification, characteristics, and criteria. *Review of Educational Research, 51,* 247–275.

Bender, W. N. (1985). Strategies for helping the mainstreamed student in secondary social studies classes. *The Social Studies, 76,* 269–271.

Benitez, H. (1994). Globalization of United States history: Six strategies. *Social Education, 59,* 142–144.

Benninga, J. (Ed.). (1991). *Moral character and civic education in the elementary school.* New York: Teachers College Press.

Benson, L. (1995). *Planning for multiple intelligences.* Raleigh, NC: Department of Curriculum and Instruction, North Carolina State University.

Berman, S. (1990). Educating for social responsibility. *Educational Leadership, 48,* 75–80.

Berson, I., & Berson, M., (2007). Exploring complex social phenomena with computer simulations. *Social Education, 71:3,* 136–139.

Beyer, B. K. (1991). *Teaching thinking skills: A handbook for elementary school teachers.* Boston: Allyn & Bacon.

Bloom, B. S. (Ed.). (1956). *Taxonomy of educational objectives, the classification of educational goals. Handbook I: The cognitive domain.* New York: David McKay.

Borich, G. D. (1996). *Effective teaching methods* (3rd ed.). Upper Saddle River, NJ: Merrill/Prentice Hall.

Bower, G. H. (1972). Mental imagery and associative learning. In L. W. Gregg (Ed.), *Cognition in learning and memory.* New York: Wiley.

Bragaw, D. H., & Hartoonian, H. M. (1988). Social studies: The study of people in society. In R. S. Brandt (Ed.), *Content of the curriculum.* Alexandria, VA: Association for Supervision and Curriculum Development.

Bransford, J. D., Brown, A. L., & Cocking, R. R. (1999). *How people learn: Brain, mind, experience, and school.* Washington, DC: National Academy Press.

Bredhoff, S. (2007). Eyewitness account of Dr. Robert King Stone, President Lincoln's family physician. *Social Education, 21:2,* 99–104.

Brophy, J. (1992). Probing the subtleties of subject-matter teaching. *Educational Leadership, 49,* 4–8.

Brophy, J. E., & Alleman, J. (1993). Elementary social studies should be driven by major social education goals. *Social Education, 57,* 27–32.

Brown, G., & Edmondson, R. (1984). Asking questions. In E. Wragg (Ed.), *Classroom teaching skills*. New York: Nichols.

Brown, J. A. (1982). Developmental transition in the middle school: Designing strategies for the social studies. In L. W. Rosenzweig (Ed.), *Developmental perspectives on the social studies*. Washington, DC: National Council for the Social Studies.

Bruner, J. (1960). *The process of education*. Cambridge, MA: Harvard University Press.

Bruner, J. (1973). *Beyond the information given*. New York: Norton.

Buckner, J. H. (1994, February). What makes a great middle school teacher? *Instructor Middle Years*, 18–19.

Bullard, S. (1992). Sorting through the multicultural rhetoric. *Educational Leadership, 49*, 4–7.

Byrnes, D. (1995). *Teacher, they called me a_____ ! Confronting prejudice and discrimination in the classroom* (2nd ed.). New York: Anti-Defamation League of B'nai B'rith.

Byrnes, D., & Kiger, G. (Eds.). (1996). *Common bonds: Anti-bias teaching in a diverse society* (Revised). New York: Association for Childhood Education International.

Caldwell, J., & Highsmith, R. L. (1994). Banks and money in U.S. history. *Social Education, 58*, 27–28.

Camperell, K., & Knight, R. S. (1991). Reading research and social studies. In J. P. Shaver (Ed.), *Handbook of research on social studies teaching and learning*. New York: Macmillan.

Carnegie Corporation. (1989). *Turning points: Preparing American youth for the 21st century*. New York: Author.

Carr, E., & Ogle, D. (1987). K-W-L-plus: A strategy for comprehension and summarizing. *Journal of Reading, 30*, 626–631.

Center for Civic Education. (1991). *CIVITAS: A framework for civic education*. Calabasas, CA: Author.

Center for Disease Control—Health Statistics. (2005). *Life expectancy hits record high. Gender gap narrows*. Hyattsville, MD: US Government Document.

Chandler, P. (2006). Academic freedom: A teacher's struggle to include "other" voices in history. *Social Education, 70:6*, 354–357.

Chapin, J. R., & Messick, R. G. (1989). *Elementary social studies: A practical guide*. New York: Longman.

Charles, C., & Charles, M. (2004). *Classroom management for middle-grades teachers*. Boston: Allyn & Bacon.

Chism, K. (2006). The Bureau of Refugee, Freedmen, and Abandoned Lands. *Social Education, 70:1*, 19–26.

Civitas: A framework for civic education. (1991). Calabasas, CA: Center for Civic Education.

Cohen, G. (1990). Continuing to cooperate: Prerequisites for persistence. *Phi Delta Kappan, 72*, 134–136, 138.

Cole, M., & Cole, S. R. (1989). *The development of children*. New York: Scientific American.

Collins, H. T. (n.d.). What's in a name? *Resource pack: Project LINKS*. Unpublished manuscript, George Washington University.

Cruz, B. C., Nutta, J. W., O'Brien, J., Feyten, C. M., & Govoni, J. M. (2003). *Passport to learning: Teaching social studies to ESL students*. (Bulletin No. 101). Washington, DC: National Council for the Social Studies.

Curtis, C. K. (1991). Social studies for students at-risk and with disabilities. In J. P. Shaver (Ed.), *Handbook of social studies teaching and learning*. New York: Macmillan.

Darling-Hammond, L., & Lieberman, A. (1992, January 29). The shortcomings of standardized tests. *The Chronicle of Higher Education*, B1–B2.

Davidson, J., & Stoff, M. (1986). *The American nation*. Upper Saddle River, NJ: Prentice Hall.

Delisle, J. R. (1991). Gifted students and social studies. In J. P. Shaver (Ed.), *Handbook of social studies teaching and learning*. New York: Macmillan.

Delpit, L. (1988). The silenced dialogue: Power and pedagogy in educating other people's children. *Harvard Educational Review, 58*, 280–298.

Dewey, J. (1916). *Democracy and education*. New York: Macmillan.

Dewey, J. (1933). *How we think*. Boston: D. C. Heath.

Dewey, J. (1961). *Democracy and education*. New York: Macmillan.

Dewey, J. (1968). *The child and the curriculum, the school and the society*. Chicago: University of Chicago Press.

Dillon, I. J. (1988). Questioning and teaching: A manual of practice. New York: Teachers College Press.

Dole, J. A., Duffy, G. G., Roehler, L. R., & Pearson, P. D. (1991). Moving from the old to the new: Research on reading comprehension instruction. *Review of Educational Research, 61,* 239–264.

Donovan, M. S., & Bransford, J. (Eds.) (2005). *How students learn history in the classroom.* Washington, D.C.: National Academic Press.

Dowd, F. S. (1990). What's a jackdaw doing in our classroom? *Childhood Education,* 228–231.

Downs, J. R. (1993). Getting parents and students involved: Using survey and interview techniques. *The Social Studies,* 104–106.

Dunn, R., Beaudry, J., & Klavas, A. (1989). Survey of research on learning styles. *Educational Leadership, 46,* 50–58.

Duthie, J. (1986). The web: A powerful tool for the teaching and evaluation of the expository essay. *History and Social Science Teacher, 21,* 232–236.

Engle, S. H. (1976). Exploring the meaning of the social studies. In P. H. Martorella (Ed.), *Social studies strategies: Theory into practice* (pp. 232–245). New York: Harper & Row.

Engle, S. H. (1977). Comments of Shirley H. Engle. In R. D. Barr, J. L. Barth, & S. S. Shermis (Eds.), *Defining the social studies* (Bulletin 51, pp. 103–105). Washington, DC: National Council for the Social Studies.

Engle, S. H., & Ochoa, A. (1988). *Education for democratic citizenship: Decision making in the social studies.* New York: Teachers College Press.

Erb, T. (2005). *This we believe in action.* Westerville, OH: NMSA.

Erikson, E. (1968). *Identity, youth and crisis.* New York: W. W. Norton & Company.

Etlin, M. (1988, May–June). To teach them all is to know them all. *NEA Today,* 10–11.

Evans, M. D. (1993). Using classroom debates as a learning tool. *Social Education, 57,* 370.

Evans, R., & Saxe, D. (Eds.). (1996). *Handbook on teaching social issues* (Bulletin 93). Washington, DC: National Council for the Social Studies.

Fancett, V., & Hawke, S. (1982). *Instructional practices in social studies. The current state of social studies: A report of project SPAN.* Boulder, CO: Social Science Education Consortium.

Fenton, E. (1967). *The new social studies.* New York: Holt, Rinehart, and Winston.

Fenton, E. (1991). Reflections on the "new social studies." *The Social Studies, 82,* 84–90.

Fernekes, W. R. (1988). Student inquiries about the Vietnam War. *Social Education, 52,* 53–54.

Frasier, M. M. (1989, March). Poor and minority students can be gifted, too! *Educational Leadership, 44,* 16–18.

Friedman, T. (2005). *The world is flat. A brief history of the twenty-first century.* New York: Farrar, Straus and Giroux.

Fuchs, L. S., & Fuchs, D. (1986). Linking assessment to instructional intervention: An overview. *School Psychology Review, 15,* 318–323.

Gagné, R. M., & Briggs, L. (1979). *Principles of instructional design.* New York: Holt, Rinehart, & Winston.

Garbarino, J. (Ed.). (1985). *Adolescent development, an ecological perspective.* Columbus, OH: Charles Merrill Publishing Company.

Gardner, H. (1983). *Frames of mind. The theory of multiple intelligences.* New York: Basic Books.

Gardner, H. (1991). *The unschooled mind: How children think and how schools should teach.* New York: Basic Books.

Gardner, H. (1993). *Frames of mind: The theory of multiple intelligences: Tenth anniversary edition.* New York: Basic Books.

Gardner, H. (1993). *Multiple intelligences: The theory in practice.* New York: Basic Books.

Gardner, H. (2000). *Intelligence reframed: Multiple intelligences for the 21st century.* New York: Basic Books.

Gardner, H. (2007). *Five minds for the future.* Boston: Harvard Business School Press.

Garrod, A., Smulyan, L., Powers, S., & Kilkenny, R. (1992). *Adolescent portraits, identity, relationships and challenges.* Boston: Allyn & Bacon.

George, P. S., & Alexander, W. M. (2002). *The exemplary middle school* (3rd ed.). Belmont, CA: Wadsworth/Thomson Learning.

Gerwin, D., & Zevin, J. (2003). *Teaching U.S. history as mystery.* Portsmouth, NH: Heinemann.

Gilligan, C. (1982). *In a different voice, psychological theory and women's development.* Cambridge, MA: Harvard University Press.

Gilligan, C., Lyons, N., & Hammer, T. (Eds.). (1990). *Making connections, the relational world of adolescent girls at Emma Willard school.* Cambridge, MA: Harvard University Press.

Gilligan, C., Ward, J., Taylor, V., McLean, J., & Bardige, B. (Eds.). (1988). *Mapping the moral domain, a contribution of women's thinking to psychological theory and education.* Cambridge, MA: Harvard University Press.

Glasser, W. (1998). *The quality school: Managing students without coercion* (3rd ed.). New York: HarperPerennial.

Glatthorn, A. A. (1987). *Curriculum renewal.* Alexandria, VA: Association for Supervision and Curriculum Development.

Glazzard, P. (1980). Adaptations for mainstreaming. *Teaching Exceptional Children, 12,* 26–29.

Global internet trends. (2001). Retrieved from **http://www.nielsen-netratings.com/pr/pr_010611_2.pdf**

Good, T. L., & Brophy, J. E. (1991). *Looking in classrooms* (5th ed.). New York: Harper & Row.

Good, T. L., & Brophy, J. E. (2004). *Looking in classrooms* (9th ed.). New York: Harper & Row.

Gottfredson, D. C., Gottfredson, G. D., & Hybl, L. G. (1993). Managing adolescent behavior: A multiyear, multischool study. *American Educational Research Journal, 30,* 179–216.

Griffin, A. F. (1992). *A philosophical approach to the subject matter preparation of teachers of history.* Dubuque, IA: National Council for the Social Studies/Kendall Hunt.

Griffin, A. F. (1992). *A philosophical approach to the subject matter preparation of teachers of history.* Washington, DC: National Council for the Social Studies—Kendall Hunt.

Gross, R. E., & Dynneson, T. (Eds.). (1991). *Social science perspectives on citizenship education.* New York: Teachers College Press.

Guild, P. B., & Garger, S. (1985). *Marching to different drummers.* Alexandria. VA: Association for Supervision and Curriculum Development.

Haas, J. D. (1977). *The era of the new social studies.* Boulder, CO: Social Science Education Consortium.

Haas, J. D. (1986). Is the social studies curriculum impervious to change? *The Social Studies, 77,* 61–65.

Hahn, C. (1996). In R. Evans & D. Saxe (Eds.), *Handbook on teaching social issues* (Bulletin 93). Washington, DC: National Council for the Social Studies.

Hanna, Paul R. (1963). The social studies program in the elementary school in the twentieth century. In G. Wesley Sowards (Ed.), *The social studies.* Glenview, IL: Scott, Foresman, and Company.

Hannah, L. (1985–86, December/January). Social studies spreadsheets and the quality of life. *The Computing Teacher,* 13–17.

Harris, J. (1998). *Virtual architecture: Designing and directing curriculum-based telecomputing.* Eugene, OR: International Society for Technology in Education.

Hartoonian, M. J. (1994). *The knowledge connection.* Madison, WI: Wisconsin Department of Public Instruction.

Hawking, S. W. (1988). *A brief history of time: From the big bang to the black holes.* New York: Bantam.

Heitzman, W. R. (1988). Sources of political cartoons. *Social Education, 50,* 225–227.

Heitzman, W. R. (2002). Teaching with cartoons: Looking at education through the cartoonist's eye. *Social Education, 64.* Retrieved June 10, 2004, from **http://www.ncess.org**

Hertzberg, H. (1981). *Social studies reform: 1880–1980.* Boulder, CO: Social Science Education Consortium.

Honea, M. J. (1982). Wait time as an instructional variable: An influence on teacher and student. *Clearinghouse, 56,* 167–170.

Howard, R. W. (1987). *Concepts and schemata: An introduction.* Philadelphia: Cassell.

Hullfish, H. G., & Smith, P. G. (1961). *Reflective thinking: The method of education.* New York: Dodd, Mead.

Hunt, E. B., & Metcalf, L. E. (1968). *Teaching high school social studies: Problems in reflective thinking and social understanding* (2nd ed.). New York: Harper & Row.

Hunt, M. P., & Metcalf, L. E. (1968). *Teaching high school social studies: Problems in reflective thinking and social understanding* (2nd ed.). New York: Harper & Row.

Hunter, M. (1984). Knowing, teaching, and supervising. In P. Hosford (Ed.), *Using what we know about teaching*. Alexandria, VA: Association for Supervision and Curriculum Development.

Hutchinson, J. (2005). Learning about the civil war through soldier's letters. *Social Education, 69:6,* 318–322.

International Society for Technology in Education. (2002). *National educational technology standards for teachers: Preparing teachers to use technology.* Eugene, OR: Author.

Isaac, K. (1997). *Ralph Nader presents: Civics for democracy: A journey for teachers and students.* Washington, DC: Center for Study of Responsive Law.

Jackson, A., Davis, G., & Tirozzi, G. (Eds.). (2001). *Turning points 2000, education of adolescents in the 21st century.* New York: Teachers College Press.

Jarolimek, J., & Parker, W. C. (1993). *Social studies in elementary education* (9th ed.). Upper Saddle River, NJ: Merrill/Prentice Hall.

Jenkins, J. M., & Tanner, D. L. (Eds.). (1992). *Restructuring an interdisciplinary curriculum.* Reston, VA: National Association of Secondary School Principals.

Jewett, A. J. (Ed.). (1960). *English for the academically talented student in the secondary school; report.* Washington, DC: National Education Association, Project of the Academically Talented Student and National Council of Teachers of English, Champaign, IL.

Johnson, D. W., & Johnson, R. T. (1986). Computer-assisted cooperative learning. *Educational Technology, 26,* 12–18.

Kates, R. W. (1989, May 17). The great questions of science and society do not fit neatly into single disciplines. *The Chronicle of Higher Education,* B1, B3.

Kearsley, G. (1996, Winter). The World Wide Web: Global access to education. *Educational Technology Review,* 26–30.

Kindler, A. (2002). *Survey of the states' limited English proficient students and available educational programs and services.* Washington, DC: National Clearinghouse for English Language Acquisition and Language Instruction Educational Programs.

King, E. W. (1990). *Teaching ethnic and gender awareness.* Dubuque, IA: Kendall/Hunt.

Kirman, J. M. (1992). Using newspapers to study media bias. *Social Education, 56,* 47–51.

Kleg, M. (1986). Teaching about terrorism: A conceptual approach. *Social Science Record, 24,* 31–39.

Kleg, M. (1993). *Hate prejudice and racism.* Albany, NY: State University of New York Press.

Kounin, J. S. (1970). *Discipline and group management in classrooms.* New York: Holt, Rinehart, & Winston.

Kozol, J. (1967). *Death at an early age.* Boston: Houghton Mifflin.

Krathwohl, D., Bloom, B. S., & Masia, B. B. (1969). *Taxonomy of educational objectives, the classification of educational goals. Handbook II: The affective domain.* New York: David McKay.

Kujawa, S., & Huske, L. (1995). *The strategic teaching and reading project guidebook* (Rev. ed.). Oak Brook, IL: North Central Regional Educational Laboratory.

Lamm, L. (1989). *Facilitating learning through the effective use of resource persons in the classroom.* Unpublished manuscript, North Carolina State University, Department of Curriculum and Instruction, Raleigh.

Laycock, F. (1979). *Gifted children.* Glenview, IL: Scott Foresman.

Leighton, M. S. (1990). Cooperative learning. In J. M. Cooper et al. (Ed.), *Classroom teaching skills* (4th ed.). Lexington, MA: D. C. Heath.

Leiner, B., Cerf, V., Clark, D., Kahn, R., Kleinrock, L., Lynch, D., Postel, J., Roberts, L., & Wolff, S. (2000). *A brief history of the internet.* Retrieved September 30, 2002, from **www.isoc.org/internet/history/brief.shtml**

Levie, W. H., & Lentz, R. (1982). Effects of text illustrations: A review of research. *Educational Communication and Technology Journal, 30,* 195–232.

Levin, J., & Pressley, M. (1985). Mnemonic vocabulary instruction: What's fact, what's fiction. In R. Dillon (Ed.), *Individual differences in cognition* (Vol. 2, pp. 145–172). New York: Academic Press.

Levstik, L., & Barton, K. (2005). *Doing history: Investigating with children in elementary and middle schools* (3rd ed.). Mahwah, NJ: Erlbaum.

Lindquist, T. (2007). *Why & how I teach with historical fiction.* [Online serial]. Retrieved August 15, 2007, from http://teacher.scholastic.com/lessonrepro/lessonplans/instructor/social1.htm

Lionni, L. (1970). *Fish is fish*. New York: Scholastic Press.

Lockwood, A. L. (1985). A place for ethical reasoning in the social studies curriculum. *The Social Studies, 76*, 264–268.

Lybarger, M. B. (1991). The historiography of social studies: Retrospect, circumspect, and prospect. In J. P. Shaver (Ed.), *Handbook of research on social studies teaching and learning*. New York: Macmillan.

Maeroff, G. I. (1991). Assessing alternative assessment. *Phi Delta Kappan, 73*, 272–281.

Maker, C. J. (1982). *Teaching models in the education of the gifted*. Rockville, MD: Aspen Systems Corporation.

Manning, L., & Bucher, K. (2007). *Classroom management: Models, applications, and cases* (3rd ed.). Upper Saddle River, NJ: Merrill Prentice Hall.

Marland, S. (1972). *Education of the gifted and talented*. Washington, DC: U.S. Government Printing Office.

Martel, E. (1992). How valid are the Portland Baseline Essays? *Educational Leadership, 49*, 20–23.

Martorella, P. H. (1991). Knowledge and concept development in social studies. In J. B. Shaver (Ed.), *Handbook of research on social studies teaching and learning*. New York: Macmillan.

Martorella, P. H. (Ed.). (1997). *Interactive technologies and the social studies curriculum: Emerging issues and applications*. Albany, NY: SUNY Press.

Marzano, R. J., Brandt, R. S., Hughes, C. S., Jones, B. F., Presseisen, B. Z., Rankin, S. C., & Suhor, C. (1988). *Dimensions of thinking: A framework for curriculum and instruction*. Alexandria, VA: Association for Supervision and Curriculum Development.

Massialas, B. G. (1992). The "new social studies"—retrospect and prospect. *The Social Studies, 83*, 120–124.

Mastropieri, M. A., & Scruggs, T. E. (1991). *Teaching students ways to remember: Strategies for learning mnemonically*. Cambridge, MA: Brookline Books.

McCabe, P. P. (1993). Considerateness of fifth-grade social studies texts. *Theory and Research in Social Education, 21*, 128–142.

McCarthy, B. (1990). Using the 4MAT system to bring learning styles to schools. *Educational Leadership, 48*, 31–37.

Medford, L., & Knorr, R. (2005). Middle aged in middle school: Career changers return to the wonder years. *Middle Ground, 8:4*, 30–32.

Medin, D. L., & Smith, E. E. (1984). Concepts and concept formation. *Annual Review of Psychology, 35*, 113–138.

Mehaffy, G. L., Sitton, T., & Davis, O. L., Jr. (1979). *Oral history in the classroom*. How to do it series. Washington, DC: National Council for the Social Studies.

Merryfield, M. M., & Remy, R. C. (1995). *Choosing context and methods for teaching about international conflict and peace* (pp. 48–49). Albany, NY: SUNY Press.

Merryfield, M. M., & Remy, R. C. (1995). *Teaching about international conflict and peace*. Albany, NY: State University of New York Press.

Merryfield, M. M., & Remy, R. C. (1995). Choosing content and methods for teaching about international conflict and peace. In M. M. Merryfield & R. C. Remy (Eds.), *Teaching about international conflict and peace* (pp. 3–40). Albany, NY: SUNY Press.

Mitchell, R. (1992). *Testing for learning: How new approaches to evaluation can improve America's schools*. New York: Free Press.

Moore, G. (1965). Cramming more components onto integrated circuits. *Electronics, 38:8*. Retrieved from **ftp://download.intel.com//abs/eml/download/EML_opportunity.pdf**

Moore, J. (2007). Popular music helps students focus on important social issues. *Middle School Journal, 38:4*, 21–29.

Morrell, E., & Rogers, J. (2006). Becoming critical public historians: Students study diversity and access in post "Brown v. Board" Los Angeles, *Social Education, 70:6*, 366–369.

Nash, G. (1982). *Red, white, and black: The peoples of early America*. Upper Saddle River, NJ: Prentice Hall.

National Center for History in Schools. (1996). *National standards for history* (revised edition). Online: **nchs.ucla.edu/standards**. Accessed Dec. 3, 2007.

National Council for the Social Studies. (1967). *Academic freedom and the social studies teacher*. Washington, DC: Author.

National Council for the Social Studies. (1979). *Revision of the NCSS social studies curriculum guidelines.* Washington, DC: Author.

National Council for the Social Studies. (1991). *Testing and evaluation of social studies students.* Washington, DC: Author.

National Council for the Social Studies. (1992). Curriculum guidelines for multicultural education. *Social Education, 56,* 274–293.

National Council for the Social Studies. (1993, January/February). *The social studies professional.* Washington, DC: Author.

National Council for the Social Studies. (1994). *Curriculum standards for social studies, expectations of excellence.* Washington, DC: Author.

National Council for the Social Studies. (2003). *Passport to learning: Teaching social studies to ESL students.* Washington, DC: Author.

National Council for the Social Studies. *Advocacy toolkit.* Online serial: **www.ncss.org/toolkit.** Accessed Dec. 4, 2007.

National Geographic Society. (1988). *Teaching geography: A model for action.* Washington, DC: Author.

Nelson, J. L., & Michaelis, J. V. (1980). *Secondary social studies.* Upper Saddle River, NJ: Prentice Hall.

Newman, D., Griffin, P., & Cole, M. (1989). *The construction zone: Working for cognitive change in school.* New York: Cambridge University Press.

Newmann, F. M. (with Oliver, D. W.) (1970). *Clarifying public controversy: An approach to teaching social studies.* Boston: Little, Brown.

Newmann, F. M., & Thompson, J. (1987). *Effects of cooperative learning on achievement in secondary schools: A summary of research.* Madison, WI: National Center on Effective Secondary Schools.

Nissman, B. (2006). *Teacher-tested classroom management* strategies (2nd ed.). Upper Saddle River, NJ: Merrill/Prentice Hall.

Noddings, N. (1991/1992). The gender issue. *Educational Leadership, 49,* 65–70.

Norton, D. E. (1993). Webbing and historical fiction. *The Reading Teacher, 46,* 432–436.

Novak, J. D. (1998). *Learning, creating and using knowledge.* Mahwah, NJ: Lawrence Erlbaum Associates.

Novak, J. D., & Gowin, D. B. (1984). *Learning how to learn.* Cambridge, MA: Cambridge University Press.

O'Shea, M. (2005). *From standards to success: A guide for school leaders.* Alexandria, VA: Association for Supervision and Curriculum Development.

Ochoa, A. S., & Shuster, S. K. (1981). Social studies in the mainstreamed classroom. In T. Shaw (Ed.), *Teaching handicapped students social studies: A resource handbook for K–12 teachers.* Washington, DC: National Education Association.

Ogbu, J. U. (1992). Understanding cultural diversity and learning. *Educational Researcher, 21,* 5–14.

Ogle, C. (1986). K-W-L: A teaching model that develops active reading of expository text. *The Reading Teacher, 39,* 564–570.

Oliver, D. W., & Shaver, J. P. (1966). *Teaching public issues in the high school.* Boston: Houghton Mifflin.

Oliver, D. W., Newmann, F. M., & Singleton, L. R. (1992). Teaching public issues in the secondary school classroom. *The Social Studies,* 100–103.

Olner, P. (1976). *Teaching elementary school social studies.* Orlando, FL: Harcourt.

Onosko, J. J. (1992). An approach to designing thoughtful units. *The Social Studies,* 193–196.

Oppenheim, A. N., & Torney, J. (1974). *The measurement of children's civic attitudes in different nations.* New York: Halsted Press.

Osborn, A. (1963). *Applied imagination* (3rd ed.). New York: Charles Scribner.

Parker, W. (1991). *Renewing the social studies curriculum.* Alexandria, VA: Association for Supervision and Curriculum Development.

Passe, J. (2006). Social studies: The heart of the curriculum. *Social Education, 70:1,* 6–7, 55–56.

Passe, J., & Evans, R. (1996). In R. Evans & D. Saxe (Eds.), *Handbook on teaching social issues* (Bulletin 93). Washington, DC: National Council for the Social Studies.

Pawloski, B. (1994). How I found out about the Internet. *Educational Leadership, 51,* 69–73.

Pearson, J., & Robertson, J. (1991). *Slavery in the 19th century.* Los Angeles: National Center for History in the Schools, University of California at Los Angeles.

Peirano, A., Wilson, E., & Wright, V. (2007). American revolution: A digital timeline analysis. In L. Bennett & M. Berson (Eds.), *Digital age. Technology-based K–12 lesson plans for social studies* (pp. 139–143). Silver Spring, MD: NCSS Publications.

Perkins, D. L. (1986). *Knowledge as design*. Hillsdale, NJ: Erlbaum.

Perrone, V. (Ed.). (1991). *Expanding student assessment*. Alexandria, VA: Association for Supervision and Curriculum Development.

Philosophy for Children. (1987). Upper Montclair, NJ: Institute for the Advancement of Philosophy for Children, Montclair State College.

Piaget, J. (1972). *The child and reality, the problems of genetic psychology*. New York: Grossman Publishers.

Plowman, P. (1980). *Teaching the gifted and talented in the social classroom*. Washington, DC: National Education Association.

Popham, W. J. (1988). *Educational evaluation* (2nd ed.). Upper Saddle River, NJ: Prentice Hall.

Postman, N. (2000). Will our children only inherit the wind? *Theory and Research in Social Education, 28:4*, 580–586.

Pressley, M., Levin, J. R., & Delaney, H. D. (1982). The mnemonic keyword method. *Review of Educational Research, 52*, 61–91.

Rasinski, T. (1983). Using jackdaws to build background and interest for reading. (ERIC Document Reproduction Service No. ED 234351). Washington, DC: U.S. Department of Education, National Institute of Education.

Ravitch, D. (1992). A culture in common. *Educational Leadership, 49*, 8–11.

Richardson, J. T. E. (1980). *Mental imagery and human memory*. London: Macmillan.

Riley, J. P., II. (1986). The effects of teachers' wait-time and knowledge comprehension questioning on pupil science achievement. *Journal of Research in Science Teaching, 23*, 335–342.

Risinger, C. (2006). Promising practices in using the Internet to teach social studies. *Social Education 70:7*, 409–410.

Roberts, N., Carter, R. C., Friel, S. N., & Miller, M. S. (1988). *Integrating computers into the elementary and middle school*. Upper Saddle River, NJ: Prentice Hall.

Robinson, A. (1990). Cooperation or exploitation? The argument against cooperative learning for talented students. *Journal for the Education of the Gifted, 14:3*, 9–36.

Rokeach, M. (1968). *Beliefs, attitudes and values: A theory of organization and change*. San Francisco: Jossey-Bass.

Rossi, J. A. (1992). Uniformity, diversity, and the "new social studies." *The Social Studies, 83*, 41–45.

Rowe, M. B. (1969). Science, soul and sanctions. *Science and Children, 6*, 11–13.

Sanford, H. (1980). Organizing and presenting social studies content in a mainstreamed class. In J. G. Herlihy & M. T. Herlihy (Eds.), *Mainstreaming in the social studies* (Bulletin 62). Washington, DC: National Council for the Social Studies.

Santa, C. M., Havens, L., Nelson, M., Danner, M., Scalf, L., & Scalf, J. (1988). *Content reading including study systems: Reading, writing and studying across the curriculum*. Dubuque, IA: Kendall/Hunt.

Santrock, J. (2008). *Educational psychology* (3rd ed.). New York: McGraw-Hill.

Saxe, D. W. (1991). *Social studies in schools: A history of the early years*. Albany, NY: State University of New York Press.

Saxe, D. W. (1992). Social studies foundations. *Review of Educational Research, 62*, 259–277.

Scherer, M. (1992). Solving conflicts—not just for children. *Educational Leadership, 50*, 14–15, 17–18.

Schmuck, R. A., & Schmuck, P. (1983). *Group processes in the classroom* (4th ed.). Dubuque, IA: W. C. Brown.

Schug, M. (2007). Why did the colonists fight when they were safe, prosperous, and free? *Social Education, 71:2*, 61–65.

Scott Foresman Social Studies. (1983). *America past and present: Teacher's edition workbook*. Glenview, IL: Author.

Shaftel, F. R., & Shaftel, G. (1982). *Role playing for social values*. Upper Saddle River, NJ: Prentice Hall.

Shapiro, S., & Merryfield, M. M. (1995). A case study of unit planning in the context of school reform. In M. M. Merryfield & R. C. Remy (Eds.), *Teaching about international conflict and peace* (pp. 41–124). Albany, NY: SUNY Press.

Sharan, Y., & Sharan, S. (1990). Group investigation expands cooperative learning. *Educational Leadership, 20*, 17–21.

Sharan, Y., & Sharan, S. (1994). What do we want to study? How should we go about it? Group investigation in the cooperative social studies classroom. In R. J. Stahl (Ed.), *Cooperative learning in social studies: A handbook for teachers.* Menlo Park, CA: Addison-Wesley.

Shaver, J. P., & Strong, W. (1976). *Facing value decisions: Rationale-building for teachers.* Belmont, CA: Wadsworth.

Shaver, J. P., Davis, O. L., Jr., & Hepburn, S. W. (1979). The status of social studies education: Impressions from three NSF studies. *Social Education, 39,* 150–153.

Siler, C. R. (1986–1987). Content analysis: A process for textbook analysis and evaluation. *International Journal of Social Education, 1,* 78–99.

Silverblank, F. (1992). *An annotated bibliography of historical fiction for the social studies, grades 5 through 12.* Dubuque, IA: Kendall/Hunt.

Simon, M. (1990). Expanding opportunities for teachers to learn about technology. *Electronic Learning, 9,* 8–9.

Singer, H. G. (1986). Friendly texts: Description and criteria. In E. K. Dishner, T. W. Bean, J. E. Readance, & D. W. Moore (Eds.), *Reading in the content areas: Improving classroom instruction* (2nd ed.). Dubuque, IA: Kendall/Hunt.

Sisk, D. (1987). *Creative teaching of the gifted.* New York: McGraw-Hill.

Slater, W. H., Graves, M. F., & Piche, G. L. (1985). Effects of structural organizers on ninth grade students' comprehension and recall of four patterns of expository text. *Reading Research Quarterly, 20,* 189–202.

Slavin, R. E. (1986). *Using student team learning* (3rd ed.). Baltimore: Center for Social Organization of Schools, Johns Hopkins University.

Slavin, R. E. (1990). *Cooperative learning: Theory, research, and practice.* Upper Saddle River, NJ: Prentice Hall.

Slavin, R. E. (1991). Synthesis of research on cooperative learning. *Educational Leadership, 48,* 71–82.

Slavin, R. E. (1996). Research on cooperative learning and achievement: What we know, what we need to know. *Contemporary Educational Psychology, 21:1,* 43–69.

Smith, E. E., & Medin, D. L. (1981). *Categories and concepts.* Cambridge, MA: Harvard University Press.

Smith, N. (2007). The flowering of identity: Tracing the history of Cuba through the visual arts. *Social Education, 71:4,* 182–186.

Sobol, T. (1990). Understanding diversity. *Educational Leadership, 47,* 27–30.

Social studies in the middle school: A report of the task force on social studies in the middle school. (1991). *Social Education, 55,* 287–293.

Sommer, R. (1978). *The mind's eye.* New York: Dell.

Sousa, D. (2001). *How the brain learns.* Thousand Oaks, CA: Corwin Press.

South Carolina Department of Education. (1987). *Guide for using guest speakers and field trips.* Columbia, SC: Department of Education.

Spindler, G., & Spindler, L. (1990). *The American cultural dialogue and its transmission.* Philadelphia: Falmer Press.

Spires, H. A., & Stone, D. (1989). Directed notetaking activity: A self-questioning approach. *Journal of Reading, 33,* 36–39.

Stahl, R. J. (1990). *"Think-time" behaviors to promote students' information processing, learning and on-task participation. An instructional model.* Tempe, AZ: Arizona State University.

Stahl, R. J. (Ed.) (1994a). *Cooperative learning in social studies: A handbook for teachers.* Menlo Park, CA: Addison-Wesley.

Stahl, R. J. (1994b). Using "think-time" and "wait-time" skillfully in the classroom. *ERIC Clearinghouse for Social Studies/Social Science Education,* ED370885.

Stanley, W. B., & Mathews, R. C. (1985). Recent research on concept learning: Implications for social education. *Theory and Research in Social Education, 12,* 57–74.

Steinbrink, J. E., & Bliss, D. (1988). Using political cartoons to teach thinking skills. *The Social Studies, 79,* 217–220.

Stevens, R., & Fogel, J. (2007). Using music to teach about the Great Depression. *Social Education, 71:1,* 15–20.

Stevenson, C. (1992). *Teaching the ten to fourteen year old.* White Plains, NY: Longman.

Stoltz, A., Banister, S., & Fischer, J. (2007). Engaging the community in civil war studies with digital video. In L. Bennett & M. Berson (Eds.), *Digital age. Technology-based K–12 lesson plans for social studies.* Silver Spring, MD: NCSS Publications.

Stotsky, S. (1990). Connecting reading and writing to civic education. *Educational Leadership, 47,* 72–73.

Strickland, D. S. (1990). Emergent literacy: How young children learn to read and write. *Educational Leadership, 47,* 18–23.

Superka, D. P., Hawke, S., & Morrissett, I. (1980). The current and future status of the social studies. *Social Education, 40,* 362–369.

Swift, J. N., & Gooding, C. T. (1983). Interaction of wait time feedback and questioning instruction on middle school science teaching. *Journal of Research in Science Teaching, 20,* 721–730.

Taba, H. (1969). *Teaching strategies and cognitive functioning in elementary school children.* (Cooperative research project 2404.) Washington, DC: U.S. Office of Education.

Task Force on Scope and Sequence. (1984). In search of a scope and sequence for social studies. *Social Education, 48,* 249–262.

TenBrink, T. D. (1994). Evaluation. In J. Cooper et al. (Eds.), *Classroom teaching skills* (5th ed.). Lexington, MA: D. C. Heath.

Tennyson, R. D., & Cocchiarella, M. J. (1986). An empirically based instructional design theory for teaching concepts. *Review of Educational Research, 56,* 40–71.

The National Education Goals Panel. (1995). *Goals 2000: A progress report.* Washington, DC: Author.

Tobin, K. G. (1986). Effects of teacher wait time on discourse characteristics in mathematics and language arts classes. *American Educational Research Journal, 23,* 191–200.

Tobin, K. G. (1987). The role of wait time in higher cognitive level learning. *Review of Educational Research, 57,* 69–95.

Tomlinson, C. (1999). *The differentiated classroom: Responding to the needs of all learners.* Alexandria, VA: ASCD.

Torney-Purta, J. (1991). Schema theory and cognitive psychology: Implications for social studies. *Theory and Research in Social Education, 19,* 189–210.

Torrance, P., & Sisk, D. (1998). *Gifted and talented children in the regular classroom.* CA: Creative Education Foundation Press.

Totten, S. (1989). Using oral histories to address social issues in the classroom. *Social Education, 53,* 114–116.

Triandis, H. C. (1971). *Attitude and attitude change.* New York: John Wiley.

U.S. Bureau of Education. (1916). *Report of the committee on social studies.* Washington, DC: U.S. Government Printing Office.

U.S. Department of Education. (1994). *High standards for all.* Washington, DC: Author.

Van Hoose, J., Strahan, D., & L'Esperence, M. (2001). *Promoting harmony. Young adolescent development and school practices.* Westerville, OH: NMSA.

Vanden, H. (2007). Bringing Latin America to life with films in the classroom. *Social Education, 71:4,* 177–181.

Vansickle, R. L. (1992). Cooperative learning, properly implemented works: Evidence from research in classrooms. In R. J. Stahl & R. L. Vansickle (Eds.), *Cooperative learning in the social studies classroom: An invitation to social study.* Washington, DC: National Council for the Social Studies.

Virtue, D. (2007). Seizing teachable moments to develop integrative middle level curriculum. *Middle School Journal, 38:4,* 14–20.

Vosniadou, S., & Brewer, W. F. (1989). *The concept of the Earth's shape: A study of conceptual change in childhood.* Unpublished paper. Center for the Study of Reading, University of Illinois, Champaign.

Vygotsky, L. (1978). *Mind in society: The development of higher psychological processes* (M. Cole, V. John-Steiner, S. Scribner, & E. Souberman, Eds.). Cambridge, MA: Harvard University Press.

Vygotsky, L. (1986). *Thought and language* (Rev. ed., A. Kozulin, Ed.). Cambridge, MA: The MIT Press.

Wade, R. (2007). Community service-learning for democratic citizenship. In R. Wade (Ed.), *Community action rooted in history. The civic connections model of service-learning* (pp. 12–19). Silver Spring, MD: NCSS.

Wallen, N. E. (1974). *Getting together with people.* Reading, MA: Addison-Wesley.

Walters, L. (2000). Putting cooperative learning to the test. *Harvard Education Letter,* May/June, 1–6.

Wesley, E. B. (1950). *Teaching social studies in high schools* (3rd ed.). Boston: D. C. Heath.

White, C. S. (1990). Interactive media for social studies: A review of *In the Holy Land* and *The '88 Vote. Social Education, 54,* 68–70.

Wigginton, E. (1985). *Sometimes a shining moment: The Foxfire experience.* New York: Doubleday.

Wilen, W. W., & White, J. J. (1991). Interaction and discourse in social studies classrooms. In J. P. Shaver

(Ed.), *Handbook of research on social studies teaching and learning*. New York: Macmillan.

Williams, P. L., & Moore, J. R. (Eds.). (1980). *Criterion-referenced testing for the social studies* (Bulletin No. 64). Washington, DC: National Council for the Social Studies.

Witkin, H. A., Moore, C. A., Goodenough, D. R., & Cox, P. W. (1977). Field-dependent and field-independent cognitive styles. *Review of Educational Research, 47,* 1–64.

Wittrock, M. C. (1986). Students' thought processes. In M. C. Wittrock (Ed.), *Handbook of research on teaching* (3rd ed.). New York: Macmillan.

Wittrock, M. C., & Goldberg, S. G. (1975). Imagery and meaningfulness in free recall: Word attributes and instructional sets. *Journal of General Psychology, 92,* 137–151.

Wood, J. W., Miederhoff, J. W., & Ulschmid, B. (1989). Adapting test construction for mainstreamed social studies students. *Social Education, 53,* 46–49.

Woyshner, C. (2006). Picturing women: Gender, images, and representation in social studies. *Social Education, 70:6,* 362–368.

Young, T. A., & Marek-Schroer, M. F. (1992). Writing to learn in social studies. *Social Studies and the Young Learner, 5,* 14–16.

Zarnowski, M. (1988). Learning about contemporary women: Sharing biographies with children. *The Social Studies, 79,* 61–63.

Zarnowski, M. (1990). *Learning about biographies: A reading and writing approach for children.* New York: Teachers College Press.

Zimmerman, W. (1981). *How to tape instant oral biographies.* New York: Guarionex Press.

Index

Abstract thinking, 13
Acceptable use policy (AUP), 295
Accommodation, 51
Accountability, 130, 132
Acheson, G., 53
Achievement, cooperative
  learning and, 130–132
ADHD. *See* Attention deficit
  hyperactivity disorder
Administrative duties, 4
Adolescence, identity
  building and, 6
Adolescent literature, using for
  social studies instruction,
  259–263
*Adolescent Portraits, Identity,
  Relationships and
  Challenges* (Garrod et al.),
  232
Advanced placement, 328
Advocacy groups, 35
Advocacy ToolKit (NCSS), 24, 26
AERA. *See* American Education
  Research Association
Affective domain, objectives in,
  93–94
Affective outcomes, groups
  and, 132
Affective processes, 49
Agency for Instructional
  Technology, 58
Airasian, P., 343
Album of American History, 211
Alexander, W.M., 304
Alibrandi, A., 67
Alleman, J., 91
Allen, H.A., 304
Allen, M.G., 304
Alta Vista, 284
Alternative perspectives
  approach, 231–232
Alternative response questions,
  347
*Amelia and Eleanor Go for a
  Ride*, 263

American Education Research
  Association (AERA),
  position statement, 335
*American Nation Teacher's
  Resource Guide*, 350–351
American Nation, The (Davidson
  & Stoff), 191, 192, 350
*America Past and Present:
  Teacher's Edition Workbook*
  (Schreiber et al.), 345
Analysis
  analyzing arguments, 197–201
  See also Research and analysis
    skills
Analysis skills. *See* Research and
  analysis skills
Anderson, T.H., 258–259
*Annotated Bibliography of
  Historical Fiction for the
  Social Studies, Grades 5
  through 12* (Silverblank),
  262
Anthropology, 55–56
Anthropology Curriculum Study
  Project, 11
Applied psychology, 57
Archaeologists, 56
ArcView, 282
Arguments, analyzing, 197–201
  detecting bias and distortion,
    197
  logical reasoning, 197–201
  syllogisms, 197–198
Aristotle, 55
Armbruster, B.B., 258–259
Armstrong, T., 341–342
Arnold, J., 63
Aronson, E., 132–133
Artifact kits, 314–318
  See also Jackdaws®
Assessing students' special
  needs, 95
Assessments, defined, 336
  See also Evaluating/assessing
    student learning

Assimilation, 51
Atkinson, R.C., 272
Atrium Society, 228
Attention deficit hyperactivity
  disorder (ADHD), 319
Attitude inventories, 221–222
Attitudes, 219–222
Attributes, concepts and, 164
Atwood, V., 12
Audiences, for writing, 269
AUP. *See* Acceptable use policy
Authentic (performance)
  assessments, 341–43
  vs. standardized testing, 342
Auth, T., 203

Backler, A.L., 58, 59
Back mapping, 110–111
"Back to School Night," 75
Backus, Lara, 233, 234
Balance of payments, 55
Baldi, S., 26
Baldwin, A.Y., 327
Banister, S., 4
Banks, J., 100–101, 229–230,
  231, 233
Barber, B., 62
Bardige, B., 238
Barham, Gail, 41
Barnes, E., 324
Barr, R.D., 10, 14, 28
Barth, J.L., 10, 28
Barton, K., 173
Basal textbooks, 41–43, 134
Baseball Saved Us, 263
Baum, W.K., 71
Beal, Amy, 48
Beal, C., 7, 49, 63, 67, 116–117,
  125, 127, 303, 312
Beane, J., 14, 50, 51, 58, 60, 62,
  94, 137, 138, 187, 256, 257
Beane's Curriculum Integration
  approach, 137
Beaudry, J., 308, 310
Becker, Carl, 54

Beck, I.L., 258, 259
Bednarz, R., 53
Bednarz, S., 53
Behavior
    students', 113–116
    study of, 57
    teachers', 114–117
    See also Psychology
Behavioral objectives, 92–93
Behavioral sciences, 9
Behind the Lines (Auth), 203
Beliefs, 219–222
Bellezza, F.S., 271
Bender, W.N., 325
Benitez, H., 232
Benninga, J., 218
Benson, L., 311
Berman, S., 241
Berson, I., 153
Berson, M., 153
Best example, 164
Bias, 197
Biographies, 263
Blaney, N., 132–133
Bliss, D., 202
Block scheduling, 16–17, 99, 112
Bloom, B.S., 93, 144
Bloom's taxonomy for the
    cognitive domain, 144
Bodily-kinesthetic intelligence,
    310
Bolton, Sarah, 8
Borich, G.D., 85, 112, 115, 140
Boundaries, 53
Bower, G.H., 271
Bragaw, D.H., 268
Brainstorming, 129, 281
    with graffiti, 253–254
Brandt, R.S., 49
Bransford, J., 162
Bredhoff, Stacey, 3
Brewer, W.F., 164
Brief History of Time, A
    (Hawking), 204
Briggs, L., 107
Brooks, Jackie, 7, 110
Brophy, J., 43, 91, 113, 116, 187
Brown, A.L., 162
Brown, G., 142
Brown, J.A., 303–304

Brown University, 60
Brown, William, 179–180
Bruner, J., 11, 302, 309
Bucher, K., 113
Buckner, J.H., 305–306
Bucks County Peace Centers, 228
Bullard, S., 231
Bulletin boards, 242
Byrnes, D., 190

Caldwell, J., 153
California Achievement Tests,
    338
Camperell, K., 250
"Canon Debate, Knowledge
    Construction, and
    Multicultural Education"
    (Banks), 233
"Cape Lookout Lighthouse
    Keeper's Trunk, The," 315
Capstone questions, 148
Captive, The (Hansen), 261
Carnegie Corporation, 305
Carr, E., 252
Carter, R.C., 290
Case studies, 181–183
    data sheet for sample,
        181–182
    defined, 182
    types of, 182–183
Causal relationships, 205
Cause-effect relationships, history
    and, 53–54
CBM. *See* Curriculum-based
    measurement
Cell phones, 281, 296
Center for Civic Education, 28
Center for Disease Control—
    Health Statistics, 195
Center for Teaching Peace,
    The, 228
Center for the Study and
    Prevention of Violence, 228
Cerf, V., 284
Certification, 17–18, 41
Chandler, P., 191
Change, 54
Chapin, J.R., 304
Character education, 222
Charles, C., 113

Charles, M., 113
Charts, 193–196
Checklists
    to assess competence, 352–353
    to assess concern, 355–356
    defined, 351
    sample, 352
Child abuse, 65–66
*Choices for the 21st Century
    Education Project* (Brown
    University), 226
Chronicles, 53–54
Chronology skills, 203–205
    comparative conceptions of
        time, 204
    recording events on time lines,
        204–205
Circle diagrams, 199
Cities, as the classroom, 64
Citizenship, 55
Citizenship education, 24–31
    alternative perspectives on a
        curriculum for effective,
        26, 28–29
    context of, 25–26
    in elementary grades, 33–34
    head, hand, heart metaphor,
        31, 33
    identifying a purpose for, 86
    in middle and secondary
        grades, 34–35
    as purpose of the social
        studies, 24–25
    reflective, competent,
        concerned citizens as goal,
        29–33
    social concern and, 218–219
    See also Concerned citizens;
        Curriculum; Effective
        citizenship; Organizing and
        planning
Citizenship skills. *See* Competent
    citizens
Civic Education Study (CivEd),
    25–26
Civil rights movement, 229
"Civitas," 28, 268
Clarifying questions, 146
Clark, D., 284
Classroom, the city as, 64

Classroom environment, 111–117
  creating and managing the, 113
  disruptive, 113
  expectations of students and
    teachers, 114–116
  rules for, 115
  social discourse in, 303
  student behavior, 114–116
  supportive teacher behaviors,
    116–117
  time allocation, 111–112
  use of space, 111
  well-managed classrooms, 116
Cocchiarella, M.J., 165
Cocking, R.R., 162
Cognitive domain
  Bloom's taxonomy for,
    144–145
  objectives in, 93–94
Cognitive outcomes, groups and,
  131–132
Cognitive psychology, 30
Cognitive socialization, 222
Cognitive styles. *See* Thinking
  (cognitive) styles
Cohen, G., 130
Cole, M., 200
Cole, S.R., 200
Collaborative learning groups,
  130–132
  See also Jigsaw Technique
Collier, C., 261
Collier, J.L., 261
Comic Life, 270
"Coming to America," 270
Committee on the Social Studies,
  1916 Report of, 8–10,
  34–35
*Common Bonds: Anti-Bias
  Teaching in a Diverse Society*
  (Byrnes & Kiger), 190
Communicating subject matter,
  266–270
  listening and speaking,
    266–267
  pupil self-evaluation form for
    discussions, 267
  RAFT technique, 269
  technology tools for, 269–270
  writing, 268–270

Communication
  with the community about the
    social studies program, 73–74
  with people with disabilities,
    321
Community
  communicating with about the
    social studies program,
    73–74
  fieldwork in, 67–71
  place and, 61–63
  publicizing school activities to,
    74–75
  social service projects, 62–63,
    237
  as sources of social data,
    64–65
Community resource persons,
  65–66
Comparative conceptions of
  time, 204
Comparing data. *See* Data,
  interpreting and comparing
  data
Competent citizens, 29, 31, 33,
  36, 118, 185–215
  analyzing arguments, 197–201
  assessing, 351–354
  chronology skills, 203–205
  conflict resolution skills,
    188–190
  interpreting/comparing data,
    190–196
  logical reasoning, 197–201
  maps, 206–211
  nature of citizenship skills, 187
  processing information from
    pictures, 201–203
  reference sources skills,
    211–214
  research and analysis skills,
    190–196
  social skills, 187–188
  spatial skills, 205–211
Completion test. *See* Fill in the
  blank test
Comprehension, 250–257
  concept maps for, 254–256
  data-retrieval charts for,
    256–257

discussion webs and, 253
  graffiti for, 253–254
  graphic organizers for, 256,
    257
  improving reading
    comprehension, 251–257
  K-W-L technique for, 252
  prior (existing) knowledge
    and, 250–251
  reading guides, 254
Computers
  individualized needs and,
    312
  See also Software;
    Technology
Concept (semantic) maps
  analyzing adolescent literature,
    260, 262
  for comprehension, 254–256
  for planning units, 101–103,
    105
Concepts
  analyses of, 164
  defined, 161
  graphic organizers, 165–167
  instructional model for concept
    learning, 165
  misconceptions and
    stereotypes, 163
  nature of, 161–162
  personal and public dimensions
    of, 161
  process of learning a concept,
    163–164
  substantive, 162
  See also Reflective inquiry
Conceptual density, 258
Concerned citizens, 29, 31, 33,
  36, 118, 216–246
  assessing, 354–356
  beliefs, attitudes, and values,
    219–222
  and citizenship education,
    218–219
  current affairs, 241–244
  discussion format styles, 226,
    227
  global education, 226
  morally mature citizen,
    219

Concerned citizens (cont.)
  multicultural education,
    229–241
  peace education, 228
  self-concept activities, 221–223
  social issues as a curricular
    focus, 224–227
  teacher positions on
    controversial issues, 244
  transforming a unit topic into a
    unit issue, 225
  See also Citizenship education;
    Multicultural education
Conflict, 54
Conflict resolution skills,
  188–190
Cognitive processes, 49
Consensus decision making, 129
Constructing knowledge, 48–50
Constructivism, 12
Consumption, 54
*Content Reading Including Study
  Systems: Reading, Writing
  and Studying Across the
  Curriculum* (Santa et al.),
  268
Content standards, 36
Context, facts and, 168
Contextualizing, 174
Controversial issues, teacher
  positions on, 244
Cooperative learning groups,
  130–132
  See also Jigsaw Technique
Copyrights, technology and, 295
Corroborating, 175
Cost, 55
Council discussion style, 227
Cox, P.W., 308, 309
Cramming, 51–52
Creating mind, 201
Criterion-referenced tests, 338
Criticism, social, 28–29
Cruz, B.C., 277
Cultural anthropologists, 56
Cultural change, 56
Cultural diffusion, 56
Cultural filters, 191
Cultural heritage, transmission
  of, 28–29, 86

Cultural pluralism, 229–230
  See also Multicultural education
Culture, defined, 55–56
Current affairs, 241–244
  strategies for analyzing,
    241–244
  teacher positions on
    controversial issues, 244
  teaching, 243
Curricular goals, 91
Curriculum
  elementary grades, 33–34
  integration of, 50, 138–139
  middle/secondary grades,
    34–35
  for multicultural education,
    235
  multidisciplinary, thematic,
    interdisciplinary, and
    integrative approaches to,
    57–60
  school, community, and sense
    of place, 61–63
  service-learning, 62–63
  social issues and, 224–228
  social service projects and, 63
  sources of subject matter,
    50–52
  See also Citizenship education;
    Organizing and planning;
    Social sciences
Curriculum-based measurement
  (CBM), 320
*Curriculum Guidelines for
  Multicultural Education*
  (NCSS), 235
Curriculum integration, 89–90
Curriculum mapping, 3–4, 87
Curriculum Renewal
  (Glatthorn), 95
*Curriculum Standards for Social
  Studies, Expectations of
  Excellence* (NCSS), 119
Curtis, C.K., 324
Cyberpredators, 295

Danner, M., 269
Darling-Hammond, L., 337, 338
Database and spreadsheet
  software, 291

Data, interpreting and
  comparing, 190–196
  charts, graphs, and tables,
    193–196
  comparing two points of view,
    192
  cultural filters and, 191
  written materials,
    191–193
Data-retrieval charts, 171–172,
  256–257
Data sheet sample, 181–182
Davidson, J., 191, 192
Davis, G., 305
Davis, O.L., Jr., 11, 71
Death at an Early Age (Kozol),
  114
Debates, 222–223, 227
Debriefing, 152, 155
Decision making
  by brainstorming, 129
  by consensus, 129
  by ratings, 129–130
Decisions Decisions simulation
  software, 290
Defining the Social Studies
  (Barr, Barth, & Shermis),
  9–10
Definitions, concepts and, 164
Delaney, H.D., 272
Delpit, L., 133
Democracy and Education
  (Dewey), 173
Democratic issues, 14
Development (of individuals),
  301–303
Development theories, 5–6, 312
  See also Erikson's theory of
    epigenesis
DeVeney, Charles, 68
Dewey, J., 8, 30, 50–51, 107,
  173, 178
*Dictionary of American
  Biography*, 211–212
Dictionary of American History,
  212
Digital archives, 3
Digital divide, 295–296
Digital libraries, 282
Dillon, I.J., 141

"Directed Notetaking Activity: A Self-Questioning Approach" (Spires & Stone), 273
Disabilities, students with, 318–326
  communicating with, 321
  individualized education plans (IEPs), 320, 322, 323
  Individuals with Disabilities Education Improvement Act (IDEA 2004), 319–320, 322
  least restrictive educational environment, 320
  mainstreaming, 322, 324–326
  types of, 319
Disciplinary mind, 201
Disclosure, 221
Discovery approaches, 171
Discrimination, based on gender, 235–236
Discussion boards, 289
Discussion form, for self-evaluation, 267
Discussion format styles, 226, 227
Discussions, whole-class, 303
Discussion webs, 253
Disequilibrium, 177
Disruptive classes, 113
Dissident minorities, 218
Distortion, 197
Diversity, 229
  See also Multicultural education
Division of labor, 55
Documenting the American South's Classroom, 270
Documents, 183
Dole, J.A., 251
Donovan, M.S., 162
Dowd, F.S., 314–315
Downs, J.R., 72
Dramatic narrative, 110
Drill and kill social studies fact-loading, 13
Dropping out, 306–307
Duffy, G.G., 251
Dunn, R., 308, 310
Duthie, J., 253
Dynneson, T., 52

Economics, 54–55
Editorials, 67
Edmondson, R., 142
Educational eras, 205
Effective citizenship, 26, 28–31
  nature of, 30–31
  NCSS definition of, 24–25
  NCSS Task Force on Revitalizing Citizenship Education list of characteristics of, 28
  as professional development, 77–78
  reflective, competent, concerned citizens, 29–30, 31, 33
  See also Citizenship education; Competent citizens; Concerned citizens; Reflective inquiry
Effective Teaching Methods (Borich), 115
Electronic books, 297
Electronic portfolios, 18
Electronic reference sources, 211
Elementary school, curriculum pattern in, 33–34
Ellis, E., 182
E-mail, 289
Enactive (doing) stage, 302, 309
Enculturation, 56
Engle, S.H., 9, 14, 28, 30, 77–78, 99, 120, 173, 218
English as a second language (ESL), 274–277, 313
Environment, 53
  Save What's Left of Florida, 68
Environmental injustice, fighting, 32
e-Pals, 23, 289
Equitable treatment, 301
  See also Individual needs
Erb, T., 304
Erikson, E., 5–6, 312
Erikson's theory of epigenesis, 5–6
ESL. *See* English as a second language
Essay tests, 343–345, 349, 355
Ethical mind, 201

Ethnicity, 12, 231
  See also Multicultural education
Etlin, M., 235
Evaluating/assessing student learning, 333–359
  AERA position statement, 335
  assessments defined, 336
  competence assessment, 351–354
  concern assessment, 354–356
  criterion-referenced tests, 338
  essay tests, 343–345, 349
  evaluation framework, 356–358
  grades defined, 336
  matching evaluation and instructional goals and objectives, 357–358
  National Assessment of Educational Progress (Nation's Report Card), 338
  national standards and national testing, 339–341
  NCSS statement, 335
  norm-referenced tests, 337–338
  objective tests, 345–348, 350
  performance (authentic) assessments, 341–343
  portfolios, 341–343
  posttests and pretests, 343
  reflective inquiry assessment, 349–351
  standards defined, 336
  test software, 348
Evaluation, of instructional software, 290
Evaluation grid, 357–358
"Evaluation of Propaganda by the Historical Method, The" (Ellis), 181–182
Evans, M.D., 222, 224
Evans, R., 223, 224, 225, 226, 227
Examples, concepts and, 164
Exchange, 54
Expanding-communities curriculum pattern, 34
Expectations, of students and teachers, 114–117

Expectations of Excellence: Curriculum Standards for Social Studies (NCSS), 40
Experiential learning, 62
Experimental psychology, 57
Explicit planning, 86
Exports, 55
Expository approaches, 171

Fact loading, 8
Facts, 167–168, 169
  compared to generalizations, 168–169
  defined, 167
  generalizations and hypotheses and, 170–171
  instructional objective, 168
  learning facts in meaningful contexts, 168
  nature of, 167
  samples of generalizations and related facts, 169
  See also Reflective inquiry
Fancett, V., 11
Federal government, curricula reforms, 10
Fenton, E., 11, 12
Fernekes, W.R., 65
Feyten, C.M., 277
Field-dependent individuals, 309
Field-independent individuals, 309
Fieldwork, 67–71
  after the trip, 71
  before the trip, 70
  during the trip, 70–71
Fill in the blank test, 346–347
First-letter mnemonic technique, 271
Fischer, J., 4
Fishbowl discussion style, 227
Fish Is Fish (Lionni), 164
Five Minds for the Future (Gardner), 200–201
Focusing questions, 149
Fogel, J., 202
Formats, for unit planning, 104–105
Format styles, for discussion, 227
4MAT system, 310, 312

Four-teacher teams, 17
Frames, 258–259
Frasier, M.M., 327
Frazee, C., 256, 257
Free will, 57
Friel, S.N., 290
Fuchs, D., 320
Fuchs, L.S., 320

Gagné and Briggs seven-step instructional model, 107
Gagné, R.M., 107
Games, 153
  See also Simulation
Garbarino, J., 61, 312
Garbarino model, 64
Gardner, Howard, 200–201, 312
  Gardner's eight modes of intelligences, 310–311
  Gardner's five minds, 201
Garger, S., 309
Garrod, A., 232
Gender issues, 12, 235–241
  sex-role stereotyping, 235–238
  women's perspectives in history, 237–241
Genealogies, 205
Generality, level of, 91
Generalizations, 168–172
  compared to facts, 168–169
  data-retrieval charts for developing, 171–172
  facts and hypotheses and, 170–171
  instructional strategies for learning, 171
  nature of, 168
  value of, 169–170
  See also Reflective inquiry
General objectives, 92
Generativity stage, 6
Genetic behavior, 57
Geographic information system (GIS), 53, 67–69, 282, 293
Geography, 53
Geography in U.S. History, 58, 59
Geography Standards Project, 36
George, P.S., 304
Gerwin, D., 173, 175

Getting Together with People (Wallen), 355
Gifted and Talented Children's Act (1978), 326
Gifted students, 326–331
  approaches to, 328
  defining, 327
  identifying, 327
  mentorship plan, 330
  in social studies classes, 328–331
  societal perspectives on, 327
Gilligan, C., 189, 191, 238, 312
GIS. *See* Geographic information system
Glasser, W., 113
Glatthorn, A.A., 95, 118
Glazzard, P., 324
Global Connections Conference, 126
Global education, 226, 244
"Global Internet Trends," 295
Globalization, 13
Global-minded citizens, 31
  See also Concerned citizens
Global positioning satellites (GPS), 53
Global School House, 289
Globes, 206–211
Glory Field, The (Myers), 261
Goals, curricular, 91, 94
Goals 2000: Educate America Act (1992), 13, 339
Goldberg, S.G., 201
Golden Owl Publishing Co., 315
Goodenough, D.R., 308, 309
Goode's World Atlas, 109, 212
Gooding, C.T., 142
Good, T.L., 113, 116
Google, 284
Google Earth, 210, 293
Governmental institutions, 55
Govoni, J.M., 277
Gowin, D.B., 102, 254–255
GPS. *See* Global positioning satellites
Grades, defined, 336
Graffiti, for comprehension, 253–254

Graphic organizers, 165–167, 256
Graphs, 193–196
Graves, M.F., 272
Gray, W.A., 330
Great Raleigh Trolley Adventure, 64, 67–68, 111
Great Transitions (Carnegie Corporation), 305
Greenberg, E., 26
Griffin, A.F., 30, 173, 177
Griffin, P., 127
Gross, R.E., 52
Grouping questions, 146–148
Grouping students for learning, 127–139
    brainstorming, 129
    consensus decision making, 129
    cooperative learning techniques, 130–132
    Curriculum Integration approach, 138–139
    decision making by ratings, 129–130
    Group Investigation Technique, 137–138
    identifying group members, 128
    Jigsaw technique, 132–137
    participation rating sheet, 353
    planning for small-group work, 127–128
    size of groups, 127
    social skills required for, 128
Group Investigation Technique, 137–138
Gudbrandsen, B., 258
Guide for Using Guest Speakers and Field Trips, 66
Guidelines, for social studies program development, 118–121
Guild, P.B., 309

Haas, J.D., 11
Hagevik, R., 67
Hahn, C., 26, 224
Hammer, T., 238
Handbook on Teaching Social Issues (Evans & Saxe), 223, 225, 227

Hannah, L., 291
Hanna, P.R., 34
Hansen, Joyce, 261
Hard copy reference materials, 211
Harris, J., 285, 289
Hartoonian, H.M., 268
Hartoonian, M.J., 52
Havens, L., 269
Hawke, S., 11, 12
Hawking, S.W., 204
Haywood Hall, 111
Head (reflective inquiry), hand (competent citizens), heart (concerned citizens) metaphor, 31, 33, 118
    See also Competent citizens; Concerned citizens; Reflective inquiry
Head Start, 307–308
Heitzman, W.R., 202
Helen Dwight Reid Educational Foundation, 73
"Helicopter" parents, 306
Hepburn, S.W., 11
Hertzberg, H., 9
Hidden curriculum, 25
High school, 16–17
    curriculum for, 34–35
    individual needs, 306–307
    magnet, 301
    See also Secondary school
High School Geography Project, 11
Highsmith, R.L., 153
Historical inquiry, 176
    SCIM-C model for, 174–175
Historical perspectives, women's, 237–241
Historical Scene Investigation (HSI), 176
History, 53–54
History Standards Project, 36
Holcomb, Lori, 209–210
Holt Social Studies, 169
Honea, M.J., 142
Honesty, 220
Horton, George Moses, 179
Howard, R.W., 49
How We Think (Dewey), 173, 178

HSI. *See* Historical Scene Investigation
Hughes, C.S., 49
Hullfish, H.G., 30
Hunt, E.B., 30, 51, 173, 176
Hunter, Madeline, 107
Hunter's model (TAP model), 107
Huske, L., 250
Hutchinson, J., 4, 71
Hypotheses, 170–171

Iconic (imagery) stage, 302, 309
IDEA. *See* Individuals with Disabilities Education Improvement Act
IEA. *See* International Association for the Evaluation of Educational Achievement
IEPs. *See* Individualized education plans
Illustrated History of the World and Its People, The, 212
Imagery, 271
Immigration accounts, 217–218
iMovie, 292
Implicit planning, 86
Imports, 55
Incidence and Effects of Poverty in the United States, The, 11
Interdependence, 130
Individual accountability, 130
Individualized education plans (IEPs), 320, 322, 323
Individual needs, 299–332
    4MAT system, 310, 312
    artifact kits, 314–318
    computers, 312
    disabilities, students with, 318–326
    enactive stage (doing), 302
    gifted students, 326–331
    for high school, 306–307
    iconic stage (imagery), 302
    individual differences among students, 307–308
    individualized instruction, 307–308
    instructional resources for, 316, 318
Jackdaws®, 315

Individual needs (cont.)
learning contracts, 313–314
learning styles and, 308,
309–312
mainstreaming, 322, 324–326
for the middle years, 303–306
multilevel reading materials,
313
multiple intelligences (MI) and,
310–312
social development and,
301–303
social discourse in the
classroom and, 303
symbolic stage (words), 302
thinking (cognitive) styles and,
308–309
Individual rights, erosion of, 14
Individuals with Disabilities
Education Improvement
Act (IDEA 2004), 319–320,
322
Inductive learning, 111
Interracial groups for learning,
133
See also Jigsaw Technique
Inferences, 174, 251
Information gathering, 49
Inquiry, 172
See also Reflective inquiry
Instant Messenger, 290
Institute for the Advancement of
Philosophy for Children, 200
Institute of Texan Culture, The,
315
Instructional devices, in
textbooks, 258
Instructional model, 165
Integrative approach, 57–60,
89–90, 138–139
Intel Corporation, 296
Intelligence quotient (IQ), 319
Interactive multimedia, 291–293
Interactivity, 292
Interdependence, 55
See also Grouping students for
learning
Interdisciplinary approach,
57–60, 89
Intermental learning, 50

International Association for the
Evaluation of Educational
Achievement (IEA), 25
International Center for
Cooperation and Conflict
Resolution, 228
International Society for
Technology in Education
(ISTE), 36, 37, 283
Internet
copyrights and, 295
digital divide and, 295–296
discussion boards, 289
e-mail, 289
future challenges and, 296–297
medial literacy and, 284–285
professional development
through, 78
real-time chat, 290
safety on, 295
telecollaboration, 285, 289–290
videoconferencing, 289–290
web-based resources, 285–289
Web logs, 289
WebQuests, 285, 287–288
See also Technology
Internment, of Asian Americans,
230
Internships, 17
Interpersonal intelligence, 310
Interpretations, of history, 53–54
Interpreting data. *See* Data,
interpreting and comparing
Interpretive questions, 147
Interviewing, 72–73
Intramental learning, 50
Intrapersonal intelligence, 310
In-your-face-behavior, 187
Iowa Tests of Basic Skills, 338
IQ. *See* Intelligence quotient
Irene M. Ward and Associates, 321
Isaac, K., 67, 68
Issue-centered curriculum,
224–228
ISTE. *See* International Society
for Technology in Education

Jackdaws®, 315
See also Artifact kits
Jackson, A., 305

James, Charity, 312
Jarolimek, J., 187, 208
Jenkins, J.M., 58
Jewett, A.J., 328
Jigsaw II technique, 134–137
Jigsaw technique, 132–133
Jim Crow era, 68–70
Johnny Tremain, 88
Johnson, D.W., 130, 132
Johnson, R.T., 130, 132
Jones, B.F., 49
Jones, R.C., 166
Jones, Thomas Jesse, 8
Journalistic historical events, 182
Journals, professional, 9, 77
Jurisprudential approach, 100
Justice, 55

Kahn, R., 284
Kates, R.W., 60
*Kathy Schrock's Guide for
Educators*, 348
Kearsley, G., 284
Keyword mnemonic technique,
272
Kiger, G., 190
Kilkenny, R., 232
Kindergarten, 308
Kindler, A., 274
King, E.W., 235
Kirman, J.M., 243
Klavas, A., 308, 310
Kleg, M., 101, 103, 231
Kleinrock, L., 284
Knight, R.S., 250
Knorr, R., 19
Knowledge
constructing, 48–50
prior, 49–50, 250–251
Kohlberg, L., 312
Kounin, J.S.
Kozol, J., 114
Krathwohl, D., 93
Kujawa, S., 250
K-W-L technique, 252, 343

Labeling questions, 146–147
Lamm, L., 65
Language, English as a second
language (ESL), 274–277

Language arts, 88
  communicating social studies subject matter, 266–270
  integrating social studies with, 265
Lateral entry teachers, 18–20
Laycock, F.
Learned behavior, 57
Learning, 57
  concepts, 163–165
  facts, 168
  generalizations, 171
  inductive, 111
  intermental, 50
  intramental, 50
  problem solving strategies, 176–183
  science of, 162
  service-learning, 62–63
  See also Concepts; Reflective inquiry
Learning about Biographies (Zarnowski), 263
Learning and teaching concepts. *See* Reflective inquiry; Concepts
Learning contracts, 313–314
Learning disabilities, 319–320
Learning How to Learn (Novak & Gowin), 102, 255
Learning styles, 308, 309–312
Least restrictive educational environment, 320
Lecture/storytelling approach, 110
Leighton, M.S., 137–138
Leiner B., 284
Lentz, R., 271
L'Esperence, M., 301
Lesson plans, 105, 107–111
  back mapping, 110–111
  formats/procedures for, 107–108
  fundamental elements of, 108–110
  Theory and Practice (TAP) model, 107
  time allocation and, 111–112

Letter disclosures, 221
Level of generality, 91
Levie, W.H., 271
Levin, J., 272
Levstik, L., 173
Library skills, 211
Lieberman, A., 337, 338
Life expectancy, 195–96
Life on the Streets, 289
Ligon History Project, 67–69
Lindquist, T., 260
Linguistic intelligence, 310
Lionni, L., 164
Listening, 266–267
Listing questions, 147
Literacy
  media, 284–285
  visual, 264–266
  See also Reading
Literature, adolescent, 259–263
Living bulletin boards, 242
Local government, 23–24
  curricula and, 24
Location, 53
Logical-mathematical intelligence, 311
Logical reasoning, 197–201
Lowry, Lois, 260, 262
Lybarger, M.B., 14
Lynch, D., 284
Lyons, N., 238

Mackie, B., 67
MACOS. *See* Man: A Course of Study
Macroeconomics, 54
Magnet high schools, 301
Mainstreamed special needs students, 17, 322, 324–326
Maker, C.J., 328
Man: A Course of Study (MACOS), 11
Managing the classroom, 113
Manning, L., 113, 304
Mapping. *See* Curriculum mapping; Back mapping; Concept mapping
Mapping software, 293
Mapping-the-field questions, 149
MapQuest, 293

Maps, 206–211
  types of information provided by, 208
Marek-Schroer, M.F., 252
Martel, E., 231
Martorella, P.H., 284, 292
Marzano, R.J., 49
Masia, B.B., 93
Massialas, B.G., 11, 12
Mastropieri, M.A., 270, 272, 325
Matching questions, 348
Mathews, R.C., 165
McCabe, P.P., 258
McCarthy, B., 310
McGlinn, Meghan, 287–288
McKeown, M.G., 258, 259
McLean, J., 238
Medford, L., 19
Media, in teaching, 12
Media literacy, 284–285
Medin, D.L., 165
Mehaffy, G.L., 71
Memorization, 8, 13
Memory
  imagery and, 271
  See also Remembering subject matter
Mental Measurement Yearbooks, 337
"Mentor-Assisted Enrichment Projects for the Gifted and Talented" (Gray), 330
Mentors, 65–66
Mentorship plan, 330
Merryfield, M.M., 59, 98, 99, 103, 150, 232, 242
Messick, R.G., 304
Metacognition, 251
Metadiscourse, 258
Metcalf, L.E., 30, 51, 173, 176
Methods of inquiry, 52
Meyer, J.L., 258–259
MI. *See* Multiple intelligences
Michaelis, J.V., 28
Microeconomics, 54
Microsoft Excel, 291
Microsoft NetMeeting, 290
Middle school, 15–17
  curriculum pattern in, 34–35
  exemplary schools, 304–305

Middle school (cont.)
exemplary teachers, 305–306
individual needs, 303–306
MidLink Magazine, 269–270
Miederhoff, J.W., 326
Miller, M.S., 290
Minorities
digital divide and, 296
dissident, 218
Misconceptions, 163
Mitchell, R., 337
Mnemonic techniques, 271–72
Mock trials, 152, 227
Monitoring, 175
Moore, C.A., 308, 309
Moore, Gordon, 296
Moore, J., 337
Morally mature citizens, 219
More at Four program (NC), 308
Morrell, E., 192
Morrissett, I., 12
Motivation, 57
Movement, between and among
places, 53
Multicultural education,
132–133, 229–241
curriculum materials for, 235
designing strategies for,
233–234
gender issues in, 235–241
goal of, 230
issues in, 231–232
multiperspective approach
to, 233
social justice activities, 234
See also Concerned citizens;
Jigsaw technique
Multidisciplinary approach,
57–60
Multilevel reading materials, 313
Multimedia editing software,
291–293
Multimedia tools for
individualized instruction,
318
Multiperspective approach, 233
Multiple causality, 170–171
Multiple choice, 346–347, 350
Multiple intelligences (MI),
310–312

*Multiple Intelligences in the
Classroom* (Armstrong), 342
Multitext approach, 42
Murphy, Fred, 5
"Murphy Taught History 30
Years, Became a Legend in
Williamsville," 5
Musical intelligence, 311
Myers, W.D., 261

Names, concepts and, 164
Nash, G., 231–232
National Alliance for Civic
Education, 35
National Assessment of
Educational Progress
(Nation's Report Card), 338
National Board Certification, 41
National Board for Professional
Teaching Standards
(NBPTS), 37
National Center for Health
Statistics, 196
National Center for History in
the Schools, 96, 173
National Council for Geographic
Education (NCGE), 77
National Council for the Social
Studies (NCSS), 9, 12, 77
Advocacy ToolKit, 24, 26
*Curriculum Guidelines for
Multicultural Education*, 235
*Curriculum Standards for
Social Studies, Expectations
of Excellence*, 119
Curriculum Standards for the
Social Studies, 36
*Passport to Learning: Teaching
Social Studies to ESL
Students*, 274–277
primary purpose of social
studies, 29
Social Education, 153, 263
Standard 9, Global
Connections, 339–341
standards, 339–341
statement on evaluations, 335
Task Force on Revitalizing
Citizenship Education,
24–25, 28

ten themes for social studies
standards, 37, 39–40, 120
website, 120, 289
National Council on Economic
Education Standards, 36
National Education Association
(NEA), 9
National Education Goals Panel,
13
National Education Technology
Standards (NETS), 18, 37,
283
*National Education Technology
Standards for Teachers:
Preparing Teachers to Use
Technology* (ISTE), 283
National Geographic
MapMachine, 293
National Geographic Society,
108–110, 118, 119, 172,
206–207
Nationalism, 31, 54, 218
National Middle School
Association (NMSA), 76–77
National Paideia Center, 106
National Research Council,
findings on learning
concepts, 162
National standards, 12–14,
36–37, 38, 339–341
See also National Council
for the Social Studies;
Standards
National Standards for Civics
and Government, 36
National Women's History
Project, 238
Nation's Report Card (National
Assessment of Educational
Progress), 338
Nazi Germany, 218
NBPTS. *See* National Board for
Professional Teaching
Standards
NCGE. *See* National Council for
Geographic Education
NCLB. *See* No Child Left
Behind
NCSS. *See* National Council for
the Social Studies

NCTEACH program (North Carolina State University), 19–20
NEA. *See* National Education Association
Needs
  of students, 85
  See also Individual needs
Negotiating skills, 189
Nelson, J.L., 28
Nelson, M., 269
NETS. *See* National Education Technology Standards
Newman, D., 127
Newmann, F.M., 100, 130, 134
New social studies, the, 10–12
  legacy of, 11–12
  projects, 11
  reforms, 10
  Woods Hole, Massachusetts, 10, 11
Newspaper articles, 67, 243–244
  reading, 264
Newspaper Association of America Foundation, 236
Newspapers in Education (NIE), 264
Newton, Heber, 8
NIE. *See* Newspapers in Education
1916 Report of the Committee on the Social Studies, 9–10, 34–35
Nissman, B., 113
NMSA. *See* National Middle School Association
No Child Left Behind (2002), 13, 19, 100, 302, 306
Noddings, N., 100, 237
Nonexamples, 164
Norm-referenced tests, 337–338
Norms, 56
North Carolina Sixth Grade Goes to Russia project, 48, 60
North Carolina State University, 60
North Central Regional Laboratory, 166
Northrup, Solomon, 180
Norton, D.E., 260

Notetaking, 272–273
Novak, J.D., 102, 254–255
Number the Stars (Lowry), 260, 262
Nutta, J., 277

Objectives, 91–94
  in the cognitive and affective domains, 93–94
  general, behavioral, and student learning outcomes, 92–93
  identifying and stating, 92
  taxonomies of, 144–145
Objective tests, 345–348
Objectivity, history and, 54
O'Brien, J., 277
Ochoa, A., 14, 30, 77–78, 99, 120, 324
Ogbu, J.U., 231
Ogle, C., 252
Ogle, D., 252
Oliver, D.W., 100
Olner, P., 224
On Becoming a Memorable Master Teacher (Brooks's approach), 7, 110
Onosko, J.J., 99
Op-ed article, 27
Opening questions, 146–147
Oppenheim, A.N., 25
Oral histories, 71–72
Organizational resources, 76–77
Organizing. *See* Organizing and planning
Organizing and planning, 3–4, 82–123
  basic issues, 85–86
  beginning the planning process, 86–90
  classroom environment, 111–117.
  See also Classroom environment
  goals, 91
  guidelines for program development, 118–121
  head (reflective citizen), hand (competent citizen), and heart (concerned citizen) metaphor and, 118

identifying a purpose for citizenship education, 86
  lesson plans, 105, 107–111. *See also* Lesson plans
  objectives, 91–94
  units, 94–105. *See also* Units of study
  variety in, 121
  See also Citizenship education; Curriculum; Social sciences
Original source documents, 8
Osborne, Susan, 324–325
O'Shea, M., 13
O'Steen, Billy, 62–63
Outcomes
  groups and, 132
  student learning, 92–93
Outward Bound, 62
Owens, V., 67
Oyez (Supreme Court's multimedia website), 249

Paideia Program (University of North Carolina at Chapel Hill), 105, 106, 249
Panel discussion, 227
Parker, W., 42, 118, 187, 208
Passe, J., 74, 226
Passport to Learning: Teaching Social Studies to ESL Students (NCSS), 274–277
Patrick, J.P., 58, 59
Patriotism, 218
Pawloski, B., 284
PDAs. *See* Personal digital assistants
Peace education, 228
PeaceJam, 228
Pearson, J., 96–98
Pearson, P.D., 251
Peirano, A., 88
People for the American Way, 43
Performance (authentic) assessments, 341–43
  vs. standardized testing, 342
Performance objectives, 93
Performance standards, 36–37
Perie, M., 26

Periodicals, 243–44
  reading, 264
Peripherals, 293–294
Perkins, D.L., 49
Perrone, V., 341
Personal development, 28–29
Personal digital assistants (PDAs),
  282, 293–294
Personal dimension concepts, 161
Personality toolbox, 6
Personal liberties, 249–250
Personal problems, 176
Perspectives, incorporating
  multiple into units, 100–101
Petroleum lesson plan, 108–110
Philosophy for Children (Institute
  for the Advancement of
  Philosophy for Children), 200
Physical anthropologists, 56
Physical development, 301
Piaget, J., 49, 51, 87, 143, 160,
  302, 304, 312
Piche, G.L., 272
Picture books, 263
Pictures, processing information
  from, 201–203, 265–266
Pie chart, 195
Place, 53, 55
  relationships within, 53
  the school and community and,
  61–63
Planning curriculums. *See*
  Organizing and planning
Planning units, 94–98, 101–105
Plato, 55
Plowman, P., 328
Pluralism
  cultural, 219, 231
  See also Multicultural education
PNI questions, 149
Political cartoons, 202–203
Political science, 55
Political systems, 55
Politics (Aristotle), 55
Popham, W.J., 338, 343
Population distribution, 53
Portfolios
  students', 341–343
  teaching, 18, 19
Postel, J., 284

Postman, N., 297
Posttests, 343
Poverty, 11
Power, 55
"Power of Oil, The," 108–110,
  118, 119
PowerPoint presentations, 48
Powers, S., 232
Presseisen, B.Z., 49
Pressley, M., 272
Pretests, 343
Print materials, 243–244
  for individualized instruction,
  318
Prior knowledge, 49–50,
  250–251
Private foundations, 10
Problem Sheets, 212–214
Problem solving, 172–183
  case studies and, 181–183
  instructional strategies for,
  176–183
  model for, 178
  real-world problems, 180–181
  related terms, 172
  SCIM-C model for the inquiry
  process (history example),
  174–176
  slavery example, 178–180
  uses of the term *problem*, 176
  See also Reflective inquiry
Process of Education, The, 10, 11
Production, 54
Professional associations, 9
Professional development
  effective citizenship as, 77–78
  through the Internet, 78
Professional journals, 9, 77
Professional resources, 75–77
  organizational, 76–77
  professional journals, 77
  through the Internet, 78
  See also Resources
Professional standards, 37, 40
Projection devices, 266
Prototypes, 161
Psychological problems,
  176–177
Psychology, 56–57
Public dimension concepts, 161

Quaker discussion style, 227
Questioning, 139–149
  Bloom's taxonomy for the
  cognitive domain for
  questions, 144–145
  desirable, 143
  duration (wait time), 140–142
  functions of, 146–147
  rehearsal and, 143–144
  sequencing of, 142–145
  Taba strategy, 145–149
  types, 140, 146–149
  undesirable, 143
Question script, 142–143
QuickTests, 348

Racism, 229
Radio technologies, 296
RAFT technique, for writing, 269
*Ralph Nader Presents: Civics for
  Democracy: A Journey for
  Teachers and Students*
  (Isaac), 67, 68
Rankin, S.C., 49
Rasinski, T., 314
Ratings, decision making by,
  129–130
Rating scales
  to assess competence, 352–353
  defined, 351
  sample, 353
Ravenscroft School (Raleigh,
  NC), 63
Ravitch, D., 231
Reading, 258–266
  adolescent literature and,
  259–263
  characteristics of "considerate"
  textbooks, 258
  concept (semantic) maps and,
  260, 262
  frames, 258–259
  multilevel reading materials, 313
  newspapers and periodicals, 264
  visual literacy, 264–266
Reading guides, 254
ReadingQuest, 166
Real-time chat, 289–290
Reasoning, logical, 197–201
Redford, Dorothy, 230

Red, White, and Black: The Peoples of Early America (Nash), 231
Reese, Lyn, 239–240
References, 211–214
    activities for introducing reference materials, 212–214
    checklist for, 352
    sample works for social studies, 211–212
    See also Resources
Reflection, questions and, 139–140
Reflective citizens. *See* Reflective inquiry
Reflective inquiry, 28–30, 31, 33, 36, 118, 158–84
    assessing, 349–351
    concepts, 160–167
    facts, 167–168, 169
    generalizations, 168–172
    hypotheses, 170–171
    problem solving, 172–183
    See also Concepts; Facts; Generalizations; Problem solving
Reflective thinking, 172
Refocusing statements/questions, 146
Reforms, curricula, 10
Region, 53
Rehearsal, 143–144
Relationships, within place, 53
Reluctant learners, 188
Remembering subject matter, 270–273
    imagery and memory, 271
    mnemonic techniques, 271–272
    notetaking, 272–273
Remy, R.C., 103, 150, 232, 242
Report of the Committee on the Social Studies (1916), 9–10
Republic (Plato), 55
Research and analysis skills, 190–202
    analyzing data, 197–201
    interpreting and comparing data, 190–196
    processing information from pictures, 201–203
Research reports, 183

Research sheets, 350–351, 354–355
Resource units, 99
Resources, 64–78, 90, 241
    in the community, 64–65
    community resource persons, 65–66
    for disabled students, 326
    fieldwork, 67–71
    genres of Web-based, 286
    for individualized instruction, 316, 318
    for issued-centered curriculum, 225
    for news, 244
    newspaper articles and editorials, 67
    oral histories, 71–72
    organizational, 76–77
    for peace education, 228
    professional development through the Internet, 78
    professional journals, 77
    school and community as, 64–65
    search engines, 284–285
    sources of units, 96–99
    surveys and interviews, 72–73
    technology, 69
    web-based, 285–289
    See also References
Resource speakers, 65–66
Resource units. *See* Teaching units; Units of study
Respectful mind, 201
Response-to-intervention, 320
Revolutionary War, 99
Richardson, J.T.E., 271
Riley, J.P. II, 142
Risinger, C., 312
Risk-free classroom environment, 139
Roberts, L., 284
Roberts, N., 290
Robertson, J., 96–98
Robinson, A., 131
Robinson, James Harvey, 54
Robinson projection, 206–207
Roehler, L.R., 251
Rogers, J., 192

Rokeach, M., 220
Role-playing, 149–152
    debates and, 227
    for social values, 227
    stage 1: initiation and direction, 150
    stage 2: describing the scenario, 151
    stage 3: assigning roles, 151–152
    stage 4: enactment, 152
    stage 5: debriefing, 152
    See also Simulations
Roles, 56
    in small groups, 127–128
Roman history concept map, 102
Ross, E.W., 38
Rossi, J.A., 12
Rowe, M.B., 142
Rubrics, 89–90, 131
Rules, 55
    in the classroom, 115
    concepts and, 164
"Russia: From Czars to Presidents and Back Again," 84–85
Russian concept map, 105
Russia Project, 125–126

Salisbury, Graham, 261
Sanford, H., 324
Santa, C.M., 269
Santrock, J., 6, 200, 201, 301
Save What's Left of Florida, 68
Saxe, D.W., 8, 223, 224, 225, 227
Scalf, J., 269
Scalf, L., 269
Scheduling
    alternatives for, 112
    See also Block scheduling; Time allocation
Schemata, 49–50, 160
Scherer, M., 189
Schmuck, P., 127
Schmuck, R.A., 127
School
    alerting the community to school activities, 74–75
    community and, 61–63
    as sources of social data, 64–65

Schreiber, Joan, 345
Schug, Mark, 3
Scientific method, 172
SCIM-C model: strategy for interpreting history, 174–175
Scripts, 143–144
Scruggs, T.E., 270, 272
Search engines, 284–285
Searle, Marah, 5
Secondary school
   curriculum in, 34–35
   individual needs in, 306–307
   See also High school
Self, 57
Self-concept activities, 221–223
   attitude inventories, 221–222
   letter disclosure, 221
   student debates, 222–223
Self-evaluation form, for discussions, 267
Semantic maps. *See* Concept maps
Sensitive issues, 99–100
Sequencing of questions, 142–145
Sequential Tests of Educational Progress, 338
Service-learning, 62–63
Service projects, 237
Sex-role stereotyping, 235–238
Shaftel, F.R., 150
Shaftel, G., 150
Shapiro, S., 59, 98, 99
Sharan, S., 137–138
Sharan, Y., 137–138
Shaver, J.P., 11, 100, 220
Shermis, S.S., 10, 28
Shuster, S.K., 324
Sikes, J., 132–133
Siler, C.R., 258
Silverblank, F., 262
Simon, M., 292
Simulations, 153–155, 227
   guidelines for conducting, 155
   managing, 153
   software for, 154–155, 290
   sources of, 153–155
   See also Role-playing
Sinclair, N., 67
Singer, H.G., 256, 257, 258

Singleton, L.R., 100
Sisk, D., 327, 328
Sitton, T., 71
Skidmore, D., 26
Skills. *See* Competent citizens
Slater, W.H., 272
Slavery, 230
   problem-based learning, 178–180
"Slavery in the Nineteenth Century," 96–98
Slavin, R.E., 130–131, 132, 134
Small groups. *See* Grouping students for learning
Smith, E.E., 165
Smith, N., 202
Smith, P.G., 30
Smulyan, L., 232
Snapp, M., 132–133
Snyder, Sam, 6
Social concern
   citizenship education and, 218–219
   See also Concerned citizens
Social consciousness, 238, 241
Social criticism, 28–29
Social data. *See* References; Resources
Social development, students' needs and, 301–303. *See also* Individual needs
Social discourse, in the classroom, 303
Social Education (NCSS), 3, 9, 153, 263
Social issues
   as a curricular focus, 224–228
   defined, 224
   See also Concerned citizens
Socialization, 56
Social justice activities, 234
Social problems, 176
   building units around, 99–100
Social sciences, 28–29
   anthropology, 55–56
   commonalities of, 52
   economics, 54–55
   geography, 53
   history, 53–54
   political science, 55

psychology, 56–57
sociology, 56
   See also Curriculum
Social service projects, 63, 237
Social skills, 187–188
   required for groups, 128
Social Studies and the Young Learner, 9
Social studies curriculum. *See* Curriculum; Social sciences
Social Studies Curriculum; Purposes, Problems, and Possibilities, 38
Social studies, defining
   1916 Report of the Committee on the Social Studies, 9–10
   alternative definitions, 14–15
   national standards, 12–14
   the new social studies, 10–12
   origins and evolution of social studies, 8–9
   working definition, 15
   See also Curriculum; Social sciences
Social Studies, The, 73
Social systems, 56
Sociological Resources for the Social Studies, 11
Sociology, 56
Socratic discussion style, 227
Software
   for databases and spreadsheets, 291
   evaluation of, 290
   for graphic organizers, 166–167
   for mapping, 293
   for multimedia editing, 291–293
   for simulations, 290
   test software, 348
   Tom Snyder Productions software for role plays and simulations, 154–155, 290
"Solving Conflicts—Not Just for Children" (Scherer), 189
Sommer, R., 201
Sorter, J., 256, 257
Sousa, D., 310
South Carolina Department of Education, 65

Southern Oral History Program, 71
Soviet launch of *Sputnik*, 10
Space, in the classroom, 111
Spatial intelligence, 311
Spatial interaction, 53
Spatial skills, 205–211
  impact of, 206
  maps and globes, 206–211
Speakers, community resource speakers, 65–66
Speaking, 266–267
Special needs, assessing, 95
Special needs students, 17
  See also Disabilities, students with; Individual needs
Speculations, 170
Spell of the Land: Sense of Place, Use of Space, 60
Spider map, 166
Spindler, G., 231
Spindler, L., 231
Spindle Stories: Three Units on Women's World History, Book Two (Reese), 239–240
Spires, H.A., 272–273
Split-page notetaking approach, 272, 273
Splittgerber, F.L., 304
Spreadsheet software, 291
Sputnik, 10
SQ3R technique, 270
Stage challenges, 6
Stage theory, 6
  See also Erikson's theory of epigenesis
Stahl, R.J., 133, 141, 142
Standard 9, Global Connections (NCSS), 339–341
Standard of living, 55
Standards
  defined, 336
  national, 12–14, 36–37, 38, 339–341
  professional standards for teachers, 37, 40
  state, 37, 43
  technology, 36–37
  ten social studies themes (NCSS), 37, 39–40

See also National Council for the Social Studies; National standards
Standardized tests, 337–338
  vs. performance (authentic) testing, 342
Stanley, W.B., 165
Statesman's Yearbook, 212
Statement of purpose, 94
Statements of curricular goals, 94
States, curricula and, 24
State standards, 37
State textbook adoption policies, 43
Statistical Abstract of the United States, 194
Status, 56
Steinbrink, J.E., 202
Stephan, C., 132–133
Stereotypes, 163
  gender and, 235–238
Stevenson, C., 304
Stevens, R., 202, 304
Stoff, M., 191, 192
Stoltman, J.P., 58, 59
Stoltz, A., 4
Stone, D., 272–273
Stories, 182
Story of America, The: A National Geographic Picture Atlas, 212
Stotsky, S., 268
Strahan, D., 301
Stream pollution, 281
Strickland, D.S., 266
Strong, W., 220
Structuring activities, 132
Student learning outcomes, 92–93
Student needs, 85
  See also Individual needs
Students
  behavior and expectations of in the classroom, 114–116
  Web-based resources for, 286
Student teaching, 17
Student will be able to (SWBAT), 92
Substantiating questions, 149
Suhor, C., 49

Summarizing, 174, 251
  questions, 147
Superka, D.P., 12
Supreme Court's multimedia website, 249
Surveys, 72–73
SWBAT. *See* Student will be able to
Swift, J.N., 142
Syllogisms, 197–198
Symbolic (words) stage, 302, 309
Synchronous online dialogue, 282, 289–290
Synthesizing mind, 201

Taba, H., 145–149
Taba questioning strategies, 145–149
Tables, 193–196
Tanner, D.L., 58
TAP model. *See* Theory and Practice model
Task Force on Revitalizing Citizenship Education (NCSS), 24–25, 28
Task Force on Scope and Sequence, 14
Taxonomies of objectives, 144–45
Taylor, V., 238
Teacher-centered approaches, 12, 110
Teacher-made materials, 314–318
Teacher-made paper-and-pencil tests, 343–348
Teacher-mentors, 222
Teacher-only talk/lecture, 110
Teachers, 15–20
  behavior and expectations of in the classroom, 114–117
  block scheduling, 16–17
  certification of, 17–18
  as developers of units, 98–99
  four-teacher teams, 17
  lateral entry, 18–20
  portfolios and, 18, 19
  positions on controversial issues, 244
  professional standards for, 37, 40

Teachers (cont.)
teaching current events,
243–244
traditional teaching pattern, 17
two-teacher teams, 15–17
Web-based resources for, 286
Teacher, They Called Me a Blank
(Byrnes), 190
*Teaching about International
Conflict and Peace* (Shapiro &
Merryfield), 98
"Teaching About Terrorism: A
Conceptual Approach"
(Kleg), 103
Teaching aids, 4
"Teaching Students How to Make
Predictions About Events in
History with a Graphic
Organizer Plus Options
Guide" (Bean, Sorter, Singer,
& Frazee), 257
Teaching units, 99
See also Units of study
Team approach to teaching, 15–17
Technology, 280–298
cell phones, 282, 296
copyrights and, 295
database and spreadsheet
software, 291
the digital divide, 295–296
emerging, 296–297
geography and, 53
GIS, 53, 67–69
incorporating new learning
environments, 283
integrating into the classroom,
282–284
Internet applications, 284–290
Internet safety, 295
mapping software, 293
multimedia editing software,
291–293
personal digital assistants
(PDAs), 293–294
simulation software, 290
standards for, 37
tools for individualized
instruction, 316
writing tools and, 269–270
See also Internet

Technology skills, 211
Technology standards, 36–37
Technology superhighway, 211
Telecollaboration, 285, 289–290,
296
TenBrink, T.D., 343, 344
Tennyson, R.D., 165
Terrorism concept map, 103
Test Generator, 348
Testing
national, 339–341
See also Evaluating/assessing
student learning
Testing hypotheses, 170–171
Test Quest, 348
Test scores, 13, 14
See also Evaluating/assessing
student learning
Tests in Print, 337
Textbooks
basal, 41–43
characteristics of
"considerate," 258
dominance of in instruction, 12
frames in, 258–259
reading comprehension and,
258–266
state adoption policies, 43
units and, 99
See also Reading
Thematic approach, 57–60
Theory and Practice (TAP)
model, 107
*Theory and Research in Social
Education* (Postman), 297
Thinking (cognitive) styles,
308–309
Think, Pair, Share, 132
Thompson, A., 67
Thompson, J., 130, 134
Time, comparative conceptions
of, 204
Time allocation, in lesson plans,
111–112
Time lines, 204–205
Timetables of History, The, 212
Tirozzi, G., 305
Tobin, K.G., 141–142
Toliver, Kay, 141
Tomlinson, C., 302, 328

Tom Snyder Productions,
154–155, 205, 224, 290
Torney, J., 25
Torney-Purta, J., 49, 270
Torrance, P., 328
Totten, S., 71–72
Traditional teaching pattern,
17, 35
incorporating into new
learning environments, 283
Traditions, 56
Transmission of cultural
heritage, 28–29, 86
Triandis, H.C., 220
Troublemakers, 113
Turning Points (Carnegie
Corporation), 305
*Turning Points 2000, Education
of Adolescents in the 21st
Century* (Jackson, Davis, &
Tirozzi), 305
Two-teacher teams, 15–17
"Two Ways to Cope" (*National
Geographic*), 172

Ulschmid, B., 326
Under the Blood-Red Sun
(Salisbury), 261
United States Institute for Peace,
228
Units of study, 94–105
assessing students' special
needs, 94, 95
concept maps and, 101–103
formats for, 104–105
for global studies, 226
interdisciplinary teams
and, 103
multiple perspectives into,
100–101
planning and creating units,
94–98, 101–105
resource units, 99
sample topics, 96
social problems/themes as
foundation of units, 99–100
sources of, 96–99
teaching units, 99
transforming a unit topic into a
unit issue, 225

University of Minnesota Project
Social Studies (K-12), 11
University of North Carolina at
Chapel Hill, 106
Upper Midwest Women's History
Center, 238
U.S. Bureau of Education, 9
U.S. Department of Education, 13

Values, 57, 219–222
See also Concerned citizens
Vanden, H., 202
Van der Grinten projection,
206–207
Van Hoose, J., 301
Vansickle, R.L., 134
Variety, in instructional
planning, 121
Venn diagram, 166
Videoconferencing, 289–290
Vietnam War, 65
Vignettes, 182
V.I.P.S., 275
Virtual Architecture, 289
Virtue, D., 58, 90
Visual learners, 201–203
Visual literacy, 264–266
von Ranke, Otto, 54
Vosniadou, S., 164
Vygotsky, L., 50, 87, 88, 127,
144, 222, 302, 303, 312

Wade, R., 60
Wait time, for questioning and
answering, 140–142
Wake County Public School
System (Raleigh, NC), 323

Wallen, N.E., 355
Walters, L., 130–131
Ward, J., 238
Warner, G., 5
Watson Institute for
International Studies at
Brown University, 226
Web logs, 289
Weblogs in Education, 289
WebQuests, 285, 287–288
Web resources. *See* Internet;
Resources; Technology;
Web Resources (at the end
of each chapter)
Wesley, E.B., 14
Westward Movement, 100–101
White, C.S., 292
White, J.J., 139, 140
White, Shannon, 68–69
Whole-class discussions, 303
Whole-language approaches, 266
"Whom Shall We Allow In"
(Cruz, Nutta, O'Brien,
Feyten & Govoni),
276–277
Wigginton, E., 71
Wilde, Lady Jane, 8
Wilen, W.W., 139, 140
Williams, P.L., 337
Wilson, A., 67
Wilson, E., 88
*With Every Drop of Blood: A
Novel of the Civil War*
(Collier & Collier), 261
Witkin, H.A., 308, 309
Wittrock, M.C., 201, 271
Wolff, S., 284

Women, perspectives in history,
237–241
*Women in the World Curriculum
Resources*, 238
Women's History Month, 238
Women's rights, ancient Egypt
and the U.S., 239–240
Wood, J.W., 326
Woods Hole, 10, 11
World Classroom, 226
World community, 9
World History for us All, 96
World hunger, 186–187
*Worldmark Encyclopedia of the
Nations*, 212
World Wise Schools, 228
Woyshner, C., 100
Wright, V., 88
Writing, 268–270
audiences for, 269
civic, 268
objectives, 93
RAFT technique, 269
technology tools for,
269–270
types of, 268
Written materials,
interpreting and comparing,
191–193

*You Forgot Your Skirt, Amelia
Bloomer*, 263
Young, T.A., 252

Zarnowski, M., 236, 263
Zevin, J., 173, 175
Zimmerman, W., 72